WOMEN AND WAR

IN THE

TWENTIETH

CENTURY

WOMEN
AND WAR
IN THE
TWENTIETH
CENTURY

Enlisted with or without Consent

Edited by

NICOLE ANN DOMBROWSKI

Routledge
Taylor & Francis Group
New York   London

First paperback edition
Published in 2004 by
Routledge
270 Madison Avenue
New York, NY 10016

Published in Great Britain by
Routledge
2 Park Square
Milton Park, Abingdon,
Oxon OX14 4RN U.K.

This edition published 2011 by Routledge:

Routledge
Taylor & Francis Group
711 Third Avenue
New York, NY 10017

Routledge
Taylor & Francis Group
2 Park Square, Milton Park
Abingdon, Oxon OX14 4RN

Library of Congress Cataloging-in-Publication Data

Women and war in the twentieth century / edited by Nicole Ann Dombrowski.
     p. cm. — (Women's history and culture ; v. 13) Garland reference
library of the humanities ; v. 1969)
    Includes bibliographical references and index.
    ISBN 0-8153-2287-9 (alk. paper)
    ISBN 0-415-97256-6 (pbk.)
    1. World War, 1939–1945—Women. 2. World War, 1914–1918—
Women. 3. Women and war. 4. Women and the military. 5. Women—
History—20th century. I. Dombrowski, Nicole. II. Series: Women's history
and culture ; 13. III. Series: Garland reference library of the
humanities ; vol. 1969.
D810.W7W653 1999
940.3'082—dc21
                                 98–36313
                                     CIP

For
Audrey Randolph

Contents

PART II
1940–1945

PART III
1946–PRESENT

List of Illustrations

Acknowledgments

This volume could not have been completed without the support of many individuals and institutions to whom I owe thanks and gratitude. The Princeton University Committee on Research in the Humanities and Social Sciences provided the financial and technical support to finish this project. The Program in Women's History at New York University sponsored the conference on Women and War out of which this volume grew. I'd like to thank MIT Press and *Hastings Women's Law Journal* for granting permission to reprint the articles of Atina Grossmann and Rhonda Copelon which were presented at the conference and serve as cornerstone contributions to the study of women, gender and war. Claudia Hirsch, Phyllis Korper, Richard Wallis, and Kristi Long at Garland Publishing all played an important part in bringing this book to print.

Throughout the course of the project many people have helped shape the ideas explored in the volume and put me in touch with people in the various fields of women's studies. I'd like to especially thank Marylin Young, Mary Nolan, Susan Ware, Darlene Levy, Atina Grossmann, Mindy Roseman, Caitlin Kelley, Lisa DiCaprio, Clara Garcia, Emily Belcher, and Tony Judt for their encouragement and advice. Arno Mayer kindly read drafts of my own work. Judy Hanson, Noelina Hall, and Philip Nord of the Department of History at Princeton offered valuable clerical aid and administrative advice. All the contributors deserve thanks for their articles and patience. I thank Kristina Cheng for her research into the book's artwork, and to Maia Wright for her computer consultation. Kathleen Cambor came through with last minute photo research and encouragement. Thank you Kate. David Herrington and his staff at "The Place," Princeton's New Media Center, have helped enormously solving the technical troubles of coordinating as many software languages as national languages which are represented in this volume. Tommy Carr deserves most thanks for serving as the book's competent and enthusiastic editorial assistant. My own energy and endurance could not have been maintained without the caring support of Jim Risser. Many thanks to all.

Finally, the views, opinions, and findings contained in this book are those of the authors and do not necessarily reflect the views of the supporting organizations or the authors' employers or institutional affiliations.

WOMEN AND WAR
IN THE TWENTIETH CENTURY

(Courtesy of the New York Public Library)

Figure 1. World War II war refugees.

ONE

Soldiers, Saints, or Sacrificial Lambs?
Women's Relationship to Combat and the Fortification of the Home Front in the Twentieth Century

Nicole Ann DOMBROWSKI

Legends of women warriors date as far back in time as wars themselves. From the jungles of the Amazon to the jagged landscape of Sparta, women as warriors have captured the imagination.[1] Likewise, the ideal of the soldier's wife in waiting has stirred and nourished the morale of fighting men. Perhaps the most evocative of all the female heroines is the defenseless victim raped or ravaged by war, an image that provokes declarations of revenge as well as pity. These three female roles---warrior, maid-in-waiting, and helpless victim---have existed simultaneously as complements to the vocation of the male soldier and as encouragement to his task. Histories celebrating women's service in the armed forces of any country must be placed alongside those of women victimized by war's violence on all sides of a conflict.

Three historical events recently have coincided to make a scholarly reappraisal of women's relationship to war and militarism timely. The Cold War and its nuclear arms race is temporarily suspended. In ex-Yugoslavia soldiers of the Serbian and Croatian armies raped women civilians, especially Bosnian Muslims, as part of an ethnic cleansing campaign, igniting debate about the specificity of war crimes committed against women. At nearly the same time, women's participation in the Gulf War revived debate on the question of women serving in combat roles in the U.S. and North American Treaty Organization (NATO) military forces. In this context, historical reassessment of women's status as agents, accomplices, opponents, and victims of wartime violence might bring more clarity to current political policies and debates.

All four of these classifications pose problems for a woman's autonomous self-expression and her subjectivity as a private individual and engaged citizen. Women who choose to fight claim a place for themselves among those men who have achieved the respect of their fellow citizens for their willingness to risk their lives for the sake of their country or their ideals. Because military service has acted as an unofficial litmus test for public leadership capabilities, many proponents of women's military service are right to point out that women's access to the highest posts of government office may well be predicated on their ability to show evidence of their capacity to command the armed services in any country. At the same time, militaries have been responsible for atrocities and unsanctioned acts of aggression, and enlisted women become complicit in these acts. How, then, can women access power without assuming the responsibility for the abuses of power as well?

Traditionally, wives, girlfriends, and soldiers' loved ones have played a more passive, but perhaps equally important, role in sustaining and supporting military culture. Politicians and generals alike have insisted that the desire to protect their families and loved ones boosts soldiers' morale. Historians and policymakers may squabble over the extent to which soldiers' commitment to defend their families inspires their acts of self-sacrifice, but the rhetoric of chivalry rings loudly enough that many opponents of women's presence in the military rely on this age-old gendered division of labor to insist upon women's exclusion from fighting forces. If women do bolster soldiers' morale, then what is their political or historical responsibility for atrocities or war crimes committed, in part, in their name? Women are home front heroines when their armies are victorious, but are they equally culpable when their troops lose?

Opponents to war, pacifists, protesters, and activists often wage their arguments for peace in absolute terms. This was especially so after the advent of nuclear armaments. Pacifists argue that we are all victims and losers in war, soldier and civilian alike. Some opponents of militarism argue that women, as bearers of children, are especially endowed to oppose the kind of violence that destroys the very humanity their bodies reproduce. But when do the opponents of war make peace with a status quo that compromises liberty, equality, or even the political freedom that their voices of opposition require in order to speak? When is New Hampshire's motto, Live Free or Die, too demanding a sacrifice?

Finally, trapped behind the lines without the means to defend themselves or exposed under the nuclear umbrella, women fall victim to war, regardless of the determination of their militaries or their own efforts to help or hinder the fight. The complexity of women's relationship to war raises the questions this volume endeavors to confront. Is women's relationship to war really more complex than that of men? The answer is yes, if only because society, with its traditional gender divisions of labor, has assigned the official task of fighting to men. What happens to our standard ideals of "feminine," "masculine," family, and country when women fight? More importantly, how is the category of woman, itself a social construction, further modified when women become warriors? And what happens to the institutions and practices of warring when women set in upon them? In many countries around the world we are witnessing these transformations. The goal in this volume is to recover the varied histories that have led up to what seems like an accelerated process of the militarization of women's lives at home and in battle.

One of the indisputable facts to emerge from the following collection of articles is that within the last century women have been enlisted into military conflicts with or without their consent. The title of the book is meant to underscore the trade-offs between the opportunities and the travesties confronting women in the context of increased global militarization. The articles clearly identify the plurality of roles and responsibilities women assume or have foisted upon them under wartime or peacetime conditions. These articles attempt to survey the personal and political interests that women have as individuals and as a collectivity when nations, ethnic groups, and political organizations wage war.

Many studies already exist that address the issues of women and the military, women and war, women and peace, feminism and pacifism, feminism and militarism, gender and war, and gender and militarism.[2] What often happens in many of these excellent volumes is that the historical trajectory and global perspective get lost in presentist debates about women's place in the military. Often celebrationist histories of women's arrival into the armed forces neglect the fundamental problem that militaries are institutions predicated on violence. Liberal feminists have argued that women should not be barred from combat positions. They contend that women are not naturally less aggressive than men. The same proponents of women's increased presence in the military have also argued that women can transform or ameliorate military institutions. The problem with the pairing of these two arguments is that one insists that women are not biologically inferior to men, yet they might well be men's ethical superiors. Women are undoubtedly the best agents to challenge sexual discrimination within the armed forces, but does that make them better suited to enforce military discipline toward enemy civilian populations? Women's entrance into combat not only reconstructs combat and its institutions but also reconstructs women in the process. It is naive to insist that women can transform military culture without understanding how military culture could transform "women." Once scholars and policymakers move beyond equal opportunity absolutism, as feminists or antimilitarists, they must address the problem of how to decrease the role of the military in conflict resolution altogether. It is our intention that this book make a contribution to such an effort.

This volume anchors women in time and geography, examining their universal as well as particular interests in relationship to war and peace. It raises the following questions: Do women, as a global category, share the same stakes in war and peace? Or does gender solidarity, either as a conscious group creation or as a category of experience, necessarily and justifiably break down when other competing identities serve as the foundation of war and peace?

Women's role in the armed services or in revolutionary units has changed to such a degree over the twentieth century that American and Russian women especially, as citizens of the world's largest military powers, must open themselves up to an understanding of the way in which superpower military hegemony affects women in other countries. As scholars and citizens, one of the challenges many of us face is recognizing that the integration of women into the existing military structures of the West in no way ensures that the world is a safer place. Also, scholars and politicians know that military women do not necessarily have a political agenda that transcends national interests. Long after women are integrated into the military, we as a society will face the task of maintaining and negotiating a just peace. Defining what constitutes a just peace in a postsuperpower world demands that female intellectuals, politicians and citizens, civilians and soldiers alike, develop a consciousness and recognition of the circumstances faced by other women and men around the world that lead to military conflict. Thus, while some women pursue liberation and equality through entry into the armed services, others continue to wage these same battles in the institutions of international and domestic politics like the United Nations.

The articles in this volume try to present a historical trajectory that pairs women's experience as victims of war with women's engagement as agents, on behalf of themselves or their countries. Furthermore, by presenting the experiences of women around the globe, the volume tries to begin to place the question of women's relationship to the institutions and the fallout of war in a global context that does not simply place the United States at the center of the story. In so doing, the volume hopes to go beyond a simple celebration of women's entry into the armed services and provoke thought about the consequences of female complicity in imperialism as well as in peace-keeping, and armed resistance movements. The volume attempts to correct assumptions and arguments made by many opponents of women's integration into military forces, that women are essentially or naturally less belligerent or less aggressive. We hope also to spark debate about the degree to which inclusion of women in combat units, whether guerrilla armies or national armies, necessarily leads to a more humane form of warfare or military policy. At the same time, the volume reveals the problems women confront as targeted civilians without self-defense training or international legal protection.

As warriors, in the U.S. military, in the Bosnian defense forces, in the Israeli army, women have moved into new roles as military aggressors. By viewing the trajectory of women as victims and agents or accomplices to these different varieties of war over the century, this volume seeks to trace women's diverse experiences and understand their options for self-defense, national solidarity, and international action as both victims and agents. In addition, we hope to provoke thought about the new problems that accompany women's self-defense and national defense. As war is transformed, how are international legal structures changing to recognize the gendering of war? In what ways are military units prepared to accommodate soldier-mothers? We are increasingly faced with the paradox of a need for child care units for soldier-mothers and abortion clinics for rape victims. Such a study is bound to raise questions and provoke debate about the responsibility women as citizens or as unrepresented subjects, as victims and as warriors, bear for the increased turn toward violent resolution witnessed during the twentieth century.

A CENTURY TRAVELED

The First World War baptized the century in a pool of blood. The nature of trench warfare in Europe limited the actual violence to the front lines until the very end of the conflict, when aviation made its mark on selected urban centers. But on the home front women were mobilized into the labor force and into civilian defense units.[3] Like many of their brethren, women answered the patriotic call to arms as an expression of their national sympathies and their family solidarities. In many cases, they hoped that their participation would earn them a larger role in public and economic affairs after the war. Several Western nations honored women's work and sacrifice with political enfranchisement. But in countries like France and Italy the molders of postwar reconstruction quickly marshaled women out of the factories and offices and back into the homes without much more than polite discussion about granting them the vote. [4]

Not all women, nor all men, in all countries responded positively to the battle cry. Pacifist movements dating from the Bismarckian era organized themselves into a vocal, internationally networked voice of opposition. Women from Europe and the United States pushed their pacifist agenda. Some of these women's opposition movements stemmed from spiritual convictions, but as Annette Becker argues, spiritual convictions could also encourage women to support and endure the sacrifices. Within Europe an important segment of women pacifists came out of left-wing socialist movements whose theoretical critique of capitalism identified war as an instrument of power wielded by the ruling elite to divide, exploit, and destroy the laboring poor. These pacifists, such as the Polish Marxist Rosa Luxemburg, spoke in internationalist terms, urging their contemporaries to rise above competitive and destructive bourgeois nationalism.[5]

The cue for pacifists on the European Left came in September 1915 when Lenin, along with his associate Gregory Zinoviev, led an antiwar conference in Zimmerwald, Switzerland. Lenin's hope was that revolutionaries in the respective belligerent countries could turn the war into a civil uprise that would lead to revolution, the blueprint for subsequent events in Russia. Most of the delegates to the conference, however, sought simply to end the conflict, which Robert Tucker believes created the grounds for the subsequent schism between communism and social democracy. But even within the parties and movements of the European Left, pacifists occupied a minority position. In Germany members of the Social Democratic party voted for war credits. In France the acclaimed leader of the socialists, Jean Jaurès, rallied French workers to the war cause shortly before his own assassination.

Back in the United States, even some prominent industrialists embraced the pacifist position. In autumn 1915 the *Oscar II,* a Norwegian vessel, waited in her berth on the Hoboken docks. Henry Ford charted her to sail over to Europe to "get the boys out of the trenches by Christmas." The *Ford Peace Ship,* as it was later named, carried an assorted crew of journalists and activists organized under the energy and conviction of a Hungarian, Rosika Schwimmer, and an American college graduate, Rebecca Shelley, who persuaded Ford that a little publicity and Ford's influence could bring the conflict to an end. The *Peace Ship* had no impact on the conflict, but it was successful in minting a small group of peace activists, mostly women, who carried the tradition of internationalism and pacifism into the interwar years through promotion by female journalists like Lella Secor-Florence.[6]

The First World War marked women's definitive entry into the war machine. For some women, it opened doors to education, as was the case for Vera Brittain. It created new spaces for participation in the various world economies. It eased entry into the political realm.[7] Entrance also implicated women in the war's destruction. By war's end, whatever victory women pacifists and patriots alike received, either in the form of the franchise, maternity benefits, or widows' pensions, was offset by some form of irreplaceable loss--a brother, father, husband, or future husband. World War I demonstrated that blind patriotism seduced women as well as men. Paul's mother in Erich Maria Remarque's *All Quiet on the Western*

Front proudly sanctioned the honorable sacrifice of her son, who himself had come to understand the senselessness of the slaughter.[8] The poem, "The Hero," by the British poet, Siegfried Sassoon, recounts the story of a soldier who must inform a mother of her son's fatal last stand. The messenger-soldier masks the real cause of the son's death, a cowardly self-inflicted wound. Instead, he lies to the old woman, telling her of her son's bravery:

> Quietly the Brother Officer went out.
> He'd told the poor old dear some gallant lies
> That she would nourish all her days, no doubt.
> For while he coughed and mumbled, her weak eyes
> Had shone with gentle triumph, brimmed with joy,
> Because he'd been so brave, her glorious boy.[9]

Sassoon's resentment of the mother's desire and need to believe that her son died a glorious death contrasts with the many postwar memorials built to commemorate lost sons and grieving mothers. In Sassoon's poem the pleasure the mother derives from the tale of her son's heroics points to the complicated system of patriotic and sentimental fervor that sustained and even sanctioned, what for Sassoon, had become pointless sacrifices. In Chapter 2, Annette Becker discusses in more depth how women's religious fervor often fueled men's patriotic spirit.

We do not have a complete count of female fatalities from the Great War, nor do we know how many children perished from attacks on civilian centers. We do know that the war began the incorporation of women into battle via patriotism and politics. The Russian Civil War witnessed women's battle service as an expression of their ideological commitment both for and against the revolution. On the European continent and in the United States, where women did make a marked entry into the public sphere, the politics of pacifism achieved more of a cease-fire during the interwar period than any kind of victory.

FASCISM'S RISE, DEMOCRACY'S FALL

During the interwar period the bellicosity of the first great upheaval continued to create shock waves across the European continent and in the colonies. In 1922 Mussolini strong-armed his way into power in Italy. He instigated violence and aggression at home and abroad, initiating the Ethiopian War in 1935. The war in Ethiopia might well mark the beginning of African liberation movements born of European repression that would explode after World War II. In Europe the Fascist party in

Italy extended olive branches to a large sector of women, offering the same type of prenatal and maternity services implemented in the French and British welfare states.[10] But while the struggles of the 1930s adopted a more ideological and less patriotic fervor, the violence committed against women reached new proportions. In Spain the burning of Catholic nuns stands out as one of the most atrocious crimes attributed to the Republican coalition against the supporters of Catholic conservativism and traditionalists who participated in Franco's right-wing coalition. Yet Spanish women joined the very forces that waged war against the obstacles to democratic reform. La Passionara (Delores Iburrai), for one, served as the figurehead of the communist/republican resistance. However, by war's end many of these women were in exile, in prison, or dead. The Franco regime subsequently implemented a policy of the restoration of traditional roles for Spanish women.[11]

In Germany women's gains during the interwar political struggle fueled the Nazis' subsequent reaction against their place in the public sphere. The Nazi determination to keep middle-class women out of the workforce may have had long-term consequences for the German defeat.[12] The German case underscores the need to investigate the responsibility of women in maintaining, supporting, and indeed nurturing bellicose military orders. We are far from concluding that the German women of the 1930s held an important enough place in society to actually challenge, halt, curtail, or topple the National Socialist project of world domination. It is still important to try to identify the level of moral and civic responsibility women actually shared in sustaining or undermining, as the case may be, antidemocratic, militaristic regimes built on violence and aggression.[13]

WORLD WAR II

The interwar remilitarization of Germany and the establishment of exclusionary racial laws meant that German women, Gentiles and Jews alike, experienced the tremors of war before the rest of the world. But by 1939 the full-scale impact of a renewed military conflict reached beyond the borders of the Reich into Poland. In Europe the familiar recruitment of women into defense industry jobs and civilian defense teams paralleled the roles cut out for women in the Great War. But by 1940, with the German invasion of France, and with the Japanese attack on Pearl Harbor in 1941, civilian men and women witnessed the tremendous attack on the home front. World War II differed from World War I not necessarily in the fact that military aircraft targeted civilian centers, but in the sheer degree to which those centers became, if not the primary assault targets, then certainly the primary pawns in the psychological game of check and countercheck played by both sides. By the time the *Enola Gay*, named for the mother of the pilot, dropped its payload over Hiroshima followed by *Bock's Car*'s bombing of Nagasaki, civilian and soldier casualties in the war totaled nearly 22,060,000, with approximately 34,400,000 wounded.[14]

Women and children figured more prominently than ever in the casualty count. We do not have a precise breakdown of the sex and age of civilian casualties. The estimated figures for the Allied and Axis powers reveal the magnitude of the plunder. The United States lost approximately 6,000 civilians, compared to the Soviet Union's 2,000,000 or more civilian deaths. One set of statistics for Japan and France seems most surprising, given France's early withdrawal from the conflict. France registered between 325,000 and 391,000 civilian casualties, whereas Japan, who suffered the atomic bombings, tallied a slightly smaller estimated loss of 280,000. According to official Japanese statistics, the number of civilians killed in Japan totaled 421,367 against a combined total loss of 2,100,000, or 3 percent of Japan's total population.[15] Between the Germans and the British the figures of civilian deaths suggest that their prolonged engagement did indeed place them in front of France in terms of the percentage of civilian population losses. The British lost approximately 60,000 to 93,000, whereas the Germans lost about 780,000. The figures for German civilian casualties actually grow larger when we add the number of deaths caused by starvation and displacement. Nearly 1,500,000 are thought to have perished due to expulsion and air raids. Another 200,000 German ethnics died largely from reprisals at the end of the war. In total, German civilian and soldier losses amount to 5,300,000, which is still far from the number of losses suffered by the Soviets in their efforts to fight off the Germans.[16] Poland and Yugoslavia registered among the greatest civilian losses, with 5,000,000 and 1,200,000, respectively.[17] The massacre of Polish Jewry greatly increased these numbers in Poland.

When we read these staggering figures, it is hard to keep in mind the individual lives they represented. The fact that France, for instance, withdrew from World War II early, or rather was beaten into submission, did play a significant role in reducing the number of French casualties. The French paid for their civilians' and soldiers' lives in exchange for their liberties and in part in exchange for their Jewish and immigrant populations. Was that price too high? Such a question attacks the very crux of the problem faced by pacifists. Is peace or appeasement at any price a "just price," to avoid the large-scale ravages of total war? In the context of ideological wars, in which people's ideas are firmly entrenched and invested in the outcome, is peace without absolute submission of one set of ideas to another really possible? Registered among the casualties of firebombings and atomic experimentation, women were not only victims of the war. Women in all countries actively participated in their country's defense. For better or for worse, women, whether in the Soviet Union, in Germany, in Japan, in Italy, or in the United States, inspired by personal motivations, political causes, and patriotic impulses, actively served their country, demonstrating their sense of duty as citizens, their desire for adventure, and their determination to carve a role for themselves in their own nation's history. Many of these women resisted being categorized into negative stereotypes that equated women with pacifism or passivity. In many cases, the pacifists' voices of rationality and even enlightened morality, which echoed loudly after World War I, became the targets of suspicion in the politicized, ideological struggle of World War II. In short, ideology came to matter for women as much as for men in a way it simply had not during the Great War. The struggle for or against fascism temporarily transcended the national passions of the patriotic battles of World War I.

In the Soviet Union women joined the Red Army to defend the motherland as well as to fight the spread of fascism. Women's antifascist leagues organized early in the mid-1930s in the USSR. Most Soviet sources on the period define "the fascist invader," and not the "German invader," as the enemy in the Great Patriotic War.[18] Yet by war's end, Stalin had urged his people to defend mother Russia. On the European continent antifascism became a political umbrella under which women and men of a variety of political backgrounds---communists, Zionists, socialists, and Catholics---made alliances. They were not necessarily fighting against Germans and Italians, but against fascism or Nazism.[19] In many cases, women who joined resistant and partisan movements during the war in France, Italy and Germany did so out of newly minted convictions of the danger of fascism. Others, somewhat disappointed by the gains made by women during the interwar years, viewed the conflict with cynicism, seeing little difference between the way fascism and democracy ruled women.

A skeptical observer, Virginia Woolf, wrote her treatise *Three Guineas* in 1938 and argued, "We [women] can best help you [men] to prevent war not by joining your society but by remaining outside your society but in co-operation with its aims. That aim is the same for us both. It is to assert 'the rights of all---all men and women---to the respect in their persons of the great principles of Justice and Equality and Liberty.' "[20] Clearly, Woolf understood the ideals at the heart of the conflict, but she felt that women everywhere had been marginalized to such a degree from the chambers of politics that had created the catastrophe, that they could now only compromise their own integrity by entering into the fray of male-dominated war games. For Woolf, the reformation of politics at home needed to precede, or happen simultaneously to, the fight against antidemocratic forces abroad.

With Europe's economic and political infrastructure destroyed, the war's end created an opening for women. In France, Italy, and Spain women finally received the vote. Only the Swiss women would have to continue to wait until February 7, 1971, for complete political enfranchisement.[21] Women also gained a share in the redistribution of postwar wealth. The welfare state expanded, increasing the number of programs improving maternity, national health insurance, education, family allowances for large families, and a number of other state-sponsored initiatives that particularly helped women.[22] At the same time the welfare state's expansion helped women, the return to a normal economy forced many women back to the home. Not unlike the normalization process of World War I, women benefited less from the economic achievements of the war. Almost uniformly from the United States to Germany governments and employers encouraged women to leave jobs previously occupied by men. Only in the Eastern bloc countries did governments encourage, sometimes insist upon, women's continued participation in industry.

DE-COLONIZATION AND COLONIZED WOMEN'S STRUGGLES FOR NATIONAL LIBERATION

Beyond the European continent, in Japan, in the overseas European colonies, and in China, the war disrupted the political stability of the colonial system and also destabilized gender relations in much the same way the First World War had in Europe. In the arenas of the newly emerging nations, women joined in the Allied and Axis struggles that then turned into struggles for national self-determination. Like American and British suffragettes of the 1910s and 1920s, colonial women sought to secure an independent political voice for themselves by supporting and enlisting in the fight for national independence.[23] The parallels between the contributions and aspirations of these women bear a striking resemblance to the fortunes of their European sisters.

In the soon-to-be former colonies, postwar reconstruction met with the obstacles of continued armed conflict. The wars for national liberation followed closely upon the heels of V-E and V-J days. The Dutch East Indies were the first to go in 1945, closely followed by the Netherlands' other struggle to keep hold of Western New Guinea, a battle that lasted until 1962. In 1946 the French began their effort to regain military respectability and international political influence. The battle in Indochina dealt the French another stunning blow and resulted in the 1954 partitioning of Vietnam. The Vietnamese civilian population became embroiled in a new type of guerrilla war that proved effective against the technological superiority of European troops and inspired other colonial countries to challenge the authority of their European overseers. The Algerians were most influenced by the success of the Vietnamese. They launched their own assault on the French in 1954, but this time French persistence dragged out the liberation process until General de Gaulle signed the Evian Accords in 1962.

The British, unlike the French, and perhaps precisely because they had not suffered defeat during the Second World War, granted India independence without armed conflict in 1947. In 1949 the residue of British and Japanese imperialism fueled the revolution in China that erupted into a full-scale civil war, enlisting women, children, and even the elderly. Beginning in the early 1960s, African liberation followed the Asian initiatives. Not all African countries became engulfed in wars of independence, but the Angolan war against the Portuguese, which lasted from 1961 to 1975, demonstrated to the world how unwillingly some of the Europeans would leave.[24]

Because the nature of the wars for national independence transpired on a less grand military scale than the European conflict, communities and families participated in or were drawn into the conflict in more intimate forms of organization than the chaotic and haphazard integration of civilians into the battles of World War II. The subversive and indirect means of fighting the colonial armies opened up roles for women on the field level. Like the female partisans in Europe, many colonial women contributed to their countries' struggles for national liberation by transporting disguised weapons, such as the female gunrunners who hiked along the Ho Chi Minh Trail supplying the North Vietnamese troops. Again in an effort to throw out the French, Algerian women actively participated as spies, munitions carriers, and guerrilla suppliers. The measure of the seriousness of women's participation in these wars can be seen in the severity with which the Europeans punished them. How did Western women respond to the prolonged military conflict that extended beyond their immediate borders? Were women as politically engaged and aware during the Cold War as they had been during World War II? One measure of Western women's consciousness about global militarization and the plight of women's struggles in the emerging nations was their response to the build up of nuclear arms at home and abroad.

COLD WARRIORS

While the underworld of empire fought for freedom, global political divisions polarized and the actual political consensus within those polarities slowly fractured. The role and responsibility of Western women in either fortifying or challenging the logics and infrastructures of the Cold War are not directly analyzed in this volume, primarily because the violence of the Cold War was either optioned for the future, capped for the time being in the missile silos built across the world, or, as the volume clearly shows, exported to the regions and hemispheres safely distanced from the actual source of the fallout. Within the United States the role of women as warriors or resisters to the Cold War immediately seems to destroy the category of woman as a useful tool of analysis.

During the very history of their country's splendid rise as imperial hegemony, American women pursued a variety of complicated paths toward their own liberation. Some historians argue that the feminist movement of the 1960s grew directly out of the anti-Vietnam War movement.[25] At the same time that young women across the country called into question their part in maintaining and legitimizing U.S. intervention abroad, they became aware of their own subjected status at home. For the segment of American women coming to political consciousness during the Vietnam conflict, liberation of native peoples abroad became intimately intertwined with sexual and gender liberation at home.

But not all American women of the 1970s became feminists, and even fewer became feminists endowed with a more or less Marxian critique of U.S. or Western imperialism. Perhaps more significantly, a small but increasingly critical number of working-class women followed a different and even more complicated road toward liberation and equality. They joined the army. Within the very bulwark of the Cold War, American women and their allies sought to carve out an equal playing field of participation. What motivated segments of young American, British, and Canadian women, relying on the example of the Women's Army Corps (WAC) of World War II, to enlist in armies recognized world-wide for better and more often for worse, as the global policemen? Did enlisted women desire to participate in the fight against communism, the same fight their middle-class female counterparts had more or less decided didn't merit the lives of American soldiers and Vietnamese men and women? Did enlisted women, like many enlisted men, see the army as a tool for upward mobility, a way to pay for a college education? Did female

GIs see the army as a better way of serving their country than staying at home and having children or as an alternative to the pursuit of a university education? Or have American women in particular pursued access and advancement in the armed forces for the simple reason that the armed forces have for so long excluded women? Studies have begun to probe these questions.[26] What is true, is that American women's increased participation in the armed forces has paralleled American armed forces' rise to global dominance. By 1989 a total of 192,373 American women counted among enlisted personnel in all occupational areas, making up nearly 10.7 percent of the armed services personnel. By 1991 the total number of women in the active and reserve forces tied to Operations Desert Shield and Desert Storm figured around 40,782, or 7.2 percent of military personnel assigned to these operations.[27]

An examination of American women's pursuit of equality and advancement in the very institution that served as one of the two important pillars of the Cold War should be accompanied by a study of those women who chose to resist the Cold War and its politics of "mass annihilation": The American women who joined the antiwar movement in the late 1960s did not necessarily end up in the antinuclear movement of the 1980s which had a much deeper critique of the destructive policies of the Cold War and its arms race. Many women joined the antinuclear movements in the United States and especially in Britain, Germany, and Italy, where it flourished first in the late 1950s and then again in the early 1980s, when President Reagan introduced the new battery of Pershing missiles in Europe. Women from SANE (National Committee for a Sane Nuclear Policy), END (European Nuclear Disarmament Campaign), andCND (Campaign for Nuclear Disarmament) often relied on an essentialist, feminist, political critique to underscore women's moral superiority, as exemplified in the protests at Greenham Common. They believed that, as mothers, they had a responsibility to the future generations to "stop the insanity."[28] These activists did not always have a political critique of militarism that extended beyond a critique of the threat of nuclear missiles. CND, for example, believed that the starting point for greater social and political change could only come after the elimination of nuclear weapons. Alison Assiter, writing on behalf of CND, declared that,

The main British peace movement, CND, is a broad, all-inclusive popular movement; it is not a political party. If we believe that the successful elimination of nuclear weaponry requires other, broader changes in society, we can put the case for this within CND. If we believe, by contrast, that every nuclear missile can be destroyed without other alterations in the world, our view will be accommodated. Participation in CND requires one belief and one only, and that is a conviction that we need to rid the world of nuclear weaponry.[29]

Only recently have Western feminist scholars such as Cynthia Enloe begun to examine the connection between U.S. militarism, U.S. economic expansion, and the supression of colonial or postcolonial peoples.[30] Many of the debates generated by the peace movements of the 1950s and 1960s championed female moral superiority and/or insisted upon peace at any price. The pacifist camp accepted the notion of a universal, transhistorical, absolute definition of "peace," demanded by the advent of nuclear weapons and the narrowed and globalized definition of war.[31] Not all proponents of the peace movement were "absolute pacifists," but like Assiter, they insisted on the nonnegotiability of peace at any price, given the potential for nuclear holocaust.[32] As this volume shows, the terms of the peace negotiated at Potsdam following World War II were politically and ideologically bound to history and geography so that, despite the new absolute of nuclear war for Westerners, war and peace had much more variegated meanings for people around the globe. One challenge of the post–Cold War world is to understand how the imperative for peace, advocated by antinuclear activists, carried with it a specific Western chauvinism and consensus about the given political order. The struggles of men and women of the developing nations continued despite the looming threat of world destruction.

The Cold War hardly ended in a whimper. While American troops begin to withdraw from overseas bases, American women press for a greater role in a diminishing force. As the makeup of the American military changes, so does its role in the world. In the post–Cold War period, the relationship between the politics of the women within the superpower camp and those in the developing nations must be measured against each other. By presenting articles that address women's experiences in the periphery, this volume attempts to begin an investigation of the areas effected by the fallout of the Cold War. It examines ways in which women in non-Western countries resorted to violence or sanctioned it as a means of liberating themselves and their nation or ethnic group from the hegemonic political hold of the West. Another volume is certainly needed to analyze more deeply the relationship between the pursuit of women's equality in the superpower-controlled West and its consequences for women asserting their individual and collective autonomy in other regions of the world.

THE ENDGAME?

The volume ends with the Balkan wars of the 1990s, another spinoff of the Cold War. While wars continue to rage on the African continent in particular, the case of the Balkan wars allows the volume to end on a concrete exploration of how the post–World War II international legal and relief structures have kept up with the increased infiltration of war into the domestic sphere. It is clear at century's end that around the globe the "civilianization" of combat has certainly incorporated women and children more directly into war's wake. As displaced refugees expelled by ethnic rivals from homes and homelands, or as rape victims instrumental in the biological engineering of new ethnic combines, women as victims have experienced the old injustices of war in newly exaggerated proportions and often by more sadistic methods.

Piecing Together the Shrapnel of Women's Experiences

MOTHERHOOD AND MILITARISM

A clear set of themes emerges from this collection of essays, suggesting that while not all women endure war in exactly the same way, similar characteristics structure their multiple experiences. One of the most significant and perhaps the most problematic themes is that of the relationship that develops between state policies toward motherhood and maternity in conjunction with the state's military aims. Mindy Jane Roseman's discussion of the expansion of state-funded maternities during the Great War in France suggests how French policymakers developed a keen interest in the prenatal and postnatal care of France's progeny. French women gained concrete advantages in the form of state-reimbursed obstetrics and expanded hospitalization for child delivery in the context of the war. Middle-class women, as well as working-class and poor women, benefited from the state's preoccupation with the reproduction of the future nation. Roseman also argues that mothers paid a certain price——
the increased assertion of the state into the hearth. Acting much like a surrogate father, the French state promoted doctors over midwives and

hospital deliveries over home deliveries as a means of ensuring the health and well-being of the infant and mother. Roseman argues that the French state's intrusion into the economy and politics of birthing created equal access to medical care among women from all class backgrounds. At the same time, these policies strengthened the state's hand in controlling and monitoring motherhood.

Elizabeth Thompson's work on the role of Syrian and Lebanese women in the liberation movements of their respective countries investigates the intersection between motherhood and militarism on an ideological plane. Organizing for independence against the beleaguered French, Syrian and Lebanese women rallied around the notion of civic motherhood. Motherhood became the politicized anticolonial identity for these women. Women asserted themselves into the new nation and supported the wars of liberation, not as independent individuals, but as mothers with a stake in each nation's future. Thompson notes that ultimately this strategy of organizing and defining themselves as mothers of the new nations actually backfired and stood as the very category used to exclude them as citizens. But in a twist of meanings, Thompson maintains that the religiously conservative definition of motherhood that emerged during the struggle for liberation rooted itself in antiwestern, anticolonial expressions of independence.

Maternity, or the fear of it, serves in a different role for the women encountered by Helen Praeger Young on the communists' Long March through China. Exploring the motivations of young and sometimes old women who volunteered or were enlisted into the Revolutionary Chinese Red Army in the 1930s, Young discovers that many women hoped that service in the military would rescue them from the burdens of child rearing at home. In China war could liberate women from their traditional responsibilities, but did it? This question is not addressed in Young's article, but, it merits reflection. Did Chinese women realize liberation from traditional family structures at least during the years of revolutionary war, or were they simply reorganized into mothers of a Communist Chinese state? The last question invokes the most problematic role of a mother appearing in Engel's article on Russian women at the front during World War II. In a brief cameo appearance Engel describes the efforts of a pregnant female soldier to push a spool of wire to the front lines. The image captures women's participation in the life cycle from reproduction to destruction, but also underscores the grey area surrounding women's struggle between self-defense and aggression.

What is clear is that, in nearly all cases, the intrusion of war greatly eroded the divide between public and private authority, especially that governing women. In France during World War I, Roseman argues, the war ruptured the concept of privacy and the previously "essential" nature of the home. Engel points out that the breakdown of privacy at the front helped to equalize male and female roles. Ivy Arai's study of women in the Japanese-American internment camps shows that the U.S. government helped destroy family and community bonds, actually freeing women, at least temporarily, from patriarchal structures, and Young shows that the Red Army promised a safe haven for young girls seeking to escape the authority of fathers and potential husbands. Together these essays explore the connection between duties provided to the state by the institutions of the military and motherhood.

DEFENDING THE NATION AND WOMEN'S HONOR

During both world wars wartime governments encouraged women's maternal roles, but they discouraged and even restricted the very means by which women became mothers—having sex. In nearly all the articles that address the question of women's sexuality one theme emerges: States feared it, whether in the United States or the Soviet Union or Great Britain. The loosening of traditional patriarchal structures during wartime, the very absence of men, created an obsession of sorts (a form of male hysteria) over women's real or perceived sexual promiscuity. Susan Grayzel examines how the British government defined female sexuality as a threat to the British nation during the Great War. By reintroducing theDefense of the Realm Act, domestic agencies tried to monitor and discourage women's sexual activity. Female sexual activity, the British feared, corrupted not only the girl but the soldier as well. Sexual moralists argued that a British victory depended on the protection of women's morality. The logic ran that by defending the nation, British soldiers implicitly defended their women's honor. Thus women ought to restrict their actions and ensure that the soldiers did not fight in vain. In Grayzel's view, a language of morality and medicine (sexually active women spread venereal disease) worked to constrict women's imagination and activity. Roseman, too, identifies the sense of unease surrounding French women's sexual activity. French medical practitioners expressed outrage at the dramatic rise in abortions during the war and the failure of women to express adequate shame. It is possible, however, that the French felt outrage not necessarily at the fact that French women engaged in sexual encounters, but rather that French women chose abortion under the very conditions in which the state tried to encourage pronatalism.

Leisa Meyer's article on the Women's Army Corps in the United States during World War II approaches the problem of female sexuality from another angle. Meyer notes that women's expression of patriotic enthusiasm through enlistment in the WAC organization stirred concern among the general population, especially among military leaders. While the U.S. military recruited women and encouraged their participation in the war effort, women's enthusiastic response sparked suspicion. WAC administrators increased their lookout for lesbians within WAC ranks. At the same time, Meyer suggests that perhaps they were right. Women did experience certain aspects of the war as an opening for sexual exploration. She argues that lesbians did have hopes that enlistment in the WACs would expand their vistas and perhaps bring them into contact with more women like themselves. Meyer's article raises important questions: Did women's enlistment in the military auxiliary forces, along with the new stimulating environment it offered, empower women to explore their sexual desires? Or conversely, did their sexual desires propel them to join the WACs? Whichever came first, women's entry into the armed services produced sexual liberation and sexual repression in surprisingly equal doses.

Soviet men and women worked side by side at the front during World War II. Women served as combatants (approximately 200,000), as physicians, and as nurses. Engel reveals how a dialectic between respect and harassment constructed Soviet women's relationships with their fellow enlisted men and officers. According to one former female soldier, a double sexual standard existed not only at the front but also in the postwar memory of women at the front. Once again, the debate about women centers on their morality, promiscuity, or honor. In the unofficial postwar discussions within the Soviet Union, frontline women were often remembered as whores. Women remember tensions over whether or not sexual relations between men and women should have been tolerated. "Mobile field wives" were women recruited to serve higher ranking officers. Their relationships to the officers were often viewed as ambiguous. The presence of such relationships at the front, thus made it easy in the postwar era, to indiscriminately soil the reputations of all enlisted women. Engel points to ways in which enlisted men nevertheless respected and protected their female compatriots. The work of Engel and Grayzel raises the question of whether contemporary and postwar officials equated female chastity with military discipline. Perhaps, in order to facilitate the maintenance of this discipline, male soldiers designated female soldiers as "little sisters," in the Soviet ranks, thus, placing an incest taboo on male/female relations. Within the Soviet context, a dialectic seems to emerge between enlisted men's respect and appreciation of women's work at the front and officers' harassment of them. What is striking about all these articles is the fact that, regardless of women's patriotism, self-sacrifice, and conduct, contemporaries and postwar evaluators, most often, defined their contributions in relation to their sexuality. The balance between women as sexual agents and women as victims of sexual abuse during wartime becomes more ambiguous and even problematic in Atina Grossmann's discussion of the mass rapes of German women during April and May 1945 by Soviet soldiers. Like Grayzel, Grossmann links the defense of women's honor to the fueling of soldiers' morale. The fear of Soviet soldiers raping German women sustained German men's own rapacious engagement on the Eastern front. While fear of rape was not the only mobilizing force bolstering Wehrmacht soldiers' morale, their fears met justification during the "week of mass rape," when Soviet soldiers entered Berlin and exacted revenge. But it is not the rapes in particular that interest Grossmann, nor her subjects, but the historical manipulation of the rapes that embeds German women's sexual honor into the postwar rehabilitation of the German nation. Here, Germany displays few signs of historical or cultural particularity. In Japan the wartime government sanctioned the suicides of the women of Saipan, who allegedly took their own lives to preserve their honor and the honor of the Japanese nation. Women's sexual honor, as well as Japanese national honor, fueled the kind of kamakaze consciousness that the government sought to promote but whose success was more ambiguous, as Haruko Taya Cook's article suggests. Were mass suicides, in the case of Japan, preemptive measures deployed against fear of mass rape? The Japanese government promoted the image of the women of Saipan as exemplary and heroic displays of patriotic loyalty. Cook questions their motivation. In the context of this volume, the reader may wonder whether these women acted out of fear of rape and American reprisals.

Most German women did not commit suicide before the threat or reality of rape. In the aftermath of the mass rapes, German women sought to redress the injustices acted upon them. They petitioned government agencies for publicly funded abortions. In a reversal of Nazi policies prohibiting voluntary abortion, the provisional German government granted rape victims the right to abortions. Grossmann says that the suspension of the antiabortion policy and the funding of abortions actually had the effect of partially perpetuating the racial policies of the Third Reich. Here is where women's right to control their own bodies and the right of nations to control their own citizenry come into harmony in disturbing ways. One could argue, as Rhonda Copelon's article suggests, that the granting of abortions to German rape victims demonstrated an expression of the progress of the German state. On the other hand, Grossmann describes how German women drew upon the racialized vocabulary of the National Socialist era that not only vilified but denigrated Slavs in racial terms, thus justifying their pursuit of abortions. Grossmann concludes that German women did not lose their honor, but preserved it by vilifying Russian men. German women, raped by Soviet soldiers, thus presented themselves as problematic subjects. They relied on their victim status to act as agents for reassigning the responsibility for their own violation. Soviet barbarism, not Nazi aggression, resulted in their rape. Thus, Grossmann provocatively argues, that in order to understand rape in wartime, it must be de-essentialized, and historicized in its particular context.

On the other hand, in the volume's last article, Rhonda Copelon suggests that, in terms of international human rights law, as defined in the Geneva Conventions governing war, it is best not to de-essentialize rape. Domestic cases of rape and wartime rape have as their goal the debilitation of the victim; the degradation implicit in the act of rape is the vehicle for the realization of that particular goal. Copelon's article demands the recognition of rape as a particular tool of warfare that requires legal sanctioning. Exploring the conditions from which the concept of crimes against humanity emerged, the Nuremberg trials, held in Germany by the Allied powers to prosecute German war crimes, Copelon shows that rape has not figured into the language or the statutes defining crimes against humanity. As such, the specific type of wartime violence usually reserved for women is ignored in current international law. The prior absence of rape among war crimes acts to further negate women's wartime suffering. Most recently, Copelon argues, rape has served as a tool for ethnic cleansing, as is the case in the Bosnian wars.

Copelon believes that rape and genocide must be considered separate atrocities. Currently, rape is considered in the Geneva Conventions as a crime against honor and not as a crime *tout court*. While the concept of a crime against women's honor embraces more profound concerns, for Copelon, this concept of rape actually "obfuscates the fact that rape is fundamentally violence against a woman's body." As a crime against a woman's body, rape further violates her autonomy, integrity, selfhood, security, self-esteem, and community standing.

For Copelon, the only way to circumvent the ambiguity surrounding the crime of rape in international law is to elevate rape to contemporary understandings of torture. Torture encompasses both the physical and psychological dimension of the crime. Conceptualizing rape as a form of torture makes the crime intelligible within an international legal framework. What does such a definition do to rape inflicted as a means of achieving genocide? According to Copelon, genocide, in the former Yugoslavia, consists of forced pregnancy, repeated rape, and the prohibition of the woman to abort so that she is forced to carry the

"Serbianized" baby to term. Historically, however, rape has not always been used as a tool of genocide. This is all the more reason for separating it out from the legal structure governing genocide. During the German genocide of the European Jews, rape served only as a tool of humiliation, and Nazi law actually prohibited Germans from engaging in sexual intercourse with their Jewish victims.[33] Nazi ideology and laws defined any Jewish-German offspring as racially inferior and therefore unworthy of life. Unlike the Serbian plan to actually colonize Bosnian women's wombs, Nazi notions of genocide, of complete annihilation, prohibited such action (which is not to say that rapes did not occur). This historical detail further underscores Copelon's claim that "to exaggerate the distinctiveness of genocidal rape obscures the atrocity of common rape."

Within legal definitions of rape, Copelon also assigns legal responsibility. Here, interestingly, responsibility rests squarely on the shoulders of commanding officers for the discipline of their troops. Thus, regardless of whether proof can be identified as to whether a rape resulted from direct orders or simple unruliness of conquering regiments, commanding officers are held accountable for the behavior of their troops. The question remains: Will the presence of international laws be effective in protecting women from the crime they have consistently suffered over the centuries under the throes of war? Furthermore, will the elevation of rape as a specifically gendered war crime obfuscate other equally and often neglected war crimes suffered by women and civilian populations such as forced starvation, forced labor, and displacement from a region or to a concentration or refugee camp? The increased awareness and reporting of sexual harassment of women within the armed forces by officers or enlisted men raise new questions about the jurisdiction of civilian and military law.

Upward Mobility: War as a Conduit for Women's Political, Social and Economic Advancement

While individual women, like individual soldiers, often suffer under war's exigencies, wartime can and has offered opportunities previously unavailable to women. The immediate question is: Could those opportunities have resulted through peaceable means, or is war just a catalyst to a process already under way? How do women's wartime gains measure against their wartime and postwar losses? In nearly every article in this volume women seem to gain something as individuals or as a collective group under the various wartime situations. Roseman clearly shows that in the First World War, French women made indisputable institutional gains in deference to the sacrifices being made at the front by their husbands. Following World War I, British and American women received the vote. More recently, in Guatemala, where military forces uprooted or chased Mayan women from their villages, women like Antonella Fabri's subject, Rosa, discovered the possibilities of self-affirmation and independent action through the struggle to relocate and reestablish herself and her family. For Rosa, the war not only physically displaced her but shook up her own received notions about women's role in society. The Guatemalan civil war stirred Rosa's personal and political consciousness, motivating her to rescue her own family and to establish survival organizations for other displaced Mayan women. The Chinese Red Army actively educated female recruits not only about military tactics but also about the political mission of the Communist party and women's role within. More often, recruits came directly out of party education units. Chinese women who joined the army thus aspired to improve themselves through education, albeit a political one, and through actively participating in the party crusade. Political consciousness and political integration in this way propel women into public roles from which they had been excluded.

The most contentious article treating the politicization of women is Carol Andreas's chapter on Peruvian women in the Shining Path, (*Sendero Luminoso*). Andreas's article intersects with many of the themes concerning women's political engagement as a conduit into military, or in this case, guerrilla/terrorist, activity. Her article, however, departs from all the other scholarly articles in this volume, in that Andreas herself takes the position of an engaged intellectual. She is at once the chronicler of women in the Shining Path and an advocate. Andreas's article is included in this volume, not as an expression of solidarity or support for Andreas or the activities of the Shining Path, but rather because Andreas and her subjects reveal the degree to which the studies and understandings of women's relationship to combat and warring are complicated, often fraught with the same moral dilemmas as those faced by men. Gender lines do blur when we actually examine how and why women and men seek to pick up arms. The women of the *Luminoso*, according to Andreas, received a very similar Marxist/Maoist political education as the one received by the women described in Young's article on Chinese revolutionaries. It is precisely this kind of violence, in some cases labeled terrorism, that demonstrates how, particularly in the post–World War II period, warfare has expanded its categories of recruits, enlisting women and children in wars, or acts of resistance, sabotage, and terrorism. Had the volume included and article on women and the intifada compared to women in the Israeli military, we might have been better able to examine the crucial similarities and differences between women who serve in legally sanctioned military units and those who serve in extra legal associations.[34]

Andreas argues that issues of U.S. imperialism and the oppressive side effects of President Fujimori's program of modernization, which hit the Peruvian peasantry especially hard, offer some of the larger macro explanations for why women make revolutionary commitments to take up arms. Andreas claims that nearly 70 years after Maoist ideas inspired Chinese women, a similar doctrine and philosophy still resonate in many of the economically desperate areas of the world. Andreas herself, in her mission to enter the political arena, can be compared to earlier female intellectual/activists who wielded their pens instead of swords.

Political violence acted out by organized militaries or illegal guerrilla troops has transformed women's place in society and in the economy. At least in the West, during the two world wars women made notable gains in terms of economic integration into the workforce. Often they succeeded in leveraging their new economic power to gain greater political sway as well. In Europe the process of economic integration that began in the nineteenth century accelerated during the First World War. But not until after World War II did women, especially in the postcolonial countries, begin to receive equal protection under unions or labor legislation. The decolonized countries presented perhaps some of the most egregious challenges to the achievement of women's economic protection. Elizabeth Thompson holds the Lebanese Comprehensive Labor Code of 1946 as one of the major prizes won by women for their participation in the war of liberation. The Labor Code guaranteed in writing women's right to work, paid maternity leave, marriage pensions, and union-scale wages.

Although many women have enjoyed permanent or temporary economic and political gains due to warfare, it is perhaps too obvious to say that many lose on the very same grounds. Certainly, whereas all German women suffered losses of political and economic participation under Nazi rule and during the war, German Jewish women (and men) suffered the abolition of all their civil rights. In the United States, as Ivy Arai's article on Japanese-American women in U.S. internment camps shows, not all American women enjoyed an improved status during World War II. While the government scouted out lesbians among the WACs for military service exclusion, West Coast Japanese-American women suffered the suspension of most of their civil rights and experienced the legal exclusion from the political body, as well as the physical seclusion from their homes.

WOMEN AS VICTIMS

The ideals of nineteenth century battle confined soldiers to well-demarcated battlefields and women to hospitals. But even in the more neatly contained battles of the nineteenth century violence and death spilled over into civilian society. The burning of Atlanta in the U.S. Civil War might be one of the most obvious parallels to the firebombings of the twentieth century. Those who survived the attacks on the home front usually did so by methods of evacuation. Displacement, the uprooting of home and hearth, thus becomes one of the ways in which women, children, and the elderly survive but also encounter new dangers away from home and the protection of local or national security forces. We have witnessed in the twentieth century the growth of the strategy of forced displacement for purposes of ethnic reorganization of areas and as a means of solidifying territorial advances, resettling conquered territories, and providing escape and salvation. Displacement has occurred simultaneously with the example of the French exodus of 1940, which is discussed later in the volume, and organized displacement, as in the case of the expulsion of Poles and Czechs from German-occupied territories during World War II.

As the century closes, the dramatic increase in refugee crises born of military conflicts spreads, and despite the presence of an international agency in the form of the United Nations High Commission on Refugees, the threat of displacement worsens, bringing with it hunger, sanitation problems, epidemics, unemployment, exile, resentment, and violence against refugees. While the physical hardships faced by refugees demand the redistribution of resources and the commitment on the part of cooperative nations to aid and mitigate the physical hardships of displacement, the more intangible result of losing statehood, and thus rights and protections founded upon such rights, can be as dangerous as the absence of food and shelter. Of course, among the growing numbers of stateless persons are first and foremost women, children, and the elderly.

The Guatemalan civil war displaced and claimed the lives of nearly 100,000 counterinsurgents, according to Antonella Fabri. In her examination of the life of Rosa, Fabri finds that displacement produces trauma greater than that experienced through the loss of physical place. Displacement and reintegration can be experienced as misplacement, and as we see for rural dwellers like Rosa, who seek shelter and anonymity in larger urban locations, displacement can be from premodern to modern or postmodern society. The displacement faced by the indigenous refugees of the Guatemalan civil war, as well as by those refugees who are forced from their rural locales into urban centers, causes the loss not only of home but also of identity.[35] Fabri argues that displacement in the late twentieth century is part of an assimilation project on the part of modernizing industrial elites who have risen to power in the newly independent countries. We know, too, that displacement can be a form of segregation as opposed to assimilation, which was the goal in the uprooting of Jews in Europe, the internment of Japanese-Americans in the United States, the expulsion of the Bosnian Muslims from Serbian territory, and more recently, the genocide carried out by Hutu extremists against Tutsi's and moderate Hutu's. In the aftermath of 1994, this affair has resulted in the restoration of a Tutsi government and the subsequent flight of a massive Hutu refugee population, which includes many of the original perpetrators. While complicated, the African crisis underscores the persistance of the horrors linked to ethnic fighting and population upheaval.

Women are not only victims of displacement. They can also be its beneficiaries, as Ivy Arai demonstrates in her study of the evacuation of Japanese-Americans to Camp Harmony.   By uprooting Japanese-Americans from their homes in urban Seattle, the U.S. government not only facilitated the loss of Japanese-American pride and property rendering both men and women equally dependent upon a military authority, but also rattled the foundation of the Japanese-American patriarchal family structure.   Evacuation and displacement had the unintended effect, according to Arai, of opening opportunities for Japanese-American women to define a new role for themselves in the family and in the community as well. These gains came at considerable consequence, but Arai shows that the consequences of displacement were more devastating for Japanese-American men than for their female counterparts. This gain is perhaps entirely predicated on the fact that the United States won the war against Japan. It is worth considering what might have happened to the interned Japanese-Americans had the United States begun to lose the war in the Pacific.

Whether it is through the transfer of birthing from the home to the hospital, or the shift of refugee populations from the rural areas of Guatemala to Guatemala City, or from Seattle to Camp Harmony, displacement brings about a shift in the structures of authority and the promise of protection and security. What we have come to see is that international and local structures play a crucial role in determining whether displacement means survival or death. Especially for women, displacement from home and often family ranks as one of the most subtle, but life-threatening, forms of violence experienced in wartime. While change of place and transformation of social structures can create opportunity and advantage, they can also render women more vulnerable to violence. Perhaps as a means of controlling for the possibility of harm to oneself or one's family, that, faced with the century's spread of violence, women are increasingly as willing as men to pick up arms for the defense of home, country, or ideology.

WOMEN COMBATANTS: FRONTLINE FEMINISTS OR MILITARIST COLLABORATORS?

Perhaps no other topic concerning women's role in war creates as great a debate as the question of women's active participation in combat units. Barbara Alpren Engel's article on Vera Ivanovna Malakhova details the role of frontline female recruits. Having earned the Red Star for battle service, Vera, in an interview nearly 50 years later, discusses her pride in having served her country. Contrasted with the 1,000 women who committed suicide at Saipan in order to preserve national honor and individual dignity, the pregnant Soviet woman at the front, described by Vera, seems more life affirming than those women asked to throw themselves off cliffs because their military had failed in its efforts to protect them. Despite the heroic tales woven through much of this volume, in sum, women do seem to fall more often into the category of victim rather than agent. Grossmann argues that the German women who were victims of rape by Soviet soldiers occupied a dual position as both victims and agents. According to Grossmann, as agents, German women could have actively consented to, or could have endured the National Socialist regime that brought the war and its subsequent reprisals about in the first place. Ultimately, for Grossmann, the challenge of the historian is to both mark the victimization of German women in mass rape, and to explore the uses of that particular national memory in exculpating German war guilt.

In the contemporary United States context, the transformations of the United States military, through the integration of women into combat and flight, span the full spectrum of experiences, raising challenging questions. Women experience integration into the armed forces as both agents and victims within the institution that they have chosen to enter, first, as a means of both serving their country, and secondly, to achieve their own ambitions for advancement. On March 31, 1997, the *New York Times* reported from the Marine Corps training base at Camp Lejeune, N.C., that 100 female Marine Corps privates were allowed, for the first time in history, to fire live ammunition from heavy weapons. Pvt. Cynthia Martinez, 20 years old, of Houston, declared, "This should have happened a long time ago." Her Captain, George Botoulas defended the new policy in logical terms, arguing, "Women received fire and they return fire." One soldier, Pvt. Tabatha

Allen, described firing a grenade launcher as "exhilarating."[36]

Nearly a month later, in Minot, North Dakota, Lieut. Kelly Flinn, the first woman in the history of the United States Air Force to fly a B-52 bomber, a nuclear-armed plane, faced the possibility of being court-martialed on charges that arose from having had a sexual affair with a married, civilian, man. Apparently, Lieutenant Flinn had been ordered not to date the married man but she defied orders. Defending the efforts to court-martial Lieut. Flinn, Capt. Chet Curtis told the *New York Times* that Lieut. Flinn's case was an example of "serious" officer misconduct and added, "How can you lead people into war if you don't uphold those standards?"[37]

Beyond questions of officer insubordination are an array of questions about women's place in the military hierarchy. What is interesting about the Flinn case is that the first woman to fly stands to be reprimanded, not in terms or circumstances pertaining to combat, but pertaining to her personal life choices and the exercise of her own sexual desires. It is by the same institutions through which Lieut. Flinn so sought to stake her claim to liberation and independence, that she is checked and repressed. That is, of course, only one possible interpretation, but what is fascinating is how male-dominated institutions express their fear of women's rise to power in persistently sexual terms. But even another question arises, which is how, from a global feminist perspective, and hopefully from a perspective that condemns nuclear war, do we make sense of Lieut. Flinn's ambitions to become the first bomber pilot in United States Air Force history?

The story of Lieut. Flinn and the United States Marine Corps privates who found exhilaration in firing grenade launchers, force feminists in particular and intellectuals as a whole to begin to cast a more skeptical eye towards the claims of finding liberation through the integration of women into combat. Lieut. Flinn's story of triumph for "women" in the military becomes less persuasive when we begin to contextualize the position of the United States military, at the end of the twentieth century, in global terms. When we really begin to think about the possibility of inserting women into the script of world history, as equals to men, we find that there are wide varieties of men to which a wide variety of women can aspire to be equal to. In the case of twentieth century military history, a few women may be moving out of the category of victim, but it is unclear that the categories they are moving into as combatants is necessarily going to improve the status of the victims.

BETRAYAL AND DISAPPOINTMENT

Regardless of the service of individual women during times of war, whether serving in combat   units, smuggling weapons, working in munitions factories, nursing wounded soldiers,   or simply keeping the hearth warm, women as a group have not always received the rewards promised for their support and enthusiasm. The theme of betrayed hopes and erasure from the historical record of the war effort have more often been women's veterans' benefits. In her article on the Syrian and Lebanese liberation struggle, Elizabeth Thompson argues that women failed to receive the benefits of citizenship that the state granted to men upon victory. For Thompson, the model of colonialism and the religious conservativism of the newly empowered regimes conspired against women's enfranchisement. Thompson argues that, in part, women end up losers in the nation because the new nation was predicated upon a masculine image. In the case of Syria and Lebanon, the new regimes adopted the conservative position of the Vichy regime and applied it to the new nation, granting women social rights instead of political rights. The most clear-cut case of women not being rewarded for their participation in the war effort is, of course, the French case from World War I.

The failure to gain political rights more often comes as a trade-off for the acquisition of social rights, as again was the case in France. But a more frequent practice until recently has been to erase women's contribution from the historical record. In many of the volume's essays we read that women's contributions have been erased, eclipsed, distorted, or even condemned in the historical narratives that commemorate the wars in which women participated.   In Guatemala the erasure of women's experience and more largely the Mayan experience is an erasure not only from the historical record but also from the newly refashioned identity of Guatemala. According to Fabri, the intention of the new elites to shape a modern-day image for Guatemala is predicated upon the violent expulsion of the Mayan culture. Through the act of killing and displacing indigenous peoples the state actively fractures their sense of who they are and thereby has been creating the possibility of assimilating "traditional" peoples into the new Guatemalan citizenry. By capturing Rosa's history in the displacement caused by civil war, Fabri facilitates efforts to resist the erasure of counter-narratives, thus preserving and documenting a history that is, for the purposes of new nation building, better off left unrecorded.

The act of recording, inserting forgotten or deliberately neglected historical narratives that include women, is the major aim of this volume. At the end of the century, it is still the domain of military historians to write the annals of war, which offer a type of official record that continues to eclipse women's experience as agents and as victims. In the postwar context of the Soviet Union, where women saw perhaps the most actual combat, the effort to erase or even denigrate women's participation at the front, as explained in Barbara Alpren Engel's article, is understandable in the context of the reconstruction of the image of the Soviet Union as a postwar superpower. Should or would superpowers require the assistance of women in their defense forces? Vera Ivanovna Malakhova's narrative is a self-conscious effort to recapture and honor the service of Soviet women's struggle against Nazism during the Great Patriotic War and subsequently against the male chauvinism of the Soviet chroniclers of World War II.

In retelling the suicide stories of the women of Saipan, Haruko Taya Cook also engages in a similar subversion of postwar Japanese and American historiography. The inclusion or manipulation of the suicides of Saipanese women, according to Cook, served the purpose of confirming what both nations wanted and needed to believe about the Japanese. For the Japanese the story of 1,000 women willingly throwing themselves off a cliff underscored the sacrificial spirit of Japan and the devotion to the fight. For Americans, the suicides shored up the image of the Japanese as a kamikaze nation that must be subdued by any means necessary, including atomic weaponry. By relocating the narrative of the suicides next to the story of women who were actually captured and refused to commit suicide, Cook paints a picture of a more complex relationship between female civilians and the war effort. She also uproots the foundation upon which Americans have based their historical argument: that the Japanese would have fought to the last man or woman. By the same token, Annette Becker's story of the faith that French women placed in God's divine will, as a means of understanding and justifying the sacrifices of their husbands, brothers, and sons in World War I, reveals the extent to which faith, honor, and determination on the part of women could sustain and prop up soldiers' motivation and conviction to wage war.

This volume, taken as a whole, pieces together fragments of many experiences from a host of different wars, different geographies, and different periods in our century's history to try to understand the complex relationship women have to war, violence, and militarism and their own political and private convictions as citizens, wives, mothers, and even warriors. The record remains incomplete. The act of recording is the first step to remembering women's contributions. Beyond remembering that women were there, historians and contemporary policymakers need to debate the ethical and political problems that stem from women's insertion into the historical record of war, as well as their incorporation into contemporary military forces.

NOTES

1. For a recent sensationalized pictorial "history" of legendary female warriors, see Tim Newark's *Women Warlords* (London: Blandford, 1989).
2. Important contributions to the field of study include Ruth H. Howes and Michael R. Stevenson, eds., *Women and the Use of Military Force* (Boulder, CO: Lynne Rienner Publishers, 1993); Margaret Randolph Higonnet, Jane Jenson, Sonya Michel, and Margaret Collins Weitz, eds., *Behind the Lines: Gender and the Two World Wars* (New Haven, CT: Yale University Press, 1989); Jean Bethke Elshtain and Sheila Tobias, eds., *Women, Militarism, and War: Essays in History, Politics, and Social Theory* (Savage, MD: Rowman & Littlefield, 1990); Laurie Weinstein and Christie C. White, eds., *Wives and Warriors: Women and the Military in the United States and Canada* (Westport, CT: Bergin & Garvey, 1997); Cynthia Enloe, *Does Khaki Become You? The Militarization of Women's Lives* (London: Harper Collins, 1988).
3. A vast literature exists on women, gender, and World War I. Much of the literature celebrates women's contributions to the total war effort but some studies look at the more long-term social and economic transformations resulting from the war that changed women's lives. See Clive Emsley, Arthur Marwick, and Wendy Simpson, eds., *War, Peace, and Social Change in Twentieth-Century Europe* (Philadelphia: Open University Press, 1989); Laura Lee Downs, "Women's Strikes and the Politics of Popular Egalitarianism in France, 1916—1918," in ed. Leonard R. Berlanstein, *Rethinking Labor History: Essays on Discourse and Class Analysis* , (Urbana: University of Illinois Press, 1993), 114—137; Françoise Thebaud, *La femme au temps de la guerre de 14* (Paris: Stock/L. Pernoud, 1986); Jean-Jacques Becker, *The Great War and the French People*, trans. Arnold Pomerans (New York: St. Martin's Press, 1986); Richard Wall and Jay Winter, eds., *The Upheaval of War: Family, Work, and Welfare in Europe, 1914—1918* (Cambridge, England: Cambridge University Press, 1988); Gail Braybon, *Women Workers in the First World War: The British Experience* (London: Croom Helm, 1981); Ursula von Gersdorff, *Frauen im Kriegdienst 1914—1945* (Stuttgart: Deutsche Verlags-Anstalt, 1969).
4. Women received the ballot in national elections following World War I in nearly all Western countries. In 1915 Denmark and Iceland fully enfranchised women. In 1917 the Netherlands, the Soviet Union, and Finland followed suit. In 1918 Sweden, Great Britain, China, Austria, Germany, Estonia, Latvia, Poland, Lithuania, Czechoslovakia, and Hungary joined the march. In 1919 Rhodesia, Luxembourg, and British East Africa continued the lead. Finally, in 1920 the United States, Canada,

Belgium, Palestine, and Ireland extended the vote to their female citizens. France waited until 1946. Quoted from Steven C. Hause and Anne R. Kenney, *Women's Suffrage and Social Politics in the French Third Republic* (Princeton, NJ: Princeton University Press, 1984), 253.

5. See Rosa Luxemburg, "To Proletarians of All Countries," in *Selected Political Writings*, ed. Dick Howard (New York: Monthly Review Press, 1971), 352—358. Luxemburg denounces the violence of the Great War and the tradition of Prussian militarism that have led to the break-up of the international union of the European working class. She laments the moment when members of her own Social Democratic party voted war credits in August 1914 to the German government.

6. For Lenin's writings on the war, see Lenin, "Socialism and War," in The Lenin Anthology, ed. Robert C. Tucker (New York: W.W. Norton, 1975), 183—95. For more information on women's peace activism during the first part of the century, see Sandi E. Cooper, *Patriotic Pacifism* (New York: Oxford University Press, 1991) and Catherine Foster, *Women for All Seasons: The Story of the Women's International League for Peace and Freedom* (Athens: University of Georgia Press, 1989). For a long view of women and peace movements in the United Kingdom, see Jill Liddington, *The Road to Greenham Common: Feminism and Anti-Militarism in Britain Since 1820* (Syracuse, NY: Syracuse University Press, 1991).

7. SeeVera Brittain, *Testament of Youth* (London: Fontana, 1979), and Lynne Layton, "Vera Brittain's Testament," in *Behind the Lines*, op. cit., 70—83.

8. Erich Maria Remarque, *All Quiet on the Western Front* (New York: Ballantine Books, 1982). First published as *Im Western Nichts Neues* (Germany: Ullstein A.G., 1928).

9. Siegfried Sassoon, "The Hero," in *The Great War and Modern Memory*, ed. Paul Fussel (New York: Oxford University Press, 1975), 7.

10. For discussions of women and the welfare state during the interwar years in Italy, Britain, and France, see Victoria DeGrazia, *How Fascism Ruled Women* (Berkeley: University of California Press, 1992), and Susan Pedersen, *Family, Dependence, and the Origins of the Welfare State in Britain and France* (Cambridge and New York: Cambridge University Press, 1993).

11. Paul Preston, *Revolution and War in Spain, 1931-1939* (London and New York: Methuen, 1984). See Martha A. Ackelsberg, "Women and the Politics of the Spanish Popular Front: Political Mobilization or Social Revolution?" *International Labor and Working-Class History* 30 (1986): 1—12. See also J. Gutiurrez Alvarez, "El Femenismo Anarquista de Las 'Mujeres Libres' 1936—39," *Historia y Vida* 20(1987): 30—39; Shirley

Mangini Gonzalez, "Spanish Women and the Spanish Civil War: Their Voices and Testimonies," *Rendezvous* 22, (1986) no. 2, 12—16.

12. For a discussion of how the Nazi regime viewed women's labor, see Jill Stephenson, "Women's Labor Service in Nazi Germany," *Central European History* 15 (1982): 241—265. See also Leila J. Rupp, "Women, Class and Mobilization in Nazi Germany," *Science and Society* 43(1979): 51—69. Rupp argues that primarily working-class women were used, to spare disruption to middle-class lifestyles.

13. Claudia Koonz has argued that German women's maintenance of "normalcy," of private life, created an important buffer from the brutality of German army officers' work at the front and in the concentration camps and thus enabled them to carry out their brutal project knowing that they could return to the civilizing environment of the home. See Claudia Koonz, *Mothers in the Fatherland: Women, the Family and Nazi Politics* (New York: St. Martin's Press, 1986). For a less empowered view of German mothers, see Gisela Bock, "Racism and Sexism in Nazi Germany: Motherhood, Compulsory Sterilization, and the State," in *When Biology Became Destiny: Women in Weimar and Nazi Germany,* ed. Renate Bridenthal, Atina Grossmann, and Marion Kaplan (New York: Monthly Review Press, 1984), 271—297. See also Annemarie Troger, "German Women's Memories of World War II," in *Behind the Lines: Gender and the Two World Wars,* eds. Margaret Randolph Higonnet et al., (New Haven, CT: Yale University Press, 1987), 285—301.

14. A Vatican study generated these figures in 1946. The exact number of casualties remains inconclusive. Norman Polmar and Thomas Allen, *World War II: America at War 1941—45* (New York: Random House, 1991), 193.

15. These statistics come from John W. Dower, *War Without Mercy: Race and Power in the Pacific War* (New York: Pantheon, 1986), 297—298.

16. Martin K. Sorge, *The Other Price of Hitler's War: German Military and Civilian Losses Resulting from World War II* (New York: Greenwood Press, 1986), 67. Sorge takes his figures from a study published in 1958 by the Federal Republic of Germany titled "Deutschland Heute." The German armed forces reported 3,050,000 combatants lost.

17. These statistics are drawn from the work of Louis L. Snyder, who also makes the claim that we cannot know for certain the total casualty count of World War II. Louis L. Snyder, *Louis L. Snyder's Historical Guide to World War II* (Westport, CT: Greenwood Press, 1982), 126. The following are the battle-to-civilian casualties for a few of the combatant countries, as counted by Snyder: USSR: 6,000,000—7,500,000/ 2,000,000—plus; United States: 292,000/6,000; Germany: 3,275,000—

4,400,000/780,000-plus; Japan: 1,219,000—2,000,000/280,000—plus; France: 200,000—400,000/391,000; Italy: 77,500—162,000/146,000; China: 1,324,000—2,200,000/none. This last figure for China seems particularly unlikely but was reported in five sources. Dower estimates that the Chinese had approximately 10 million war dead, including casualties of the famine. Trying to distinguish civilians from soldiers seems nearly meaningless. Despite the heavy toll suffered by China, the Soviets still lost a greater number of their total population.

18. Historians have argued that Stalin coined the title "Great Patriotic War," as opposed to the "Great Revolutionary Struggle" or "Great Battle to Save Communism," because it would have been more difficult to rally the Soviet population to defend ideology over country. So, while the motherland was not defined in specifically ideological terms, the enemy was defined in ideological rather than hereditary or racial terms. Of course, ideology did not present a problem for Stalin when he signed the Hitler-Stalin Pact of 1939.

19. The *Union Sacrée* of World War I succeeded, if only briefly, in the suspension of intranational class tensions and political divisions for the pursuit of the higher patriotic cause, but the result of that uneasy union was exactly the radical politicization that resulted in the creations of extremist politics on the Right and on the Left. That was a result of the war, not a feature of it.

20. Virginia Woolf, *Three Guineas* (New York: Harcourt Brace Jovanovich, 1938), 143.

21. Thomas Wanger, "Mannerherrschaft ist Krieg: Waffenkult und Politischer Frauenausschluss," *Homme* 3, no. 1, 45—63. Wanger examines the fact that Swiss men in Appenzell Ausserrhoden wore daggers and swords to prove their right to vote and now, since 1990, men and women carry cards.

22. For excellent discussions about postwar welfare states and women, see Robert G. Moeller, *Protecting Motherhood : Women and the Family in the Politics of Postwar West Germany* (Berkeley: University of California Press, 1993), and Linda Gordon, ed., *Women, the State and Welfare* (Madison: University of Wisconsin Press, 1990).

23. Not all of the European colonies, however, capitalized on the war as an opportunity to assert independence. In fact, many colonial subjects fought valiantly or served their respective mother countries with unwavering commitment despite racism and   exclusionary policies. See Ben Bousquet and Colin Douglas, *West Indian Women at War: British Racism in World War II* (London: Lawrence and Wishart, 1991).

24. For a basic narrative on the history of African liberation in the context of the Cold War, see Peter Calvocoressi, *Independent Africa and the*

World (London: Longman, 1985).

25. See Sara Evans, *Personal Politics: The Roots of Women's Liberation in the Civil Rights Movement and the New Left* (New York: Vintage Books, 1980).

26. For a celebrationist history of the rise of women in the U.S. and British armed services, see Kate Muir, Arms and the Woman (London: Sinclair-Stevenson, 1992). Muir hails the arrival of women in the military as a sign of women's gains to equal access to male bastions of privilege arguing, "Apart from the priesthood, the military is the only institution still standing up to the onslaught" (Muir, 97). She further stakes out the position that as armies increasingly assume peace-keeping responsibilities requiring close contact with civilian populations, women bring an important perspective to the new military mission. Such an argument is, of course, based on an essentialist notion of women's innate attributes, which would, if they were really innate or biological or sex-specific emotional predispositions, act in such a way as to prevent them from enlisting in militaries in the first place.

27. Figures taken from data provided by Defense Manpower Data Center, cited in Mady Wechsler Segal, "Women in the Armed Forces," in *Women and the Use of Military Force*, op. cit., 87—98.

28. For an excellent discussion of the problems of essentialist and separatist strategies for achieving peace, see Janet Radcliffe Richards, "Why the Pursuit of Peace Is No Part of Feminism," in *Women, Militarism, and War: Essays in History, Politics and Social Theory* , ed. Jean Bethke Elshtain and Sheila Tobias (Savage, MD: Rowman & Littlefield, 1990), 211—227. Richards argues that separatist political strategies hark back to nineteenth century notions of separate spheres. She further suggests that by making "peace," a women's issue is a mistaken approach since peace is not just good for women. Unfortunately, Richards errs in assuming that there exists something like "bad male values," war, that can be replaced with "enlightened female values," like peace, a logic that rolls back into the very essentialism Richards asks the women of Greenham Common to rise above.

29. Alison Assiter, "Womanpower and Nuclear Politics: Women and the Peace Movement," in *Over Our Dead Bodies*, ed. Dorothy Thompson (London: Virago, 1983), 204.

30. Cynthia Enloe, *Bananas, Beaches, and Bases: Making Feminist Sense of International Politics* (Berkeley: University of California Press, 1990).

31. For manifestos written by members of different peace movements in Britain, see Alice Cook and Gwyn Kirk, *Greenham Women Everywhere* (London: Pluton Press, 1983), and Dorothy Thompson, *Over Our Dead Bodies* , op. cit.

32. Books exploring the variety of American approaches to the elimination of nuclear weapons include William Chaloupka, *Knowing Nukes: The Politics and Culture of the Atom* (Minneapolis: University of Minnesota Press, 1992); Allan M. Winkler, *Life Under a Cloud: America Anxiety About the Bomb* (New York: Oxford University Press, 1993); Carole Gallagher, *American Ground Zero: The Secret Nuclear War* (Cambridge, MA: MIT Press, 1993); and Marilou Awiakta, *Selu: Seeking the Corn-Mother's Wisdom* (CO: Fulcrum Publishing, 1993), all reviewed by Jane Caputi, "Nuclear Visions," *American Quarterly* 47, no. 1 (March 1995): 165.

33. The Law for the Protection of the Blood prohibited marriages and extramarital relations between Jews and Aryans. For an in-depth discussion of Nazi racial laws, see Michael Burleigh and Wolfgang Wippermann, *The Racial State: Germany 1933-1945* (New York: Cambridge University Press, 1991), 82.

34. For a review of recent literature on women in the Middle East, see Suad Joseph, "Women, War and History: Debates in Middle East Women's Studies," *Journal of the History of Sexuality* 4, no. 1 (1993): 128—136. For a study of the formation of Palestinian women's consciousness see Amal Kawar, "National Mobilization, War Conditions, and Gender Consciousness," *Arab Studies Quarterly* 15, no. 2 (1993): 53—67. For an overview of Palestinian women's lives under occupation read Fawzy Didar, "Palestiniennes de l'Interieur" *Mediterranean Peoples*, 22-23 (1983): 131—147.

35. For a more theoretical analysis of how violence, especially collective sexual violence, against women erodes their communal identities and ties, see Ruth Seifert, "The Second Front: The Logic of Sexual Violence in Wars," *Women's Studies International Forum* 19, nos. 1—2 (1996): 35—43.

36. Michael Janofsky, "Women in the Marines Join the Firing Line," *The New York Times*, March 31, 1997, 1.

37. Elaine Sciolino, "From a Love Affair to a Court-Martial," *The New York Times*, May 11, 1997, 1.

Part I
1914–1939

Figure 2. Women greet returning World War I soldiers.
Arras, France, September 1918.

TWO

Tortured and Exalted by War
French Catholic Women, 1914–1918

Annette BECKER

> Our Father, you are the Lord, but it is the tenderness of our marriage which is eternal....I wait for no one else..because you will never return...my God, make me understand, give me the strength to bear....My love given for France, abandoned in order to please God....How has my heart consented to such a wrenching....Oh! We must love God terribly to make such a sacrifice. To love him, I give up my loved one. To love more than love itself?...You are not dead and I am not a widow...There is this infinite, dear, grief because the unchanging and deep darkness is the image of the sad and tenacious fidelity....Widowhood which is nothing more than a long test of conjugal fidelity...now all contact is over, that is the sacrifice, but hearts hold on to each other.[1]

From April 3, 1915, the world catastrophe that soldiers were already calling "the Great War" crashed down on Mireille Dupouey. Like millions of women across the globe, Mireille already understood the horrors of a separation that she believed to be only temporary. She and her husband, Dominique-Pierre Dupouey were united above all in a common love of God. In 1911, at the time of their marriage, Mireille sponsored the young naval officer, before God, in his conversion to Catholicism.[2]

Like Mireille Dupouey, each of the contemporaries of the Great War, regardless of nationality or side, was a product of a late-nineteenth or early-twentieth-century education, determined by country, religion, and family. Each person had acquired by this time the values that he or she defended—or believed to defend—during and after the conflict. These values, put to the test before suffering, anxiety, wounds, or death, were to resist, then transform themselves and give birth to new values. In this way, combatants and civilians existed in a series of affective and political relations that would take them away from their loved ones and to the

State. The members of families, parishes, professions, neighborhoods, and villages carried an individual destiny situated within a collective destiny determined by their local community, the Catholic Church, and their country. This is the heart of a culturally totalizing process of a conflict from which no individual escaped because each participated in the enormous fight for the civilization, from the period of the war proper through the 1920s, "from death to memory."[3]

If war is formally a military battle between military men, it cannot but be considered as an ensemble of fluctuations, of comings and goings between the front and the home front: munitions and supplies, propaganda and love, religious and patriotic fervor, hope and disappointment, death and mourning, male sensibilities and female sensibilities. The majority of combatants were married men and fathers, and they had the impression that to resist meant above all to dignify whatever experience awaited their loved ones, to ensure the security of their own.[4] In the context of this male/female give—and—take, history has, to this point, been mainly interested in what men thought about combat and separation.[5] In this essay, I try to recover the words of those women of a very specific milieu of intellectual practicing Catholics, indeed militant believers: intellectuals, because these women were in the habit of entrusting to pen the ideas that preoccupied and sustained them; Catholic practitioners, because they were in the avant-garde of the fervor for a crusade that spirited the heart of the war culture.[6] How many among them were entirely persuaded that this war was indeed a "religious war"?[7] Their war might be read as a diptych: If it separated them from the men they loved, from husbands, sons, brothers, and friends, then the war also brought them together via values, both shared and reaffirmed by the war.

WAR'S SEPARATION

The war upset all the material and affective habits of society. In August 1914, all healthy men joined their units, whether they were career officers, enlisted men, or volunteers. Women did not participate in war, not in this manner. The separation began. The fact that the large majority of French men and women imagined a short and victorious war explains why they moved beyond their intense sadness and parted with conviction: "It seemed to me, my Pauline, that it was you being sent to war, that one robbed me of . . . my love, I am sad and tired. I am alone. I would like to fight immediately."[8]

In a few weeks the assumed temporary separation evolved into indefinite time. The war was not won as rapidly as expected. The troops entrenched themselves and at a terrible price: Some were wounded or killed, others lost in action, perhaps taken prisoner. Separation became waiting: waiting for letters, for news, for certainty of life. For Jacques

Maritain, an enlistment exemption, due to poor health, resulted in a continual reporting to duty throughout the entire war. For Raïssa, Jacques' wife, this back and forth pattern brought with it a paradox, several times over, the terror of departure, increasingly more potent, as one by one, their friends died at the front:

> Jacques is declared fit for the armed services. What a joke. But how upsetting for me. I said it, "God's will," as soon as possible, without waiting for my heart to taste the pain . . . intense contemplation but in anguish and sadness. God and Jacques exist at the same time in my heart. Agony. From this point forward I can only consider myself as good as dead. What kind of life for me if Jacques departs! More importantly what might happen to me. This thought strengthens me. By this test, God asks for the expansion of my love. . . . There is within this trial a humiliation that is good, an apparent abandonment made to bolster hope and unite us to the crucified savior. Our good mother of the sky. It seems that she too is made of a bronze heart for us. But what, has she not sustained us for three years of waiting for this awful war? Could it not in fact be that this strong woman fixes us to the tree of the Cross in order that we carry the fruit of the welcomed redemption?[9]

This enormous mysticism Raïssa Maritain confided only very rarely to her journal of notations, which, beyond her love for God and the force of the contemplative life, expressed her very human love for Jacques Maritain. She had the unbelievable luck though never to see her husband depart farther than the artillery depot of Versailles, where he was declared definitively unfit for service.[10] She probably felt a little shame and extreme anxiety at such a moment, accepting, however, "God's will." She reasoned that to consent to sacrifice, gave proof of one's Christian purity. Among their friends, everyone rejoiced at Jacques's exemption; Not one condemned him, or put into question their patriotism. Their Christian pacifism gave them the certainty that, above all, God decides. The letters from their friend Christine Van der Meer of Walcheren demonstrated this very well. In a rare example of woman—to—woman wartime correspondence, she wrote:

[in 1914] . . . Jacques has been definitively exempted and that was a great joy for us; that at least he was spared the horrors of the war. There is a nobler and more useful task to fulfill than to kill and destroy others. Alas, that God wishes to have pity on France and to chase the barbarians who dirty his dignified soil....That which takes place in Belgium and in France is incredible. Is it really necessary that the *wrong* should be so grave and that the punishment should be so reprehensible [in 1917] Jacques enlisted . . . that adorable hand of the master is sometimes so sad and incomprehensible! It seems too stupid and absurd to the point that it must be, it seems to me, his expressed desire. . . . Jacques will have more of a chance to do good and his example will lead others to God. . . . But the suffering is immense and I pray to God . . . to spread his grace over you so that you wear it as a valiant soldier of Jesus Christ. . . .[11]

Jacques Maritain, the intellectual, battled against Germany from 1914 on, with his own kind of arms, those of philosophy and theology.[12] One can hardly prevent oneself from thinking, however, that others, intellectuals or not, beginning with their friends Ernest Psichari and Charles Péguy, had paid for the same engagement with their lives. Some of the Maritains' closest friends lived a definitive separation—definitive, as they believed, uniquely on earth.

Isabelle Rivière was forced to wait for many weeks without news of her loved ones. Her brother and her husband were reported missing in combat. Jacques Rivière had been captured. Henri Alain-Fournier[13] was dead, but like hundreds of thousands of soldiers of the Great War his body was never found. Alain-Fournier had become an unknown soldier. Isabelle and Jacques Rivière thus began a difficult dialogue between France and eastern Prussia: The delay of shipping letters was very long, and it was impossible to really respond to each other. Letters had to pass by the military censor, and perhaps even more difficult, the censor of the heart. Jacques and Isabelle were tortured by the death of Alain-Fournier to the point that Isabelle continued to refuse to believe. "My Jacquot dear, today it is one month since I've learned that you are alive; I am brought back to life....I only ask to receive similar news about Henri as I have received about you."[14] Rivière, on his part, suffered a form of double guilt. On the one hand, he lived the collective guilt born from having been taken prisoner; on the other hand, he grappled with the personal guilt of a man who continued to love another woman as well as his wife. Like so many of his contemporaries, he considered having been taken prisoner a failure, a humiliation, "an interminable mortification."[15] Furthermore, he was tempted to escape in order to resume his place in the combat, but in 1917 he hesitated to benefit from a transfer to Switzerland for medical reasons.[16]

Isabelle tried to show him that they were stronger than the war, than the "failure," but she was occasionally discouraged: "I received your letter with the second photo. You are the same in one as in the other: yet there is something changed in you. . . . Are we going to continue much longer to age and to change so far from each other?"[17]

Isabelle and Jacques Rivière had 3 years to learn how to live with separation, which is described by Isabelle as another fashion to love and to live: "To speak to you of me, my poor love! What can one say. I only exist in thought and in waiting. I dream that we will be two new beings, that it is necessary to reacquaint ourselves with each other entirely: It will be like a new love, and at the same time my sadness and my consolation."[18]

It is in this manner that the weight of the war and the price of death were the reality not only of the front; via correspondence and leaves, the entire society was visited and very soon traumatized by death long before Verdun, the Somme, or the *Chemin des Dames*.[19] Widows and orphans soon multiplied. In November 1914, Pierre-Maurice Masson wrote to his wife: "I ask myself how the French soul can survive among such sadness....How will budding youth, love, and dreams of happiness ever bloom again on this devastated soil?"[20]

The correspondence of Mireille Dupouey is exemplary since she continued to write to her husband after his death. This practice did not dissipate until well into the 1930s, when she died: "I sort through the letters in my mailbox, five, not a single from you!—How can it be? *Voilà* the mystery of death. Is it because there is a mystery in grief which I can believe in like I believe in the beneficent mystery of the divine religion?"[21]

Henceforth death reigned: The war accomplished its work. And indeed, this dramatic vision had to be complemented in some less pessimistic expression. Our witnesses knew, and were able to find in the depths of the loss brought by the war, the loss of faith. One lost oneself in the war, but one could also find oneself on the other side of death as well: "Oh how the war had revealed everyone to himself; in the triage that it so meticulously achieved, it is evident that all the doubters have fallen." Isabelle Rivière thus judged her contemporaries in very harsh terms, whereas her husband accepted the idea of choice made by the war and reminded her of her duty of Christian indulgence: Each person struggles with himself or herself in war at his or her own rhythm of grieving and hoping.

WAR RECONCILES AND REUNITES

Pierre-Maurice Masson wrote to the widow of one of his cousins: "That which is moving and magnificent in this death, is that death has accepted in these last few months the most peaceful of the courageous, and that he seems to only love you all the more for his ability to sacrifice himself to his duty; showing thus, as in a final gesture of a Christian knight, that there are times when, to achieve the beauty of a life one must know how to lose it."[22] The exalted vision of the war, extending its charitable aspects to include death, was largely shared by Christian women. One finds in their writings this insistence on the sacrifice and its inherent virtue. A fascination with suffering is expressed in such a manner. The sublimation of sadness into human love is at the heart of the different dialogues, mixing a love for France with a love of Christ: "I feel myself ready to defend savagely the beautiful French order which has made blossom the wise melody of my life by the light of your eyes."[23] All evoke the communion of saints; they feel themselves "enlisted in this grand 'army' of saints which God is at once the limit and the ferment."[24] The *choice* to offer one's life to God was seen as giving meaning to combat, from the front to the home front.

A few short hours before being killed at the front, Dominique-Pierre Dupouey described to his wife the horrors of night combat. Then, in what would be his last letter, he concluded in the following manner: "Let us not force ourselves to tears when God makes us see the 'motifs' of joy . . . at the bottom, to make the great prayer for each of us, continue to be the magnificent cry of the French poet, PaulClaudel: 'Lord, deliver me from myself.'"[25]

The war effectively reunited the Dupoueys in the certainty of their values. It only separated them in appearances. Mireille all her life would maintain a friendship with Henri Gheon, whom her husband helped to convert to Catholicism. In the same way, the Rivières rejoiced at the conversions for which they were the vectors during the conflict. These wartime conversions could be viewed as victories achieved between the front and the home front, responses to the miracles of God and miracles in and of themselves. It is in this manner that Alain-Fournier saw the conversion of Pauline, who he described as, "my young Jewish wife with whom I present myself before God," to marry. [26]

These conversions were taken as a sign of the mediation of the living or of the dead in the war. The war itself was thus converted, transformed into a spiritual exercise: A collective imitation of Christ, the war engendered the new spiritual births that individually imitated Christ. Conversions and deepenings of faith, thanks to the test of war, allowed the faithful to find serenity and even occasionally joy. Jacques Rivière was persuaded that the force of his wife at his side was a "profound miracle,"[27] saying that she "has always been for me something of the incarnation of France herself."[28]

Even in discouraging moments, when the suffering of absence seemed to overwhelm, the French Catholic women found comfort in prayer.

They drew upon the lesson of Christ's passion. Life arises from death. God, in offering his son to men, gave to them the gift of hope from expiation. The Catholics of the Great War lived this example day after day. To imitate the sufferings of Christ was not seen as an act of hopelessness. There was no paradox; the more one suffers, the more one is convinced that the kingdom of God is near. Not only did the they *not* fear suffering and death, but they desired it as a sign of election. It is one thing to proclaim in such a manner that one loves the suffering by intellectualizing the sacrifice through faith, wishing to serve as an example to contemporaries and indeed to future generations. However, it is something else to find serenity in the absolute horror, in the catastrophe.

The task remained to adapt faith to the reversibility of suffering and devotion. In this manner, one can get at the desire for intercession, from the desire to imitate the Virgin on the one hand, and the desire for consolation on the other. The faithful could be described as existing in three concentric circles: that of the religion of daily life, lived in the parish; that of the collective manifestation of pilgrimage or of the cult of saints, as defined by the Catholic church; and that of the popular forms of devotion, often on the fringes of what the church was willing to tolerate, bordering on superstition.[29] The "ordinary" and "the extraordinary" were thus inextricably mixed among the faithful, the believers, as well as the baptized skeptics, who formed the immense majority of those who lived the war.

Certain devotions, even if they were strongly encouraged by the church, such as to the Virgin, to Sister Thérèse de Lisieux, and to Jeanne d'Arc, were so clearly the favor of the faithful that they seem to obscure a nice hierarchy that was more often rather strict. The Virgin, of course, was the chief consoler: "For you, the young heroic men, the war is the battle...the danger, the victory. For we women it is the tears, the desperate prayers, the stone slabs where we genuflect, the desire so strong, ...so superhuman, that you should be protected. . . .Some of these women go to the statue whose knees they kiss—I have stayed a long time, my dearly beloved, crying in her shadow, thanking the Virgin who protected you."[30]

In March 1918, in the middle of the bombardments on Paris by "Big Bertha,"[31] Jacques and Raïssa Maritain made preparations to depart for Rome to plead, in front of Pope Benedict XV, the cause of the Virgin who had appeared in La Salette. On April 2, 1918, the couple met with the pope to pressure him to read a manuscript edited by Jacques Maritain in 1915.

Jacques Maritain: "The Virgin wept before La Salette, it is due to these tears."

Raissa Maritain: "These tears correspond to the actual state of the world."[32]

The Maritains insisted on the unprecedented capacity of the Virgin to suffer. It is this capacity that made her so popular during the war. Mother before all mothers, such was the Virgin of Seven Sadnesses: "Someone showed me at the back of a chapel...a Virgin holding a branch. It was the Virgin of charity [Bon Secours]. On her head, against a wall was draped a large tricolor [Republican flag], and all around her were plaques of marble either attached to the wall or placed on a large marble table and engraved with thank you notes offered by the parents of soldiers at the front or from spouses or from sons. My mother had bought a photograph of the Virgin and instructed me to hide it among the flowers and the marble. I'd say an Our Father, and each time that she came to the village she would go to genuflect before this Virgin and pray for me. . . ."[33]

In a number of regions, people fixed to the walls of churches ex-voto paintings or photographs depicting different miracles of the war or of what they understood as such—expressions of theatricalized prayers. These were hymns of life, brought by men and more often by women, who survived through the mass of deaths.

After the Virgin, Jeanne d'Arc and Thérèse de Lisieux were the two most popular intercessors prayed to during the war. As with Thérèse de Lisieux, Jeanne d'Arc had not yet been canonized.[34]

Indeed, during the entire the war, the faithful prayed to both as if they were already saints. The two young female heroines of the faith, the one dating as far back as the fifteenth century, the other who had just recently died, owed their canonization in the 1920s to their popularity during the war. Jeanne, like the Virgin, was thought to bring victory; Thérèse, like the Virgin, protected and consoled. The two future saints, as if they represented the two different strengths of Mary, offered the certainty of a miracle, both collective and individual. As such, they presided over many conversions. The belief in the reversibility of suffering was at the base of this fervor. From the drama of the crucifixion, from the martyr of Rouen, to the long dialogue with the invisible in a death at 24 years of age, Thérèse taught that the greatest sadness gives birth to the greatest happiness. The masses of women and of men who suffered in the Great War shared the youth of Jeanne and of Thérèse. The "statue mania" of the ninteenth century affected more than Republican heroes seen in public spaces. The most popular saints of the nineteenth century had been sculpted and thousands of replicas were placed in the smallest parish churches. Above all of them were the mediators. As women, they had been prayed to by women, as the books of prayer had been above all read by women. These prayer books had been written by men, the sculptures created by men, for a public whose vast majority was female.[35] During the war, a world of men began to discover them. The correspondence of soldiers often makes reference to these spiritual encounters during the war. The men took great pleasure in the mention of these awakenings to their wives and their mothers, reminding them that the women were more pious than they were before the conflict. The common prayers and devotions thus became a fundamental link between the front and the rear, between men and women. Many would send pious medals, prayer books, and religiously inspired images on post cards. One young girl wrote to her brother: "Mama is making you a parcel. You will find a bottle of iodine that if by bad luck, something happens to you, you can pour it on the bandage, tying it very tightly. Along with the medicine you must also wear Saint-Antoine and the other medal, which mother is parting with so as to give them to you. Wear these and they will bring you good luck."[36]

One finds additional traces of this fervor in the correspondence of Louise de Bettignies, a young woman of Lille who was arrested and condemned to death by the Germans for acts of resistance. As a woman, she transgressed by taking an active part in the war. As a good Christian, she waited only for God's final decision.

From the fortress of Siegburg, where she awaited her execution or her pardon, the heroine, who had engaged herself, at the risk of her life, in a mission for the Intelligence Services, did not forget her desire to enter into the Carmelite order and take anew the example of Thérèse: "I have discovered that this time in prison was an excellent *noviciat* . . . Is this not the moment to live the prayer of oblation of the little Sister Thérèse? This dear sister keeps me company, as well as the memory of Mother Isabelle. Adding of course Christ, you are familiar with my cellmates."[37]

For these Catholic women, faith in God and their country—"the oldest daughter of the Church"—carried them through the war. In the 1920s and 1930s, the "survivors" of this ideology would express the endurance of their double certitude: "We do not have the right to permit ourselves to give into such sadness....I have never really known such joy before this war; but since the beginning it increases in me little by little, it is a joy which nourishes all the sadness. Do not believe for a moment that I am, from this point, pure and perfect; if God brings himself so close to me, it is by an indulgence which fills me with confusion, of love and fear. You will help me to earn, my loved one; pray to God for me in knowing that I pray to him for you, with all my love."[38]

During the 1920s and well after the conflict of World War II, this type of thought could only be seen as stupefying, indeed, terrifying, for those who considered the war as nothing more than one long, completely negative atrocity. This expression of a richness found at the bottom of the sadness of the war could no longer be understood other than as a kind of propaganda destined to deflect from the real and immediate fight, and against war in general. This virtual consent to the tragedy that claimed ten million lives could not come from anything except a kind of "brainwashing," which should not reproduce itself again. Even for the historian of today, the task is not simple, because the fervors of a different age have been so occulted. The eschatology of pacifism has long since replaced that of victory at all cost and redemption by faith. We have to begin to pose the difficult question in sifting through the different *a posteriori* sources of interpretation on these men and women, the combatants above all: How did they make it through those four and a half years? We come closer to responding accurately to this question when we are able to know better the range of consent and refusal of the women of that time.

Translated by Nicole Ann Dombrowski

NOTES

1. Mireille Dupouey, "Lettres à l'absent," *Cahiers 1915—1919* (Paris: Cerf, 1944), July 28, 1915, December 31, 1916, and March 20, 1917.

2. On the conversion of Dominique-Pierre Dupouey, who became in his own turn a sponsor to the faith during the war, see the contribution of Frédéric Gugelot, "Henri Ghéon ou l'histoire d'une âme en guerre," in *Chrétiens dans la Première Guerre mondiale* , ed. Nadine-Josette Chaline (Paris: Cerf, 1993), 67—94, and Frédéric Gugelot's doctoral thesis, *Conversions of Intellectuals to Catholicisme, 1880—1930* (under the direction of Etienne Fouilloux). Since a certain number of the women that I study converted, I must especially thank F. Gugelot for his generous contribution and thoughts.

3. Annette Becker, *La guerre et la foi, de la mort à la mémoire, 1914—1930*, (Paris: Armand Colin, 1994). English translation: *War and Faith: The Religious Imagination at War, France 1914—1930* (New York: Berg, 1998).

4. As it was again repeated 80 years after the fact by a veteran interviewed on the radio program "History Direct," broadcast over France-Culture, March 1995, "In front of me there were ten departments invaded by the enemy, behind me was my family—what would you have liked me to do?"

5. Three recent works begin to fill this void. Françoise Thébaud, ed., *Histoire des femmes*, le XXème siècle, vol. 5 (Paris: Plon, 1992); Christine Bard, *Les filles de Marianne: Histoire des féminismes, 1914—1940* (Paris: Fayard, 1995); Mary Louise Roberts, *Civilization Without Sexes: Reconstructing Gender in Postwar France, 1917—1927* (Chicago: University of Chicago Press, 1994).

6. Stéphane Audoin-Rouzeau and Annette Becker, "Pour une histoire culturelle du premier conflit mondial," *Vintgième siècle, Revue d'histoire* (January 1994), Jean François Sirinelli and Jean Pierre Rioux eds., *Pour une histoire culturelle du Vigntième siècle* (Paris: Le Seuil, 1997), and J.J. Becker, G. Krumeich, and J. Winter, eds. *Guerre et cultures, 1914—1918* (Paris: Armand Colin, 1994).

7. We find the same expression coming from Jacques Rivière as often as from Henri Massis: "But, more than ever before, what better reason to hope for to re-waken our faith! The war we were fighting was a war of religion: There you have it; the profound explanation for the re-awakening." Letter from Henri Massis to Jacques Maritain from November 7, 1914, study circle on Jacques and Raïssa Maritain, Kolbsheim. I thank René Mougel for his warm introduction to these archives.

8. Alain Fournier-Madame Simone (Henri and Pauline), *Correspondance, 1912—1914* (Paris: Fayard, 1992), August 3, 1914, 258; August 5, 1914, 263.

9. Raïssa Maritain, *Journal* (Paris: Desclée, 1963), April 30 and May 1, 2, 3, and 7, 1917, 40—41.

10. On the love of the Maritains, see René Mougel, "A propos du mariage des Maritain: Leur voeu de 1912 et leurs témoignages," in *Cahiers Jacques Maritain* 22 (1991): 5—44.

11. November 13, 1914, and April 30, 1917. Archives of Jacques and Raïssa Maritain, Kolbsheim, dossier of Christine and Pierre Van der Meer de Walcheren.

12. Jacques and Raïssa Maritain, *Oeuvres complètes: Vol. 1. 1906—1920*; (Suisse: Editions Universitaires Fribourg; Paris: Editions St. Paul). Jacques Maritain, *Le rôle de l'Allemagne dans la philosophie moderne*. Title given by the journal *La Croix* to 22 lessons given by Maritain at the Institute Catholique of Paris in 1914—1915, of which long summaries were published in *La Croix*.

13. Jacques Rivière was the editor in chief at N. R. F. Henri Alain-Fournier was the author of *Grand meaulnes* (First published in 1913).

14. "Correspondance Jacques et Isabelle Rivière, 1914—1917," *Bulletin des Amis de Jacques Rivière et d'Alain-Fournier* 51(1989): 7.

15. Jacques Rivière, *Carnets, 1914—1917* (Paris: Fayard, 1974), August 1915, 253.

16. On prisoners and humanitarian organizations, such as the CICR of Geneva, see Annette Becker, *Oubliés de la Grande Guerre. Humanitaire et culture de guerre: populations occupées, déportés civils, prisoniers de guerre,* (Paris: Noësis, 1998).

17. "Correspondance," op. cit., January 30, 1916, 28.

18. Ibid., February 7, 1915, 11.

19. The *Chemin des Dames* was the path by which French women delivered supplies from the home front to the trenches during World War I. Annette Becker, "La mort des écrivains," in *La très Grande Guerre, 1914—1918* (Paris: Le Monde Edition, 1994). Id. *Les croix de bois, sépultures de la Grande Guerre,* (Paris: Communio, 1995).

20. Pierre-Maurice Masson, *Lettres de guerre, 1914—1916* (Paris: Hachette, 1918), November 5, 1914, 20. Graduate of the *Ecole Normale Superieure,* professor of French literature at Fribourg, Switzerland, Masson should have defended his doctoral thesis on Rousseau at the Sorbonne. Instead, he was killed April 16, 1916 at Verdun. His leave had been canceled.

21. M. Dupouey, op. cit., October 1, 1915, 39.

22. Op. cit., February 22, 1915, 55.

23. D.P. Dupouey, op. cit., November 25, 1914, 112.

24. Masson, op. cit., All Saints Day, November 1, 1915, 151.

25. D.P. Dupouey, op. cit., April 2, 1915, 199.

26. Fournier-Madame Simone, op. cit., August 3, 1914, 258.

27. J. Rivière, op. cit., 120.

28. Ibid., February 26, 1915, 194.

29. See the remarkable demonstration of Alphonse Dupront in *Du sacré* (Paris: Gallimard, 1987).

30. Fournier—Madame Simone, op. cit., Pauline to Henri, September 28, 1914, 308. Alain-Fournier was killed September 22. Upon the archeological discovery of his body in 1991 and its interest in the Great War, see the film of Jean-Pierre Helas and Alain Ries, *A fleur de terre.* (Expressions, 1995).

31. Annette Becker, "The 'Big Bertha' Strikes Saint-Gervais," in *14—18 la très Grande Guerre* (Paris: Le Monde-Editions, 1994), 209—214.

32. Jacques Maritain, *Carnet de notes* (Paris: Desclée, 1965), 124.

33. Testimony of Marius Hourtal, edited in 1978. Cited by R. Cazals et al., *Années cruelles 1914—1918* (Gué: Atelier du Gué, 1983), 56. The church Saint-Vincent of Carcassonne shelters to this day statues and ex-voto dating from the Great War.

34. Jeanne d'Arc: Cause introduced in 1894, beatified in 1909, canonized in 1920. Thérèse: Cause introduced in 1914, beatified in 1923, canonized in 1925.

35. Jean Delumeau, ed., *La religion de ma mère: Le rôle des femmes dans la transmission de la foi* (Paris: Cerf, 1992); Claude Savart, *Les Catholiques en France au XIXème siècle: Le témoignage du livre religieux* (Beauchesne, 1985), 673; C. Savart, A la recherche de "l'art" dit de Saint-Sulpice, *Revue d'histoire de la spiritualité* 52(1976): 265—282.

36. Postcard of the sister of Joseph Foulquier, 1915. Cited in Rémy Cazals et al., op. cit., 69.

37. Cited by Antoine Redier, *La guerre des femmes: Histoire de Louise de Bettignies et de ses compagnes* (Paris: Editions de la Vraie France, 1924), 255—56.

38. Isabelle Rivière, op. cit. April 13, 1916, 39—40.

Figure 3. A Russian mother-soldier talks with her daughter.

THREE

The Great War
and Modern Motherhood
La Maternité and the Bombing of Paris

Mindy Jane ROSEMAN

On April 11, 1918, while most Parisians were taking refuge from the harassment of Germany's long-range cannon "Big Bertha," the staff of the Clinique Baudelocque—the state-of-the-art maternity facility attached to the older Maternité Port-Royal—were making their usual rounds. When the bomb fell, Mademoiselle Lère, a student midwife, had just delivered a newborn back into the hands of its mother. The midwife was killed in the bombardment; the mother and child were spared.

Like the debris and lives this bomb scattered, much could be said about this event. At the time, little mention was made of the attack. Little mention was made, however, of any civilian war casualties, whether from industrial accidents or enemy fire. So all that history has left of Mademoiselle Lère is a commemorative plaque affixed to the outside of Porte-Royal.[1] Even fewer traces remain of the mother. So why single out this bombing among the many others, even the more celebrated attacks on the maternity hospitals in Reims and Arras in 1915?

The short answer is that the bomb fell in Paris, and in 1918: Paris, being behind the lines yet under military administration, suggests the mutually constructed and dependant nature of the home and battle fronts; 1918, because the social upheaval caused by the war's long duration had become the status quo. This rare event provides, therefore, an opening to reconceptualize the home front. If there is a commonplace in the characterization of the Great War, it is in the conceptual line drawn between the battle and home fronts—*l'avant* and *l'arrière* —with the war being equally, but differently, waged. Thus John Williams' standard history, *The Other Battleground: The Home Fronts Britain, France and Germany, 1914—1918,*[2] reminds us on page one that the impact on the civil and domestic life of the nations involved was nothing short of revolutionary. The wholesale dedication of the belligerent powers to the waging of war brought changes to the civilian scene unprecedented in any previous conflict. War was no longer a matter almost exclusively for the fighting man, an isolated affair of clashing armies on some distant battlefield. The wearing of a uniform ceased to be virtually the sole criterion of service, privation or suffering. It was now, indeed, that the phrase "Home Front" was first coined.

This passage is curiously clichéd, even odd. Williams's formulation erases the experience of the siege of Paris during the Franco-Prussian War. There was nothing terribly distant about submitting to a siege.[3]

What is so terribly "new" about the Great War, was the "home front," but not in the way Williams analyzed. We need to pursue more conceptually the idea of the home. What did "home" mean in France at the beginning of the twentieth century? How was home "experienced"? How did the structuring assumptions that defined "home" define the "home front"?

Such questions bring us back to the bombing of the Maternité; who was the mother in the Paris maternity complex who narrowly escaped death? And what does home have to do with her location? Her identity is unknown, for reasons that have as much to do with a policy of anonymous admission as a loss of records. We must therefore rely on a statistical profile to establish a social location for her. Had the bomb fallen on the Maternité 18 years earlier in 1900 rather than 1918, she would likely have been a single woman employed in domestic service or the needle trades. In order to be admitted to the Maternité, she would have had to be eligible for public assistance—in other words, poor. And most significantly, she would have come to the Maternité only because she had no other alternative. The Maternité, despite three decades of political and medical reform, was still considered a place to be avoided.[4] The Paris municipal government and the Office of Public Assistance (referred to hereafter as OPA or Assistance Publique) in fact officially discouraged poor and destitute women from using the Maternité. Assistance Publique would pay for the home health care services of a midwife or medical doctor. The operative word here is "home."[5] The woman needed to have a home, or an adequate home, in order to avoid the Maternité. A domestic servant might live on the sixth floor of her employer's lodging, if she hadn't been discharged due to the pregnancy. Or she might live in a small furnished room elsewhere. But the Assistance Publique would have considered her materially, and affectively, homeless. To be *sans domicile* meant more than simply without shelter: it meant without the support and care—emotional work—that bolstered it.   It meant often not to be living in a proper "*ménage*".   It meant to have no mother, sister, or aunt to help with a birth, to be bereft of the emotional infrastructure necessary to be a normatively "Republican" mother.[6]

But a "fact" emerges in the course of the Great War: The women becoming mothers in Paris increasingly received public assistance, from approximately 60 percent in the years immediately preceding the war, to over 97 percent in 1918. And of those 97 percent, 80 percent of the births occurred in a Maternity hospital.[7] As will be discussed, the class complexion of the hospital population increasingly became middle class.[8] For all we know, in other words, the new mother whom fortune spared was a shopkeeper's wife who lived in the apartment in back and walked the family's dog in the Luxembourg gardens.

This change in social morals, then from home to hospital, with the potential destablizing effacement of class, is the historically significant rupture, which calls for a rethinking of the home—the meaning of home—particularly the imbrication of "women," that is to say, mothers into the home.   Home was the site where Republican virtue would be reproduced[9]—father and mother of the family, each with their appointed roles inside and outside their refuge—their repository of love and patriotism—home sweet home.   Of course, this home was always under construction, and the relative stability it achieved in the Third Republic was more apparent than real; the panic of "depopulation"—dating from the 1890s and lasting well into the twentieth century—spoke to the deep anxiety about the grounding of the bourgeois home and the continuation of the happy family. Women, as wives and especially as mothers, were the vehicles through which this discourse ran; their construction as emotional care providers and reproducers was the foundation. It is this discourse that holds interest—from home and reproduction to nation and population. The instability of the idea of home, its production through the discourse of nationhood, led to the profound irony of the Great War.[10] That the Great War prompted this shift in modern motherhood is particularly revealing, for despite certain continuities with prewar policies and tendancies, mostly the change was viewed (by those in authority) with anxious alarm. I want to suggest that the magnitude and duration of the Great War ruptured the conceptual "privacy" of the "essential" nature of the home—the reproduction of affective relations. With the "man of the house" mobilized for war, the idea of home became unimaginably threatened and weakened, which then led to the dislocation and displacement of caring, affective relations on to other institutions at best, or into fantasies and anxieties at worst. My concern is with those displacements—the shift in the site of childbirth from the home to the maternity hospital. Such a shift could be viewed in Habermasian terms as an encroachment of the "systems" world the "life" world,[11] or the ever-increasing medicalisation of women and motherhood.[12] I would simply like to interpret it as the displacement of the first gesture of emotional reproduction—coming into the world—not "at home" but "at hospital," a soulless institution. I would further argue because of the other dislocations in the emotional and reproductive worlds—the general mobilization of men, the governmentally managed provision of foodstuffs and heating material[13]—the meaning if not the purpose of home was profoundly disturbed by the Great War and can be measured by the overidealized and sentimentalized durge for home and hearth that characterized immediate postwar French politics.

The trend was anticipated immediately.   Dr. Bonnaire observed as a reporter to the supervisory board for the OPA that "the number of births remains the same. There is, however the chance that it could increase, due to the fact that many women who would not have wished to resort to public assistance in times of peace are willing to come to 'maternity' wards in a time of war."[14] That these comments were made to the Conseil, a body concerned above all with ensuring the fiscal health of the OPA, is not so astonishing. A sharp increase in the number of births in maternity wards would require considerable expenditure. What is worth noting is Bonnaire's assumption that women, who ordinarily did not seek help, would leave their homes and turn to the maternity hospitals. But this was not the only option: They could have stayed home, and a midwife would have been provided for them. Bonnaire knew this, as he had been the obstetrician of the Central Bureau de Bienfaisance (charity) in Paris, as well as the medical director of the school for midwives at the Maternité. Each municipal district of Paris had on its inscription list qualified midwives whose fee was paid by the city. Why, then, did Bonnaire insist on women's recourse to the maternities? There were two possible answers neither one mutually exclusive. Without their able-bodied male partners women might have been more impoverished.[15]   I read Bonnaire's statement as an expression of masculine anxiety, which elided the absence of men into the loss of home.[16]

The director of the OPA called attention to "the strain brought about by the state of war on the number of births performed in hospital maternity wards."[17] He mentioned the initial flight of women to the provinces, where the better-off stayed for the duration (and these were the middle and upper middle classes who used the city's midwives): "The city's midwives' clientele....in the difficult times we are going through, no longer exist, in a manner of speaking; women who give birth at home, assisted by a midwife, prefer to bring themselves to the hospital and give birth there, free of charge."[18] One year into the war midwives themselves commented on the increased use of maternity hospitals. Lina Roger, the head of the largest union, wrote that "according to statistics, even if the number of births is diminishing due to the length of the war, the number of hospitalized births is on the rise."[19]   She claimed that the increase in hospital use was due to "bourgeois" use of the facilities. She wrote to the director of the OPA to demand that more be done. The director replied that he too "deplored" the state of affairs; he believed that despite inquiry many women "illicitly benefit from free care in the maternity wards." Those who are honest, he added, preferred to pay 5 francs per day to Public Assistance "in order not to stay at home."[20]   To add further insult to injury, most maternity wards, but most famously the Maternité and Clinique Baudelocque, had "consultations for babies," where sterilized milk for infants was distributed gratis, or for a nominal charge.[21] At this maternity ward there were 9,920 consultations in 1914, 11,050 in 1915.[22] Such a tangible offer to Parisian mothers and their young children clearly was welcomed. Whatever inquiry there was into a woman's financial situation must have been cursory, due to the predominant assumption that if the man was "absent," the woman was needy. OCAMI (Office Central de l'Assistance Maternelle et Infantile or Central Administration of Assistance to Mothers and Children) itself admitted that it had no mechanism for sufficiently investigating an applicant's financial status.

The director of the OPA tried to reverse this trend by shutting down a number of maternity services (not without controversy);[23] but this only had the effect of making the OCAMI more efficient. In fact, the presence of middle-class, married women giving birth in the hospital remained constant, and continued after the war. This meant that in absolute and relative terms, these women were no longer giving birth in their homes.[24] Bonnaire again offered an explanation: "An antinomy seems to exist between these two findings which is explained by the fact that from the beginning of the war, and above all since the rise in the cost of living, pregnant women prefer to check into the hospital where they find themselves without expense in the maximum tranquillity, security or care.[25] In 1917, 25,161 women were cared for at a maternity hospital in Paris; 20,981 in 1916, with the same birthrate:

And the social conditions of these births are themselves even modified—one comes across in our maternity ward, a number of female employees of small business owners, who previously gave birth at home under the care of a midwife from the village. These women constitute in a time of peace, the half of the clientele of these midwives which is now escaping them. Thus while salaries have risen everywhere, all administrations, public and private, have allocated to all categories of personnel, allowances for the high cost of living, the midwives have seen their clientele disappear in part; they find themselves today in a more difficult situation.[26]

Immediately after the war the situation was unchanged. In a letter to the Paris Municipal Council, dated December 26, 1919, the largest association of midwives in France noted the soaring increase of paying clients of modest means choosing to go to the "facilities offered by hospital maternity wards."[27]

The specter of an impoverished corps of midwives was as troubling as the increasing female population in the hospitals. The unstable cultural space the hospital occupied easily recalled the old canard of midwives, abortionists, and marginalized women. Noted Bonnaire:

For many years, the medical establishment has been alarmed by the congestion in hospitals due to abortions: multiplying in proportion which increases singularly at this hour of the difficulty of maternal life, a disruption thrown into their conjugal home by the absence of...soldier husbands.[28]

A home without the presence of a man was perverse—a realm antithetical to caring, nurturance, and reproduction. The supervisory council of the OPA, along with the Academy of Medicine, investigated. Dean Roger, of the Paris Medical School, announced his findings: Only one-third of the women admitted to maternity hospitals "naturally miscarried." Therefore, two-thirds of all women whose births did not terminate with a live child had "induced" their abortion.[29] He identified the means of transmission of this "epidemic." Women's increased employment during war time was suspected: "It was in these feminine agglomerations that the contagion spreads, in factories, workshops, stores and even in the quarters of the hospital...."[30] This was truly a horror, in Roger's estimation, but worse, the perpetrators were predominantly midwives (38 licensed, 24 unlicensed, and according to criminal convictions, 1 doctor and 11 herbalists).[31] Most women declared matter-of-factly that they aborted. "All these examples show an important change of mentality. Abortion . . . is no longer considered by certain women to be a criminal act which one hides and is embarrassed by. One looks upon it as a lawful operation."[32] The conclusions of Roger's report, would form the basis for the 1920 anticontraception/antiabortion legislation read as a blueprint for the reconstruction of motherhood that had suffered much war damage. The report called for the regulation of the practice of midwifery, the control of lay midwives and the sale of probes, a propaganda campaign against abortion, with posters in hospitals and factories, an annual "celebration of motherhood" to glorify mothers of large families, and, finally, the regeneration of religious sentiment—"To make them understand that maternity is a virtue and divine sacrament."[33]

The immediate effect of this report was the establishment in each maternity hospital of an "isolation" room for suspected abortions, under strict surveillance, "in a fashion to make clear to them that they were considered criminals and not to be confused with the mothers cared for in the neighboring hallway."[34] This internal segregation of moral space underscores the process of class effacement the Great War brought to motherhood. Good middle-class mothers—mothers in the maternity hospital there through no fault of their own—needed to be cordoned from the evil ones who chose abortion. That religiosity was invoked was ironic, for the entire effort to reform the maternity hospital and motherhood was part of the secularization of public culture—the civilizing mission—of the Third Republic.[35]

The final point relates back to Third Republic policies. The creation of home for those who had a less than normative one had long been part of the Republican social agenda. In 1891 Adolphe Pinard, a physician, obstetrician, and legislator whose life spanned two republics and one empire, at a public conference at the Sorbonne on aid to mothers spoke of the great Republican project of providing assistance to all mothers and children in need.[36] Throughout his long career Pinard built institutions, concrete ones—such as the Clinique Baudelocque, of which he was the director—and abstract ones, such as puericulture, the science of "child nurturing," of which he was the founder, to assist, protect, and transform motherhood from unenlightened misery into Republican perfectibility.[37] As the professor of clinical obstetrics at the Paris Medical School and the author of many texts and treatises, a member of the Academy of Medicine, a member of the extra-parliamentary commission on depopulation, and coauthor with Nobel Prize—winning Charles Richet of the commission's report on depopulation, Pinard was extraordinarily influential. His opinion carried weight. And his *idée fixe* was "improving" the quality of infant life; (he founded the French Eugenics Society in 1912 and defined eugenics in those terms).[38] His puericulturally inspired eugenics knew no class and ethnic division— improving France la République was his aim. His eugenics program was relatively mild: At a minimum, he wanted all pregnant women to rest and eat well so their babies would be vigorous and beautiful, as he put it (in a word, fat).[39] He was a tireless and vociferous opponent of industrial war work for women (because of the higher rate of prematurity among infants born to mothers so employed) and the driving force behind the regulation requiring on-site day care centers, breast-feeding breaks, and health inspections there.   I address him here at length because at the age of 70, Pinard was named by the military government of Paris as the director of the OCAMI, and it was through the instrumentality of the OCAMI that Paris would compensate for the displacement of the home.   Under Pinard's direction, all women "domiciled" in Paris—but especially those "homeless in Paris because they came from the provinces or were refugees of regions engulfed in battle"[40]—would receive "a shelter" until they could be "placed" and find work.   There was supposed to be an inquiry into a woman's means, but the requirement was not rigorously enforced. All women who registered at the Mairie and then came to the Maternité, Clinique Baudelocque, or Tarnier received 1 franc and a half per day for 30 days—that is to say, a month before delivery, and for 20 days after delivery.   Ten new shelters were opened to accommodate mothers temporarily without homes.

On March 18, 1915, the OCAMI further specified which women could receive aid: women not yet 8 months pregnant, women 8 months pregnant, new mothers less than 1 month, and nursing mothers for more than one month (ie., all pregnant and nursing women). As far as Pinard was concerned this was the program the nation should have undertaken 30 years earlier.   But material aid was not sufficient; the goal of the OCAMI was to reform motherhood, make it fit for the battle: "In reality, in these hospital works, breast feeding is rigorously supervised and managed in a manner that doesn't require mothers to deviate from hygenic practices; indeed it was even imposed in the 'convalescent refuges' as they were properly referred to.   From this point of view, the importance of the role of the OCAMI is felt in terms of a social order rather than as a charitable order."

But there was a limit to social reordering, and it is on that note that I will conclude.   The OCAMI and those who composed it were quite aware that institutions were not home—that the emotional qualities, the soul, could only with much difficulty be reproduced.   So when Leon Bourgeois, a senator, and former prime minister and the "architect" of what was considered the official "social philosophy" of the Republic,[41] praised Pinard's efforts with the OCAMI, he drew attention to its attempt to "care":

Let us direct our thoughts to the trenches which is what preoccupies our men who fight, who are risking their lives; it is crucial to know what has become of the wives and children that they have left at home behind them. They know that from a material point of view, an allocation is granted to all those who are wives or companions of mobilized men . . . thanks to you [Pinard], they will know that not only this allocation, insufficient without a doubt, is accorded to them but that they are surrounded by an atmosphere of active and vigilant tenderness which has been created, placing them consequently, not only in a shelter from material difficulties, but from moral worries too.[42]

After the war was over and the effort to reconstruct all that had been destroyed was under way,[43] the lace that bound motherliness and "hominess" was rethread ever more tightly. During the very long discussions in the Academy of Medicine and later in the National Assembly concerning the establishment of a national network of "maternity hospices,"[44] it was acknowledged that something had gone wrong by "institutionalizing" motherhood:

It is illogical to proceed from a physiological act, like giving birth, and arrive in the same house where one cares for the ill; it is illogical and dangerous. This hospitalized character of many maternity wards is often disheartening for the mothers, and the moral atmosphere of a maternal hospice, a house entirely devoted to the career of the mother and not only to the obstetrical intervention, is without a doubt different than that of a hospital maternity ward. In this "milieu" mothers develop a taste for their task.[45]

The recognition of the sterility of institutional forms of reproduction defined the other end of the spectrum, which sentimentalized home and family life after the war. The experience of the Great War for mothers was one of increasing opportunities for institutionalization, and from a mother's perspective it is not altogether clear that this meant a "loss." To liberal practitioners of midwifery, it was. But what was feared at the time, by the policymaking men, was homelessness, a loss of a place in the world, a displacement of the taken-for-granted division of emotional labor and so on. These anxieties, more imagined than real, nevertheless help our understanding of French politics in the interwar, Vichy, postwar, and contemporary periods.

NOTES

1. Archives de l'Assistance Publique [AAP], *Liasse* 678, July 24 1919. "So it is a terrible catastrophe that has struck our students, our mothers who have just given birth, and our newborns. Mlle. Lère, who was killed, was a charming person, with a joyous character. She has left among you all an enduring memory," 45.

2. John Williams, *The Other Battleground: The Home Fronts Britain, France and Germany, 1914—1918* (Chicago: Henry Regnery, 1972), 1.

3. See Michael Walzer, *Just and Unjust Wars* (New York: Basic Books, 1991), in which he writes that "siege is the oldest form of total war," 160. In light of the Serbian aggression in Bosnia and the Russian bombing of Grozny in Chechnya, one might remark that modern European warfare has all become total in the sense that it refuses the distinction between combatants and civilians.

4. If literature is any guide, the maternity incubated disease, be it of a medical or moral nature. See Edmond de Goncourt *Germinie Lacerteux* (Paris: Union générale d'éditions, 1979), for an example.

5. There is no equivalent word in French for "home." *Foyer* comes close to the sentimentality. Also interesting is Luc Boltanski's *Prime education et la morale de classe* (Paris: Mouton, 1977), for a fantastic schema of the Republican reorganization and rationalization of the *foyer*.

6. See Rachel Fuchs, *Poor and Pregnant in Paris* (New Brunswick, NJ: Rutgers University Press, 1994). This accretion of meanings is expressed in another supposed motivating factor driving women to give birth at the Maternité—the intention to abandon their newborn. I wish to bracket this entire issue except to note a discursive connection between having an adequate home and reproducing affective relations (i.e., nurturing a child) and being homeless and having to relinquish one's child. I do not mean to imply that women who abandoned their children did not love them, or were incapable of loving them. Rather, I am trying to suggest that at the cultural level the discourse of homelessness carried this connotation. If these women had a home, they would not abandon their children.

7. Statistics from the *Bulletin hebdomadaire de statistiques municipal de la ville de Paris*. See also Fuchs, *Poor and Pregnant in Paris*, op. cit.

8. Certainly, these brute statistics ought to be qualified. The birthrate during the Great War was below its already depressed average of approximately 900 births per month in Paris, dropping to a low of approximately 550 per month and approximately 700 per month in 1918.

The well-to-do population of Paris had initially fled south, and while some returned, many remained. Furthermore, many women and their dependent families did seek refuge in Paris.

9. See Phillip Nord, "Republican Politics and the Bourgeois Interior in Mid-Nineteenth-Century France," in *Home and Its Dislocations in 19th -century France*, ed. Susan Nash (Albany: SUNY Press, 1993). "Placed at centre-stage in the new middle-class interior is the femme de foyer: angel in the hearth, devoted wife and, above all, loving mother" (193).

10. Although Benedict Andersen's *Imagined Communities* (London: Verso, 1992) makes no mention of gender, his writings on nationhood and nationalism have been influential in the field. See also Mary Louise Roberts, *Civilization Without Sexes* (Chicago: University of Chicago Press, 1994), for the gender relations and the bitter irony of the Great War.

11. See, generally, Jurgen Habermas, *The Theory of Communicative Action*, vol. 1, trans. Thomas McCarthy (Boston: Beacon Press, 1984), and Nancy Fraser, "What's Critical About Critical Theory? The Case of Habermas and Gender," in *Feminist Interpretations and Political Theory*, ed. Mary Lyndon Shanely and Carole Pateman (London: Polity Press, 1991).

12. This literature is vast. See, for example, Yvonne Kniebielher and Catherine Fouquet, *Histoire des mères* (Paris: Editions Montalba/Pluriel, 1977), Ornella Moscucci, *The Science of Women* (London: Cambridge University Press, 1989), and Judith Waltzer Leavitt, *Brought to Bed: Childbearing in America, 1750—1950* (New York: Oxford University Press, 1986).

13. See Theirry Bonzon, "Society, State and Municipality: Provision Issue in Paris During the First World War" (Unpublished paper delivered at "Mobilizing for Total War 1914—1918" conference at Trinity College, Dublin, 23—25 June 1993).

14. AAP, *Proces verbaux du conseil surveillance* (PVCS), 13 August 1914, 615.

15. See, generally, Jean Jacques Becker, *The Great War and the French People* (New York: Berg, 1990), in which he studies the material effect of the mobilization on morale and misery, concluding that by 1915, "the overall material situation...[was] not so intolerable" (28).

16. For some women, evacuees and refugees, their homes were lost. But I don't believe that was what vexed them.

17. AAP, PVCS, op. cit., 3 December 1914, 36.

18. Ibid.

19. *La Sage Femme*, 5 January 1916, minutes from the general meeting of 8 December 1915.

20. Midwives were paid 15 francs per birth in 1915 (this included 9 days of follow-up care), 20 francs in 1916, 25 francs in 1917, and 35

francs in 1918 by Public Assistance. AAP, op. cit., "Liberal" practitioners of midwifery charged, on a sliding scale, approximately the same rates.

21. Layettes were also distributed free of charge.

22. Archives de Paris, minutes, Conseil Municipal de Paris, 31 March 1917, 164. "Ces deux chiffres montre assez les services rendus par l'Institut de la Maternité alors que les naissances diminunent, le nombre de consultations augment." So profoundly tied was milk provisioning to the well-being of the *foyer* that Adolphe Pinard as the director of the Office Central de l'Assistance Maternelle et Infantile (OCAMI) insisted that the military maintain a herd of cows in the city. When for financial reasons the army wished to put the cows out to pasture as it were, Pinard availed himself of Sen. Paul Strauss and had the herd reinstated. The *troupeau de Paris* produced 9,200 liters per day. *Bulletin de l'academie nationale de la medicine* 80(1918): 566.

23. AAP, PVCS, op. cit., 3 June 1915.

24. To this day in France virtually all births take place in a public hospital or private clinic, there being little "alternative" health activity. There is a small movement to bring birth back into the home.

25. AAP, PVCS, op. cit., 214.

26. Ibid.

27. Archives de Paris, Minutes, Conseil Municipal de Paris, December 26, 1919, 1584.

28. AAP, PVCS, op. cit., 8 November 1917, 112—13.

29. AAP, PVCS, op. cit., 25 September 1919, 21.

30. Ibid., 22.

31. Ibid. Dr. Potacki, a well-regarded obstetrician, defended midwives, stressing that just because most abortions were preformed by midwives it did not follow that most midwives were abortionists.

32. For a longer historical regard on the "licit" and complicit nature of abortion in France, see Nancy Jaicks, *Les Faiseuses d'Anges* (Ph. D., Columbia University, 1993).

33. AAP, PVCS, op. cit., 9 October 1919, 34.

34. Ibid., 35.

35. See Mindy Jane Roseman, *Birthing the Republic: Midwives, Medicine and Morality in France: 1870 to 1920* (Forthcoming Ph. D., Columbia University), chapter 3.

36. "De l'assistance des femmes enceintes," Conference at the University of Paris, 9 May 1891, reprinted in Adolphe Pinard, *Clinique Obstetrical* (Paris: Steinheil, 1899).

37. See Roseman, *Birthing the Republic*, note 39, chapter 4. Pinard held up as a model middle-class mothers who wanted for neither family, material, nor rest as the "situation ideale pour toute femme enceinte." "De

l'assistance," 29—30. The Republic, Pinard would argue, had the mission to realize this classless ideal of motherhood for all French women. As late as 1928 Pinard admonished that the Republic had to do better. See "Ainsi parle Dr. Adolphe Pinard," *Les cahiers de l'enfance* (Paris: 1954), 15.

38.   See William Schneider, *Quality and Quantity* (Cambridge: Cambridge University Press, 1990).

39.   This is, of course, a simplification.

40.   AAP, PVCS, op. cit., 10 September 1914, 638.

41.   J.E.S. Hayward, "The Official Philosophy of the French Third Republic: Leon Bourgeois and 'Solidarism,' " *International Review of Social History* 6 (1961): 20—32; Judith Stone, *The Search for Social Peace* (Albany: SUNY Press, 1985).

42.   *La Guerre et La Defense de L'Enfant*, 55.

43.   See especially Steven Hause, "More Minerva Than Mars: The French Women's Rights Campaign and the First World War," in *Behind the Lines* , ed. Margaret Randolph Higonnet et al. (New Haven, CT: Yale University Press, 1987), for a particularly insightful account of the gendered nature of reconstruction.

44.   Anne Cova, "Louise Koppe et sa maison maternelle," in Actes du 115e Congrès National des Sociétés Savantes (Paris: Association pour l'Etude de l'Historie de la Sécurité Sociale, 1991), 49—78; Alisa Klaus, *Every Child a Lion: The Origins of Maternal and Infant Health Policy in the United States and France, 1890—1920* (Ithaca, NY: Cornell University Press, 1993).

45.   *Bulletin de l'academie nationale de la medicine*, 14 March 1922, 305.

Figure 4. 'A Call to Arms.'
World War I British recruitment poster.

FOUR

The Enemy Within
The Problem of British Women's Sexuality During the First World War

Susan R. GRAYZEL

> There is no doubt that the wave of patriotic feeling and general excitement that passed like a flame over the land during the first months of the war did result in a dangerous heightening of sexual passion.
>
> Mary Scharlieb, *The Hidden Scourge* (1916)

A few months after the outbreak of war, in November 1914, Colonel East, commander of the Severn Defenses, cited the newly created Defense of the Realm Act (DORA) when he issued an order in Cardiff "to certain women . . . prohibiting them from being out of doors between the hours of 7 P.M. and 8 A.M."[1] The first five women arrested for this pleaded guilty and were subsequently sentenced to detention for 62 days; other women arrested for the same offense were sentenced in early December to a total of 56 days of hard labor.[2] These actions prompted a quick public outcry. By late December, newspapers reported that several protesters, including Labour party leader George Lansbury, had met with East to challenge the military orders. They argued that such restrictions on behavior, if necessary, should be applied to everyone, not merely women listed by the police. East listened, but claimed his interest was in the health of the soldiers and not morals, which led the *Herald* to comment that "the military authorities only take action to secure the health of the men. The physical and moral degradation of women does not count with them." They urged all who felt contrary to join in "emphatic protest" against the measures.[3]

The case of the Cardiff women presented the first use of Defense of the Realm regulations to legislate the behavior of women with reference to immoral behavior and prostitution. That it was read as a return to the nineteenth-century Contagious Diseases Acts—which targeted women who spread venereal disease—was evident in an angry feminist response published in the suffragette periodical *The Vote*. Here, C. Nina Boyle made use of the popular vocabulary of outrage prevalent in wartime propaganda by referring to the "Prime Minister and a 'Scrap of Paper.' " Boyle thus implied that Prime Minister Asquith's refusal to abide by his previous declaration opposing the return of the Contagious Diseases Acts was comparable to Germany's violating the treaty guaranteeing Belgian neutrality. Worried about the arbitrary application of regulations and that the accused women would be tried in courts-martial, Boyle denounced the way in which women's rights were denied and their good names besmirched as "utterly sickening." She tellingly observed that prostitution typically went unnoticed, but "[w]hen inconvenient and dangerous—to men, not to girls—there is an immediate resort to persecution of a peculiarly dastardly kind."[4]

That such "persecution" of women would be necessary in the wartime climate of Europe is suggestive of the kind of victory that the governments of countries like Britain and France promised to their inhabitants as the First World War progressed. Victory came to hinge upon two factors: the preservation of the fighting forces and the conduct of the civilian population. At a moment when the concept of "morale" began to be associated not just with the military but with noncombatants, the moral behavior, particularly the sexual behavior, of women came to be seen as potentially imperiling the nation. New campaigns for understanding the threats posed by venereal diseases were launched even as attempts were made to stem the social disorder that female promiscuity seemed to unleash.

Drawing on debates that examined female sexuality in relation to the nation and as a threat to the fighting man, this essay analyzes the extent to which debates about female sexual morality that developed during the First World War became arenas for the expression of anxiety about general social disorder. Many contemporaries saw internal threats to the nation's welfare being posed by women in the so-called home front who instigated sexual misconduct. A virulent response to anxiety over women's sexuality may be seen in British legislation, in which a woman found to have a venereal disease could be criminally punished for infecting "members of His Majesty's forces." While using an occasional comparative lens to illustrate how France became the important counterexample, what follows will focus on Britain as a case study of attitudes and policy toward disease and sexual immorality during the First World War. By making women the objects of scrutiny in debates about prostitution, venereal disease, and the perceived decline in moral standards and behavior, the regulations transformed immoral women into a type of internal enemy.

"SOMETHING MORE THAN FLIRT"

As Allied nations like Britain and France prepared for war in 1914, public debate intensified about the effect of military mobilization on the women left behind. Women were held accountable for their incomparable moral influence on men, an influence that could be compromised if they acted inappropriately in public. Many newspapers commented on women's general influence on soldiers and approved inquiries into "the moral aspect of the occupations of certain young women" in London's streets that denounced their "painted faces" and their "suggestively ogling and hanging on to the arms of khaki-clad soldiers."[5]

When prosecuting the Cardiff women in November 1914, Colonel East felt that he was acting on behalf of the well-being of such soldiers. Others concerned with the behavior of women both around old and new centers of military activity and in major cities and towns, believed regulation could not solve a moral problem. The National Vigilance Association (NVA) spoke of the need to appoint "women patrols" to safeguard the behavior of the women and girls around the base in Cardiff.[6] Patrols were also proposed as a solution to "scandalous conduct" in Bristol, where there was "great excitement" among the young women of the city. According to the NVA, "Very young girls, indeed, owing partly no doubt to a kind of silly hero-worship, were trying to flirt, or do something more than flirt, with young soldiers."[7] Thus innocent excitement about heroes in uniform had a dangerous potential. While women were urged to preserve the morale of the fighting forces and the soldier became the epitome of all that was desirable, those concerned with immorality feared that such sentiments could corrupt both young women and men.[8]

These feelings persisted after the first wave of enthusiasm. On Monday November 22, 1915, twenty young women, ages 18 to 25, were charged at London's Tower Bridge Police Court for "frequenting Waterloo-road for immoral purposes." They were charged with "soliciting" and brought before a magistrate, who commented, that "for their own safety," the women ought to be detained indefinitely. "It is hopeless and almost worse than useless," he went on, "to treat these cases as if they were *ordinary* misdemeanours. It is not only the girls who require protection against themselves, but the soldiers also call for some protection from persistent solicitation."[9]

As the war dragged on, the "useful girl" was contrasted with the "frivolous girl", as these two categories became a common way to distinguish between patriotic and detrimental ways to act. The epitome of the "girl not doing her bit" became personified for some in the flapper— representative of, in one attack, a "very numerous class of women— especially young women, who are absolutely hindering victory through...thoughtlessness" and for whom "war means nothing but men in uniform with whom they can flirt."[10]

Women's and girl's allegedly scandalous public behavior also provoked studies that searched for solutions, and several conferences on these questions took place in London during the first six months of 1917, one held by London Borough authorities and another sponsored by the NVA on "The Moral Condition of the Streets of London."[11] The Bishop of London, Arthur Winnington-Ingram, presided over the latter and called particular attention to the continued presence of "hundreds of women... soliciting for prostitution in the streets" that proved how much was still to be done "to clean up this heart of the Empire." Speakers such as Sir Edward Henry, the chief commissioner of police, addressed specific problems facing London and detailed the misuse of parks as locations where, throughout the night, "couples may be seen behaving in a most scandalous manner." Lieutenant-General Sir Francis Lloyd, the officer in charge of London forces, then spoke on behalf of soldiers, urging the audience not to be quick to condemn their behavior, because "it is difficult when you have been working in dirty wet trenches with bullets flying about...to come to London with all its pleasures and temptations, and if you are a virile soldier, not to 'have a go' of some sort." Mrs. Louise Creighton, the final speaker and head of the National Union of Women Workers, concluded that public action had to be taken to create a morally pure London. Not only did Londoners have to fight prostitution, drunkenness, and debauchery, she declared, but they had to struggle to prevent ordinary boys and girls from becoming practitioners of these vices.[12]

While denounced at various intervals throughout the war, the behavior of this "girl in the street" attracted increased national and metropolitan interest in 1918 with the arrival of American troops. The *Daily Express* first ran a series of articles in September 1918 criticizing the women of London.[13] The *Express* aimed its call for action at General Sir Nevil Macready, London's new commissioner, calling on him to ban "strumpets" from all places of "soldiers' recreation" and instead to make them "save themselves by honest labour."[14] Here again, the distinction between the socially useful and frivolous illustrated the gap between two kinds of womanhood—the patriot working to save England and the corrupt, urban pleasure-seeker.

Following this cry to arms, an article by Edward Bok, editor of the American *Ladies' Home Journal*, reinvigorated the debate.[15] In an interview after a 2-week visit, Bok said that nothing "surprised and depressed" him so much as a recent visit to London. Comparing London with his experience "in a great many large cities," Bok claimed to have never witnessed more "disgraceful" scenes than those he found in London streets, where American "boys [we]re openly solicited, not only by prostitutes, but by scores of amateur girls." All successful American efforts to halt the spread of vice and disease would be of no use, he lamented, if America's "clean-blooded and strong-limbed" soldiers came "over here only to be poisoned and wrecked in the London streets. We should not be asked to send our boys here to be morally crucified."[16] Bok further called for direct government action. If an individual soldier, for instance, sought out a brothel, he would be responsible, but "where the temptation is allowed to beset him on every hand in street, hotel and restaurant," then the responsibility was that of the "Government which allows such a traffic to go on apparently with its sanction." Bok was particularly shocked by the apparent "public acquiescence... based on the argument that the men who are making the great sacrifice must be permitted certain indulgences while away from home." He even, perhaps most threateningly, implied that the failure to eliminate this threat to American soldiers might lead to the withdrawal of U. S. troops for their own safety.

Following a denunciation that so thoroughly questioned the moral basis of the British people and government, confirmations and rebuttals came from various quarters. Some defended both American soldiers and London: "Even if solicitation is practised, the solicited need not respond....The temptation of the streets does not come from the woman, as much as it comes from the men." Others clarified the government's legal position, that while prostitution, as such, was not recognized as "legal," a woman could come and go in public, provided she was not "disorderly"; thus the "morality" of her behavior would not necessarily lead to her being stopped. Moreover, those defending London noted that "the necessities of war have placed the sexes on a different relationship, and that this freedom which has broken down so much of woman's reserve, appears to...be a greater evil than it really is." The problem was thus redefined as one of perception; the behavior of London's women was not immoral. Bok had failed to recognize that the war had created "different" and "freer"—but no less moral—relationships between the sexes.

Editorially, *The Evening News* appeared to disagree with this line of argument in defense of London's women. While declaring that there was no need to panic, *The Evening News* noted that war required all of the nation's strength— "we should make up our minds not to allow ourselves to become weakened by the idle and the vicious"—personified by the prostitute and the girl in the street.[17] Once again, morality—women's morality—at home was seen as holding the key to British victory.

The NVA offered its own rebuttal to Bok's comments about London's streets. It cited with approval the response of Edward Price Bell, the editor of the *Chicago Daily News*, who particularly scorned the idea that

American soldiers were "good enough men to fight the Hun,...[but] not good enough men to venture into British streets unescorted."[18] American soldiers themselves echoed such views, and a letter in the *Evening Standard* from an American serving with the Grenadier Guards defended London's women, protesting that "this rot on London's morals reflects upon their character generally, and we resent it."[19] This soldier also asserted men's control over their own morality and their lack of fear of the alleged dangers lurking in London streets. *The Vigilance Record* concurred, lamenting Bok's "wild and unfounded statements."[20] Despite the fact that the British themselves were quite critical of the behavior of women in wartime London, the hyperbolic attack by an American caused an emotive defense.

Certainly, as *The Vigilance Record* and others pointed out, the scandal of London's streets made for "good copy." Although scandal sold papers, the debates about the public behavior of women in the capital were not just about creating news. The reasons for the perceived dangers of London's "amateur girls," particularly for overseas troops, can be explained, in part, by the defensive observation recorded above: that war had altered the relationship between the sexes.[21] These changes in social and public behavior did not go unnoticed nor, as we have seen, unchallenged. The sexual double standard was not loosened in these debates, but it was shifted. Women were still regarded as the guardians of moral virtue, held to higher standards of behavior, and even granted influence over even the most "virile" soldier. If relationships between the sexes had become freer, even seduction could be reversed. Women, even young girls, were accused of "accosting" soldiers in training or on leave. Whether such accusations were valid or not, the anxieties disseminated in public about women displayed the extent to which alleged changes in appropriate feminine behavior could send shock waves through the entire society.[22]

It is not possible to evaluate the extent to which the moral standards of women, particularly the generation that came of age during the war, "declined" or even if their sexual activity increased. Commentators like Justice Darling of the Old Bailey claimed that "the harm the war had done to the morals of the people...was far beyond any material damage that had been done. In nothing had it done more harm than in the relaxation on the part of the women of this country."[23] However, in response, Lady Burbidge, while professing to understand what caused the justice's opinion, criticized Darling. Instead, she defended women who entered new spheres and engaged in new occupations by insisting on their patriotic motives. If work for the national good brought "girls without any experience of the world...into contact with men of all social and moral grades in circumstances strong with emotional appeal," they, overwhelmingly, she argued, did not yield to temptation. Women's morals were unaltered; rather, the war, according to Burbidge, had "weakened for the time being the barriers restraining criminal activities and immoral tendencies. The less daring of the criminal and immoral types took advantage of this fact."[24] She might also have noted that the war intensified the attention paid to women. It can, perhaps, be seen as a sign of their increased importance in this new modern war that their morale and morality became such objects of public scrutiny.

DEFENDING THE REALM

Discussions of women's sexual behavior around soldiers had the spread of venereal disease as a subtext. In Britain, the passage of DORA in 1914 and the public issuance of the report of the Royal Commission on Venereal Disease in 1916 indicated government concern. This reintroduced debates about the Contagious Diseases Acts, along with other measures such as the Criminal Law Amendment Bill, and thus attempted to prosecute all women, perhaps lulled into moral lapses by the war, suspected of infecting soldiers.

Before the war, concern with the spread of venereal disease had led to the creation of the Royal Commission on Venereal Diseases (RCVD) in 1913. This commission concurred with those who had opposed the Contagious Diseases Acts of 1864, concluding that there was decisive evidence that this legislation had helped to fight against these diseases.[25] Among the RCVD report's contributions to the larger debates about women and their behavior were its conclusions that no practical legislative action could prevent the spread of disease among single or sexually promiscuous people.[26] Furthermore, it concluded that while these diseases might result from "vicious habits," it was "equally true that large numbers of sufferers are absolutely innocent." Significantly, the RCVD based its call for action on the fact that in wartime society, along with the "heavy losses of the best manhood of the nation," venereal diseases "must tell heavily on the birth-rate and on the numbers of efficient workers." Efforts to check the spread of such disease therefore became, during wartime, "of paramount national importance."

Two organizations—the National Council of Public Morals (NCPM) and the National Council for Combating Venereal Diseases (NCCVD)— took the report as a call to action and began to educate the public. The latter claimed it acted in response to "the need to anticipate, and if possible to check that exacerbation of venereal disease which always follows in the wake of a great war."[27] Under the auspices of the NCPM, the president of its Ladies' Council, Dr. Mary Scharlieb, published *The*

Hidden Scourge, a work aimed primarily at women to provide them with knowledge about venereal disease.[28] Here, Scharlieb echoed the RCVD's condemnation of the Contagious Diseases Acts, claiming that any such measures had the pernicious effect of "intend[ing] to make wrong-doing safe"—to "enslave" women and to "dupe" men. For Scharlieb it was crucial not to condemn sufferers for some "mistaken ideas of morality," because the entire community was at risk.

Most importantly, Scharlieb made the war's harmful influence on the spread of disease unmistakably clear.[29] Since the war began, both men and women "were too often swept off their feet by unrestrained emotion." She was adamant that the British Empire was at a crisis point, that venereal diseases posed "a national danger as great and more insidious than defeat on sea, on land and in commerce." Awakening the nation to this "internal" enemy was the first step toward a complete victory. With its emphasis on maternal responsibility and education as a means of combating the spread of the disease, Sharlieb's text seemed to live up to its aim of addressing women, not sheltering them, by providing them with moral and medical lessons meant to be taken "home."

Other commentators called for the regulation of human behavior: "In war there is only one way, and that is State control, to localise the evil, coupled with the immediate clearing-up of all young girls from the streets." It would certainly not be "more moral or dignified to allow 'flappers' to infest the streets and infect the soldiers rather than introduce the system which all Europe knows to be the only preventative measure."[30] Others spoke of the vital work that had to be done to inform British and Colonial soldiers about venereal disease.[31]

After the release of the RCVD's report but before the enactment of legislation in 1917, a group of women launched a letter-writing campaign demanding official notification of venereal diseases. Signed by such well-known women as Emmeline Pankhurst, Margaret Macmillan, and Mrs. Lloyd George, the letter spoke on behalf of "soldiers' mothers" who "have given their sons willingly to die for the Empire, but not like this." Urging legislative action on behalf of the "race," the writers demanded notification and compulsory treatment for those suffering from these diseases, inviting "the mothers and wives of the Empire to join with us in demanding that these diseases should be treated as other dangerously infectious ones are."[32] In response, feminists representing the United Suffragists as well as Charlotte Despard of the Women's Freedom League denounced such demands, because of the "social ban" attached to sufferers and the fear that notification would cause people to avoid treatment and thus increase the chance of the diseases' spread.[33] *The Englishwoman* questioned the fundamental mechanism of the proposal in its reporting on the letter "given wide publicity in the press." How, it asked, were the infected persons to be discovered?[34] Advocates of the more lenient guidelines set up by the RCVD continued to stress the importance of education, not notification.

A. Maude Royden, a leading suffragist, was one of several feminists who attempted to popularize information about venereal diseases to civilian audiences. Her 1917 *The Duty of Knowledge* denounced any attempts to regulate prostitution as providing men with a false sense of security and punishing women. She reminded her readers that "if men are infected by women, the women themselves must, in the first instance, have been infected by men."[35] She argued that women, in addition to their other wartime roles—acting in "rescue, preventative, or reformatory work, in schools for mothers, in crèches, as probation officers"— all had a vital role to play in the battle against this indigenous foe.

Other feminist participants in wartime debates about venereal diseases noted how the mass mobilization and absence of men affected society. Millicent Garrett Fawcett, leader of the largest British women's suffrage organization, the National Union of Women's Suffrage Societies, wrote in 1917 that as a result of the war, among other things, "the very feeling of gratitude and admiration for what our soldiers are doing for us has led numbers of inexperienced girls into a frame of mind which makes them think that anything and everything which these men wish for must be given to them." While excusing the girls' behavior as the result of naivete, Fawcett remarked that the disease could be seen as "one of the penalties which war exacts." Applauding the conclusions of the RCVD report and, in particular, its evidence that the Contagious Diseases Acts had not worked and should not be reinstated, Fawcett also raised an older issue lurking at the back of the debates: that the real enemy to be rooted out was not the disease but prostitution, and that the core of such a fight was the need for men to exercise self-control and to lead chaste lives.[36]

After the initial uses of the broader terms of DORA and in the aftermath of the RCVD's report, in 1917 the British government introduced legislation into Parliament to deal with sexual immorality: the Criminal Law Amendment Bill. A wide range of measures were covered in the bill, including raising the age of consent for women from 16 to 18 and introducing penalties of imprisonment with hard labor for knowingly spreading venereal disease.[37] It also proposed criminalizing advertisements for abortifacients and alleged cures for disorders spread by sexual contact. The most controversial aspect of the bill proved to be its provisions, in the infamous clause 3, that if a girl under 18 was found guilty of loitering for the purposes of soliciting, actively soliciting, or behaving in "a riotous or indecent manner," then "by reason of her mode of life or associations" the court could "in lieu of awarding any punishment, order the girl to be detained until she attains the age of nineteen, or any less period."[38] Clearly, this measure responded to the ongoing public outcry over the "scandal of the streets" and the allegedly loosened morals of young girls, and the NVA, for one, endorsed this idea of reforming rather than merely punishing the girl.[39]

On the other hand, feminist organizations quickly attacked the bill as doing more harm than good. They objected to compulsory examinations for venereal disease and pointed out that, despite proponents' claims that both men and women would be subject to the same laws, women were still far more likely to be blamed and punished. Members of the Women's Freedom League pointed out that making the transmittal of venereal disease a legal crime as well as a moral one would do nothing for wives infected by their husbands, since "very few married women in their present state of economic dependence could afford, for themselves or their family, to dispense with the breadwinner, and many would hesitate to imprison the father of their children." Leaders of this organization, including Charlotte Despard, denounced this aspect of the bill by claiming it was a backhanded way of reestablishing the Contagious Diseases Acts and had to be opposed.[40] This and similar opposition led the government to withdraw this provision from the bill.[41]

Although this aspect of the Criminal Law Amendment Bill was meant to be an indirect means of fighting venereal disease by regulating prostitutes and other suspicious women, its failure led to new efforts. Instead, under DORA, the British government revived some provisions of the Contagious Diseases Act of 1864. In the eyes of opponents to the acts, the first of these direct attempts occurred with regulation 35C. This regulation made it possible for the police to "control" or "regulate" the "presence, movement or behavior" of anyone "likely to prejudice the training, discipline administration or the efficiency" of those people engaged in making or "handling munitions of war." Such suspected miscreants could be reported to the police or the military authorities, and anyone who had been "convicted...of any offence against public order and decency" could be prevented from residing in select areas.[42] Although the wording of the regulation avoided either the terms "prostitutes" or "women," those opposed to the Contagious Diseases Acts believed that not only could it easily be turned toward prostitutes, it implicitly addressed them.[43] What was at stake in such regulations was discipline, not disease; indeed, they recast disease as a question of order.

Despite receiving criticism over the ambiguously worded regulation 35C, in late March 1918 the government issued a new Defense of the Realm Regulation, which was designed to prevent the spread of disease among the armed forces.   This regulation, 40D, stated that "no woman who is suffering from venereal disease in a communicable form shall have sexual intercourse with any member of His Majesty's forces" nor could she "solicit or invite" such sexual intercourse.   Women charged under this regulation could then be taken into custody for at least a week and subjected to any medical examination that could ascertain if they were suffering from venereal disease.   An accused woman would be "informed of her right to be remanded" and could choose to be examined either by "her own doctor or by the medical officer of the prison."[44]   Some of the most disputed aspects of the Contagious Diseases Act thus returned with 40D, including the fact that women were held accountable for the spread of disease and, even if merely suspected, could be subjected to an intimate medical examination with or without their consent.

Outraged by the sweeping tone of regulation 40D, organizations such as the Association of Moral and Social Hygiene demanded its immediate withdrawal.[45]   On June 27, 1918, at a protest meeting in Fabian Hall, representatives from the leading feminist organizations gathered to voice their strenuous objections.[46]   Women and "social purity" campaigners did not provide the only voices of protest.   An editorial in the *Manchester Guardian* asserted that while the "evil" that was being combated was also "a source of serious military weakness," it did "not follow that the remedy proposed is wise or even tolerable."[47]   Like other editorials, the *Guardian 's* denounced both the inequality of charging women and not men and the dangerous "French" precedents that were being followed.   As an editorial in the *Herald* mused, this was but the slippery slope toward the "logical end" of the *maison tolerée* with its certified occupants."[48]   Although France did not subject any woman suspected of "inviting" soldiers' sexual intercourse to arbitrary arrest and physical examination, its very maintenance of legalized brothels made it the emblem of a system that regulated and thus tolerated the 'evil' of prostitution.

Regulation 40D was not abolished until after the war's end, and a number of women were "successfully" prosecuted under its aegis.   Cases drew both publicity and public protest, but the Home Office, while responding to criticism, did not alter its policy during the war.[49]   The history of 40D is certainly not a "new" story, although it has not been widely analyzed, but its brief life is nonetheless instructive.   First, while the British often compared themselves to the French when constructing policy around venereal disease, eventually the British regulations under DORA were even more widespread.   In Britain, moreover, a severe split existed between its military and public health directives regarding venereal disease.[50]   Defense of the Realm regulations 35C and 40D directly contradicted the government's own report from the Royal Commission on

Venereal Diseases. Although the range of options regarding venereal disease was not extensive and was similar across Europe, Britain appeared more regimented during the war because it established (or rather reestablished) a regulatory system that went beyond prostitution, targeting both the prostitute and the "new" amateur girl.[51]

ENSURING VICTORY AT HOME

During the war concern with social order and the moral battles that *had* to be won if the war was to be a true victory became intensely caught up with the behavior of women. The appearance of women in new arenas, acting in a less "restricted" manner, suggested to many, throughout the war, that drastic changes in the relationships between men and women were under way. Others insisted instead that the "freer" behavior being discussed reflected a new "comradeship" between them. However, if the war brought a greater openness in discussions of venereal disease or in the kinds of public space available to unsupervised women, these changes were observed with a good deal of trepidation.

The problems posed by an allegedly rampant female sexuality were threefold. First, "amateur girls" and increased casual sexual encounters were read as signaling a moral decline in the nation's great metropolis that suggested the country could be felled by the seeds of moral decay eating away from the inside. Second, professional female sexuality and the interactions between prostitutes and soldiers in particular became the most obvious areas of concern. Venal sex was read as a threat to discipline and order as much as it was seen as spreading disease, but most at issue was women's, not men's, sexual misbehavior. Nonetheless, the third issue of the physical toll of venereal diseases and their debilitating effect on the fitness of the fighting forces was met with some provisions of a previously used and nationally specific response: the return of the Contagious Diseases Acts.

By characterizing venereal diseases as internal enemies, as deadly to soldiers as to the "race" that the postwar world would rebuild, the female carriers of disease tainted the public roles of all women. It therefore became difficult, for many, to distinguish between prostitutes and women who slept with soldiers out of desire or "misplaced" patriotism. National morale came to be associated with female sexual morality, even as a new vocabulary marked out sex-specific roles meant to foster military morale, and the war years marked not only the appearance of the "flapper" and the "amateur girl," but the allegedly overpaid and uncontrollable new female war worker. As such, the threat that women posed went far beyond disease.

NOTES

My thanks to Laura Lee Downs, Tom Laqueur, Susan Pedersen, Sonya Rose, Joe Ward, and Nicole Dombrowski for their comments on earlier versions of this essay.

1. The order was issued in November 1914, and the first women arrested were brought before a military court on November 28, 1914. This information was reported in "Undesirable Women and the Army," *The Vigilance Record* (December 1914).

2. Details that the women pleaded guilty are recorded in "Undesirable Women and the Army." Information about sentencing can be found in W[ar] O[ffice] 32 5526/040564, PRO Kew.

3. "The Cardiff Outrage," *Herald*, 19 December 1914. This was Lansbury's paper.

4. C. Nina Boyle, "The Prime Minister and a 'Scrap of Paper.' C.D. Acts Re-established in a New Form," *The Vote* (December 1914). Outrage over the German chancellor's tearing up the treaty of 1839 guaranteeing Belgium's neutrality as being only "a scrap of paper" fueled pro-war sentiment and became a pivotal part of British propaganda. Posters reprinting the treaty's signatures and labeled "The Scrap of Paper" were circulated in Britain in 1915. For a reproduction of one such poster, see Walton H. Rawls, *Wake Up America! World War I and the American Poster* (New York: Abbeville, 1988), 44. See also the discussion of the "scrap of paper" in Nicoletta Gullace, "Women and the Ideology of War: Recruitment, Propaganda, and the Mobilization of Public Opinion in Britain, 1914—1918" (Ph.D. diss., University of California at Berkeley, 1993), ch. 1.

5. See "The Girl in the Street," *Daily Express*, 3 November 1914, and "Women and the War," *Daily Call*, 19 November 1914. Angela Woollacott, " 'Khaki Fever' and Its Control: Gender, Class, Age and Sexual Morality on the British Homefront in the First World War," *Journal of Contemporary History* 29 (1994), and Philippa Levine, " 'Walking the Streets in a Way No Decent Woman Should': Women Police in World War I," *Journal of Modern History* 66 (March 1994), analyze some of the complaints raised in the *Daily Call* article. See also Lucy Bland, "In the Name of Protection: The Policing of Women in the First World War," in *Women in Law: Explorations in Law, Family and Sexuality*, ed. Julia Brophy and Carol Smart (London: Routledge and Kegan Paul, 1985), and Susan Kingsley Kent, *Making Peace: The Reconstruction of*

Gender in Interwar Britain (Princeton, NJ: Princeton University Press, 1993).

6. "Cardiff and Women Patrols," *The Vigilance Record* (December 1914). See Levine, " 'Walking the Streets,' " op. cit. on the formation of the Women Police out of a number of such "patrols".

7. "Bristol Vigilance Association," *The Vigilance Record* (March 1915). The article attributed a change in this behavior to the early closing of pubs and the creation of woman patrols. The following month *The Vigilance Record* approvingly cited the warning of a judge from the Gainsborough County Court to young girls who should be kept indoors at night for their own good.

8. See Woollacott's analysis of this phenomenon in " 'Khaki Fever,' " op. cit.

9. "Soldiers and Young Women," *The Vigilance Record* (December 1915). Emphasis added.

10. Mrs. Flora Annie Steel, "Women Who Are Hindering Instead of Helping," *Sunday Herald*, 10 May 1918.

11. M.H. Mason, "Public Morality: Some Constructive Suggestions," *Nineteenth Century and After* 32, no. 485 (July 1917): 186; "Conference on the 'Moral Conditions of the Streets of London,' " *The Vigilance Record* (July 1917). The conference was adjourned and continued on July 30, as reported in *The Vigilance Record* (August 1917).

12. Bishop of London Arthur F. Winnington-Ingram, Sir Edward Henry, Lieutenant-General Sir Francis Lloyd, and Louise Creighton all quoted in "Conference on the 'Moral Conditions of the Streets of London,' " *The Vigilance Record* (July 1917).

13. "Scandal of the Streets," *Daily Express*, 20 September 1918.

14. "The Land Cure," *Daily Express*, 20 September 1918.

15. "London Street Women—An American Editor's Endictment," *The Evening News*, 24 September 1918. The interview was originally published in the *London Times*, which this article acknowledged, and reprinted elsewhere. All further references in the following two paragraphs are to this article.

16. Bok added that it was unfair not only to the soldiers but to "the American mother." An outcry against the war could result if news of the condition of London reached "the American woman."

17. "The State of Our Streets—A Warning From America," *The Evening News*, 24 September 1918.

18. Edward Price Bell, as quoted in "The Moral Condition of the London Streets," *The Vigilance Record* (October 1918). Emphasis in the original.

19. G.S. Graves, Letter to the Editor, *Evening Standard*, reprinted in

The Vigilance Record (October 1918).

20. "The Moral Condition of the London Streets," *The Vigilance Record* (October 1918).

21. "London Street Women—An American Editor's Endictment," *Evening News*, 24 September 1918.

22. Proposed wartime alternatives to conventional bourgeois sexual morality provoked anxieties in many quarters in France as well. See Susan R. Grayzel, "Mothers, Marraines, and Prostitutes: Morale and Morality in First World War France," *International History Review* 19, no. 1 (February 1997).

23. Quoted in Lady Burbidge, "Woman and the War—Has She Degenerated?" *Sunday Times* 1 June 1919.

24. Ibid.

25. The Contagious Diseases Acts were suspended in 1883. Douglas White, "Synopsis of the Final Report of the Royal Commission on Venereal Diseases," *Report of the Royal Commission on Venereal Diseases* (1916). Reprint. London: National Council for Combating Venereal Diseases, (1921). Dr. Douglas White, a leading member of the committee, provided a footnote to the reprinted version of the report, pointing out that in May 1917, Parliament outlawed the treatment of venereal disease by any except qualified medical personnel. Further references will be made parenthetically. For more on the original Contagious Diseases Acts, see Judith R. Walkowitz, *Prostitution and Victorian Society* (Cambridge: Cambridge University Press, 1980). The reintroduction of some equivalent of the Acts can be attributed to pressure from Dominion military leaders. See Suzann Buckley, "The Failure to Resolve the Problem of Venereal Disease Among the Troops in Britain During World War I," *War and Society* 2 (1977), H[ome] O[ffice] 45 10802/307990 and 10894/359931, PRO Kew, and the discussion below.

26. It suggested that venereal disease was grounds for annulling a marriage, and if the annulment resulted in the children becoming illegitimate, then the state should ensure "that disabilities of illegitimacy should not follow." See *Report of the Royal Commission*, op. cit., 47—49.

27. Douglas White et al., "Draft of Letter on the Inaugural Meeting of the National Council for Combating Venereal Diseases," 21 October 1914. Fawcett Library, FL, Association for Moral and Social Hygiene [AMSH] Collection, Box 311/1. The first meeting, according to this letter, was scheduled for 11 November 1914, at the Royal College of Medicine. The NCCVD thus began distributing leaflets in advance of the publication of the RCVD's report

28. Mary Scharlieb, *The Hidden Scourge* (London: C. Arthur Pearson, 1916). The book's foreword was by the Bishop of London. Scharlieb also

publicized these ideas in two articles, "New Remedies for Old Diseases," *The Englishwoman* 88 (April 1916), and "Royal Commission on Venereal Diseases: Education," *The Englishwoman* 89 (May 1916).

29. Scharlieb brings this up in reference to "war babies," the scandal of an alleged increase in illegitimate births due to the war. For more on war babies, see Susan R. Grayzel, "'The Mothers of Our Soldiers' Children': Motherhood, Immorality, and the War Baby Scandal, 1914—1918," in *Maternal Instincts: Visions of Motherhood and Sexuality in Britain, 1875—1925*, ed. Claudia Nelson and Ann Sumner Holmes (New York: Macmillan Press, 1997).

30. Civis, "A Word About Venereal Disease," *The English Review* 23 (December 1916).

31. George A. Wade, "The National Campaign Against Venereal Diseases," *The World's Work* (February 1917). In France, no less than the French Academy of Medicine was enlisted to issue a set of guidelines to advise military personnel what they could do to avoid venereal disease. See Grayzel, "Mothers, Marraines, and Prostitutes," op. cit.

32. "Letter to the Editor," *Manchester Guardian*, 25 October 1916. The letter originally appeared in the *Times* 23 October 1916. A press cutting of the *Manchester Guardian* copy can be found in Folder 15, HO 45 10802/307990.

33. See Letters to the Editor, *Manchester Guardian*, 25 October 1916. Also in HO 45 10802/307990.

34. "Echoes," *The Englishwoman* 95 (November 1916).

35. A. Maude Royden, *The Duty of Knowledge: A Consideration of the Report of the Royal Commission on Venereal Disease, Specially for the Use of Social Workers* (London: NCCVD, 1917).

36. Mrs. Henry [Millicent Garrett] Fawcett, "The Problem of Venereal Diseases," *Review of Reviews* 55, no. 326 (1917): 155, 158.

37. The bill received a good deal of attention from various organizations, and its various clauses were reprinted and discussed in *The Vigilance Record* (March and April 1917). See also HO 45 10711/244320 for a discussion of attempts to promote comparable legislation in the spring of 1914 and of the dangers of doing so during the war.

38. Clause 3, Criminal Law Amendment Bill, reprinted in *The Vigilance Record* (April 1917).

39. "Opposition to Clause 3," *The Vigilance Record* (April 1917).

40. The copy of a letter sent to the prime minister, the home secretary and members of Parliament and the press from Charlotte Despard, Florence A. Underwood, and E. Knight of the Women's Freedom League was reprinted in *The Vote*, 2 March 1917. *The Vote* also recorded that the National Union of Women's Suffrage Societies, the Free Church League

for Women's Suffrage, and "many prominent individual women" also opposed the measure.

41. An overview of debates surrounding the Criminal Law Amendment Bill can be found in E.M. Goodman, "The Criminal Law Amendment Bill," *Review of Reviews* (April 1917); see also Dr. Jane Walker, "Recent Proposal on the Moral Question," *The Englishwoman* 100 (April 1917), and "Beware of Constructive Legislation," *The Englishwoman* 115 (July 1918).

42. Regulation 35C, Defense of the Realm Act, 14 April 1917. See *Defence of the Realm Regulations: Acts and Regulations* (London: HMSO, 1917).

43. It could also be used against aliens, an issue that was brought up in a statement from the National Council for Civil Liberties sent to the Association of Moral and Social Hygiene. See FL ASMH Collection, Box 311/1.

44. 40D, Defense of the Realm Act, 22 March 1918. See *Defence of the Realm Regulations: Acts and Regulations,* op. cit. This regulation was further publicized in the *London Times,* 27 March 1918, and reprinted in *The Vigilance Record* (April 1918).

45. Alison Neilans, secretary, Letter, 28 March 1918. FL AMSH Collection, Box 311/2.

46. These included Helena Swanwick (representing the Women's International League), Florence Underwood (Women's Freedom League), Mrs. Broadley Reid (Women's Liberal Federation), and others from the Catholic Women's Suffrage Society, Friends Social Purity League, and National Union of Trained Nurses. See the account of the meeting dated 27 June 1918, in FL AMSH Collection, Box 311/2. Other letters in the AMSH collection demonstrate opposition from the National Union of Women Workers, and the AMSH both amassed press cuttings concerning 40D and actively sought out information as to the impact of 40D on local communities

47. *Manchester Guardian,* 27 March 1918. Reprinted in "Extracts from Editorial Notes," FL AMSH Collection, Box 311/2.

48. *Herald,* 6 April 1918. Reprinted in "Extracts from Editorial Notes," FL AMSH Collection, Box 311/2.

49. For more on 40D, see HO 45 10894/359931. Regulation 40D was amended on 19 July 1918, to include not only members of "His Majesty's Forces" but also those "of any of His Majesty's Allies" and was revoked on 25 November 1918. See regulation 40D in *The Defence of the Realm Regulations Consolidated* (London: HMSO, 1919), 151.

50. Buckley, "The Failure to Resolve," op. cit., 81, notes that this split accounted for some of the inefficiency with which venereal diseases were fought.

51. For a more thorough discussion of these issues, see Susan R. Grayzel, "Women's Identities at War: The Cultural Politics of Gender in Britain and France, 1914—1919" (Ph.D. diss., University of California at Berkeley, 1994), ch. 4.

Figure 5. Red Army soldiers after the Long March, 1938.

From left to right: Chen Zongying, Cai Chang, Xia Ming, Liu Ying.

FIVE

Why We Joined the Revolution
Voices of Chinese Women Soldiers

Helen Praeger YOUNG

In 1934 the beleaguered Chinese Communist armies, under constant attack by Chiang Kai-shek's Nationalist forces, withdrew from the Chinese Soviet base areas in central and south China. This 6,000—mile retreat west and north across China became known as the Long March. In the late 1980s I had the good fortune to interview twenty-two Chinese women who had participated as Red Army soldiers in the Long March.

These women told stories of leaving children behind with peasant families, of crossing glacier mountains in the third trimester of pregnancy, of leaving babies where they were born, or of carrying them along a day or two after birth. They described the work they did as women soldiers, carrying stretchers, spreading propaganda, recruiting laborers and male soldiers, and carrying gold for the army. Rich as these stories are, the greatest wealth of material came in response to the question, "Why did you join the party and the army?" Their answers, framed by their understanding of Marxist ideology at the time of the interview, contained details from their childhood, their family situations, how they perceived their future, how and when they were politicized, and how they understood their own decision to join the revolution. From the responses of these women, it is possible to find ways to understand what motivates women anywhere to become revolutionaries and go to war.

All the women, those who joined communist organizations before entering the army, as well as those who enlisted in the Red Army directly, spoke not of joining the army but of "participating in the revolution." What "becoming revolutionary" meant was as varied as the women themselves. To some, it meant freedom from exploitation and abuse at home, the hope of escape from the chaos of poverty, and the safety of a secure, regimented environment with enough food to eat; for those whose futures were unsettled, it was a way of avoiding marriage into a strange family, or remaining an unmarried, unpaid worker on the lowest rung of the family ladder; for the educated and educable, it was an exciting way to fight for social justice and work for national sovereignty. For almost all, participating in the revolution meant finding a place to belong. One, echoed by several others, said, "The party was my family." However, the revolution, unlike their families, offered them opportunity to allow their unsubmissive, independent traits to surface.

When asked "Why did you join?" the women spoke about (1) the social and economic situation in their families and the level of education they received; (2) the geographical setting of their home cities or villages, including the proximity of their home to the Chinese Soviet base areas or the path of the Red armies; and (3) the opportunity to learn about the revolution from communist underground workers in the village, revolutionary organizations in the village, progressive teachers in school, and family members, usually men, already in the revolution.

From the founding of the Chinese Communist party (CCP) in 1921, the male party members had been serious about equality of the sexes, although they interpreted equality within the boundaries of their own cultural consciousness.[1] They organized schools for their sisters, wives, and mothers; established literacy classes for women workers and peasants; and wrote sexual equality into their documents, advocating emancipation of women and an end to child marriages of all kinds. They guaranteed protection for women and offered them access to the economic and cultural life of the society.[2] The CCP has continued this top-down policy of liberation of women within the patriarchal society.[3]

FAMILY SITUATION, CLASS, AND LEVEL OF EDUCATION
During the first three decades of the twentieth century, there was little institutional support for girls and women in China. In the poorest families, baby girls were unaffordable luxuries, to be disposed of as quickly as possible by death, sale or marriage. Unlike sons, daughters were part of the birth family only until they married and joined their husband's family, giving rise to the common Chinese saying, "When a girl is married, it is like throwing water on the ground."[4] In those harsh economic times, girls from poor families were sold into marriage as *tongyangxi*.[5]

Tongyangxi
Four of the twelve *tongyangxi* among the women interviewed were infants under 1 year old when they were given to other families. Li Jianzhen, born to poor peasants in Guangdong, was sold to another poor family for eight copper coins when she was 8 months old. She spoke of the plight of some girls in rhyme:

Eighteen-year-old wife, three-year-old husband.

At night the wife puts the little husband to bed,
Works hard to take care of him until he grows up;
When the husband is grown up, the wife is old;
The dream has been hidden away.[6]

There were two different situations [she continued]. There were younger baby brides as well as younger husbands. In the old society, families with money would buy a girl, but actually she would be a servant or daughter rather than a wife.

My own mother had twelve children: four dead, eight living. The three of us girls were sold, leaving five. Four of my brothers were sold abroad in Southeast Asia. Finally, there was only one younger brother left.

In the old society, we called it "selling baby pigs." There was no alternative. You bore one child, gave it away, and bore another.

In Sichuan, Liu Jian's destitute family gave their first child, a daughter, to another family when she was 3 days old. Then two more daughters were born and, Liu explained, "People didn't have any choice but to put them in the urine bucket and cover it."[7] She was more fortunate than her sisters. When she was born in a paddy field and left to die, her grandmother picked her up. A year later, when her mother gave birth to a son, "They said I was good luck, because I brought my mother a boy." A son was old-age insurance for his parents. His wife came into his family to work and to continue the male family line. Together, husband and wife took care of his parents when they were too old to be productive.

The girls who became *tongyangxi* when they were older had a much more difficult time. Four of the five women who were sold into another family between the ages of 6 and 8 spoke of maltreatment. Their experience was typical.[8] The abuse of *tongyangxi* was widespread and for all four, their mistreatment was a crucial factor in the decision to run away and join the revolution. Two believed they would be beaten to death by their "in-law" families and chose the uncertainty of life and death in the military over the certainty of death in their adoptive families. The other three *tongyangxi* were sent to their "in-law" families just before puberty, in one case to prevent her from joining the army.

None of the twelve *tongyangxi* was educated as a child. Several, however, spoke of standing outside the schoolroom, listening to the teacher after they had taken the boys in the family to school. Two, whose designated "husbands" were revolutionaries, received some schooling as teenagers, one in a CCP school, the other in a progressive work/study school.

Daughters in Birth Families

The three who were from poor peasant families but not sold as *tongyangxi* had no education. The other seven, who grew up in more comfortable families, received some schooling. Even in wealthier families, however, girls were seldom educated with their brothers, since girls were not highly valued. Money spent on education for girls was thought to be a waste. Lin Yueqin, from a mountainous area in Anhui province, explained:

> At that time, China was governed by feudalism and there was no equality between men and women. Chinese women had no freedom, no right to education. Boys from rich families could go to school, but girls from rich families could not. They had no right to choose freely whom they would marry. When you were in your mother's belly [laugh], your parents arranged your marriage. Women had no status. They were at the lowest level of society, doing household chores, home labor.

> My father was a businessman in our small town and was comparatively accepting of the idea of equality between men and women advocated by Sun Yat-sen after the May Fourth Movement.[9] So, although men and women were not equal, I did get some schooling. I studied at home, first, and later went to a primary school for three years.

Liu Ying, an educated woman from Hunan province, came from a family ruled by a traditional father. She had to fight for her education with some support from her mother, who was herself literate.

> The sons were more important than the daughters in my rather feudalistic family.[10] My father wanted the sons to go to school, not the daughters. But I also wanted to go to school. I struggled and struggled, studying by myself until I could pass the entrance exam for the Women's Normal School in Changsha. [At that time, boys and girls didn't go to school together.] An early communist revolutionary, who had just come back from studying in France, established this progressive girls' school where we didn't have to pay tuition. Many of our men teachers had been classmates of Mao Zedong when they were students in the No.1 Normal School in Changsha. Under the influence of these teachers, we joined the revolution.

Later, Liu Ying continued her schooling at the college level in Moscow, the only one of the women interviewed to receive tertiary education before the Long March.

Four of the others also attended progressive schools and became political activists as a direct result of what they learned from their teachers. They did not follow the usual pattern in society of the time, for they came from families that were more enlightened than Liu Ying's. Jian Xianren, also from Hunan, was educated in the village, along with her little brother.

We started school together when I was 8 and my brother was 6. Old Chinese people favored boys over girls, but in our family, boys weren't considered more important than girls. They just thought I was old enough to take care of my younger brother, so they let my little brother and me start school together.

However, when it was time for Jian Xianren and her brother to go on to middle school, her grandmother became ill. She was kept at home to help, while her brother went on to school in the provincial capital. He became a revolutionary and brought her material to read. After her grandmother died, she joined her brother, entered the same school in Changsha that Liu Ying attended, and also became a political activist.

He Manqiu, in Sichuan province, did not attend a progressive school.[11] She explained that her father and grandmother raised her, because her mother did not like her: "She thought I was ugly and wanted to throw me away."[12] Her grandmother wanted her to follow traditional Confucian principles, to be a proper daughter and become a proper wife. When she was 6 or 7, her grandmother bound He Manqiu's feet, to which process the child agreed in spite of the pain. After her father took her to meetings advocating unbound feet, however, she decided to take the bindings off before her feet were too badly crippled, an even more painful process.[13]

Not at all the modest, submissive female her grandmother wanted her to be, He Manqiu was something of a tomboy. Her comparatively open-minded father hired a tutor for her, then sent her to middle school in Chengdu, the provincial capital. She was brought back home when she was 14, because warlord armies were fighting in Chengdu. At home, she was bored and increasingly "afraid my grandmother would find a mother-in-law for me."[14]

GEOGRAPHY

He Manqiu came from Sichuan, a vastly overpopulated and opium-riddled province. In addition to warlord armies living off the land as they fought each other, the Nationalist and communist armies were fighting near He Manqiu's village. He Manqiu describes how the Nationalist soldiers had two guns—a rifle and a "smoking gun" [an opium pipe]. My father said we'd better stay out of the way of these soldiers because they tried to take everything they could from the local people, so we hid for several days. When we returned to the town to see what was happening, we heard firecrackers, drums, and gongs as soon as we got close to the village. I had never experienced such an exciting scene in all my 15 years! My father was cautious and didn't dare go further, but I wasn't at all afraid. I squeezed into the crowd and stood next to a neighbor, who was a good friend of my father's. I asked him what the matter was.

He said, "What do you mean, what's the matter? This is the Red Army!"

Beginning from that time, I began to think about participating in the revolution.

Chinese Soviet base areas were established in poor, remote mountainous regions, often straddling provincial borders. The advantage to the communists included proximity to a supportive population, terrain favorable for guerrilla warfare, and distance from the scrutiny of national and provincial authorities. Of the twenty-two women interviewed, sixteen lived in or near Soviet base areas, in places where the Red armies were fighting, or in the path of a moving Red Army. These areas, poor in normal times, were even more devastated by the depredations of the warlord and Nationalist armies on the civilian populations. Not only did these armies feed and clothe themselves by living off the land, they also took the young men to be   soldiers and laborers. Like He Manqiu, however, the women interviewed remembered the Red Army positively. When the Red Army stopped moving, even for a brief time, they established local communist government and mass organizations. They redistributed the land and shared the landlords' grain with the local peasants.

As early as 1928, the Party Congress passed a resolution emphasizing the need to bring women into the revolution and linking women's interests with revolutionary activities.[15] Three of the seven women from Sichuan and Anhui who lived near the 4th Front Army cited the CCP propaganda advocating women's liberation as one of the reasons they joined the revolution.[16]

OPPORTUNITY

Many of those who lived in proximity to the Red armies reported that nothing in their village had ever been as exciting as the   coming of the army. Certainly, the attraction of adventure existed for all the women, although it was never directly cited as the reason they joined. None was quite as straightforward as Li Yanfa who said, "Why did I join the army? To go find food to eat. There was no food at home." Several others mentioned hunger as a factor, but they also spoke of the effects of propaganda that promised equality between men and women, and a chance to change the social and economic structure in China. The powerful attraction of a different way to live life, an alternative to being a wife in a poor family, was clearly important for many. Even Li Yanfa, like the others, expressed several reasons for joining, although her basic reason for joining the army was simply hunger.[17] She found life in Sichuan with her opium-smoking father intolerable, and her life, after he sent her to her "in-laws," even worse.

> The first time I saw the Red Army [Li Yanfa explained], I went to the meeting in a big village. My father was lazy—you know, he smoked. I went by myself. Children weren't afraid any more. The meeting was led by a woman. At the first meeting, I didn't dare say anything. At the third meeting, I asked if I could join the army. They said yes, but asked, "What about your family?"
> I answered, "My mama died. My two brothers don't live at home and my father smokes opium." I told them everything. And they said, "Yes."

When her father found out that Li Yanfa wanted to join the army, he told her, "If you join the army, I'll pull the tendon out of your leg!" Then he insisted that she get married immediately into the family to which she had been betrothed before she was born.

> "Whatever you say, it's okay with me," I said. I knew that I was going to join the army anyway, so I went to my "in-laws."

> The bed that the family gave me was only a frame with a shabby rain cape made of palmleaves on it, not even any straw or stalks on the bed. When I got up in the morning, I had to take the ox out to graze. Five families owned one ox. I carried pails of water on a shoulder pole for the five families. After I fetched water for each family, I gathered kindling and cut grass while the ox was grazing. You know what I ate when I got back? They fed the dog sweet potato leaves mixed with the rice that had stuck to the pot and some water. After the dog ate, I would eat what was left.

Li Yanfa bided her time until she could safely run away to the army headquarters one morning while the ox was grazing.

I ran ten miles without stopping, but they wouldn't let me in. There were two guards at the gate.

"What do you want? What's a little girl doing here?" they shouted. I was thirteen.

I said, "The team leader says I can be a soldier."

"Let *you* be a soldier?" they replied.

My clothes were shabby, just hanging in threads.

"*You* join the army?" one guard repeated. He went inside to see if the team leader knew anything about it. Then he said, "Come in." I saw the team leader and ran to her, crying in her arms.

After we filled in some papers, I had a bath in a basin of water. Then they took me to eat. I ate one bowl of meat and vegetables, one bowl of rice.

"Is it enough?" they asked.

"Give me one more serving," I said. I finished, and they asked again,

"Enough?"

Still not enough, so I got another, until I had three bowls of meat and vegetables, three bowls of rice. The salty vegetables were so tasty—sweet potato, pumpkin, tofu, pork, all mixed up together. They wouldn't let me have any more. They said I'd burst!

"We eat this every day," they told me. "Don't eat any more now."

The shabby clothes I came with were burned and they gave me a set of clothes that had been taken from the local tyrants—two sets of underclothes and one set of padded clothes. We used red cloth for the epaulets and the star on the hat.

That was how I joined the army. No one in our village joined with me. There was no food at home. When you join the army, you have food to eat and clothes to wear.

Proximity to Army Route or Base Area

Zhong Yuelin emphasized the accident of life that put her in proximity to the Red Army. She had been sold to a family living in a larger village in Jiangxi province when she was 8 years old; a happy circumstance, she said, because if I had stayed in my mother's village, I probably wouldn't have taken the revolutionary road. My mother's village was in a mountain valley. It was rather backward and isolated from outside ideas. When I went to the family as *tongyangxi*, I had more opportunity because the village was larger, much more open and receptive to Communist party propaganda.

There were quite a few people who could read and write because many young people were concentrated there. They officially organized the local government and some mass organizations like the Children's Corps, the Young Pioneers, the Women's Unit. I joined the Young Pioneers by myself, just because I thought it was good.

At that time, we believed that women had been oppressed for thousands of years. One time I was told to go to a women's meeting. At the meeting they asked what my name was. I said, "I don't have a name."

I hadn't had a name before that!

All of her life, Zhong Yuelin had been called "Old Zhong's daughter." The Communist party organizations not only gave individual women the most basic recognition but also provided social legitimacy for women who occupied the lowest position in the family as well as in society.[18]

Underground Communists Working in the Villages

Among the women who lived near the Soviet base area in Jiangxi province, where the central communist government was based, only Wei Xiuying joined the army directly, before joining a local communist organization. After carrying messages for the soldiers, she joined the army with several men from her village. They encouraged her to enlist with them, she said, because of the daily abuse she suffered from her "in-law" family.

Deng Liujin followed the usual pattern for the women in this area and joined Communist organizations before joining the army. She described a woman who came to her village, befriended her, and persuaded her to make a revolutionary commitment:

I was still waiting for the son who hadn't been born yet. My foster parents half-adopted a son, borrowing him from another family. I was supposed to be his fiancé, but I didn't like him at all. Later he got sick and died.

I lived this way until 1929, when Mao Zedong, Zhu De, and Chen Yi brought the army to western Fujian where I lived. Because of the Nationalist reactionary propaganda, most of us ran away to the mountains to hide when the Red Army arrived. We were naive at that time, so we believed what the Nationalists said and didn't trust the Red Army. Gradually, we began to understand and we moved back to the village.

I know now that even before the Red Army came there was an underground organization in the township. A woman who often came to visit us asked me if I wanted to become active in helping the poor people. I knew my family wouldn't interfere if I tried to do this kind of work, so I said, "Of course, but what can I do? Nothing can be done."

"Why not?" she asked me. "You are so poor, you've suffered a lot—you have to liberate yourself."

"How can I liberate myself?" I said.

She suggested that we two be the first to cut our hair, to set an example. At that time, I wore a pigtail. As a married woman, she wore her hair in a bun. In the old society, nobody had short hair, so cutting hair was abnormal. If you cut your hair, everybody laughed at you. She had to persuade me several times until I finally gave in. We cut our hair. People stood around and looked at us but we thought, 'Think what you please, we're cutting our hair.'

After we cut our hair, and after I accepted the things she told me, she said, "Now that the Red Army is here, we want to overturn the landlords. You are a poor person. Would you like to join the party to help in the work to liberate the poor people?" So in 1931, three years after the Red Army came, I joined the party and she was my sponsor. Before I joined the party, I didn't participate in any revolutionary activities. I just had advanced ideas.

CCP Organizations in the Villages
Cutting away the symbol of marital status in cutting hair, joining communist organizations, and running errands for the army were all paths to involvement for the women living near the Central Soviet base area on the Jiangxi-Fujian border. In some cases the families supported the girls, especially childbrides like Deng Liujin, who had no one in the family to

marry. In Li Guiying's case, she was compromised by the revolutionary act of joining a literacy class and had to make the break with her "family," not unwillingly:

> I was sold when I was 7 years old. My foster family was also poor. I was just sold to this family—there was no husband for me. The son was much older than me and had left, so it was only the old woman and me. That old woman was very fierce, terrible. She wasn't good to me. I had to do almost everything—men's work, women's work. I shouldered everything in the house. At that time we led a bitter, hopeless life. Then, Chairman Mao and General Zhu came to our county. I was about 18 or 19.

When the mass organizations were established, Li Guiying secretly joined a literacy class organized by the communists:

> I'd go to the class when that old woman wasn't home. When she was at home, I didn't dare go. When she found out, she threatened to kill me with the kitchen knife and tried to beat me to death. She gave me a black eye. The comrades in the literacy class told me to go back to class, but I said, "I don't dare go. It's all right as long as you're here, but when you leave, that old woman will beat me to death!"

They made that old woman wear a tall hat and paraded her through the village, shouting, "Don't abuse child brides!"

After Li Guiying joined the army and began the Long March, her husband was wounded in battle. She and her husband were sent to join a guerrilla team near her husband's hometown. She was wounded during a skirmish, and her husband died. Pregnant at the time, she endured terrible physical suffering, especially when she was captured and jailed. When Li Guiying talked about the difficulties she experienced, both before and after she joined the army, she spoke in a matter-of-fact voice, neither dramatizing nor minimizing the violence she suffered. She gave no indication that she was aware of the irony of escaping domestic violence only to experience military violence, but seemed, in retrospect, to understand violence as simply a part of life. Neither she nor the others interviewed expressed any regrets over their initial decision to join the revolution.

Progressive Teachers and Relatives
Jian Xianfo gave more complex reasons for joining the Red Army. Her sister, Jian Xianren, already politicized by her brother before she entered the Women's Normal School in Changsha, was a student activist wanted

by the Nationalist police. In order to avoid putting her family in jeopardy, Xianren left and joined the Red Army. Xianfo, 7 years younger, explained that her thinking was influenced by the political ideas of her older brother and sister, by the patriotism of progressive teachers, and by the Nationalist threat to her family.

My older sister and brother went to school in Changsha, but in 1927, after Jiang Jieshi[19] betrayed the revolution, there was an official order to arrest them. They escaped to our hometown, but the official order was sent to all the counties, so they were on the run and joined the Red Army. Afterwards, our family life wasn't peaceful anymore. I was always haunted by that.

Of course, I was influenced by my sister and brother. They told me about the October Revolution and described how the Soviet Union was building socialism there. I listened very eagerly, and although I was young I understood.

After the older children found refuge in the Red Army, the family was harassed by the Nationalists, who arrested Jian Xianfo's father. When the family bought his release, he worried about his vulnerable 16-year-old daughter and sent her away to the Women's Normal School in Changsha.

When the September 18 incident occurred, I was in school.[20] During our lessons, our teachers told us how our country was humiliated. We felt so sad when we listened—sometimes we were in tears. After the September 18 incident, Jiang Jieshi refused to put up any resistance against the Japanese. The Nationalist policy was to establish internal peace before resisting foreign aggression.[21] They wanted to fight the Red Army in a civil war.

Under such circumstances, I couldn't go on with my education. I had gone home during vacation and hadn't wanted to go back to school. My father comforted me and said, "When there is an opportunity, go join the Red Army and fight the Japanese." I already had such a thought. In December 1934, the 2nd Route Army Group guerrilla troops came to our town. Some of the guerrillas knew about my family, and they welcomed me to join the army.

"What can I do in the army?" I asked them.

"You are a student, you are educated, there are a lot of things you can do," they said. "You can be a teacher, you can do propaganda." I was very happy and I followed them. At that time, my younger brother went with me. He was 15 and I was 18. But, of course, when I left I knew the Nationalists would not leave my family in peace.

While the Jian sisters' stories about the entire family suffering because of the political activism of the children were the most poignant, all those who belonged to revolutionary families told stories of ostracism, execution, and incarceration of members of their families. In several accounts by women from revolutionary families, there is a hint of inevitability, a suggestion that they never considered any choice other than participating in the revolution. This was probably due both to the propensity of Chinese family members to engage in the same work and make the same commitments as others in the family, and to the fact that, in the eyes of the authorities, the whole family was guilty of the crimes of one family member. Since they were already compromised by the activities of a revolutionary family member, they may well have felt they had no choice but to become revolutionaries themselves. When they talked about their earlier life, they either detailed their growing intellectual commitment, as the Jian sisters did, or they simply recounted the experiences with no evaluation of the nature of their commitment.

Xie Xiaomei, whose life was marred by bad luck, had one brother who was a communist and another, not a communist, who helped his brother. When her noncommunist brother was executed, Xie Xiaomei was briefly jailed, then exiled from her hometown, along with her mother. She continued working for the party, married a fellow worker, fought in skirmishes and battles with the communist guerrillas, and in 1934 left on the Long March—after first finding a family who would provide a home to her newborn child. Although she and her husband were eventually turned out of the party and not readmitted until the 1980s, she spoke only about the circumstances that made her life so difficult, expressing no regret about joining her brothers to work for the revolution.

The younger Jian sister and Ma Yixiang were the only interviewees to credit a female family member with contributing to her involvement in the revolution. Ma Yixiang joined the army to save her life. She had been placed as a *tongyangxi* after her siblings had died of malnutrition. When her "in-law" family threatened to kill her, she ran away to her aunt, who was already working with the Red Army. Her aunt then took her to a Red Army field hospital. The doctors and nurses took pity on her and let her work in the laundry, although she was only 11, to keep her safe from her vengeful "in-laws." Her safety didn't last long, however, for not long after she joined, she was expelled from the army over a misunderstanding about her class background. She and other women also expelled followed the army until they were finally reinstated.

Usually, the revolutionary relatives who brought women into their work were men: uncles, brothers, fathers, male cousins. In three cases, it was the "husband" of a *tongyangxi* who played a role in the process.

Chen Zongying, who went to her husband's family as a *tongyangxi* at 12, was the only one who stayed married to the husband her father had arranged for her. The two families were related by marriage and the youngsters had developed a strong relationship before they knew the details of the betrothal. Her husband was one of the early communist leaders, and, she said, "I just followed him. I knew what he was doing must be good." But she also explained that she had been politicized through the influence of a woman with whom she worked, and at a work/ study school she attended briefly.

Qian Xijun's "husband" was also an early communist. He told her that he considered her his sister, not a wife, and arranged for her to attend schools organized by the communists for their female relatives. She joined the party, did underground work in Shanghai, married Mao Zedong's brother, then moved to the Chinese Soviet base area with her husband.

The third *tongyangxi* whose "husband" helped her was Zhong Yuelin, who did not have a name before she joined the communists. She worked into jobs of increasing responsibility until she was assigned one that took her out of her village. Her "husband," also a revolutionary, helped her run away from his family. In most cases, the women had to run away from their "in-law" families to join the army; the family of a girl who joined the army would not only be looked down on in the village, but the *tongyangxi* were economic assets to the "in-law" family.

Joining from Political Conviction

Of the sixteen women who mentioned having revolutionary relatives, only six indicated that the relatives' involvement was crucial to their decision to join the revolution. Most of the ten who only mentioned revolutionary relatives in passing spoke of their own political participation in local organizations.

Kang Keqing said she didn't know of her father's involvement in the revolution until the guerrillas came to her village a second time. At 14, she had joined the underground communist organizations and had already made up her mind to join the army. There was no son in her "in-law" family for her to marry. The army returned to her village when she was 17, and she ran away to become one of the most fearless fighters in the Red Army.

Recruited

Of the six who had not mentioned having revolutionary relatives, Zhang Wen's story is unique. She was the only one who used the plural when she told of joining the army. She was working in a clothing factory when the Red Army came to her town and set up headquarters near the factory: "That year, 1933, hundreds of men and women joined the Red Army, not as soldiers but as laborers, because they had to make clothes for the army." The entire factory, male supervisors and female workers, were recruited. After she became politicized and adept at propaganda, Zhang Wen was transferred to more interesting work during the Long March.

Although the women themselves did not suggest that age was a factor in joining the revolution, twenty-one of the twenty-two women interviewed joined the army or other communist organizations when they were under 21, fourteen of them before they were 18 years old. They had not yet borne children, and had the time and opportunity to work for the revolution that older women, bound to their husband's family by marriage and children and ground down by poverty, did not have. Chen Zongying, who joined the Communist Youth League (CYL) at 24, had transferred her loyalty to her husband even before they were married. She did not, however, sever ties with his family: Two of her daughters were brought up in her husband's family.

WOMEN'S PERSONAL AND POLITICAL PATHS TOWARD REVOLUTION

The reasons the women joined the revolution were primarily gendered, for the men who joined for similar reasons did not have the same impetus as the women. For example, the men with whom Wei Xiuying joined may have been looking for safety and for the thrill of adventure as she was, but they, as males, had not been sold into an abusive family; the revolutionary "husbands" of Chen Zongying and Qian Xijun joined from political conviction that came from the schools they attended - schools their "wives" were prohibited from attending. On the other hand, men as well as women were brought into the revolution by their fathers, brothers, sisters, and cousins. Men also joined the local communist organizations in their villages and became active in the CYL and the party, finding security in a strong organization and a cause to believe in. And they also were predominantly in their teens and early twenties, ready to leave home on their own terms.

Although the attraction of participating in the revolution as a path to a new life was certainly a factor for both sexes, the urgency that impelled the women to join the revolution rose directly from their being women. They expected even greater changes in the way they would live their lives than the men did. As the nameless Zhong Yuelin so clearly demonstrated,

Chinese girls had no place, no status, apart from their relations to a male in the male families. They had little legitimacy or social identity, or, to borrow Linda Kerber's concept in the context of the American Revolution, no citizenship.[22] As part of the communist revolution, they were no longer just the property of the men in their families; they demonstrated their independence by cutting their hair and thus cutting the symbol of marital status. The army paid off the families they ran away from, sheltered them from abusive families, gave them jobs that took them outside the prescribed confines of their homes, and taught them to read and write. The appeal of belonging to the revolution was powerful to a woman who had been sold into child servitude, prevented from going to school, or physically abused, and offered her a way to avoid being married into a strange family, or living the half-life of an unmarried servant in her "in-law" family. In offering an end to *tongyangxi* and an end to unequal treatment of girls and women, the revolution held a gendered attraction for those women who were strong and independent, an essential element for the participation of women.[23]

The men were joining by the thousands, but the women interviewed were often the only women in their village to join the revolution. Why did these particular women join, when most other women did not? Some, of course, followed their revolutionary "husbands" or male relatives into the revolution, not really making a clear-cut choice for themselves. For more assertive women, the CCP propaganda advocating equality for men and women persuaded them that the revolution would allow them to be strong and aggressive.[24] Even the women whose subsequent experiences had included disgrace, physical suffering, and death of those close to them expressed no regret over their decision to become revolutionary activists. While helping them escape from hunger, physical abuse, low status, boredom, and marriage, the revolution drew them into an exciting new life, a safer and more interesting place in society, and granted them a sense of belonging and a patriotic purpose.

NOTES

1. There are many good sources that give a clear picture of women in the male-dominated China of these years. See Christina Gilmartin, "Gender, Political Culture, and Women's Mobilization," in *Engendering China*, ed. Christina K. Gilmartin, Gail Hershatter, Lisa Rofel, and Tyrene White (Cambridge, MA: Harvard University Press, 1994), 195—225; Christina Gilmartin, *Engendering the   Chinese Communist Revolution*

(Berkeley, 1995); Kay Ann Johnson, *Women, the Family and Peasant Revolution in China*, (Chicago: University of Chicago Press, 1983); Judith Stacey, *Patriarchy and Socialist Revolution in China* (Berkeley: University of California Press, 1983); Margery Wolf, *Revolution Postponed, Women in Contemporary China*, (Stanford: Stanford University Press,1985), especially chapter 1.

2. "At the First Congress of the Chinese Soviet Republic in November 1931, a provisional constitution was written and adopted for the areas administered by the Communists. It held:

> It is the purpose of the Soviet government of China to guarantee the thorough emancipation of women; it recognizes freedom of marriage and will put into operation various measures for the protection of women, to enable women gradually to attain the material basis required for their emancipation from the bondage of domestic work, and to give them the possibility of participating in the social, economic, political and cultural life of the entire society.

Conrad Brandt, Benjamin Schwartz, and John Fairbanks, eds., *Documentary History of Chinese Communism* (Cambridge, MA: Harvard University Press, 1952), 223.

3. Even today, the top-down policy statements and laws concerning women's liberation have not greatly changed the basic attitudes of male superiority in China, especially in the rural areas. During the period of economic reforms in the 1980s and 1990s, many of the practices resulting in violence against women and male control of women's lives that were in existence in the earlier years of the century reemerged in China.

4. *Jia chuqude nu, po chuqude shui.* The sense is that once water is poured away, it can never be returned to the jar. In the same way, a daughter is lost to her birth family once she marries.

5. There are a variety of terms used to describe the practice of selling or giving away daughters into servitude and/or marriage in China. I use the term *tongyangxi* (pronounced TOONG YAHNG SHE) throughout, as that is the term used by all of the women interviewed, although their particular circumstances and the practices in their localities were not the same. The translations for *tongyangxi* such as "child wife," "affianced daughter-in-law," and "little foster-daughter-in-law," while descriptive, can be awkward and sometimes misleading. Therefore, I have chosen to use the Chinese word itself without translation. The family relationships for *tongyangxi*, such as "in-laws" and "husband," are in quotes, as there was no true marriage for most of the women interviewed.

6. According to a soldier who sat in on the interview because she was collecting the mountain rhymed songs created by Li Jianzhen, the songs

were all original. It seems more likely that Li Jianzhen remembered many songs to which she added her own twist or her own verses. Ono Kazuko, *Chinese Women in a Century of Revolution, 1850—1950* (Stanford: Stanford University Press, 1989), 144, quotes a version of this poem from a collection of mountain songs, without attributing authorship to any particular person.

7. Yi Haining, who helped with this translation, said peasants in Sichuan used a large wooden bucket to store urine for later use as fertilizer. This was where a baby girl would be drowned if the family could not afford to raise her. In a conversation in Beijing in1988, Isabel Crook explained that the bucket was about 10 inches in diameter. She said in theory people didn't approve of killing baby girls. The neighbors would bang on the door and shout, "Save the child! Save the child!" but they wouldn't actually prevent the drowning.

8. See Arthur Wolf and Chieh-shan Huang's mortality statistics on adopted daughters, *Marriage and Adoption in China, 1845—1945* (Stanford: Stanford University Press, 1980). Although the statistics are from Taiwan, there is no reason to believe that the trend was different in the provinces the interviewees came from, during the same time period.

9. The May Fourth Movement of 1919 was a widespread political and cultural movement against foreign imperialism and traditional Chinese practices.

10. A loose translation of the Chinese saying *Zhong nan, qing nu* (Emphasize boys, treat girls lightly), which many of the women quoted repeatedly.

11. He Manqiu's story appears in Helen Praeger Young, "He Manqiu: From Doctor to Soldier on the Long March," *Science & Society* 59, no. 4 (Winter 1995—1996): 531—547.

12. In the mother's defense, her own position in the family depended on giving birth to sons. Even in families that could afford to raise daughters, they were still considered to be only temporarily in the family, since they joined their husband's family at marriage. While deplorable, He Manqiu's mother's attitude toward her daughter was probably not unusual.

13. For a personal description of footbinding, see Ida Pruitt, *A Daughter of Han* (Stanford: Stanford University Press, 1967), 22.

14. Marjorie Topley and Janice Stockard discuss the strategies of marriage resistance by a group of women silk workers in Guangdong province. He Manqiu and the others who were avoiding marriage by joining the revolution had no access to groups such as Topley and Stockard describe, but acted independently. Janice Stockard, *Daughters of the Canton Delta* (Stanford: Stanford University Press, 1989), and Margery

Topley, "Marriage Resistance in Rural Kwangtung," in *Women in Chinese Society*, ed. Margery Wolf and Roxanne Witke (Stanford: Stanford University Press, 1975), 67–88.

15. "Resolutions of the 6th Congress of CCP in Moscow, July to September 1928:

> It is of the greatest importance to absorb the masses of peasant women into the struggle for victory in the revolutionary movement in the rural villages. As they directly participate in the economy of the villages, occupy an important place among the troops of the poor peasants in the villages, and have enormous influence in the life of the peasants, they must participate in our movement. Our experience of peasant movements in the past teaches us that peasant women are the bravest of all fighters. . . . The main task of the Party is to consider as a positive fact that the peasant women are positively participating in the revolution and that they must be absorbed into the peasant organizations, particularly into the Peasant Associations and the Soviets, to the fullest extent.

M.J. Meijer, *Marriage Law and Policy in the Chinese People's Republic* (Hong Kong, 1971), 38.

16. In "Mobilization Without Emancipation: Women's Interests, the State and Revolution in Nicaragua," *Feminist Studies* 11, 227—254, Maxine Molyneux develops the argument that political strategies linking gender interests with revolution must include practical gender interests in order to appeal to women.   ". . .it is the politicization of these practical interests and their transformation into strategic interests that women can identify with and support which constitutes a central aspect of feminist political practice" (234). Certainly, the promise of equality between men and women would have special appeal in Sichuan province, where many of the men smoked opium, leaving the women to do the bulk of the agricultural work without being able to own property or participate in political decisions.

17. Hill Gates suggests that desperately wanting to find security in a "government" job may have been a compelling force for these women, as it was later for Latina revolutionaries who called it "employamania." (Conversation, Stanford University, August 1995)

18. Linda Kerber, in "May All Our Citizens Be Soldiers and All Our Soldiers Citizens: The Ambiguities of Female Citizenship in the New Nation," in *Women, Militarism, and War* ed. Jean Bethke Elshtain and Sheila Tobias (Totowa, NJ: Roman and Littlefield, 1990), 89—103, suggests that joining the army and the revolution resulted in a kind of citizenship to which women previously had no access: "Sometimes

women considered themselves to be citizens and sometimes the nation referred to them as citizens in the same way as men, but not always.   The notion that there are alternative forms of citizenship, not just the right to hold public office and to vote, but the right to engage in certain kinds of public activities, indicates a broadening of the definition of citizenship" (87).

19.   Jiang Jieshi, more familiarly known as Chiang Kai-shek, was leader of the Nationalist army.   In 1927 the cooperation between the Nationalists and communists ended, and the Nationalists began the period of "White Terror" against Red activists.

20.   The Japanese invasion of Manchuria, northeast China, on September 18, 1931.

21.   *Rang wai bi shu an li.*

22.   Kerber, "May All Our Citizens Be Soldiers," op. cit.

23.   Molyneux, "Mobilization Without Emancipation," op. cit.

24.   Kathleen B. Semergieff, *The Changing Roles of Women in the People's Republic of China, 1949—1967* (Ann Arbor: University Microfilms International, 1985), 8—9.   "However, despite the economic circumstances of a woman, before or after marriage, individual assertiveness was rare indeed.   This was not because she did not desire it, nor because it was lacking in her personality, but because there was not place for it within the highly structured social order."

Part II
1940–1945

Figure 6. Distressed mother searches for her
lost children. Gea Augsbourg.

SIX

Surviving the German Invasion of France
Women's Stories of the Exodus of 1940

Nicole Ann DOMBROWSKI

> We saw something very strange happening to Paris. A very dark fog
> began to pass over the city.   —Jackie De Col

The black fog and the sirens' blarer, triggered by the passage of German bombers, delivered an ominous message to the people of Paris. An end to the "funny war" neared as German troops advanced and French troops retreated.[1] For the civilians of Paris who had feared the German arrival since the inception of the invasion on May 10, 1940, the day of reckoning had arrived. A city of cafe philosophers and fashion icons would have to decide to stay and greet the invading forces or to flee.

On June 10, exactly one month after the start of the blitzkrieg, Parisians and members of the French government joined the retreating masses of Belgian refugees, French civilians from the Champagne and Ardennes regions, and French troops in a mass exodus to southern France. Among the fleeing civilians, women, children and elderly struggled to rescue themselves and their loved ones from an army rumored to have cut off the hands of children during World War I. Even France's literary treasures, such as Joseph Kessel, Simone de Beauvoir, and even the aging Colette, descended with the masses into the abyss.

Jackie, then an unremarkable young Parisian schoolgirl, age 17, observed the shadows cast in the sky and lived to recall how the darkness of the war encroached not only on the future of her country but on the rest of her life. Jackie's story of survival of the Battle of France in June 1940 recaptures the fear and excitement of the inaugural days of World War II and the German occupation. In the retelling of her war story, 50 years after the event, Jackie unleashes the power of personal and collective memory and offers the contemporary reader a clear view of history at the intersection of personal and public experience. Her memoir captures the civilian side of battle, enriching our understanding of how the military defeat engulfed civilians and cleared the way for the establishment of bureaucratic structures that conditioned the daily struggles for survival during the German occupation.

By June 10 most civilians and French army units had evacuated the northeastern region of France. In an intermingled dance of children and soldiers, the French eluded the German invaders, hoping to make a stand at the Loire River. Many of the Parisians who had evacuated the city at the beginning of hostilities in September 1939 displayed an initial reluctance to displace themselves again. But by late afternoon on June 10, the government led by example. It made its way to Bordeaux to establish operations. Rumors ran wild through Paris nearly as quickly as the Germans rode through the Ardennes forest. "Paul Reynaud [the Prime Minister] had fled with his mistress," one such rumor reported. Others repeated the story that "the British have surrendered" and reactivated the stereotypes of the "Boches" of World War I.

This atmosphere of fear propelled Parisians from their sedentary positions. In a   six-floor walk-up in the Marais district, Jackie and her family consulted with neighbors about whether they should stay or leave.[2] "I don't want my daughter to serve as a welcome mat for the Germans," decreed Jackie's neighbor, who showed concern about the safety of her 20-year-old daughter. Jackie's family, the DeCols,[3] contemplated their neighbor's fear. Contact with German soldiers might well bring rape or death. After a brief debate, the family decided to split up. Jackie, her mother, then 38 years old, and her grandmother, nearly 68, would join the flood of refugees. Jackie's father and uncle would stay and enlist in the civil defense forces (*la défense passive*) to participate in the anticipated defense of Paris.

MEMORY AND HISTORY

Jackie's memory of her departure from Paris cannot be separated from the knowledge of the events that followed. Indeed, for Jackie the exodus marked the beginning of the end to a way of life she and her family had taken refuge in. Once before the DeCols had fled. In 1925 her father and paternal grandparents "were chased out of Russia," as she remembered.

"My father began his life in Odessa, traveled for 15 days before reaching Paris with his family, and ended his life in a camp at Auschwitz," she recalled. For Jackie, the exodus symbolizes something larger than France's defeat. It marks a watershed in her own life, and a revision of her identity from *française* to *française d'origine juive*. This transformation of consciousness took place on the roads of France in the summer of 1940.

In this essay I want to draw upon Jackie's memories of the exodus of 1940 in order to re-create a sense of how the horror of defeat took shape in the mind of a child and survived as a symbolic marker throughout the life of a private individual and a citizen of a larger collectivity, the French nation. By retracing the past through the life of one individual, I hope to gain a clearer perspective of the way in which the national catastrophe of military defeat spilled over into the lives of individuals and families. What we learn is how the war shattered families and communities. Government and German military policies thus intervened to structure their means of survival during the occupation. We also gain an understanding of how postwar national histories about defeat and occupation are integrated into, challenged by, and also transform the documenting of individuals' private memories, themselves enriched and edited through the oral transmission of postwar family discussions.

I have chosen Jackie's oral history because it is representative in detail and in its broader scope of many of the oral histories I have taken of French men and women who at the time of the exodus ranged in age from 9 to 25. Her narrative is also somewhat distinct in that she was half Jewish, a label that held practically no meaning for her at the time of the war or before, but came to be a living category of experience through the ideological transformations brought about by Nazi and Vichy racial policies. Therefore, Jackie's narrative tells not only a story about the different paths that some French Jews stumbled upon, but also the story that Jackie, a non-practicing French Jew, tells herself about her relationship to her own Jewish identity both at the time of the war and in its aftermath.

For Jackie, as for me, the exodus cannot be separated from her family's quest to find a place of security and happiness amidst the historical turbulence of twentieth-century Europe. Her own consciousness of that struggle only dates from her family's reintegration into occupied France following the exodus of the summer of 1940. The following narrative re-creates and examines the trajectory of one family who left Paris as Parisians in 1940 and returned later that summer as European Jews.

The details of the DeCols' journey create a sharp image of individuals' plight in the tidal wave of world historic events. Furthermore, the details tell of how gender and race constructed the survival strategies of French refugees. In the first days of the exodus a general pattern emerged: The women left and the men stayed behind to finish business, enlist in defense initiatives, and settle family affairs. Women defined the immediate task as one of shepherding themselves, children, and grandparents to safety and salvaging family valuables. Often their first question was not so much where to go, but what to bring.

FAMILY FORTUNES LOST AND FOUND

"We decided to take only precious items. But what did we have that was precious?" Jackie recounted, laughing.

"Boots! New boots and books. I brought along my favorite book, *La joie des moeurs*." She shook her head to think that a book was the most valuable possession she owned at age 17. Of course, her mother held up the practical end and like most women on the road packed up a portable kitchen.

Like many Parisians following the flow of civilian foot soldiers, the bifurcated family of women left through the Porte d'Orleans. The women followed the path that overpasses the Seine River and carried them past Versailles, through Rambouillet, and across the wheat fields that extend toward Chartres. Other cars and pedestrians routed themselves south through the Porte d'Italie or through Ville Juive. What all the refugees shared in common was the absence of a firm sense of where they would actually end up at the end of the day's long and sun-soaked walk.

The DeCol women were not the only French to select their most valuable objects. As the young girl and two women tracked along the road to Chartres, they encountered a museum of items discarded along the road. To their great fortune the women found a three wheeled cart apparently abandoned by a magazine vendor. Grabbing the wagon and stocking it with their own valuables, the women lightened their load. Jackie was struck that items that refugees had deemed valuable at the moment of departure lost their value in direct proportion to their weight and the distance people had to carry them. Only the smallest and most useful objects maintained their value during the exodus. Even sentimental companions like puppies wandered abandoned along the road. Seemingly banal items like baskets, pots and shoes soared in value as refugees exchanged items between each other or with the road.

The cathedral town of Chartres, known best for its stained glass windows depicting biblical scenes in a colorful visual display, is about an hour's ride on today's train from Paris. The trip can be made in about 8 hours on bike. By foot, under the hot sun, the refugees moved at a slow, encumbered pace. After some time Jackie's grandmother, like so many other elderly refugees, felt unable to continue the journey. The two younger women searched among the stalled cars, the jockeying bicycles, and the prodding pedestrians, trying to persuade a willing driver to accommodate an elderly person. The DeCols found a good samaritan, but for families less fortunate, the strain of the road forced younger generations to part with older generations, hopeful that the Germans would take mercy on the elderly fallen behind. Many narrators often admitted that the young represented the future and had to be saved before those of the passing generation. Other stories of selfishness and competition between refugees permeate refugees' memories of life on the road. It is impossible to gauge whether generosity outweighed selfishness, but in many postwar narratives the selfishness of the French toward each other often is invoked as an explanation of why the Germans so easily defeated the country. The theme of selfishness transcends issues of practicality and serves as a kind of moral explanation of why the nation suffered the punishment of occupation. The theme of "just punishment" pervades refugee narratives and will be further discussed later in this essay.In the case of the DeCols, their efforts to find their grandmother transportation met with reward. At an early juncture in their journey, the grandmother took her place in the back seat of a slow-moving sedan. All three women said their good-byes and promised to meet up in Chartres. Jackie's mother instructed her mother-in-law to check into a hotel room and to wait for them at the train station.

VIOLENCE AND DEATH SHATTER ILLUSIONS
"We had no sense of reality," Jackie exclaimed. "We thought that we'd be able to actually find a vacant hotel room in the midst of the exodus." The moment of illusion had nearly passed; however, the women did not expect what awaited them. They returned to their pilgrimage without delay.

"Soon we began to hear airplanes firing. Everyone said they were Italians, but I didn't really know." With excitement and horror Jackie explained the sound of the planes, still vivid in her imagination after a half century.

"The planes fired—tac tac tac—bombing these completely innocent refugees," she said. According to Jackie, no soldiers lingered among the refugees to warrant such a blatant attack on harmless civilians. For the refugees, this first air attack unleashed the surreal sense of the situation and regardless of where refugees were on the road, they seem to universally have been at the same place when the Italian air strike occurred. Such is the imprint of cultural lore on individual narratives. Confronted with the violence, Jackie lost all connection with her former world. Her narrative description of that moment in her flight changed, too. Rather than describing a scene from her own life, Jackie, like many others who remembered their encounters with violence, described their own story relying more on the tools of fiction.

"At the bottom of it all, I was excited by the adventurous aspect of the moment," she remembered. Jackie likened herself to her cousins, who also had "fond" memories of being attacked.

"I found the experience exalting, like it was an astonishing and dangerous vacation, and I'm not some kind of idiot," she proclaimed in self-defense.

What is remarkable and fascinating about civilians' stories of their encounters with combat, especially young boys and girls, is that they resemble so much soldiers' stories of combat adventure and bravery. They, too, hold on to the categories of casualties and survivors. For Jackie, the banal and the extraordinary combined in such a way that her own life seemed scripted by someone else. Of course, her life, along with the millions of other French and Belgian refugees, was being controlled by someone else, the German, and to a lesser degree, the French high command.

From the vantage point of the road, however, the responsible parties seemed very far away from the pit where Jackie and her mother sought shelter against the Italian bombers' artillery.

"Everyone yelled to take refuge in the ditches next to the road, but I didn't want to. I absolutely didn't want to get pricked by thorns. And there were dogs urinating all over." For Jackie, the dangers of nature seemed worse than the threat from the sky. Nevertheless, the two DeCol women survived the attack. As the planes passed, the refugees gathered up their things and assessed the damage—destroyed cars, burning shrubs, dead animals, and worse, wounded and killed companions.

Jackie's memory of the aerial attack actually pairs pain and pleasure. Her narrative passes immediately from the horrors of the war to the sumptuousness of the French countryside, a seeming non sequitur, but more likely a mental crutch. "We continued a ways and then stopped alongside a huge field of strawberries," she said. While others farther down the road suffered under the Italian bullets, Jackie consumed strawberries.

FINDING NEW FRIENDS AND OLD ACQUAINTANCES

In the evening her mother found a barn for the two to sleep in. Her mother informed her that they were going to sleep inside with a few of the other refugees. The two women made a bed for themselves and fell asleep. In this way, the shape of Jackie's story alternates between recounting the horrors of exposure and attack with descriptions of sanctuary and communal comfort.

"*Voilà* declared Jackie. Safe in a barn somewhere between Chartres and Paris, she encountered the next threat, the dreaded Fifth Column. Rumors and reality spun tails of the Fifth Column among the refugees. Allegedly, the Fifth Column included Hitler's spies and German sympathizers planted among the masses and ordered to stir up fear while at the same time encouraging the French to surrender. The Fifth Column, much like the occupation that followed, symbolized an invisible force of French working against French and in collaboration with Germans. Jackie remembers this particular encounter in the barn as the moment when a few people woke the peacefully sleeping refugees with cries of "Hurry up! hurry up! The Germans are coming! They are massacring everyone! Hurry! Hurry!"

In reality, the two women only came into contact with one German at this juncture in their journey. The straggler was by himself, weeping and running in front of the crowd of refugees. Apparently he had been wounded and was searching for his superior.

"I remember this sight so well because it made me so sad," Jackie reminisced of the German soldier. What is so striking about Jackie's compassionate comment is that it is representative of a large portion of French attitudes toward the first Germans they encountered. While this is a theme I want to return to, it is worth noting that two types of French observations of the invading army seem to emerge on the road. The most frequent is that the German army appeared more organized and disciplined than the French troops. Second, the Germans, seemed polite or, as the French say, "correct." It is important to remember the first impressions held by the French of Hitler's invading army—important because the German command had planned it that way, demonstrating again the significance German tacticians ascribed to psychological combat; important also, because many French felt deep humiliation when viewing the differences between their disorganized band of weary soldiers and the effectiveness of the German troops.

Despite the danger, and because of it, the mass of refugees continued the journey south. For Jackie and others, the sight of wounded and dead bodies scattered over the ground seemed strange, yet after a moment someone would place an abandoned mattress over a body and passersby would carry on without delay. The seeming indifference and coldness displayed by the abandonment of the dead and wounded were tempered by the coincidental encounters of neighbors and friends. Along the way, Jackie and her mother stumbled upon people they knew from Paris, like their concierge.

"We'd see people whom we'd seen or spoken to earlier...there was a sort of solidarity after sleeping in the same barn or in the same rooms and giving each other some ham," she said.

Jackie spoke of solidarity with other refugees after she experienced the attack. One sees again how the recurring dialectic between solidarity and selfishness structures not only Jackie's personal narrative but also the historical evaluation of the period. Solidarity and selfishness serve as major poles between which individuals and the nation as a collective make sense of their experience and the defeat. After the moment of solidarity forged by the air attack, Jackie and her mother moved on, independently of the crowd, in order to try to find her grandmother. Their independent advances were sustained and nurtured by intermediary encounters with these floating communities. Often such exchanges served as a means of sharing information about the location of food, shelter, or the whereabouts of lost family members.

A SECOND FRONT OR SECOND FARCE:
CROSSING THE LOIRE

Upon arriving in Chartres, the two travelers found a town charged with panic. According to Jackie, agitators, most likely members of the Fifth Column, urged civilians to cross the Loire River. Jackie remembers the push toward the Loire as the work of the internal enemy, yet it is interesting that many refugees and historians have seen the push toward the Loire as a last stand against the German advance. Without any sign of her grandmother, Jackie and her mother followed the crowd across one of the bridges of the Loire.

"The Loire was a tiny stream! It had no strategic importance whatsoever," Jackie said. "You could cross it jumping from one leg to the other!"

With 50 years of public debate on the subject and her own remembered crossing, Jackie ridiculed the rush across the Loire River. People were panic stricken trying to push across the bridge. Jackie recalled one woman who had gone mad because she'd lost her child in the crowd. The vivid image of a woman tearing at her breast with grief etched itself in the young girl's memory. The panic of the crowd and the seemingly utter lack of purpose in the flight finally forced Jackie and her mother to take a rest from the exodus.

In Jackie's own narrative of the crossing of the Loire, all the national tropes of the exodus appear: mothers separated from their children; a nation of cowards seeking refuge behind Maginot Lines and shallow rivers; a retreating army fallen behind the advancing enemy. Not only are the themes of Jackie's narrative familiar ones that are repeated in a host of oral and written sources on the exodus and therefore must be understood as a production of the mingling of her own personal recollections and the public commemoratives she encountered after the war, but the structure of her tale is also quite standard.[4] Juxtaposed against the irrational crowd, Jackie and her mother stand out as rational actors, competent enough to judge the implausibility of the protective possibilities of the Loire River. In her mind and in her memory of her mind, she acted rationally and against the masses. She and her mother retreated from the crowd to regroup and redefine their strategy. But what choice might she have in remembering her actions? As a survivor, must she remember herself as an agent and not as a victim in the flow of chaos?

One of the markers of a society under siege is the absolute dissolution of the former barriers between public and private life. Ownership of home, of one's property, of one's body, of one's nation may fall completely to chance. Home or *foyer*, one of the most protected and sacred spaces of French society, a sanctuary of family life, is what the army had failed to protect and what many families tried to preserve on the road. Given the upheaval, many refugees tried to salvage the few vestiges of private life, in other people's abandoned houses. Jackie and her mother can be counted among that group. While many continued the push across the bridge, Jackie explored an abandoned house. She described the scene as bleak. Household items lay scattered about. In the rear of the house, she heard people milling about. Assuming that they must be refugees like herself seeking shelter and relief in someone else's abandoned house, she advanced to investigate. She shouted and walked toward the kitchen. Making themselves at home, she caught the tired squatters rummaging through the cupboards. With a welcoming hail the refugees offered Jackie something to drink, a little soda water with strawberry juice. Apparently the official residents had forsaken the "syro." These intermediary hosts had simply arrived slightly before Jackie, and they extended their hospitality to her as if it were their own house.

"There was even this guy there who had a beard," Jackie remembered.

"He said, 'Come with me,' but I said, 'No!' I said that I'd come with my mother to find my grandmother and he said, 'Just come with me. We can live together. It's much better to wait for death while making love.' "

Jackie said that she ran away from her would-be Romeo. It was unclear where her mother had disappeared to during this episode, but she clearly reunited with her. When the war resumed, the Goldilocks-like figures actually reappeared. Jackie later spotted the bearded Don Juan among the crowd in the exodus. Apparently he had found another woman with whom to end his story, and he ran pushing along her baby carriage. These types of strange encounters with other French refugees pepper many exodus narratives. Indeed, the encounters with strangers reinforced the thin line between danger and solidarity within the crowd. One must remember that real danger did exist. Much of the law enforcement apparatus had disbanded, as had prisons for that matter. Faced with abandoning prisoners to the Germans or staying to stand guard over them, many local prison officials chose to let prisoners have their liberty rather than turn them over to the Germans.[5]

At about the same time that Jackie spied her fickle-hearted suitor, she and her mother decided again to halt their march. Unaffected by their previous encounter, the two women eyed another house off the road. One after another house stood empty and open. Jackie remembered the extraordinary quality of these empty homes: "We found a table still covered with plates, cups and saucers half full. We found books....A house where an hour before there was life, now stood silent."

Everything had been abandoned in the same haste as when the DeCols had left their own home.

"We had the feeling that cadavers lingered there, but there were no cadavers," she recalled.

The feeling of death so marked the house that Jackie refused to sleep inside. The two women left the house, and on their way back to the road they crossed another woman, a nurse who was an army major, accompanying a neighbor child of about 13 years old. Apparently the child, described as tall and scrawny, had been separated from his parents during the Italian aerial attack. The major recognized him and took him under her wing. Together the three women and the boy summoned up the courage to go back into the haunted house. Still spooked by the lugubrious atmosphere and encouraged by the warm June nights, the group removed some blankets from the house. They set up camp in the garden. Jackie's memory of drifting off to sleep that night highlighted her sense of rupture from the crowd but also underscored her mental and physical exhaustion, which had rendered her indifferent to the cries of the distant agitators.

"From time to time we heard in the distance people shouting, 'The Germans are coming, the Germans are coming! They are killing everyone! Leave! Leave!' But we stayed put, the only civilians remaining near Chartres," she recalled.

Jackie and her mother drew upon personal resolve and a sense of stubbornness to justify and support their desire to unhinge themselves from the destiny of the masses. The failure of finding Jackie's grandmother also provided sound reasoning for wanting to remain near Chartres. Jackie recalled with troubled emotion the debate about whether or not she and her mother should stay and try to locate the older woman. With little sense of where the older woman might be, Jackie's mother decided that they would have to hope that the grandmother and her companions had found shelter. Without telephones and without any fixed point of meeting, the women had little choice but to abandon hope of reuniting with Jackie's grandmother at that particular juncture. Decisions such as the choice to continue without a family member caused intense anxiety and guilt, but in time, fear undermined even the most solid convictions, and many refugees continued their journey south.

The nurse-major, now their sworn travel companion, reminded the two women that if the Germans arrived, they would all surely be raped. In an attempt to face down an unpleasant probability, the women decided to take preventive measures. Drawing upon tradition and folklore, (and perhaps desperation), the women undertook a search in the kitchen for a pot of mustard. With an air of confidence and self-assuredness, Jackie recounted how the three women equipped themselves with packets of mustard so that in the case of an approaching German soldier, they could smear the mustard on their intimate areas.

"That way, when the soldier finished his act, he'd be stung by the mustard as he withdrew." Jackie laughed when retelling the story, adding that she prayed that they wouldn't encounter any Germans because she had no desire to smear herself with mustard. The laugh subsided after a brief moment, and she seemed to relive the moment of fear. Very seriously, she corrected the tone of the conversation,

"We did stay there for a while, but we were afraid, you know. Really afraid."

SOMNOLENT SOLDIERS AND SCARRED CIVILIANS

Suddenly, as if the regeneration of excitement conquered her memory of fear, Jackie remembered a huge noise, followed by an encounter with a French soldier. It sounded like a steamship. Still in their condition of squatters, the women felt overcome by the sense that indeed the French must have lost. Everything was lost, everything. But instead of a battalion of German soldiers, a French straggler approached the small group and their Goldilocks-like home. For the first time in her life Jackie saw before her eyes someone who was genuinely sleepwalking. Tired, nearly mesmerized, the French soldier made his way toward the door of the house. The women watched. Suddenly, before reaching the garden, the boy fell forward onto the ground and remained in a deep sleep. The women ran to check if he had died. The nurse tried to revive him, but her efforts failed to draw a response. The boy only snored.

Soon Jackie and her mother realized that the boy belonged to a retreating French battalion taking refuge in a small hotel a few kilometers down the road.

"We saw the soldier's fatigue and knew instantly that little hope remained," she said. For Jackie, this incident marked the first vivid memory of the mingling of French soldiers and civilians on the road.

Immediately after confessing that the sight of the boy deflated their hopes, Jackie then added somewhat peculiarly, "Actually, their presence reassured us. We felt protected by the French army. We gave them some of our ham."

The forward march of the troops left the women with no other choice than to follow the crowd. The nurse-major, a ranking officer, invoked her rank to requisition a truck inching by the women on the road. The driver behind the wheel protested. He did not want to stop. When he pulled over, the nurse-major simply requisitioned his vehicle.

"She had the right to do it. She even had the paperwork," Jackie said defensively, as though she were still face to face with the dissenting truck driver.

Indeed, French authorities requisitioned many privately owned cars and trucks during the course of the exodus. However, many personal narratives and even official reports document that authority fell short of what it took to make the machines run. Many an authorized official abandoned his or her requisitioned vehicle once it had run out of gas. By mid-June gas had become a more valuable commodity than a car or truck. Stories abound about how refugees swindled other refugees for gallons of gas or milk. If you had a car, gas called the higher price. If you cared for a hungry child, milk was liquid gold. Refugees who succeeded in driving all the way to the Spanish border in order to flee abroad remember with bitterness how, having survived the gas exploiters, they only met their match with French border guards who forced them to turn over their vehicles for "official" use.[6] These unlucky pedestrians continued their journey over the Pyrenees on foot.

Back among the crowd, the truck driver, a newly appointed chauffeur, drove his companions along the road to Angoûlème. The nurse and Jackie's mother copiloted in the cabin. Meanwhile, Jackie sat like a pioneer on a bundle strapped by a leather belt to the back of the truck. The 13-year-old boy sat fastened to Jackie's lap. Like a caravan of gypsies, the women finally departed from the outskirts of Chartres and made their way to Angoûlème.

"We rolled and rolled and rolled at a snail's pace," Jackie recalled, sighing. Unable to maneuver with all the crowd, the truck had no choice but to roll right over two dead horses. Sirens commanded occasional pauses in traffic. But by this time, perhaps at least 4 days into the exodus, the crowd had mastered the drill. The sirens sounded. The carts, cars, trucks, wagons, and horses halted. Refugees jumped for cover under the cars, the mattress, or in the prickly ditches. For everyone except the Germans, trek to Angoûlème continued at a slow, steady pace, toward little more than disappointment and displacement.

Lucky enough not to run out of gas, the cohort of women and children finally arrived at their destination. Located in the uppermost region of France's southwest, Angoûlème provided a resting point for many refugees determined to make their way farther south to Bordeaux or the Mediterranean Sea. A region rich with wine and wool, Angoûlème offered a sampling of the bounty of France's southern region, an area foreign to many northerners, including Jackie and her mother. This quality of the exodus, the encounters with previously unseen or unimagined regions of one's own country, accounts for the fact that so many refugee narratives, despite the presence of fear and disaster, resemble travel journals of the more adventurous type.

THE END OF THE ROAD
On June 18, Marshal Pétain announced the signing of an armistice with

the Germans. France was divided into Free France, or Vichy France, and German Occupied France. Angoûlème rested squarely on the Line of Demarcation. East and toward the interior, the French would maintain control. West of Angoûlème, encompassing the Atlantic seaboard and the city of Bordeaux, the Germans would administer and police. While the remaining French officials carved up the country with the German Armistice Board, thereby sequestering millions of refugees in the overcrowded villages of the south, Jackie and her mother found refuge in the home of a southwestern family.

"Families were both ordered and volunteered to lodge refugees from the north," remembered Jackie. "We were assigned to lodge with a family that was absolutely adorable. Their son was still fighting the war. He was in the army." Jackie and her mother occupied the room of the enlisted son.

"I simply remember that they had a beautiful library. I read their books during the remainder of the exodus, you see, because we stayed with these folks for about a month."

During that month the flow of refugees continued. Unable to find lodging or determined to escape the clutches of the Germans, northerners, joined now by some members of the southern region, continued their procession towards the Mediterranean or the Spanish boarder. On June 19, Pommerey, then acting minister of the Interior, issued a formal halt to the exodus. He charged that the mass of French men and women cluttering the roads encumbered the military retreat and lacked the expression of dignity characteristic of the French people.

July 1940 was as close as the French nation has perhaps ever come to occupying that uncomfortable place in the Catholic imagination—purgatory. For nearly a month refugees meandered in a sort of national limbo, wondering if they'd been saved or condemned by their government's actions.

French representatives led by Prefect Marlier, director of the Commission on Refugees, negotiated with the Germans the details of the repatriation of the eight million refugees back to German occupied territory. During these negotiations the French officials agreed to German categories of exclusion from occupied territory. "Israelites," mixed-bloods, communists, and former public officials would be banned from return to the German territory. In addition, any Alsatians or Lorrainians refusing to accept German citizenship would be refused readmission. These restrictions on admission to the occupied zones represented the first step in the collaborative enforcement of Nazi racial laws.[7] They also marked the first steps in redefining French citizenship, a category Jackie would soon be excluded from, once she crossed over the Line of Demarcation.

The growing overpopulation crisis in the south, coupled with the fear of political unrest, provided the pretext for both, hesitant and opportunistic, Vichy officials to sign on to the German demands in order to get the repatriation process under way. With the stroke of a pen, millions of people received marching orders—back into enemy territory, except, of course, those who fell outside the legal categories of citizenship—Jews, communists, socialists, and foreigners.

Meanwhile, as a means of fighting off boredom and to make a contribution to resolving the refugee crisis, Jackie enlisted herself in local relief efforts. Unemployed, homeless, and without word of their loved ones, many refugees sought to lend a hand with the maintenance of their own surplus population and to assist with the return of wounded soldiers.

The nurse-major immediately took a job at the hospital in Angoûlème.

"Because I wanted to make myself useful, I'd accompany her to the hospital each day and do tasks that nurses would assign to me since I was not a nurse," explained Jackie. "I helped out with the wounded soldiers. I was in charge of maintaining soldiers' morale, if you will. I talked with them. They were happy to have someone to chat with. I did their shopping for them. I helped them wash up."

With delight and tenderness, Jackie remembered one soldier in particular: "There was one officer who was 22 years old. He suffered from a bullet that hit a part of his genitalia, rendering him permanently impotent. Happily, his wife was already pregnant from a leave he had spent earlier in the war."

Jackie helped the young wounded soldier to try to locate his pregnant wife. Separated from her for over a month and without the ability to communicate via telephone or post, the young officer turned to Jackie who intervened to try to obtain information from the local mayor's office. Refugees inundated local city officials with letters and inquiries, attempting to locate relatives and loved ones lost in the chaos of the road. Local newspapers printed the names of lost children and registered refugees in an attempt to help people find each other. The Red Cross and Christian women's organizations ferried letters from town to town within the permitted areas. From June to late July, the Germans prohibited the transfer of mail from the free zone to the occupied zone fearing that military secrets or resistance plots would be passed from zone to zone. But by late July the pressure from French officials to loosen up the surveillance on the communication from one zone to the other was so severe that the Germans buckled. The Armistice Bureau in Paris received hundreds of inquiries each day about the whereabouts of refugees in the south. Finally, by the beginning of August some mail began to circulate between zones. Of course, the censors inspected nearly every piece.

Shattered by the nation's capitulation to the superior German army, refugees were made increasingly anxious by the uncertainty of the condition and whereabouts of family members. Demobilized soldiers struggled to locate their wives and children, who had counted among the refugees. Conversely, families displaced from home navigated official and unofficial channels trying to find their fathers, brothers, or husbands' disbanded regiments. While Jackie helped the soldiers locate their loved ones, she and her mother tried to find out the location of her grandmother, her father, and her uncle.

"FREE FRANCE": RELIEF WORK AND REPATRIATION

As the exodus slowed and as refugees began to settle into their new localities waiting anxiously for directions from their new leaders, a sense of general relief seemed to have momentarily lifted the nation's sense of fear. For a moment, it seemed to many that the horror had passed. Defeated, the nation could now collect itself and move on. Jackie's memory of this transition shares this sentiment with many other refugee narratives. She fondly recalled the work she performed in Angoûlème, aiding soldiers. In many respects, the immediate period after the defeat seems more animated with a sense of national solidarity than the chaotic months and weeks preceding France's fall.

"I fed the soldiers. I wrote their letters. There were five or six officers who said very nice things about me, that I was their sunshine. I sang for them since radio transmission ceased. I even think I sang rather well at that time," Jackie boasted.

"Progressively, they found their families. There was one captain, a very handsome man with very blue eyes who was the brother of a known French writer, Pierre Cleraque. He wrote books on French pedagogy, which I actually later read as a teacher."

While Jackie worked at the hospital, her mother volunteered her time at the train station, feeding refugees, organizing train departures, and working at the missing persons office.

"It was not at all a period of terror," Jackie recounted. As though dismissing the Germans and casting a stone at her own nation, Jackie further insisted, "The horrible things happened much latter, and not necessarily just because of the Germans; there was the French *milice*, the French political police."

Jackie, like many French refugees, held on to positive impressions of her first encounters with German soldiers:

"There were many German soldiers....they obeyed orders. Plenty of them were not Nazis. There were plenty who were not zealots."

Jackie associated positive attributes to the German soldiers at the beginning of the occupation, remembering good deeds: "At the beginning, they tried to aid the population...for example, among their ranks were Czechs and Austrians who weren't Nazis and who hurt no one. I once saw a German who arrived in Angoûléme, and who spotted a small French girl. He was so moved by her because she must have resembled his own daughter. He could not speak French, but he took out a photo of her to show us. He offered some candy to the little girl, but her parents refused to allow her to accept it. They ran away like some children."

Jackie's memory of kind Germans offering candy to little French children is probably not a mistaken one. German soldiers received strict orders not to offend the French population. Propaganda leaflets dropped early in May near the front urged French soldiers to throw down their arms and to welcome the benevolent Germans, who only had the interests of Europe at heart.[8]

A quantity of quaint tales accompany the arrival of Germans on French soil. The warm images serve in the larger reservoir of public memory to set up a stark contrast against which to measure the memory of the Germans of 1942: terrorists, recruiters of forced labor, racists, and torturers of the Resistance. The desire for a kinder memory of the Germans' first days in France certainly resonates with a real remembered experience, but it also tempers the degree of dishonor attributed to the submitting populace. Implied beneath the layers of collective and personal memories of "good" Germans is the question: How were we to know they would turn out to be such murderers? Can history comprehend why the French of 1940 did not immediately recognize the Germans of 1942 beneath such disarming grins?

Jackie's memory of Germans also reconstructed them as slightly naive: "The Germans would also go to local restaurants, the ones that were still open. Many of them had never seen seafood. They had never even eaten clams. So they didn't even know how to eat them. They'd try to open them with their fingers or to crack them with their teeth." She laughed and said that tales like the clam story offered the French a little comic relief from the real tragedy of events. But more than offering comic relief, the stories of kind Germans underscore the fact that German planning worked, at least temporarily. Repeatedly, Nazi leaders displayed a sophisticated understanding of the importance of winning the psychological war as well as the ground war. I would not claim that all French civilians encountered well-behaved Germans. Indeed they did not. However, the German army displayed, on the whole, a degree of control and self-discipline in the early days of invasion that contrasted dramatically with the demobilizing French troops and, more importantly, that challenged French expectations of a dramatic reenactment of the violence associated with the German invasion of World War I. The

Germans both disarmed the French military and the French psyche.

After about a month in Angoûlème, Jackie and her mother received authorization to repatriate to the occupied zone. The repatriation of northern refugees from the nonoccupied zone took place over a period of 4 months, until the Germans closed the Line of Demarcation on November 20, 1940. By the end of the summer of 1940 and the beginning of autumn over seven million refugees traversed the line by train or by automobile. Strict policies negotiated in Paris, during July, at the Majestic Hotel regulated entry into the occupied zone. Among those refugees excluded from reentry were French citizens of the regions of Alsace and Lorraine who were unwilling to swear allegiance to Germany. As of July 7, Vichy authorities agreed with the German Armistice commission that Jews would be prohibited from reentering the occupied zone. Inhabitants of France's northern coastal region sought permanent lodging and employment in the south, forbidden from repatriating to their region, which was newly designated, "the forbidden zone." By the time the Line of Demarcation closed in November, nearly one million refugees remained displaced in the unoccupied zone.

Despite Jackie's Jewish heritage, she and her mother made it across the line without any problems. In reality, the system of racial and nationality verification remained weak during the summer months, and in many cases authorities could not rely on anything more than refugees' word of honor. French authorities did require repatriating refugees to sign a sworn oath that they were not "Israelites." While the archives demonstrate that this policy was in full force throughout repatriation, few refugees, Jackie included, have any recollection of having signed the oath either way.

As for Jackie, she reunited with her father and grandmother in Paris and learned that the family had experienced very different fates during the turbulent summer months. Apparently her grandmother had not gone much farther than Chartres with the benevolent family in the automobile. Her path intersected with a convoy of frustrated German soldiers. According to Jackie, these Germans were not as nice as the candy giver. Having encountered some resistance along the route, they displayed signs of aggravation when coming across Jackie's grandmother and her companions. These Germans rounded up the refugees and forced them to line up against a wall. Jackie's grandmother claims to have heard a trigger click, but for some reason the soldiers never fired.

Within their family history, Jackie's grandmother's close escape was remembered as a miracle. The rough treatment she received from the Germans, however, was considered as having had no connection to her status as a French Jew. However, the lesson that the family drew from the tale was that the safty net for French Jews had contracted. Jackie's father and uncle, however, never departed from Paris. Upon their appearance at the recruiting office, fleeing bureaucrats turned them away. Discouraged but determined to defend the capital, the two men stayed on, only to be able to see the Germans enter Paris without a pause. The two men aided units of the Civilian Defense forces but never coordinated with the official army. Because the two men did not leave, they inadvertently avoided the first administrative identity checks faced by French and foreign Jews at the Line of Demarcation.

Jackie's story of the exodus ends with the happy unification of all members of her family in Paris. During the first 2 years of the occupation, Jackie tried to resume normalcy and continued her studies, beginning her career as a student teacher, hiding her Jewish heritage. But the years following the exodus were rigged with as many dangers as those she and her mother faced on the open road. In those years, she came to terms with her identity as a French Jew. In 1942 she lost her father and her uncle to the Gestapo, who successfully deported the two men to Auschwitz, where they eventually died.

MEMORY AS A BEGINNING AND AN END

For Jackie, the exodus marked the beginning of the end of a way of life. Her memory of life under the occupation forms part of a different story. The story of her life on the road captures the departure from her sense of security and belonging. Jackie's story of displacement and upheaval during the summer of 1940 is remembered as the end of innocence, of a nation and of a girl. While not all refugees on the exodus lost the security of their identity as French citizens, many French Jews like Jackie, along with thousands of Alsatians and Lorrainians, confronted a geographic displacement as well as the displacement of their identity as French citizens. As the Vichy government drafted and implemented policies for repatriation that grouped the French into racial, religious, and political categories, new identities were forged and the state charted a different course for many of its citizens' futures. What is striking about both the individual and the collective memory of that institutional shift is the degree to which it is obscured and forgotten.

Few civilians protested their scheduled return to German-occupied territory, including French Jews. In fact, many tried to hide their identity so as to cross the Line of Demarcation. Only Alsatians and Lorrainians as a group refused the terms of repatriation from the beginning of the policy, and even they tried to return to their homes to recuperate their furniture and other family heirlooms to bring back to their new homes in southern France.

And why wouldn't these displaced, unemployed, and impoverished refugees not want to return to their homes in the occupied territory in the summer of 1940? For the most part, their initial encounters with Germans on the road suggested to them that their conquerors would be polite, organized, and efficient, allowing them to get on with the business of reconstructing a new France within a united Europe. It is interesting to note in Jackie's story, that only upon returning home and exchanging road stories with her grandmother does she encounter the idea of a threatening or malicious German. In the late summer and early autumn of 1940 the French regrouped in their homes and communities, a defeated nation. Only after the turmoil began to settle were they able, as individuals and as a newly diminished collectivity, to weigh the consequences of the defeat. For the average citizen, the August—September period of reunion was crucial for exchanging experiences and information in order to better understand the nature of the German rule, as well as the nature of the Vichy position of initial accommodation and subsequent collaboration.

By recuperating personal narratives, we, as historians and heirs of history, begin to reassemble the neglected fragments of the past. When civilians' individual experiences and memories are pieced together with evidence of state policies, military maneuvers, and historical events, a sharper picture emerges of the complexity of the conditions and concerns that weighed upon individuals' and institutions' decisions and actions. Individual narratives especially illuminate how race and gender intersect with historical events and institutional policy, carving out separate paths of historical experience. Had Jackie been a boy, her perspective of the defeat would have more likely clarified the military experience. From Jackie and millions of other survivors of the exodus we see how personal memory intersects with national history in a manner that generates a clearer historical perspective from which we can better understand the impact of past politics on the lives of individuals and communities alike. By comparing Jackie's narrative of the exodus to other civilian experiences, we could trace the different stages through which the French began to make meaning of the defeat and the intentions of the Nazis, thereby constructing individual and collective ways of coping with occupation, exclusion and deportation. By reconstructing a more complete narrative about the failures (or even successes) of the past, perhaps we, as members of an international community, can generate more informed ideas about how to alleviate such catastrophes in the present and the future. The casualties of World War II, especially in France, did not only fall on the battlefield. Recognizing and documenting the process of destroying and rebuilding civilian populations challenge traditional methods of military history, urging the historian to uncover and recover fragments of the past housed not only in archives but also in the treasure chests of individual and collective memory.

NOTES

1. The *drôle de guerre*, has been translated as the phony war, but if literally translated it also converts to "funny war," and until May 1940 it had been funny (as in strange) for France in the sense that it had been a war without combat.

2. Jackie was one of thirty men and women I interviewed about their experience in the exodus of May and June 1940. I met Jackie in 1992 at her home in Ville Franc, a suburb just outside Paris. I've chosen to write about Jackie's oral history because it raises most of the themes addressed in the sum of oral interviews I conducted. Jackie became a schoolteacher and as such had a great knack for collecting historical memorabilia. At the time of the interview, she lived with Madeline, another survivor of the exodus. Madeline's family traveled a distinctively different road since, unlike Jackie's family, Madeline and her parents never had to face the problem of anti-Jewish legislation. When the women met me and told their stories, they were as surprised as I was to learn of what totally different memories they held about the exodus and about the war.

3. All names have been changed at the request of the individuals.

4. Nicole Dombrowski, "Beyond the Battlefield: The French Civilian Exodus of May—June 1940" (Ph.D. diss. New York: New York University, 1995), 233—301.

5. Dombrowski, op. cit., 98—166.

6. James Vladimir Gill, "Panhard (A Memoir)," *The Kenyon Review* 105, no. 4 (Fall 1993): 24—31.

7. Dombrowski, op. cit., 317—386.

8. Dombrowski, op. cit.

Figure 7. Vera Ivanovna Malakhova:
Decorated for her service in the Soviet Army.

SEVEN

The Womanly Face of War
Soviet Women Remember World War II

Barbara Alpern ENGEL

> We left the battle together with the soldiers. It was terribly hard.
> We'd had nothing to drink for two days, and our lips were cracked
> and bloody. My clothes were rumpled and filthy....We went from
> village to village, each of them occupied by the Germans. Finally,
> we found one that was ours. "The German's were here, but they've
> left," the villagers said. "Give us water," we yelled. And as we
> passed through the village, our guns and rifles at the ready in case
> someone fired on us, they poured water over us, and whoever got
> so much as a drop was happy. They simply poured water over us.
> And we couldn't even stop, we had to break out of the
> encirclement! [1]

Women played a role unprecedented in modern warfare during the four
terrible years that the Soviets fought in World War II. Women mobilized,
as men did, because of the Nazi threat. The Germans carried on a vicious
war of extermination in the East: They aimed to destroy the USSR, wipe
out the communists, and turn the survivors into slaves. Making no effort
to conceal their intentions, they treated the Slavic populations in captured
areas with stunning brutality. In response, Soviet citizens rallied to the
defense of their homeland, some because of their feelings about the
government, the Communist party, and the leadership of Joseph Stalin,
others despite their feelings. Convinced that their cause was a just one,
Soviets entered World War II much as Western Europeans had entered
World War I—their patriotism firm, their faith in victory strong, their
willingness to fight and die untroubled by the doubts about warfare that
had circulated so widely in postwar literature in the West. [2]

Women constituted a substantial minority of those who went to the
front. Initially, they fulfilled "traditional" women's wartime roles,
washing the filthy and bloodstained clothing of the fighting forces,
preparing the kasha (food), and serving it to the soldiers. They served as

telegraph workers, nurses, and physicians, but even in noncombatant positions, few of these women served "behind the lines." Due to the central role that women already played, as well as to the relentless demands of total war, early in 1942 the Central Committee of the Communist party agreed to allow women to join the fighting forces. By the end of 1943, over 800,000 women volunteers served in the armed forces and the partisans, constituting about 8 percent of military personnel.[3] Most of these women fought at the front, about 200,000 of them in the air defense forces; thousands more fought the Germans as rank-and-file soldiers, as machine gunners, as snipers, as sappers, and as driver-mechanics in tank units. A few female officers led battalions of men into battle. Women won military awards for their bravery and distinguished service, often posthumously. Although Russian women had served at the front and taken up arms at earlier stages of the nation's history, in particular during World War I and the civil war that followed the Bolshevik revolution, they had never before served in such numbers, nor had their role been so important to military success.

Despite this exemplary record, women's frontline responsibilities received relatively little attention during the war, and their role as fighters even less. Writes historian Jeffrey Brooks, "The war as portrayed in *Pravda* [most authoritative paper in the Soviet Union] was largely a male experience, despite the enormous role of women in the struggle."[4] In the immediate aftermath of war, women's frontline participation was effaced almost completely from the record. The appearance of a few articles and books devoted to women's wartime role broke this virtual silence in the mid-1960s. Within a decade, the number of publications devoted to women and the war had grown substantially, although it continued to be tiny by comparison with literature on the war itself, which in the former Soviet Union amounted to nearly 20,000 books and countless articles.[5] Nevertheless, in Russian and increasingly in English, there is a body of literature devoted to the accomplishments of the Soviet women who served in World War II, describing their participation, assessing their contributions to the war effort, and chronicling their truly remarkable courage, endurance, and self-sacrifice under horrific conditions. This essay will draw upon that literature but proceed in a different direction. Instead of asking about women's contribution to the Soviet war effort, I want to ask what the war meant to the women who took part in it, and what their experience tells us about the authorized memory of World War II.

WOMEN PHYSICIANS AT THE FRONT

Vera Ivanovna Malakhova, the main subject of this essay, was one of thousands of women physicians who served at the front.[6] Born in 1919 to a worker's family in the Siberian city of Tomsk, she was the beneficiary of Soviet efforts to advance people of her class and gender in the decades following the Bolshevik revolution. She began medical school in 1936 and, supported by a small stipend, completed her training in June 1941, on the eve of the Nazi invasion. Malakhova served for 4 years as a frontline physician and was present at the Battle of Stalingrad. She was wounded twice and decorated many times for courage under fire, receiving the Red Star, the second-most prestigious medal for military service that the Soviet government awarded. After the war, Malakhova returned to Tomsk to practice as a physical therapist in a clinic for athletes, where she worked until her retirement. She married, bore a son, separated from her husband, and took a lover. So long as she had the strength, she remained engaged in public activity, organizing cultural events and commemorations of the war. However, if women's narratives can be said to "recount a process of construction of the self,"[7] then the 4 years she served in World War II remain most central to Malakhova's sense of her own identity. The fact that Malakhova spent the war years at the front and had direct experience of combat distinguished her from the majority of her female contemporaries, for whom the drama and travails of World War II constituted an important episode but not a defining experience.[8] Every other event in Malakhova's life seems to pale in comparison with the role she played in defending her homeland[9] from the enemy, the solidarity she felt with others at the front, and no doubt, the pride she takes in the adventures she had and the dangers she overcame. She began to speak of her wartime experience almost as soon as her interview commenced, resisting the efforts of her interviewer to encourage her to talk about her earlier life and education. Every topic, whatever it was, led almost inexorably to the war. Finally, about an hour into the interview, her interviewer stopped trying to stem the tide and let Malakhova's memories of the war take over the narrative.

Malakhova's narration of her experience in World War II comes to about 4 hours of taped interview and over 120 double-spaced pages of transcription. The interview follows no chronological order once she starts talking of war: she begins in the very thick of things and only much later, and only because she was asked, does she tell us where she was when the war broke out and why it was she went to the front. The narrative consists of a series of vivid stories in no particular temporal sequence, each of them relating to some aspect of her wartime experience. Many of these stories are vivid and dramatic—she tells what it was like to come under bombardment, to escape from German encirclement, to suffer almost unbearable physical deprivation. The stories also offer a kind of memorial to the men and women with whom she served. She names them and describes their character, actions and experiences, as if rescuing those she knew from the anonymity of the millions of dead.

At the same time, Malakhova's account serves as a critique of the official, Soviet-era narrative, which extolled the achievements of the party and the state. During her interview, she condemns the practice of abandoning the wounded during retreats from German attack, for example, and the brutal Soviet treatment of those of its citizens who fell into German hands. She refers with contempt to the conduct of Special Service officers, sent to the front to oversee the former political prisoners who had volunteered to fight. Malakhova is at her most vehement when she speaks of abuses of power.

Gender often inflects both Malakhova's critique of the powerful and her celebration of ordinary women and men. A central theme in her stories is the experience of women at war. In that sense, too, her narrative is self-consciously revisionist: She explicitly sets out to tell the truth about Soviet women's experience of war, a truth that in her opinion has never before been told. "No one speaks of this," or "I've never read about this anywhere," she sometimes says, and tries to set the record straight by incorporating women into a narrative of war that has excluded them or included them only in limited and stylized ways.[10]   Let us look at what she tells us.

Malakhova provides a straightforward account of her reasons for going to the front and is almost matter-of-fact about its hardships and dangers. Neither she nor her friends at medical school ever doubted that they would serve, she says: "What was there to talk about? We had graduated, they had given us our diplomas. Naturally it was our duty to go to the front."[11] Three months after the war broke out, she left Tomsk with her division.   Her responsibility as a physician was to run a mobile field hospital that served soldiers in the infantry. This meant that she and her aides marched alongside the troops and did their work wherever and whenever there was combat. They would put up their tent, lay out their instruments, and deal with the carnage. Like all field physicians, they were constantly in physical danger, and their rate of mortality was high: Only the troops themselves had greater casualties than women physicians who served with rifle battalions, as Malakhova did.[12] Malakhova herself narrowly escaped death several times.

But, as in the quote with which this chapter begins, Malakhova's emphasis is on the "we" as much as on the "I"; on the experiences people shared as much as on experiences that were uniquely her own. For that reason, her narrative sometimes effaces the differences between women and men. Even more commonly, she minimizes the distinctions between those who actively engaged in combat and those who "supported" them at the front. Repeatedly in her interview, Malakhova speaks of herself as someone who "fought [*voevala*]" (rather than served) at the front. My dictionary translates the verb *voevat'* as "to fight," "to wage war on." Soviet war propaganda reinforced that sense of unity by portraying everyone in the nation, wherever they were, as fighting the fascist invader. "Our country has turned into a single armed camp," as one wartime leaflet addressed to women put it.[13] "I could shoot very well with a carbine," Malakhova notes, comparing herself favorably with raw recruits who were sent into battle without knowing how to handle a rifle.[14]

However, even as she emphasizes the commonalities of life at the front, the dangers and struggles that women shared with men, Malakhova draws attention to the particularity of women's experience, which, in her opinion, has been unjustly neglected. For instance, she tells us at some length about the laundresses—their blouses worn and bleached from washing, their hands in dreadful condition: "Their hands—impossible to describe! Their hands were constantly in lye and soap, which was itself very coarse....After all, they had to wash the pus-covered and bloody shirts of all the soldiers and the sheets from the field hospital....Everything was covered with blood and pus, and they washed it all." These are girls who merit attention, she says, but no one has ever written about them. "There have been many injustices done to women who served at the front, very many," [15] she concludes, meaning both the painful work that laundresses performed and the way that history has ignored them.

Malakhova's focus on the corporeal, gendered female body serves to highlight its uneasy fit into the masculine world of war. Take, for example, her discussion of uniforms. Although the Soviet government drafted women physicians for frontline duty and after 1942 permitted women volunteers to fight, it did not modify the procedure for women's sake or initially, even provide uniforms for them.[16] At first, women fought in clothing manufactured for men. They went off to war wearing men's undershirts and underpants beneath men's uniforms and military greatcoats. Women clumped about in heavy boots designed for the larger feet of men. Malakhova remembered how women improvised: "They gave us these blue and red bands....We were supposed to use them to take out the wounded. They were made of knitted fabric. And we sewed them into socks for ourselves. They never issued us socks! We went around in men's underpants and undershirts. There were no bras. We sewed them ourselves from some of the [stuff] they gave us for bandages. The [male] senior doctors scolded us, but what could we do?"[17] We learn from Malakhova how women dealt with their bodily functions at the front, in the absence of special sanitary arrangements for women or separate toilet facilities. Many women ceased to menstruate altogether, she tells us, because of the fear and stress. She herself experienced a flow so heavy and painful it debilitated her for days. If a woman became pregnant, she had to continue to serve until her seventh month. What this could mean in practice becomes clear from Malakhova's description of a pregnant signalwoman: "She already had a belly like some kind of chariot, and poor thing, she had to wheel 10 kilos, if not more, 10 kilos of wire wound on a spool with a metal base; and she had not only to pull it along, she had to drag it from company to company. And while she was pregnant!" [18] In other ways, too, women's very anatomy proved a disadvantage.

> Of course we sometimes had these physiological moments, and this was very hard, very hard, because you're marching along and the men are everywhere. You march at night....You couldn't during the day, because then the infantry and other forces were on the move and they'd bomb you....So you'd move only at night. You'd march along emaciated and exhausted, and all of a sudden you'd need to... But how? ... To move off was dangerous, because the land was sometimes mined. So three of [the older men] would turn their backs in a circle and open wide their greatcoats and say: "Little daughter, come here, don't be ashamed. We see that you can't walk away." And we'd squat and pee....

It was much simpler for the men. "The men didn't even pay attention to us: They simply turned their backs and that was it, if you please." [19]

In the above incident, as elsewhere in Malakhova's account, ordinary soldiers emerge as remarkably chivalrous in their treatment of women. In reply to a question about the danger of rape at the front, Malakhova talked about how safe she felt among rank-and-file male soldiers, even when she was sleeping alongside them in the trenches, as she did late one night when she had nowhere else to lie down: "I lay down in the very midst of the soldiers. They all moved aside, so I would be warmer. No one did a thing. There was nothing crude at all!" Soldiers had a "chaste" attitude to the women, she concluded. [20] The soldiers' (although not the officers') use of the term "little sister" (*sestrechka*, in Russian) reinforced the asexual, comradely character of wartime relations between women and men. Soldiers used the term *sestrechka* to address women of all ranks and responsibilities who served as medical personnel in the military: "They called all of us 'little sister.' It didn't make any difference whether you were a doctor, a doctor's assistant, or a medical orderly. To them, we were all 'little sister.' "[21] As sisters, servicewomen were "off-limits," because to make sexual overtures was to violate the incest taboo. As one male veteran of the war put it: "We did not look upon them as women....We looked upon them as friends....They were our friends who carried us from the battlefield....You don't marry your own sister, do you? They were our sisters."[22]

By contrast with the ordinary soldier, invariably depicted as chivalrous in his relation to women's chastity and protective of women's person, Malakhova sometimes portrays men of high party status and military officers as sexual predators. In fact, men's sexual abuse of power provides one of the themes of Malakhova's narrative. She mentions sexual harassment about half a dozen times.[23] The first time, she observes that "this is something about which no one has ever said anything," and she is correct.[24] The discussion of harassment is one of many occasions in which her talk of prewar events moves unfailingly to the war. She begins by explaining why she never became a Komsomol (member of the League of Young Communists) or a Communist party member, despite her working-class origins and the prerogatives that party membership would have brought her, and despite her avowed support of the Soviet system. Then she goes on to assure her interviewer that she fought no worse than many party members, and that in fact, some party members were cowards who sought to escape the front: "They tried somehow to get assigned to support services in the rear outside the line of fire—even officers did it. But this was just a few. So I wouldn't say that rank-and-file communists.... You know, some commissars behaved very dishonorably." There was one "disgusting" commissar who attempted to take advantage of her.

> Once he summoned me at night. So. "Sit down," he said, "we need to talk." I say, "I am listening, comrade Major." I don't sit down. He spreads out his overcoat.... It was cold. "Sit on my overcoat." I say, "I'll stand." "'No, no, no, you sit down." Well, I had no right to disobey; I was still a junior officer, while he was a major. I sat down on the corner. He began to move toward me. He moved and moved and all of a sudden—whap! His hand was under my skirt. I jumped up and said, "Ah, so that's why you summoned me." You know, I was really upset. I remember that I was shaking all over. If things had been different, I'd have simply slapped him in the face. But here I couldn't, he was my superior. But he kept his cool. "I wanted to test you," he said. I said, "You know what, you can test your wife. But you have no reason to test me." He really tried to get his revenge later. And two other officers tried to do the same thing.[25]

According to Malakhova's account, whether or not they belonged to the Communist party, officers also "felt their superiority" and used it to gain access to "intimacy."[26] Once, the commander of a medical battalion threw a grenade into a trench where women were bathing, forcing the women to run naked into the open air.   In this case, the commander's superior, an "amazing commissar," "the only political worker I respected," punished the commander for his offense.[27]   Another time, a group of officers forced Malakhova and another woman (Tasia) to join a New Year's Eve party in their dugout, despite the women's desire to celebrate with their own platoon.

> So what did the officers do? They forced us—we didn't have the right to refuse—they subjected us to military discipline. Tasia and I went almost with tears in our eyes. At that time the chief surgeon was courting me, and he, obviously, had designs....With his enormous paw he seized hold of me and sat me down on his knees, put my hands like this behind my back. By this time all the officers were very drunk. "Penalize her!" I struggled and struggled, but they simply poured some vodka in my mouth. In order not to choke, I gulped it down and immediately became drunk. And so I poisoned myself, for two whole days I threw up and he had to keep watch over me for those two days to be sure I didn't die.[28]

Rarely did women take such abuses passively. They warned each other about commanders who abused their power and encouraged each other's defiance. Malakhova tells us how her friend, Lida, cursed out an officer who tried to seduce her, despite the possibility of suffering punishment for insubordination. "Lida really knew how to curse [*byla takaia matershchina*]!" [29]

Voluntary unions and romantic love were a different matter. "Love must be love," Malakhova declares. "That is the best human feeling, the most elevated! If you really love a person, you can scale the highest mountains."[30]   She herself loved in this way, and this love is one of her most treasured memories.   Her lover was another physician, a senior officer who at one point saved her life by helping her to escape from a German encirclement.   Later, as she lay in the hospital recovering from shellshock at the Battle of Stalingrad, he risked his life to swim across the Volga with a birthday present for her, a package of raisins, a scarce item that he had saved. Not long after, he was mortally wounded and died in her arms, uttering as his last words, "How will you live without me?" The memory of her wartime lover is still fresh. Although almost 50 years have passed, during which Malakhova married, bore a son, separated, then entered a free union that lasted many years, it is to this lost love of her youth that her memories often turn.

LOVE AND WAR

Malakhova's romantic language conceals an uneasiness she shares with other women veterans concerning the subject of love. "I want to write you about something which you cannot write in books," one woman wrote to Svetlana Aleksievich, the editor of a groundbreaking book on women veterans' memories of war. "On the theme of woman and war, it is shameful to sidestep one major question—the question of the PPZh [*Polevaia Pokhodnaia Zhena*, or mobile field wife] as they were called and are still called....[31] Sexual relations occured at the front and were part of the truth of human life there, of "earthly love," in the writer's words: "Legitimate, illegitimate, it [earthly love] existed at the front, and it degraded people and elevated people and saved their lives." The writer herself had had such a love and the feeling lasted her entire life, although the man had not loved her as she loved him and abandoned her, pregnant, when the war was over.[32] The acronym she uses, PPZh, circulated widely during the war and in the postwar period, always with a derogatory meaning.

Malakhova also employs the term PPZh. She, too, is ambivalent about sexual relations at the front, sometimes adopting a critical attitude toward women's sexual activity, sometimes a very down-to-earth one.   Thus Malakhova can say that "everyone has sexual desires, everyone!"; can laughingly describe how the nurse who served as her "right hand" became pregnant by a lady-killer who cut a broad swath among the women; and can assert several times about casual sexual relations, "Youth will be youth."[33]   Yet she is ready to condemn an "excellent surgical nurse, excellent!" because she lived with their commander, a "wonderful man," and when he summoned her, "she would throw aside everything, leaving others to do the work, and she would do his washing and ironing and look after him." Because he was such a good commander, "they forgave him" for this behavior. But not the woman.[34]

For Malakhova, the PPZh are women who failed to resist or acquiesced to sex with a powerful male because of a desire to obtain the privileges that such an association might bring. "We didn't like them at all," she remembers of the PPZh in general.   With one exception, Malakhova portrays such women negatively.   The exception was Anna Georgievna, who was involved with the commander of their regiment ("a splendid man!") and who was so modest and self-effacing, so very industrious, that she concealed her status and claimed no privileges.[35] But the remaining PPZh are distinguished from other women primarily by their purported privileges. "We [women] lived honorably, we conducted ourselves honorably and disliked the PPZh.   They had privileges.   We who served in the infantry had to walk 35—40 km at night, while they rode horses...."[36] But in fact, the lines were never so clear-cut in the minds of those who applied the labels. When they called a woman a PPZh, people rarely knew whether she felt "real love" or merely sought a privileged status.[37] Malakhova herself blurs the distinction at one point, referring to the PPZh in the language of love: "Perhaps, that love was the only one of their [the purported PPZh's] lives. I don't know...."[38]

CONTEXTUALIZING MEMORY

Malakhova's pained, sometimes contradictory efforts to speak of women's sexuality in a way that honors female subjectivity are in part the result of the problematic status of women and their sexuality in Soviet culture. After the revolution of 1917, the Bolsheviks undertook far-reaching efforts to emancipate women and to equalize their social status with men's. Family law ended women's subordination to men at home and made divorce readily accessible. In 1920 abortion became legal if performed by a physician. The industrialization drive of the early 1930s brought a huge influx of women into the labor force. Women from lower class backgrounds, Malakhova among them, enjoyed unprecedented opportunities for education and upward occupational mobility, although they never enjoyed so many as men. Then in the mid-30s, after Stalin consolidated his hold on power, family policy took a conservative turn: Abortion became illegal, and divorce became both complicated and expensive. The 1920s had been a period of relative sexual freedom. In the 1930s, by contrast, free love itself was labeled "bourgeois." The government began to trumpet the virtues of the "socialist" family and monogamous love and to celebrate motherhood. A "cult of stereotyped, hyperbolized masculinity," which combined elements of physical might, technical and industrial prowess, and military style, increasingly characterized the public sphere, while the new female ideal demonstrated "sweet naivete" and "modesty," as well as abiding maternal instincts.[39] Nevertheless, the original aims of involving women in social production did not disappear. But now women were supposed to support the masculinized values of the public sphere while displaying the virtues of femininity.

These changes narrowed the definition of women's sexuality. In the Soviet Union, there was no iconographic sexualization of women in the form of advertising, pinups, or posters, thanks to the censorship of every public image and word and to the prudery of official Soviet sexual discourse. Instead, the state-controlled media portrayed Soviet women as chaste and pure. Women's very sexual agency was negated by the law of 1936, which made homosexuality illegal. The law specified only the homosexuality of men, presumably because women's autonomous sexual feeling as expressed toward other women was literally beyond the imagination of those who formulated the law.[40] Trained in the 1930s, even a woman physician such as Malakhova lacked a knowledge of the potentialities of her own body. She remembers: "We had no conception of sex at all, none at all....We didn't even have a medical conception of it. No one taught it to us."[41] Thus, by the late 1930s, there was no longer a language in public circulation with which women might speak of their intimate lives.[42]

After the Nazi invasion of June 1941, wartime propaganda drew on this highly gendered imagery and reinforced it, even as it summoned both sexes to do everything in their power to repel the enemy. Literature and poetry presented women as the embodiments of home and family for which men risked their lives, as in the lines of the love poem "Wait for Me," beloved of millions:

> Wait for me and I'll come back,
> Wait with might and main.
> Wait when you are drowned by grief
> In floods of yellow rain
> Wait amid the driving snow,
> Wait in torrid heat.
> Wait when others cease to wait
> Forgetting yesterday.[43]

A high proportion of memorable figures in wartime films were women exemplifying the virtues of loyalty, constancy, endurance, and self-sacrifice.[44] Even women who took on nontraditional roles at the front were usually presented as gentle and domestic. By contrast with brave and manly men, women soldiers were girlish, shown in terms of their "spiritual qualities rather than through the actions which confirmed their exceptional status."[45]

To be sure, in films one might sometimes see peasant women taking up rifles and machine guns to resist the German invader; and a woman partisan fighter, the legendary Zoia Kosmodemianskaia, was glorified in print and film. Kosmodemianskaia, a teenage Komsomol member, joined the partisans and in November 1941 set afire a stable of German horses. Captured by the Germans, she was tortured and publicly hanged. She became a national symbol of courage and self-sacrifice, and her life and martyrdom eventually became the subject of a play and feature film (*Zoia*). However, representations of Kosmodemianskaia, like those of other women, stressed her suffering and sacrifice over her heroic action.[46] Although the occasional article might refer to the Soviet Union's fighting women, no posters represented them and few films portrayed their heroism, as films consistently portrayed the heroism of men.[47]

Wartime propaganda portrayed women as passive sexually as well. When women were eroticized in wartime writing, it was as chaste victims, not as seductresses, as in the following poem, in which the violated woman represents the innocence of the violated Mother Russia and serves as a foil for the brutal German occupiers, who perpetrate ghastly crimes. This poem, like the preceding, was written by Konstantin Simonov, one of the most important wartime writers.[48]

> If you do not want to have
> The Girl you courted
> But never dared to kiss
> Because your love was pure—
> If you don't want fascists to bruise and beat
> And stretch her naked on the floor
> In hatred, tears and blood
> And see three human dogs despoil
> All that you hold dear
> In the manliness of your love...
> Then kill a German, kill him soon
> And every time you see one—kill him.[49]

Thus Soviet culture offered women a highly circumscribed repertory of words and images with which to speak of their sexuality.

Malakhova's difficulty in speaking about women's sexuality is also very much affected by the way that servicewomen were regarded after the war was over. As victory drew near and the chaos and upheavals of the early wartime period gave way to order and renewed control, gender distinctions became exaggerated in ways they had not been earlier. Thus in 1943, coeducation, in practice since 1918, was abolished in secondary schools in order to give proper attention to "the different requirements of their [boys' and girls'] vocational training, practical activities, preparation for leadership and military service."[50] A new family code of 1944 reinforced marital ties by making divorce more expensive and complicated to obtain. The code was also intrusively pronatalist: Single people were taxed, as were people who had fewer than three children. The cult of motherhood intensified. "Motherhood medals" were awarded to women with five or more children; those with ten or more received the honor of "Heroine mother." Gender stereotyping continued in the postwar period. Although the state-controlled media continued to praise women for their accomplishments and sacrifices on the home front, it virtually effaced their military role.[51] And in postwar monuments, fiction, art, and film the warrior is invariably male and only men fight at the front.

TRANSFORMING THE WOMAN WARRIOR

Gender stereotyping and the erasure of women's wartime achievements contributed to a radical popular derogation of women's role at the front that developed seemingly independently of any official impetus. Allusions to women's sexual reputation played no role whatever in official commemoration of the war, but they dominated popular discourse. Despite the iconographic emphasis on women's purity and courageous self-sacrifice and the absence of sexualized public images, despite women's extraordinary achievements, their collections of medals and awards for bravery, and heroic action under fire, popular opinion in the Soviet Union insisted on stereotyping women who served at the front as "camp followers."[52] "They'd look at you askance and say, 'We know what you did there!' " one woman veteran remembered of the postwar period.[53] My colleague Anastasia Posadskaia, born in the late 1950s, remembers that the unsavory reputation of women who had been at the front continued to be well known by women and men when she was young, but she was unable to tell me where she first learned about it. Such attitudes were so widespread that women veterans became fearful of wearing their uniforms and medals in public. "I didn't like to show myself [with my medals]," Malakhova remembers, "because many people thought I was some kind of front-line "W" [whore]—unfortunately, many people called us that." Once, when she did put on her medals and uniform to participate in a victory commemoration with other veterans, she was accosted on the street by a stranger who said, "Ah ha! There goes a frontline whore!"[54] Thus, even as women's heroic actions, their suffering and self-sacrifice at the front were downplayed or effaced by government silence in the postwar period, postwar popular discourse transformed their feats into sexual transgression, enabling the "mobile field wife" to crowd out the woman warrior, at least for a time.

No historian of Soviet women and World War II has discussed this transformation, in part, I think, to avoid detracting from women's achievements and perpetuating slander best forgotten. Yet, if one turns from women's achievements to women's experience and memory, this transformation becomes very important. In her discussions of sexuality (and not only sexuality), Malakhova is grappling with it, sometimes to deny the reputation of frontline women, sometimes to endorse it in particular cases. She never satisfactorily resolves the dilemma. Women veterans as a group had to grapple with their reputation, too. Some persisted in affirming their wartime record; others became "as silent as fish." "I tell you honestly, we hid it, we didn't want to say that we had been at the front, " reports one of Aleksievich's respondents. "We wanted to become ordinary girls once again. Marriageable girls." In this inability to take public pride in their accomplishments or to wear the medals they had earned at risk of their lives, the women differed from men, who in the words of one female veteran, "as victors, heroes, and suitors could wear their medals; they had a war, while people looked at us [women] as if we were completely different."[55]

To be sure, as Nina Tumarkin has argued so eloquently, all public commemoration of the war was saturated with politics and bore little relation to the experiences even of the men who fought it. Soviet representation of World War II was intensely politicized. For over 40 years, only a single narrative line was permitted, reflecting the self-image, priorities, and propaganda needs of the government-controlled press and media.[56] In this official version of the war, the heroic Soviet people, inspired by the party and/or (depending on the politics of the time) in Stalin's name, fought fascism to defend the socialist motherland and proved that their system was superior. War stories became part of authorized history, and only authorized versions could be told, while the terrible human costs of victory, some of them easily avoidable, some of them directly due to government policy, were kept from the record. To preserve a sanitized public memory, the physical needs of those who were wounded were ignored, and their damaged bodies literally concealed from view.[57] Until very recently, public commemorations of World War II were "elaborately orchestrated galas...meant to infuse the body politic with national pride and a spirit of allegiance to the party," to quote Tumarkin. The propaganda extolling grieving mothers and triumphant soldiers came down to one thing: 'Socialism had triumphed.' "[58] However distorted the celebration of wartime achievements, women's comments suggest how painful it was to be excluded from them in the decades following the war.[59]

REVISING THE WAR STORY

It is in the context of public memory, not only valorized but masculinized, that women's memories of war must be understood. By the late 1920s, the official version of the Soviet past had become the only acceptable one. Because authentic personal narratives threatened to provide "access to hidden domains of the past...obliterated by the official version of history,"[60] they played almost no role in its creation. In the 1930s, the traumas of collectivization and terror completed the Soviet Union's transformation into a   society "where remembering [was] dangerous."[61] As a result, oral history practice was virtually impossible until very recently, and even now it remains very difficult.

Nevertheless, circumstances have changed dramatically in the past few years. Malakhova's oral history is part of a new and widespread quest for authentic versions of the Soviet past that was unleashed in the late 1980s.

This period saw unprecedented explorations of the Soviet experience. Not a week went by without the appearance of a new film, book, article, or television program challenging accepted interpretations of history. Nothing remained sacred—not the character of V. I. Lenin, hitherto an iconographic figure; not Soviet conduct of World War II, hitherto regarded as a spotless record. By ending political repression and allowing people to speak publicly and for the first time of the unspeakable, *glasnost'* legitimized people's memories and enabled them to tell their own stories.

However, *glasnost'* discourse is also inflected by gender. Across much of the political spectrum, critics agree that communism destroyed the family and undermined women's "natural role" as wife, mother, and guardian of the family hearth. From that perspective, Malakhova, as well as the women who told their stories to Svetlana Aleksievich, can be seen as contesting aspects of the very *glasnost'* discourse that has enabled them to speak. In telling their stories of World War II as they themselves experienced it, they insist that women, too, "had a war," just as did the men who wore their medals without fear for their reputation. Their stories are filled with pride and a sense of accomplishment. They figure as actors, as heroines, and as doers rather than as victims: As nurses and physicians, they carried wounded men from the battlefield under a hail of bullets; as snipers, they took out dozens of German tanks; as officers, they proved to the men they led that they were capable of taking command. They stood firm under bombardment and despised the men who ran away. They showed how they all "fought honorably," in Malakhova's words.

Oral histories of women thus serve a dual function. First, oral histories allow the historian to recapture women's hitherto undocumented experience. Second, women's oral histories permit us to problematize accepted narratives, in this case, the national narrative of war. In Soviet narratives, as in others, the battlefield is depicted as a male domain, the warrior generically male. Soviet discourse on militarism also stressed "masculine" qualities, even as the circumstances of modern war, with its bombing of civilians, refugee populations, and, at least in the Soviet case, women carrying guns, coming under bombardment and occupying combat roles, made the gendering of actual combat experience increasingly arbitrary. Oral history allows us to see how women inserted themselves into the highly male-gendered discourse of war. Although these women are by no means the first to tell such tales of Soviet women's courage and heroism, their stories differ from those published in the Soviet period. They take the individual as their focus, by contrast with Soviet-era narratives, which used the deeds of Soviet women (and men) to celebrate the achievements of the Soviet state. For the first time, the women discuss the particularity of their experience as women, as well as the dynamics of gender, making their narratives, among other things, "stories of how women negotiate[d] their 'exceptional' gender status" on the frontlines of war.[62] Malakhova's oral history is unique, however, in linking gender, sexuality, and power. Taking advantage of the possibilities of speaking openly about the hitherto unspeakable after the collapse of the Soviet Union and the delegitimation of the Communist party, she uses her tales of sexual abuse to critique the party and the men who abused their power. This is part of a broader critique of Soviet conduct of the war. The way that Malakhova's narrative gives the (sometimes gendered) human body a central role contributes to that critique as well, because it emphasizes the human cost of war. Malakhova is as attentive to the bodies of others as she is to her own. We learn the names of comrades; how they looked and acted; the ways they lived and died. She makes no attempt to diminish the physical suffering of war, nor to conceal war's ugliness and pain. Wounded bodies, bleeding bodies, bodies mangled beyond recognition figure often in her account.[63] Yet despite Malakhova's critique of abuses of power and privilege, she never questions the necessity of Soviet participation in World War II, or the justice of the Soviet cause, nor do any of the other women whose testimonies we have; instead, she shows us the price that people paid for victory, some of that price unwarranted.

In arguing that Malakhova gives us a different version of the war story, I do not mean to suggest that she or other women were impervious to the gendered discourse. Despite their own role in the war effort, many of them, Malakhova included, accepted many of the gendered conventions of their era. They express doubts about whether women should be permitted to fight, for example. "Of course, women shouldn't be in the infantry," Malakhova says. "They really shouldn't be! What about the men? How many of them hid out behind the lines? How many?!...While we girls...were right at the front!"[64] Most of the women who told their stories to Aleksievich uncritically embraced their culture's definitions of femininity: They wept when the military barber cut off their braids; they did up each other's hair in the bathhouse; they darkened their brows, kept mirrors handy at the front, and in general, tried as best as they could to "remain women." "Although we passed through the terrors of war, we were nevertheless able to give birth to beautiful children....And that's the main thing," said one of them.[65] But their testimonies make it clear that a gendered discourse cannot eradicate their sense of having played a major role in the most significant event of their era, however much it encouraged others to deny or misrepresent their actions. So the women take the opportunity to speak of their accomplishments and to insert their experience into a narrative that has excluded it until recently.   The last word here belongs to Vera Ivanovna Malakhova.   A response to her interviewer's question about what she would like most in life right now, it is also the conclusion of her interview:

> I only want my health....There is so much I would like to do.   I want to celebrate my division, I've given everything to celebrate my division.   Now they spit on us, on all the veterans.[66]   And all the same I fought....Especially women, it's unfair....   I think that your project of interviewing women is very significant and I hope you complete it.   Because we are dying out....Because we women who served at the front don't deserve to be called whores, forgive me for saying that so directly, we don't deserve it, we weren't that way. There were very few PPZh and even those lived with just one man; there were a few promiscuous women, but really very, very few. Not many at all....We lived honorably, fought honorably, and I don't know, I consider that we had good girls.... I wish you and I had more time.   I could tell you so much, so many good stories. But no one is interested.   Journalists simply latch onto one thing. "That's all, Vera Ivanovna, that's all," they say, "don't tell us anything else."   They write a tiny article, wham, bam, and that's it. That's the end of it.   No one is interested now, absolutely no one, and we are dying out, most of us are gone, and we are the last. And that's that.

NOTES

1. Transcript of interview with Vera Malakhova, Hoover Institution Archives, Oral History Collection, 55. The interview was conducted by Anastasia Posadskaia, a part of a larger feminist project designed to retrieve the voices of old Russian women. A section of the interview appears in Barbara Alpern Engel and Anastasia Posadskaia-Vanderbeck, ed. *A Revolution of Their Own* (Boulder, CO: Westview Press, 1998). The interviews were made possible by a grant from the John D. and Catherine T. MacArthur Foundation. I am very grateful to the Rutgers Center for Historical Analysis for generously supporting the research and writing of this article, and to the center's community of scholars for creating a most congenial and stimulating intellectual environment.

2. By the end of the 1920s, state censorship of publications insulated

the Soviet population from critiques of World War I. That war, officially entitled the First Imperialist War, was presented in Soviet history as a political war over the spoils of colonialism.

3. K. Jean Cottam, "Soviet Women in World War II: The Ground Forces and the Navy," *International Journal of Women's Studies* 3, no. 4 (1980): 345.

4. Jeffrey Brooks, "*Pravda* Goes to War," in *Culture and Entertainment in Wartime Russia*, ed. Richard Stites (Bloomington: Indiana University Press, 1995), 21. For the portrayal of women in official iconography, see Richard Stites, *Russian Popular Culture: Entertainment and Society Since 1900* (New York: Cambridge University Press, 1992), 98—116. Ilya Ehrenburg and Konstantin Simonov, *In One Newspaper: A Chronicle of Unforgettable Years* (New York: Sphinx Press, 1985), gives a good sense of the place of women in Soviet wartime reportage.

5. John Garrard and Carol Garrard, eds., *World War 2 and the Soviet People: Selected Papers from the Fourth World Congress for Soviet and East European Studies*, (New York: St. Martin's Press, 1993), 8. My reading of the attention given to women's wartime roles in the decades that followed is based on B.S. Murmantseva, *Sovetskie zhenshchiny v Velikoi Otechestvennoi voine: 1941—1945* (Moscow: Mysl', 1974), and B.S. Murmantseva, "Noveishaya literatura o ratnom i trudovom podvige zhenshchiny v gody Velikoi Otechestvennoi voiny," *Voprosy istorii* 9 (1983). I may have somewhat underestimated the numbers.

6. Women constituted 41 percent of frontline physicians and 43 percent of assistant physicians. K. Jean Cottam, "Soviet Women in Combat in World War II: The Rear Services, Resistance Behind Enemy Lines and Military Political Workers," *International Journal of Women's Studies* 5, no. 4 (1992): 366.

7. "Origins," in *Interpreting Women's Lives: Feminist Theory and Personal Narratives*, ed. Personal Narratives Group (Bloomington: Indiana University Press, 1989), 5.

8. Of the twenty-five interviews conducted by Anastasia Posadskaia for our collaborative oral history project, only Malakhova had a record of such service and only she chose to concentrate her narrative on the war.

9. Malakhova's homeland and the socialist state appear not to be differentiated in her mind, as they were not in the minds of many of the women Posadskaia interviewed. By the 1940s, it would seem, the two had become melded.

10. Malakhova transcript, 33, 64, 89, 159.

11. Malakhova transcript, 36—7.

12. John Erickson, "Soviet Women at War," in Garrard and Garrard,

World War 2, op. cit., 62. Everywhere at the front, women risked their lives. Of the approximately eighty women from Tomsk who went to the front with Malakhova, only four others lived to see the defeat of the Germans.

13. *Sovetskie zhenshchiny v otechestvennoi voine: vsesoiuznyi miting zhenshchin uchastnits otechestvennoi voiny v Moskve 10 Maia 1942* (Moscow: OGIZ, 1942), 11.

14. Malakhova transcript, 36.

15. Ibid., 63-4.

16. See the discussion in Erickson, "Soviet Women at War," op. cit., 67—69.

17. Malakhova transcript, 71. The need to divest themselves of their own clothing and hairdos and to go off to war with short hair and in men's uniforms is one of the themes in other testimonies, too. See, in particular, Svetlana Aleksievich, *U voiny ne zhenskoe litso* (War's Unwomanly Face) (Moscow: Sovetskii pisatel', 1988), 85. Aleksievich published this book with the purpose of setting straight the historical record: "Our memory of war and all our ideas about war come from men," Aleksievich observes with good reason in her introduction. The book is a collection of comparatively brief excerpts from oral histories and personal letters of women who served at the front in both combatant and noncombatant roles. At the time of its publication, the volume was groundbreaking, because the women's testimonies about their own experiences diverged from the practice of treating women's wartime roles in terms of a narrative of national heroism; instead, the book explores in depth women's memories of the war as they themselves experienced it.

18. Ibid., 64.

19. Ibid., 72—3.

20. Ibid., 68—9; 72. Other women report much the same thing. "At the front, the men were wonderful to us, they protected us," remembered one woman, who recalled how soldiers covered women with their own jackets and shared with them their last remaining crust of bread. "We never experienced anything from them besides kindliness and warmth." Aleksievich, op. cit., 85.

21. Malakhova transcript, 88.

22. Quoted in Nina Tumarkin, *The Living and the Dead: The Rise and Fall of the Cult of World War II in Russia* (New York: Basic Books, 1994), 183—4.

23. The women whose testimonies Aleksievich cites never mention sexual harassment, but references to it can be found in the published diary of a male physician who served in the Soviet army, although without the

note of outrage that is so strong in Malakhova's account. See Nikolai Amosoff, *PPG-2266: A Surgeon's War* (Chicago: Henry Regnery, 1975), 172, 179. I am very grateful to Nancy Frieden for bringing this book to my attention.

24. Malakhova transcript, 33.

25. Ibid., 33—4. The role of the political commissar was to maintain the ideological purity of the armed forces.

26. Ibid., 72.

27. Ibid., 94—5.

28. Ibid., 105—6.

29. Ibid., 34.

30. Ibid., 45—50. With a nod to the cult of maternity, she is quick to add that really, a woman's most elevated feeling is when she suckles her own child: "In my opinion, a woman has no better feeling. Being a mother is simply a heavenly feeling, a heavenly feeling."

31. Here, as in all future references to PPZh, I will retain the Russian acronym, because that is the reference people used.

32. Aleksievich, op. cit., 174.

33. Malakhova transcript, 49, 107.

34. Ibid., 66.

35. Ibid., 65.

36. Ibid., 65. Only high-ranking officers had horses; everyone else went on foot. A relationship with a man with a horse could make a woman's life much easier.

37. The physician Nikolai Amosoff, who served as a surgeon during the war, was prepared to go to considerable lengths in order to keep the woman he loved from acquiring the label of a PPZh: "One thing I have decided: I will never put Lyda in a position where she could be referred to as a PPZh. We must be more careful," he wrote in his diary. Amosoff, *PPG-2266*, op.cit., 206.

38. Malakhova transcript, 66—7.

39. Beth Holmgren, *Women's Works in Stalin's Time: On Lidiia Chukovskaia and Nadezhda Mandelstam* (Bloomington: Indiana University Press, 1993), 13.

40. We know that in the 1970s and '80s, male homosexuals were still persecuted under that law; lesbians might be harassed, but their sexual behavior remained safe from legal penalties.

41. Malakhova transcript, 48—9. The proscription against women speaking of women's sexuality continues to this day. The "intimate" aspect of women's lives remains "deeply hidden," in the words of my colleague, Anastasia Posadskaia. Women never discuss it in public and discuss it rarely and with difficulty in the family, between mothers and daughters.

42. Discussions of women's sexuality had become problematic by the late 1920s, as official treatment of the ideas of Aleksandra Kollontai became more negative. Kollontai was the major Bolshevik thinker and writer about women's sexual relations. Allegedly, she preached that having sex was like drinking a glass of water.   On Kollontai, see Barbara Clements, *Bolshevik Feminist: The Life of Aleksandra Kollontai* (Bloomington: Indiana University Press, 1979).

43. Quoted in Stites, *Russian Popular Culture*, op. cit., 101. The popular response to this song is discussed in Robert Rothstein, "Homeland, Home Town and Battlefield: The Popular Song," in Stites, *Culture and Entertainment*, op. cit., 84—5.

44. Peter Kenez, "Black and White: The War on Film," in Stites, *Culture and Entertainment*, op. cit., 169.

45. Katharine Hodgson, "The Other Veterans: Soviet Women's Poetry of World War 2," in Garrard and Garrard, *World War 2*, op. cit., 81; also Stites, *Russian Popular Culture*, op. cit.,100.

46. Stites, *Russian Popular Culture*, op. cit., 115; Hodgson, ibid., 81; see also the discussion of Kosmodemianskaia in Tumarkin, *The Living and the Dead*, op. cit., 76—78.

47. References to wartime articles on women fighters can be found in B.S. Murmantseva, *Sovetskie zhenshchiny v Velikoi Otechestvennoi voine*, op. cit. See also Jeffrey Brooks, "*Pravda* Goes to War," op. cit., 9—27.

48. Stites, ibid., 111, 115. See also Argyrios Pisiotis, "Images of Hate in the Art of War," in Stites, *Culture and Entertainment*, op. cit., 143. Compare this to the sexualization of women elsewhere in times of war, as noted in Margaret Higonnet and Patrice Higonnet, "The Double Helix," in *Behind the Lines: Gender and the Two World Wars*, ed. Margaret Higonnet et al. (New Haven, CT: Yale University Press, 1987), 37.

49. Quoted in Stites, 100.

50. Rudolf Schlesinger, ed., *The Family in the USSR: Documents and Readings* (London: Routledge and Kegan Paul, 1949), 363.

51. In the last days of the war, the president of the Soviet Union publicly thanked women for their participation in all spheres of national defense; thereafter, women were removed from combat positions in the army.

52. Cynthia Enloe, *Does Khaki Become You? The Militarization of Women's Lives* (Boston: South End Press, 1983), 2, 106.

53. Aleksievich, op. cit., 171. Amosoff refers to the term PPZh and notes it was commonly used by soldiers to refer to women who became involved with men at the front. D'ann Campbell has observed that women who fought in the U.S. armed forces during World War II acquired a similar reputation, but the numbers were much smaller.

D'Ann Campbell, "The Regimented Women of World War II," in *Women, Militarism, and War: Essays in History, Politics and Social Theory*, ed. Jean Elshtain and Sheila Tobias (Savage, MD: Rowman and Littlefield, 1990), 115—6.

54. Malakhova transcript, 146.

55. Aleksievich, op. cit., 85, 171, 175—6.

56. Tumarkin, *The Living and the Dead.*

57. Mutilated war victims were swept off the streets two years after the war had ended, and sent to the colonies in the north to end their days. See Tumarkin, 98-9.

58. Ibid., 28.

59. After the mid-1960s, participation of women in public commemorations probably grew, as their frontline role was increasingly acknowledged and as they aged and became less vulnerable to sexual slurs. No one has documented this evolution. Malakhova herself became very active in veterans' affairs and organized reunions of her division at anniversary celebrations; still, she is quite aware of the difference between those commemorations that genuinely honor veterans and those that co-opt them.

60. Patrick H. Hutton, "Collective Memory and Collective Mentalities: The Halbwachs-Aries Connection," *Historical Reflections/Reflexions Historiques* 15, no. 2 (1988): 318.

61. Daria Khubova, Andrei Ivankiev, and Tonia Sharova, "After Glasnost: Oral History in the Soviet Union," in *Memory and Totalitarianism*, International Yearbook of Oral History and Life Stories, ed. Luisa Passerini (New York: Oxford University Press, 1992), 89. People not only have trouble finding their own voice; many are reluctant to speak with it. Some women approached for our project refused to be interviewed; fourteen others, having initially agreed, declined when my colleague, Anastasia Posadskaia, tried to set up an appointment or arrived with her tape recorder.

62. "Origins," in *Interpreting Women's Lives*, op. cit., 5.

63. The women who shared their stories with Aleksievich are equally graphic about the maimed bodies of soldiers: They tell of men reduced to pieces of meat; of how people looked after bombing and shelling or being buried alive.

64. Malakhova transcript, 70.

65. Aleksievich, op. cit., 111, 113. See also 112, 136—148.

66. This is in reference to the current attacks on the cult of World War II, which are described in Tumarkin, *The Living and the Dead*, op. cit.

Figure 8. German refugee raped on train by Polish hoodlums, orphaned by the war. Original newspaper caption reported that Poles rode trains into Berlin in 1945 to loot German refugees.

EIGHT

A Question of Silence
The Rape of German Women
by Soviet Occupation Soldiers

Atina GROSSMANN

> Until that time I had lived so happily with my husband and the children. I had four children; the youngest I had to bury on May 18; it was 4 months old. Now I am in a desperate condition and do not want to have this child under any circumstances.[1]

This statement, submitted to the Health Office of Berlin's working-class Neukölln district on December 16, 1945, by a woman requesting a medical abortion on grounds of rape by a Soviet soldier, encapsulates the extraordinaily convoluted nature of my topic. I came to it unintentionally, quite unwillingly but irresistibly, through my research on the politics of abortion and birth control in postwar Germany. Finding this affidavit among the 995 cases approved for abortion on the grounds of rape recorded in the Neukölln district office (Bezirksamt) files on "Termination of pregnancy" between June 7, 1945, and June 17, 1946,[2] I was both moved (despite myself) by the poignancy and desperation of a woman's and mother's statement, and horrified (despite all I know) at the notion that anyone could describe herself as having lived happily—and normally—in Germany until the defeat of the Third Reich and the arrival of the Red Army.

The question of rape of German women by occupation, mostly Red Army, soldiers during and after World War II is intricate as well as richly and perilously overdetermined. It partakes of two highly developed discourses that continually intersect and threaten to block each other—so much so that the silence referred to in the title of this chapter is at least as much that of the historian trying to figure out how to tell the story as about the events discussed.

On the one hand, the feminist discourse on rape, its representation and construction, while not trusting every single story, validates and publicizes the voices of women who speak of sexual violation and tries to integrate rape into its analysis of "normal" heterosexual relations. On the other hand, the historical discourse on Germany's confrontation with its Nazi past (*Vergangenheitsbewältigung*) tends to distrust any narrative that might support postwar Germans' self-perception as victims insofar as it might participate in a dangerous revival of German nationalism, whitewash the Nazi past, and normalize a genocidal war. This fear became dramatically clear in the *Historikerstreit* of the mid-1980s and continues to haunt current historical and political debates in Germany, as well as among observers abroad.³ It is compounded by the renewed nationalism and xenophobia in a reunited Germany, which seeks, among other things, to claim Wehrmacht soldiers as heroic and beleaguered fighters on the eastern front holding back the Stalinist Slavic onslaught. Indeed, just announcing apparent "facts" about the massive incidence of rape perpetrated by soldiers of the Red Army that smashed the Nazi war machine is enough to provoke enormous anxiety and resistance among many who are otherwise not averse to documenting the widespread existence of male violence against women. Historical analysis becomes even more difficult in the current context of anguish and confusion about the proper analysis of, and response to, the rapes in the former Yugoslavia and especially in Bosnia.⁴

The ironically titled documentary film *BeFreier und Befreite*, on precisely this topic, made by the noted West German feminist filmmaker Helke Sander, highlights my dilemmas—as the child of German—Jewish refugees working as a feminist historian of modern Germany. Much as I respect Sander's efforts to document a complicated and important history and to create a public space for its discussion, I find her approach deeply problematic, at times wildly self-righteous and historically disingenuous. Sander claims finally to be breaking the silence on a story long subject to taboo and ignored either as exaggerated anticommunist propaganda or as the "normal" by-product of a vicious war, a story sacrificed on the altar of the "myth of antifascism" or of East-West rapprochement. But in many ways, the criticism Sander hurled at Gertrud Koch's negative review—"Du machst es Dir viel zu einfach" (You make it much too easy for yourself)⁵— needs rather to be applied to the film. Oblivious to historians' analyses of the ways in which the stubborn (and noncontextualized) search for "real information" can distort far more than illuminate, Sander insists that she just wants to present the "hard facts."⁶ These are represented for her by numbers and in a quite peculiar manner, indeed, one that borders on parody, for the pencil and blackboard wielded by her demographic expert, Dr. Reichling, hardly seem the instruments of modern statistical analysis.

But hard—or even soft—facts are hard to come by and unreliable. It has been suggested that perhaps one out of every three of about one and a half million women in Berlin at the end of the war were raped—many but certainly not all during the notorious days of "mass rapes," from April 24 to May 5, 1945, as the Soviets finally secured Berlin. The numbers cited for Berlin vary wildly, from 20,000 to 100,000, to almost one million, with the actual number of rapes higher because many women were attacked repeatedly. Sander and her collaborator, Barbara Johr, speak, perhaps conservatively, of about 110,000 women raped, many more than once, of whom up to 10,000 died in the aftermath.[7] At the same time— and despite their virtual fetishization of statistical clarity—they announce on the basis of Hochrechnungen (projections or estimations) that 1.9 million German women altogether were raped at the end of the war by Red Army soldiers.[8] This may be a horrifically accurate estimate, but one wonders whether or not the focus on numbers has something to do with precisely a competitiveness about the status of victim ("*ein Verbrechen mit dem anderen aufgerechnet*"), so sensitive in the context of World War II, that Sander claims to resist in her work; it even suggests a lust for generally portraying women as victims that seems central to her particular historical and feminist agenda.[9]

When telling this important and tangled story, the point cannot be to argue about numbers or to gather "just the facts." As the historian Norman Naimark concludes in his careful history of the Soviet zone, "It is highly unlikely that historians will ever know how many German women were raped by Soviet soldiers in the months before and years after the capitulation."[10] At the same time, however, he demonstrates that, despite all necessary caveats about similar episodes of violence and lack of discipline on the part of other occupation troops,

> rape became a part of the social history of the Soviet zone in ways unknown to the Western zones....It is important to establish the fact that women in the Eastern zone—both refugees from further East and inhabitants of the towns, villages, and cities of the Soviet zone—shared an experience for the most part unknown in the West, the ubiquitous threat and the reality of rape, over a prolonged period of time.[11]

Sander's film opens with a familiar still frame of shattered Berlin, 1945, women searching through the ruins and Red Army soldiers swaggering down the street. The voice-over, however, comes as a provocation. "Just like in Kuwait, just like in Yugoslavia," the narrator intones, as we see newsreel footage of soldiers grabbing bicycles from women or posing with newly acquired loot. This is the film's essential (and essentialist) message; even as it deals with a particular historical moment, it posits the horrific universality of rape. The universal soldier, whether in the Red Army or the SS, in the U.S. Army or the French Foreign Legion, the Iraqi Army or the Serb irregulars, rapes and pillages innocent women; women as universal victim are the booty of every war, the unrecognized and uncompensated targets of war crimes.

However, as the African-American literary critic Hazel Carby has pointed out, "Rape itself should not be regarded as a transhistorical mechanism of women's oppression but as one that acquires specific political or economic meanings at different moments in history."[12] In other words, even as we struggle to name sexual violence and to create community among women in order to combat it, we must understand it as both an intensely personal and a public, politically and historically constructed event. In one particularly gruesome moment in the film, the camera darts back and forth between grainy shots of women's disheveled, disemboweled bodies while a female voice repeats, "German women, Russian women, German women, Russian women," all united by one vicious male orgy of transhistorical, transpolitical patriarchal violence. But these are not any (or all) women: What the film does not make clear is that these pictures intended to represent the "equality" of male violence affecting women are in fact taken from the *Deutsche Wochenschau*, the Nazi war propaganda newsreels, and were used to demonstrate the "bestial" and "animalistic" actions of the Red Army "horde" against *German* women. Ironically, the very image Sander uses to establish that she is not limiting her critique to Russians is lifted from a Nazi film showing German victims.[13]

In this particular case, then, on the most mundane (and melodramatic) level, the problem is that this is not (yet another) "universal" story of women being raped by men, as Helke Sander would have it, but of German women being abused and violated by an army that fought Nazi Germany and liberated death camps. Mass rapes of civilian women also signaled the defeat of Nazi Germany—a historical event I learned to call *Befreiung* (liberation) but which Germans usually described as *Zusammenbruch* (collapse). Therefore, beyond arguments about the veracity of women's reports or pseudostatistical investigations (although I do think that much conventional historical research remains to be done), I am interested in "de-essentializing" and historicizing the rapes Sander addresses in her film; these events cannot, I think, be usefully understood by quick comparison to Kuwait or Yugoslavia, nor can they gain macabre comic relief by editing in clips of U.S. Army antivenereal disease films.

In particular, I want to examine two points that seem to me important when thinking about German history and how feminists might approach the place of these events in German history. First, the massive experience of rape, the fear of rape, and the incessantly repeated stories of rape—both at the time and years later—need to be solidly located within a pervasive German self-perception and memory of victimization so strong and enduring that it continues to surprise many Americans, and especially Jews, as it repeatedly pops up. Second, I want to read the language of the various rape narratives quoted here as offering clues to the continuing impact within the immediate postwar period of both Weimar and National Socialist population and social welfare policy, and the links and differences between the two.

We need to ask how the (eventually privately transmitted and publicly silenced) collective experience of the rape of German women in the absence of (protective) German men insinuated itself into postwar Germans' view of themselves as primarily "victims" and not "agents" of National Socialism and war. The mass rapes of 1945 inscribed indelibly in many German women's memory a sullen conviction of their own victimization and their superiority over the vanquisher who came to liberate them. Mass rapes confirmed Germans' identity—both the women who were assaulted and the men (dead, wounded, maimed, or in prisoner of war camps) who could not/would not protect them—as victims of *Missbrauch* (abuse). The term was ubiquitous when used by women to circumscribe their experience but was also deployed more generally to suggest all the ways in which the German *Volk* as a whole had been woefully abused—by the Nazis, by Hitler, who reneged on his promises of national renewal and led them into a war that could not be won, by the losses on the front and the Allied bombing raids, and then by defeat, occupation, and a de-Nazification that was generally perceived as arbitrary and unfair.

Let me be clear: I am not suggesting that raped German women were not victims (as long as we are stuck with this somewhat insufficient vocabulary); there must be no doubt that they were. The problem is that Sander's eagerness to integrate German women into the international transhistorical sisterhood of victims of male violence leads to a problematic historical slippage and displacement in which German women seem to become the victims primarily of National Socialism and the war, rather than of the failure of National Socialism and defeat in the war. It both leads to, and is symptomatic of, the exasperating insistence of some German feminists that women as a group were only the victims (and not also the agents, collaborators, and beneficiaries) of National Socialism.[14] Sander's own deliberately innocent narrative style (she is the righteous and beleaguered investigator who just wants to know the truth) undergirds this slippage. It is critical, however, to remember that in the case of mass rape of German women, it was not the Third Reich but rather its collapse (*Zusammenbruch*) that led to women's violation.

Given the current preoccupation (especially in Germany) with "taboo-and silence-breaking" in discussions of World War II and genocide and the relative crimes of Nazis and Soviets—and Sander's film is a significant contribution to this growing genre—it is also important to clarify that these were not, initially at least, rapes that had been silenced. They became an official problem located in the public sphere because they had social health and political consequences that required medical intervention: venereal disease and pregnancy. They were immediately coded as public issues, not as an experience of violent sexual assault, but as a social and medical problem that needed to be resolved. And it was in that context that women received, at least some help—medical treatment and abortions—and that some of the documents cited in this chapter were produced.

Nor were these rapes silenced among the women themselves, again at least initially; as I looked at the literature of the postwar years—diaries, memoirs, and novels—I found rape stories everywhere, told matter-of-factly, told as tragedy, told with ironic humor and bravado.[15] Women told their stories to authorities from whom they expected specific forms of redress, and they also obsessively retold their stories to each other and to their daughters. They lived, interpreted, and represented their rapes in a particular historical context that they participated in creating. We need to understand how the experience of, the reaction to, and the memory of these rapes were framed by the specific historically toxic conjuncture in which they took place.

THE EXPECTATION OF RAPE

It is crucial to note how massively these rapes had been prefigured in Nazi propaganda. Women living in self-styled "cellar tribes" in ravaged Berlin were already transfixed by intense fear of rape as the Red Army advanced. Horrific images of invading Mongol barbarians raping German women were a vital part of the Nazi war machine's feverish (and successful) efforts to bolster morale on the eastern front and keep the home front intact. Nazi propaganda had been relentless in characterizing the Russians as subhuman and animalistic (*das viehisches Treiben dieser Untermenschen*). The threat of a surging Asian flood and marauding Red Beast tearing through what was supposedly still a pacific, ordinary German land was used to incite desperate resistance even long after it was clear that the war was fundamentally lost. By the end of the war most German women had already seen graphic newsreel footage of the bodies of "violated women, battered old people, and murdered children" (*geschändete Frauen, erschlagene Greise, und ermordete Kinder*) left behind as the Red Army pounded westward. Indeed, the very last newsreel released in 1945 showed a white fence with the desperate message scrawled on it, "Protect our women and children from the Red Beast."[16]

Moreover, Germans knew enough of *Wehrmacht* and SS crimes in the East to have reason to believe that vengeful Russians would commit atrocities and to make the oft-repeated (but never proven) account of the Jewish-Russian writer Ilya Ehrenburg's infamous call for Soviet soldiers to seek retribution by raping "blond" German women plausible.[17] Whatever the level of ordinary Germans' detailed knowledge of the systematic extermination of European Jewry, it was no secret that *Wehrmacht* actions on the eastern front (in contrast to the western front) went well beyond the standards of ordinary brutal warfare. German soldiers had been explicitly commanded to liquidate all putative "Bolsheviks," and during their "scorched earth" retreat, as a matter of policy, not from a lack of discipline, they laid waste to huge territories of civilian population and massacred entire villages. Again and again in German recollections of what Russian occupiers told them, the vengeful memory summoned was not a parallel violation by a German raping a Russian woman, but of a horror on a different order: It was the image of a German soldier swinging a baby, torn from its mothers arms, against a wall—the mother screams, the baby's brains splatter against the wall, the soldier laughs.[18]

The embittered defense by the retreating *Wehrmacht* forced exhausted and in part disbelieving Soviet commanders to continue hard fighting right into the center of devastated Berlin. By February, they were only 35 miles east of Berlin, and still the Germans would not surrender as they tried to carve out escape routes for themselves to the west and north. Fortified by huge caches of alcohol conveniently left behind by the retreating Germans, reinforced by brutalized Soviet prisoners of war liberated along the way, and enraged by the street-to-street, house-to-house German defense, loyally carried out by young boys and old men as well as regular soldiers, the Red Army pushed through East Prussia toward Berlin in what the military historian John Erickson has called "a veritable passion of destructiveness."[19] In a remarkably infelicitous sentence, Erickson concluded: "The fighting drained both sides, though Russian lustiness won through."[20]

Official Soviet policy, reflecting Stalin's pronouncement that "the Hitlers come and go but the German *Volk* remains," obstinately refused to acknowledge that the Red Army would engage in atrocities on anything more than the level of "isolated excesses." Ilya Ehrenburg himself (whose line "We shall be severe but just" was in any case being pushed aside by Stalin's new interest in mollifying the *Volk*) insisted that "the Soviet soldier will not molest a German woman....It is not for booty, not for loot, not for women that he has come to Germany."[21]

In this instance, however, Goebbels' propaganda—for once—turned out to be correct. So much so that many women reported feeling that they were reenacting a scene in a film they had already seen when the drama they were expecting actually unfolded: Soldiers with heavy boots, unfamiliar faces (invariably coded as Mongol), and shining flashlights entered a darkened cellar, searched for weapons and watches, and then, revolver in hand, commanded the proverbial "*Frau, Komm.*"

Even the public policy response to the rapes—the unofficial but generally accepted suspension of paragraph 218, which had criminalized all nonmedical or noneugenic abortions—had already been set into motion by the Nazis. The other side of harsh wartime regulations limiting abortion and access to contraceptives were secret directives permitting—or coercing—abortions on female foreign workers and women defined as prostitutes and non-"Aryans," as well as on the growing number of German women who became pregnant, via consensual sex or rape, by foreign workers or prisoners of war. Already in 1940, the Minister of the Interior had issued a secret memo instructing local health offices to consider "voluntary" extralegal abortions not provided for in the 1935 amendment to the 1933 Sterilization Law (which sanctioned eugenic abortions prior to sterilization), in "urgent, proven" cases of rape or undesirable racial combinations (with someone "racially alien," *artfremd*).[22]

By the beginning of 1945, the encroaching Red Army had advanced to such a point that the possibility of mass "violations" of German women by Soviet troops was acknowledged and indeed widely publicized. Since rapes were already supposedly resulting in many pregnancies, the Ministry of the Interior even suggested the establishment "in large cities [of] special wards for the care of such women."[23]

THE EXPERIENCE OF RAPE

For German women in 1945—certainly in Berlin and to its east—rape was experienced as a collective event in a situation of general crisis. While frightful and horrific, it seemed to provoke no guilt; if anything, it confirmed their expectations and reinforced preexisting convictions of cultural superiority. Rape came as just one more (sometimes the worst, but sometimes not) in a series of horrible deprivations and humiliations of war and defeat: losing your home, becoming a refugee, having your menfolk killed, maimed, or taken prisoner, your children die or sicken of disease and malnutrition. It is not even clear to me that rape claimed a particularly privileged status in the long litany of miseries women confronted. The story of rape was told as part of the narrative of survival in ruined Germany. As one observer noted, "Rape had become routine."[24] Margaret Boveri, a German journalist who published in 1968 what she presented as her "Survival Diary" of the Battle of Berlin, laconically noted for May 8, 1945:

> Rode [on her bicycle] a ways with a nice bedraggled girl...imprisoned by Russians for 14 days, 'had been raped but well fed....May 8, 1945. The usual rapes—a neighbor who resisted was shot....Mrs. Krauss was not raped. She insists that Russians don't touch women who wear glasses. Like to know if that is true...the troops were pretty drunk but did distinguish between old and young, which is already progress.[25]

If many German women felt confirmed as well as violated, Jews and antifascists who emerged from hiding to welcome the liberators only to have to flee again from the threat of rape felt betrayed, or simply grimly accepting. Inge Deutschkron, in hiding with her mother, remembered her growing joy and relief as she heard the rumble of Russian tanks approaching Berlin. But one of the soldiers she welcomed with a happy smile grabbed at her clothes, muttering the already classic phrase, "*Komm, Frau, Komm.*" At first uncomprehending, she ran to her mother, who sighed, "So it is true after all," and added hopefully, "We must show them our Jewish identity cards"—they had been hidden in the goat shed for just this occasion—"they will understand." But Deutschkron adds, "They understood nothing. They couldn't even read the identity cards." Another kind of chase began: flight and hiding not from deportation to the death camps but from sexual violation. Eventually the shooting was over, the Nazis gone, and a semblance of order restored, but Deutschkron noted, "I could no longer be really happy."[26]

Anne-Marie Durand-Wever, an anti-Nazi physician, emerged from "gruesome" nights in her cellar in bombed-out Berlin and returned to work in a first-aid station; she hastened to test women and girls for venereal disease and to ferret out gynecological instruments since, as she reported in her diary, "I guess we'll have to do abortions." Durand-Wever was sure that "our" soldiers had comported themselves no differently, but on May 23 she made a sad note about her own daughter: "This afternoon Annemie was here with her child. Four Russians. Swab inconclusive. In any case sulfa medication (*Albucid*). For this one tends one's child!" Still in February 1946, she portrayed a "loathsome" situation of continuing rapes, venereal disease, unwanted pregnancies, and mass abortions.[27]

But in this situation of wartime and occupation, women were not only victims but also agents; as caretakers and providers, they scrounged and bartered for food and shelter, and negotiated protection for their children and themselves with occupation soldiers. They also reported extremely diverse experiences of what they variously named as rape, coercion, violation, prostitution, or abuse. Some women and young girls were brutally gang-raped in public with a line of soldiers waiting for their turn. In some cases, women's bodies were slit open from stomach to anus, or they were killed afterward. Others were forced to have sex alone in a room with a lonely young soldier for whom they occasionally even developed ambivalent feelings of hate, pity, and warmth; still others consciously offered themselves in exchange for protection of a daughter; some made deliberate decisions to take up with an occupier—preferably an officer with power—to shield themselves from others and to garner privileges. And of course there were also moments of genuine affection and desire. Women recorded brutality, but also, at times, their own sense of confusion about the fine lines between rape, prostitution, and consensual (albeit generally instrumental) sex. In a recurring trope in memoirs and diaries, women are gathered at water pumps in bombed-out streets, exchanging "war stories" with a certain bravado and *Berliner Schnauze* (sarcastic humor). Almost gleefully they revealed their strategems to trick Russians as gullible as they were brutal: masquerading as men or ugly old women disguised by layers of clothing or faces smeared with dirt and ash, pretending to have typhus or venereal disease. But they also marveled at soldiers' apparently indiscriminate "taste" in women, the fact that they seemed to prefer fat ladies, or their astounding sexual prowess even when utterly inebriated.

The anonymous narrator of *A Woman in Berlin*, a compelling diary—albeit of unclear provenance and authenticity—to which Sander accords a prominent place in her film, explained her reaction after a series of brutal rapes during the first chaotic week of April—May 1945:

> Then I say loudly, "Damn it!" and make a decision. It is perfectly clear. I need a wolf who will keep the wolves away from me. An officer, as high as possible, Kommandant, General, whatever I can get. For what do I have my spirit and my little knowledge of foreign languages? As soon as I could walk again I took my pail and crept onto the street. Wandered up and down...practiced the sentences with which I could approach an officer; wondered if I didn't look too green and wretched to be attractive. Felt physically better again now that I was doing something, planning and wanting, no longer just dumb booty.[28]

THE CONSEQUENCES OF RAPE

Women's rape stories were framed in incredibly complicated ways, shaped by their audience and the motives behind their telling. Their experiences were ordered and given meaning within a complex grid of multiple images and discourses. Most immediately, there was the political fact that doctors in Berlin, driven by a complicated set of health, eugenic, racist, and humanitarian motives, and with the support of the Protestant bishop, quickly decided to suspend paragraph 218 prohibiting most abortions and to perform abortions on raped women who wanted them. And as Durand-Wever later reported, "They all wanted them."[29] The ad hoc decision was quickly institutionalized by a highly organized medical and social hygiene system that had never really broken down, at least in the cities. Throughout most of the first year after May 1945, a medical commission composed of three or four physicians attached to district health offices approved medical abortions—almost up until the last month of pregnancy—on any woman who certified that she had been raped by a foreigner, usually but not always a member of the Red Army. (There were also abortions granted to women who reported being raped by American and French military personnel, or foreign workers; I found no reports of rape by a German.) All these applications were carefully recorded with name, marital status, address, month of pregnancy, and date of request, date of approval by the medical commission.[30] With dubious legality but with virtually full knowledge and tolerance by all relevant—both German and occupation—authorities, indeed with the consent of the Protestant—although not the Catholic—church, abortions were, it would appear, performed on a fast assembly line in the immediate postwar period.[31] Rapes were immediately medicalized and their consequences eliminated (*beseitigt*). The plans already in place for setting up abortion wards to eliminate unwanted Mongol and Slav offspring were in fact instituted after the Nazis had been defeated. In the summer of 1945 a young German army surgeon just released from an American POW camp in France and ordered to work for no pay in a Berlin hospital noted in his diary:

> There is much medical work on the gynecological ward. On orders of the British and American authorities all pregnancies which can be proven to have resulted from rape (mostly by Russians) are to be terminated. There are also many illegal abortions by quacks which are then admitted infected into the hospital.[32]

Abortions were performed in public hospitals at public cost. The physician in charge of the Neukölln district health office, Dr. Brandt, was an antifascist who had been newly appointed by the occupation authorities; however, at least some of the doctors on the commissions approving the abortions and probably many of those performing them in hospitals were former committed Nazi party members who had been (temporarily) suspended from private practice and forced to serve in public positions as part of their de-Nazification proceedings. It seems likely that the techniques used to abort women at extremely late stages of pregnancy had previously been tested on wartime foreign female forced laborers.[33]

This background has led some historians to characterize these postwar abortions as a continuation of Nazi race policy.[34] But the picture is more complicated and overdetermined, the discontinuities at least as dramatic as the continuities. All women applying for medical abortions were required to submit certified statements detailing the events that had led to their unwanted pregnancy. The individual letters are all different, but somehow also the same; among the approximately one thousand that I read, certain narrative codes do emerge (on the other hand, the pattern of events described are no different from those reported in memoirs or diaries). The affidavits are in women's voices, but they are framed by the necessity of appealing to political and medical authority and by certain preexisting available languages.

In interpreting the rape experience to officials and also to themselves and their friends or family, and in making their case for abortion in the affidavits submitted to health offices, women (and the medical authorities approving the abortions) relied on a mixed legacy of Weimar and National Socialist population policy discourses, as well as current occupation policy. They repeatedly referred to both the social and racial/eugenic grounds on which their abortion should be sanctioned—despite the presumably compelling and popularly known fact that neither of those indications but only rape by an occupation soldier was recognized as justifying an "interruptio."[35]

Thus, women utilized rhetoric that was helpful in avoiding guilt and managing recourse. First, they hearkened back in narrative terms to the social hygiene, sex reform, and maternalist discourses of the Weimar welfare state—which predated Nazi racialist formulations and would outlast them—and couched the abortion issue in terms of medical, social, and eugenic indications. Women matter-of-factly and pragmatically asserted their right to terminate pregnancies that were not socially, economically, or medically viable—in the name of saving the family or preventing the birth of unwanted or unfit children. Within this framework of social necessity, the problem was not a moral one of bearing a child resulting from an act of violence and terror, nor even necessarily a racial one of bearing inferior offspring, but quite directly social and economic—the problem of any unwillingly pregnant woman who could not care for a child or another child. Invoking this discourse of social (not moral or racial) emergency, one woman wrote to the Neukölln health office: "I am pregnant due to rape by a Russian on April 27, 1945. I request removal of the fetus since I already have an illegitimate child and live with my parents who themselves still have small children."

After April and early May when women had mainly been raped in their cellars, public spaces became sites of danger as women ventured out to look for food, fuel, or water, scrounge through ruins, try to locate relatives, or recuperate belongings. A woman who had been robbed of her bicycle and raped while on her way to the suburb of Potsdam wrote on November 9, 1945: "Since I am single, my mother dead for fifteen years, my father a half-Jew from whom I have had no sign of life for six years, it is impossible for me to set a child into the world under these conditions."

Another letter dated August 6, 1945: "I have three children aged five to eleven years. My husband, a former soldier, is not yet back. I have been bombed out twice, fled here in January from West Prussia, and now request most cordially that I be helped in preventing this latest disaster for me and my family."

Women also drew upon the Nazi racial hygiene discourse, which banned "alien" (*artfremd*) offspring (indeed, when rapes by other occupation forces were certified, the perpetrator was frequently identified as Negro if American or North African if French). They availed themselves of the rich repertory of Nazi racial imagery of the barbarian from the East, especially the Mongol from the Far East, associated with the cruel frenzy of Genghis Khan. A letter from July 24, 1945: "I hereby certify that at the end of April this year during the Russian march into Berlin I was raped in a loathsome way by two Red Army soldiers of Mongol/Asiatic type." Even Inge Deutschkron, who had initially been so happy to greet the Soviets, described her first "Russian" as small, with crooked legs and "a typical mongolian face with almond eyes and high cheekbones, clad in a dirty uniform with his cap perched lopsided on his head."[36]

In the (successful) affidavits presented to health offices, multiple and overlapping voices all talked at once, often in the same document. In an interesting indication of the dissimultaneity of social welfare understandings in the immediate postwar period, many statements freely mixed the social necessity discourse familiar from the Weimar debates over abortion reform and the racial stereotypes popularized by the Nazis, with threats of suicide or descriptions of serious physical ailments that might have legitimated a medical indication under any regime. A letter from August 20, 1945:

On the way to work on the second Easter holiday I was raped by a Mongol. The abuse can be seen on my body. Despite strong resistance, my strength failed me, and I had to let everything evil come over me. Now I am pregnant by this person, can think of this only with disgust and ask for help. Since I would not even consider carrying this child to term, both my children would lose their mother. With kind greetings.[37]

In a matter-of-fact but also desperate manner, women mobilized existing discourses, entangled them, and deployed them to tell their own stories for their own purposes.

Although such remarkably similar tropes are evident in virtually all the recorded rape stories, whether official depositions requesting abortions or diaries and memoirs, the image of the *Russe* was also complicated and multifaceted. The Russian was split into good and bad on many levels. Inevitably, there was the drunken, primitive Mongol who demanded watches, bicycles, and women and did not even know that a flush toilet was not a sink. He was generally counterposed, however, to the cultivated officer who spoke German, had memorized Dostoyevsky and Tolstoy, deplored the excesses of his comrades, and could be relied on for protection even as he sought to educate his captives about German war crimes. (Incidentally, such "cultivated" status was rarely achieved by American occupiers, who were persistently categorized as primitive and vulgar, even if not so dangerous, since they could supposedly achieve their conquests with nylons and chocolate rather than by rape. As Durand-Wever recalled, there were those who quipped, "The difference is that the American and the British ask the girls to dinner and then go to bed with them, while the Russians do it the other way round.")[38]

But even the "primitive" Soviets were cast in a dual if ultimately consistent mold: The ignorant peasant soldier with the peculiar racial features associated with Slavs or Mongols (finally anyone who did not look German was identified as Mongol) could be cruel but also a child—or perhaps puppy—like character, easily distracted by a playful baby or even dominated by the proper amount of authoritative response on the part of women who ordered him about as they might a child or a pet animal. Invariably there was mention of Russians' pleasure in small children and their tenderness toward babies (in explicit contrast to the stories the Red Army soldiers told of German behavior in the East). But this positive characteristic was, of course, only another aspect of their underdevelopment. And in an indication of the highly variable nature of Soviet occupation, some officers were even known to shoot an offending soldier on the spot—although this display of "justice" often served only to confirm Germans' sense of Russians as uncivilized. Strikingly—and disturbingly—the former Soviet soldiers Sander found to interview for her film conform to such stereotypes and resemble, in quite uncanny fashion, the grotesque "primitive" figures of Soviet prisoners of war the Nazis paraded in their *Wochenschauen*. Sander further reinforces these prejudices with her filmic stance: A more respectable-looking former soldier is interviewed with his back to her; the toothless Russian with a crooked grin holding forth about male sex drives is filmed head-on.

German women at the end of the war did not, however, reserve their contempt for Soviet men alone. Indeed, some narratives favorably compared Russian officers with contemptible, defeated German men who were now pathetic parodies of the manly Teutonic genus valorized by the SS; even if not dead, wounded, or detained in Soviet POW camps, they were unable and unwilling to defend the women for whose safety they had supposedly been fighting. Preoccupied only with saving their own skins, they were not above pressuring women to go with Russian soldiers, in order not to endanger themselves—rape, after all, was a less horrific fate than Siberia or getting shot.

Thus women's negative and prejudiced image of the Russians helped them to distance the horror of their own experience. The narrative of the Russian primitive or exotic curiously absolved him of guilt, as it also absolved women themselves. Such childlike, primitive, animal-like creatures could not be expected to control themselves—especially when tanked up with alcohol—or adhere to rules of civilized behavior. Nor could women be expected to defend themselves against such an elemental force, backed up in many cases, of course, by rifle or revolver. In the end, German women lost their honor, but they also preserved it. They managed to maintain the conviction of their own superiority, not only against the former enemy but also against their own men, who either abetted their humiliation or sought to punish them for it. Speaking of the major she has finally cornered into her bed, hoping that he will fend off rivals, the anonymous narrator of *A Woman in Berlin* wrote (not untypically but in an analytical style somewhat improbable for a diary composed at the time):

> On the other hand, I do like the Major, I like him the more as a person, the less he wants from me as a man. And he won't want a lot, I can feel that. His face is pale, his wounded knee gives him trouble. Probably he is searching for human, womanly companionship more than the purely sexual. And that I give him freely, even gladly. Because among all the male creatures of the last several days he is the most tolerable man and human being.[39]

For the most part, however, Russians might be terrifying or sometimes amusing, but certainly not on the same level as Germans. To Germans in the spring of 1945, after all that had happened, it was clear who had more *Kultur.*

THE AFTERMATH OF THE RAPES

After the rubble was cleaned up and the men were home, the pregnancies aborted (at least 90 percent apparently were, especially in Berlin) and the VD treated, the initial explosion of speech about the rapes was muted, at least in public. This was certainly the case in the East, where the Soviet Military Administration stymied all efforts by German communists to broach the subject as a potential block to public support for the occupation and above all to the electoral chances of the Communist party against the Social Democrats (SPD) in Berlin's first open elections in 1946. (The communists lost, certainly in part because a majority female electorate had not forgotten what the Soviet "friends" had done.)[40]

Not even in the West where, presumably, such tales might have served as a useful Cold War propaganda tool did the public discussion continue. With the return of prisoners of war and the "remasculinization"[41] of German society, the topic was suppressed, not as too shameful for women to discuss, but as too humiliating for German men and too risky for women who feared (with much justification, given the reports of estrangement and even murder) the reactions of their menfolk.

German women, especially in the East and among refugees from the East in the West, were left with memories that had not been worked through, that had no easy access to public space even as they were, whether directly or indirectly, constantly invoked or alluded to. There were no rituals of guilt and expiation, as in commemorations of persecutions of Jews and the Holocaust, no structures of compensation, and memory as in veterans' organizations and benefits.[42] And this, of course, provides the resonance for Sander's claim to breaking the silence. In their privatized but pervasive discourse, women remembered and passed on to their daughters their experiences: of bombing raids and flight with women and old people from the advancing Red Army, rapes and fear of rape, and also pictures of sturdy *Trümmerfrauen* tidying up the ruins of the bombed-out cities. In an analogue to their heroic and pathetic brothers, fathers, husbands, lovers, and sons on the eastern front—who also felt no shame or guilt because they perceived themselves as having had no choice—women, too, invented themselves as both victims and heroines. They expressed little shame or guilt even though many of their menfolk expected it of them—a circumstance that left its depressing traces in postwar gender relations.

The memories, if suppressed, remained raw and distorted but hardly, as Sander's film would claim, completely silenced. Their abundant traces can be found in postwar literature, film, and government documentation.[43] Women felt victimized, violated, humiliated, but finally not guilty or responsible—a sentiment feminists laud when confronted by survivors of sexual assault but historians deem highly problematic in the context of the general German unwillingness to acknowledge responsibility for the misery they endured and the crimes that they perpetrated. In the postwar period, women's stories were combined with men's more openly validated tribulations on the eastern front and as prisoners of war, to construct a new national community of suffering that served not only to avoid confrontation with Nazi crimes but also, of course, as a strategy for reauthorizing and reestablishing the unity of the Volk, providing the basis for a "sick" Germany to "recover" once again (a metaphor much used by postwar women's groups from all political camps).

At the beginning of the recent upsurge of research and discussion about guilt and complicity, German women's historians and feminists felt themselves especially exempt from charges of this kind and sought assiduously to document and certify women's status as victims of a patriarchal regime. Now, in a curious kind of way, they are perhaps particularly faced with the task of confronting and working through the problem of acknowledging their agency during and after the Third Reich and as contributors to the reworking of national identity in both West and East Germany.

We are now, after unification, hearing women's war stories again, some for the first time since the 1950s, and beginning to record and study them. I think that the care with which we tell those stories, in each historical case, matters and may help us to find a usable language to talk about rape—so universal and so specific—as well as German history. It is finally this responsibility to address a particular, complicated historical legacy that Helke Sander has evaded, as a filmmaker, as a documentarian or historian, as a feminist, and as a German.

NOTES

An earlier version of this essay appeared in German in *Frauen und Film* 54/55 (April 1994). Permission to reprint the English version is granted by MIT Press, Cambridge, Mass., who printed it in *October* 72 (Spring 1995): 43—63. It also appears in *West Germany Under Construction*, ed. Robert Moeller (Ann Arbor: University of Michigan Press, 1997), 33—52.

1. December 16, 1945, Landesarchiv Berlin (LAB) Rep. 214/2814/ 221/2 (Gesundheitsamt Neukölln).

2. The interruption of pregnancy records are from the Landesarchiv Berlin, Gesundheitsamt Neukölln, Rep. 214. Neukölln seems to be the district that has the most completely preserved Gesundheitsamt records, so it is difficult to judge—at this point at least—whether the number of applications and near universal approval rate were similar in other Berlin districts.

3. See, among many other considerations, Geoff Eley, "Nazism, Politics, and Public Memory: Thoughts on the West German Historikerstreit 1986–1987," *Past and Present* 121 (November 1988): 171—208, Charles S. Maier, *The Unmasterable Past: History, the Holocaust, and German National Identity* (Cambridge, MA: Harvard University Press, 1988), and the special issue of *New German Critique* 44 (Spring/Summer 1988).

4. See, for example, the uproar about Catherine MacKinnon's analysis of the connections between rape and pornography in the former Yugoslavia in *Ms.* cover story (July/August 1993): 24—30. See Erika Munk's critique, *Women's Review of Books* (January 1994).

5. Helke Sander, "Du machst es Dir viel zu einfach," *Frankfurter Rundschau*, 26 November 1992.

6. Helke Sander and Barbara Johr, eds., *BeFreier und Befreite: Krieg, Vergewaltigungen, Kinder* (Munich: Verlag Antje Kunstmann, 1992), 11. See Joan Scott, "The Evidence of Experience," *Critical Inquiry* 17 (Summer 1991): 773—97; see also the exchange between Laura Lee Downs and Joan Scott in *Comparative Studies in Society and History* 35 (April 1993).

7. Barbara Johr, "Die Ereignisse in Zahlen," in Sander and Johr, *BeFreier und Befreite*, ibid., 48, 54—55. See also Erich Kuby, *Die Russen in Berlin 1945* (Bern/Munich: Scherz, 1965), 312—13.

8. Ibid., 48, 54—55, 59.

9. See Sander, op. cit. The insistence on the critical importance of precise figures seems especially ironic given that Sander in a notorious short story (which refers to the "exterminatory will" of the five books of Moses and the "literally murderous patriarchy" of the Old Testament) is so contemptuous of the focus on numbers in discussion of the Final Solution. See "Telefongespräch mit einem Freund;" in *Die Geschichten der drei Damen K.* (Munich: Weissmann Verlag, 1987), 140—41 (translated by Helen Petzold as "A Telephone Conversation with a Friend" in *The Three Women K.* [London: Serpent's Tail, 1991], 118—30). Inevitably, once one enters the realm of millions, one enters the terrain of Holocaust and of women's claim to equal or similar status with Jews as victims—a hallmark of some German feminist writing.

10. Norman M. Naimark, *The Russians in Germany: A History of the Soviet Zone of Occupation, 1945—1949* (Cambridge, MA: Harvard University Press, 1995), 132—33.

11. Ibid., 106—7.

12. Hazel Carby, *Reconstructing Womanhood: The Emergence of the Afro-American Woman Novelist* (New York: Oxford University Press, 1987), 18. See also Kathryn Gravdal, "Chretien de Troyes, Gratian, and the Medieval Romance of Sexual Violence," *Signs* 17 (Spring 1992): 558—85.

13. See Deutsche Wochenschau nos. 755/10/1945, 754/9/1945, and 739/46/1944. Filmarchiv Barch (Koblenz).

14. This debate about whether German women should be studied primarily as *Opfer* (victims) or *Täter* (perpetrators) has now been played out in many forums, notably the bitter arguments between Gisela Bock and Claudia Koonz over the latter's book *Mothers in the Fatherland: Women, the Family and Nazi Politics* (New York: St. Martin's Press, 1987). See my review essay "Feminist Debates About Women and National Socialism," *Gender and History* 3 (Autumn 1991): 350—58.

15. For further references see the (different) German language version of this article, "Eine Frage des Schweigens: Die Vergewaltigung deutscher Frauen durch Besatzungssoldaten. Zum historischen Hintergrund von Helke Sanders Film BeFreier und Befreite," *Frauen und Film* 54/55 (April 1994): 15—28.

16. Deutsche Wochenschau no. 755/10/1945. Sander's film uses clips from this newsreel of a radio reporter interviewing German women about rapes committed by Soviet "bestial hordes." See also nos. 754/9/1945 and 739/46/1944.

17. See Susan Brownmiller's discussion in *Against Our Will: Men, Women and Rape* (New York: Simon & Schuster, 1975), 70—71.

18. This terrifying image obviously has a long lineage not limited to memories of World War II. For a specific reference in this context, see Ingrid Strobl's response to Sander's film, "Wann begann das Grauen?" *Konkret* (September 1992): 55. There is no reliable comparative data on rapes committed by the *Wehrmacht* because, whereas rape by German soldiers on the western front was generally severely punished, "In the Soviet Union, however, we no longer hear of soldiers being tried, let alone executed, for acts of violence and plunder against Soviet citizens." See Omer Bartov, *Hitler's Army: Soldiers, Nazis, and War in the Third Reich* (New York: Oxford University Press, 1991), 70. See also the recent film *Mein Krieg*, in which German veterans talk about their experiences on the eastern front.

19. See (among many sources) John Erickson, *The Road to Berlin: Stalin's War with Germany*, vol. 2 (London: Weidenfeld and Nicolson, 1983), 512; Omer Bartov, *The Eastern Front 1941—45: German Troops and the Barbarization of Warfare* (New York: St. Martin's Press, 1986), and Richard Evans, *In Hitler's Shadow: West German Historians and the Attempt to Escape from the Nazi Past* (New York: Pantheon, 1989), chapter 2.

20. Erickson, *Road to Berlin*, ibid., 603.

21. Ilya Ehrenburg, *The War: 1941—1945*. Vol. 5: *Of Men, Years—Life* (Cleveland: World Publishing, 1964), trans. Tatiana Shenunina in collaboration with Yvonne Kapp, 175. See also Erika M. Hoerning, "Frauen als Kriegsbeute. Der Zwei-Fronten Krieg. Beispiele aus Berlin," in *Wir kriegen jetzt andere Zeiten. Auf der Suche nach der Erfahrung des Volkes in antifaschistischen Ländern. Lebensgeschichte und Sozialkultur im Ruhrgebiet 1930 bis 1960*, vol. 3, ed. Lutz Niethammer and Alexander von Plato (Berlin: Verlag J.H.W. Dietz Nachf., 1985), 327—46.

22. Sterilization was recommended as a follow-up. Barch (Koblenz), Schumacher collection 399, RMI, September 19, 1940, secret memo to health offices and local governments. I am grateful to Gabriele Czarnowski for sending me copies of these materials.

23. RMI to RMJ, express letter, Berlin, February 26, 1945, in Barch(Koblenz) R22/5008.

24. Michael Wieck, *Zeugnis vom Untergang Königsbergs. Ein "Geltungsjude" berichtet* (Heidelberg: Heidelberger Verlagsanstalt und Druckerei, 1990), 261.

25. Margaret Boveri, *Tage des Überlebens: Berlin 1945* (Munich: Piper, 1985, first published 1968), 121—22, 126.

26. Inge Deutschkron, *Ich trug den gelben Stern* (Munich: Deutscher Taschenbuch Verlag, 1987), 179—81.

27. Anne-Marie Durand-Wever, *Als die Russen kamen: Tagebuch einer Berliner Ärztin.* Unpublished diary, with kind permission of Dr. Madeleine Durand-Noll.

28. Anonymous, *Eine Frau in Berlin: Tagebuchaufzeichnungen* (Geneva and Frankfurt: Helmut Kossodo Verlag, 1959), 78; in English, *A Woman in Berlin*, with an introduction by C.W. Ceram, trans. James Stern (New York: Harcourt Brace, 1954). Uncertainty about authorship and authenticity notwithstanding, the language used and the experiences reported are consistent with other reports.

29. Anne-Marie Durand-Wever, "Mit den Augen einer Ärztin. Zur Kontroverse zwischen Prof. Nachtsheim und Dr. Volbracht," *Berliner Ärzteblatt* 83 (1970), offprint, n.p.n.

30. For example, from November 8, 1945, until February 1, 1946, 7 to 9 months after the height of sexual violence in April/May 1945, of the 253 pregnancies approved for termination, 4 were in the first to second month, 34 in the second month, 26 in the second to third month, 87 in the third month, 15 in the third to fourth month, 38 in the fourth month, 4 in the fourth to fifth month, 22 in the fifth month, 3 in the fifth to sixth month, 15 in the sixth month, 1 in the sixth to seventh month, 6 in the seventh month, and 1 in the seventh to eighth month. LAB Rep. 214/2814/220 (Bezirksamt Neukölln). See also Rep. 214/2814/ 221/1–2, 2740/156.

31. See (Probst) Heinrich Gruber, *Erinnerungen nach sieben Jarhzehnten* (Cologne: Kiepenheuer and Witsch, 1971). The alacrity with which German and occupation officials turned to abortion as an obvious remedy contrasts sharply, for example, with the French response to reports of rape by German soldiers in the First World War. See the excellent article by Ruth Harris, "The 'Child of the Barbarian': Rape, Race and Nationalism in France During the First World War," *Past and Present* 141 (November 1993): 170—206.

32. Unpublished diary, Dr. Franz Vollnhals. By kind permission of Mrs. Itta Vollnhals.

33. See Michael Burleigh and Wolfgang Wippermann, *The Racial*

State: Germany 1933—1945 (Cambridge: Cambridge University Press, 1991), 263.

34. See especially Ingrid Schmidt-Harzbach, "Eine Woche im April. Berlin 1945. Vergewaltigung als Massenschicksal," *Feministische Studien 5* (1984): 51—62, and Hoerning, "Frauen als Kriegsbeute."

35. All depositions quoted from LAB Rep. 214/2814/220.

36. Deutschkron, *Ich trug den gelben Stern*, op. cit., 178.

37. LAB Rep. 214/2814.

38. Durand-Wever in *Proceedings of the International Congress on Population and World Resources in Relation to the Family*, August 1948, Cheltenham, England (London: H. K. Lewis and Co., n.d.), 103.

39. *Eine Frau in Berlin*, 138.

40. See Wolfgang Leonhardt, *Child of the Revolution* (Chicago: Regnery, 1958); Naimark, *The Russians in Germany*, op. cit.,120—21; Schmidt-Harzbach, "Eine Woche im April," op. cit., 51—65.

41. I borrow the term "remasculinization" from Robert Moeller; he refers to Susan Jeffords, *The Remasculinization of America: Gender and the Vietnam War* (Bloomington: Indiana University Press, 1989).

42. Rape victims were not completely ignored by the Federal Republic. In the 1950s, some women in the West were minimally compensated, not for rapes, but in the form of support payments for any living children that had resulted. See BArch(Koblenz) 189 (Federal Ministry for Family and Social Welfare) 6858 and especially 6863 for records of children of rape.

43. See, among many sources, the massive documentation of Soviet crimes (prominently including rape) against Germans, gathered in the 1950s by the West German Ministry for the Displaced and Refugees (*Vertriebene und Flüchtlinge*), *Ostdokumentation*, Barch (Koblenz). American references include James Burke, *The Big Rape* (Frankfurt: Friedrich Rudl Verleger Union, 1951), and Cornelius Ryan, *The Last Battle* (London: Collins, 1966); for the GDR, see Konrad Wolf's DEFA film, *Ich war neunzehn* (1968).

(Courtesy of the Chisholm Gallery, Wamsutta Mills, New Bedford, MA)

Figure. 9 Women's Army Corps recruitment poster.

NINE

The Lesbian Threat
Within the World War II Women's Army Corps

Leisa D. MEYER

After her visit with the New Zealand women's army corps in 1944, American Women's Army Corps Captain Ethel Hoffman reported:

> The wisdom of the Director's emphasis on maintaining femininity was certainly stressed. Apparently nothing has been done along that line and the masculine characteristics of some of their leaders, added to the natural tendency of regimentation, probably have influenced the women to adopt mannish haircuts, long strides, etc. It...has been responsible, I think, for many of the depreciating [sic] comments I heard made by some of the civilians I met.[1]

Understanding the construction of female homosexuality within the Women's Army Corps (WAC)[2] during World War II requires analysis of the tensions between masculinity and femininity that shaped the construction of the "lesbian threat" within the corps. In other words, one must address the relationship between gender and sexuality contained within the public connections between female soldiers, "mannish" Wacs, and lesbians. While historians have analyzed the respective challenges gay men and lesbians posed to the military, they have not addressed the precarious position of women within the U.S. Army, either as a group or as individuals. Gay men were perceived as a threat to the military because they were homosexual, but their presence did not endanger *men's* position within the military generally; joining the military reinforced men's claim to a "masculine" identity that was presumed to be a heterosexual one as well. In contrast, accusations of lesbianism within the WAC were the apotheosis of cultural anxieties over women's entrance into the military, the seeming renunciation of feminine values for the embrace of the masculine, and threatened the legitimacy of all "female soldiers."[3]

During World War II public anxieties about "mannish" women were part of broader cultural concerns with female sexual agency. Thus, in a culture increasingly anxious about women's sexuality in general, and homosexuality in particular, the formation of a sex-segregated women's unit within an otherwise wholly male institution sparked a storm of public speculation as to the potential breakdown of heterosexual norms and sexual morality. These concerns focused on the potentially "masculinizing" effect the army might have on women, and especially on the disruptive influence the WAC would have on sexual standards.[4] The lesbian was the epitome of the sexually autonomous woman, not even requiring a male presence to satisfy her sexual desire. Assumptions of predilection, however, rather than individual acts of homosexuality were most critical overall in the public discourse addressing the lesbian "threat" in the Women's Army Corps. A woman's expressed desire to join the military could in itself be cause for suspicion, because "real women" would not want to be "soldiers" at all.

Consequently, articulated fears of the kind of woman who might flourish in a martial environment, regardless of suspicion of particular sexual behaviors, were rife with allusions to lesbianism and followed the corps from its inception. Jack Kofoed, a reporter for the *Miami Florida News*, could imagine no "female soldiers" other than "the naked Amazons...and the queer damozels of the isle of Lesbos."[5] Another female reporter, pleasantly surprised at the appointment of the "feminine" Oveta Culp Hobby to head the women's corps, wrote, "Left to guess, most of us would have said that if ever a woman's army got under way in this country a man or an unmarried woman with worlds of experience and a *Gertrude Stein haircut* [author's emphasis] would direct it."[6]

Within the WAC the issue of female masculinity or "mannishness" became one of the major frameworks within which issues of lesbianism were addressed. Women's entrance into the military and their assumed usurpation of men's duties also became a symbol of women claiming traditionally male power. Fears that the WAC would either attract or produce lesbians were in part generated by what historian Esther Newton has called the "fusion of masculinity, feminist aspirations, and lesbianism."[7] The connection between mannishness, female power, and lesbianism was also made by the WAC director, Colonel Oveta Hobby, in a postwar interview in which she drew an analogy between women's claim to suffrage and women's entrance into the military: "Just as a startled public was once sure that woman's suffrage would make women unwomanly, so the thought of 'woman soldiers' caused some people to assume that WAC units would be hotbeds of perversion."[8] As WAC historian Mattie Treadwell recalled, during World War II there was a "public impression that a women's corps would be the ideal breeding ground for [homosexuality]" because of the "mistaken" popular belief that "any woman who was masculine in appearance or dress" was a homosexual.[9]

The nonoverlapping categories of "woman" and "soldier" informed popular connections between lesbianism and women's entrance into the military. Cultural associations between "masculine" women and female homosexuality formed the basis for suspicions that at least some female soldiers would be lesbian.[10] Within this framework a woman's entrance into the WAC and her donning of a masculine style of dress seemed a clear example of cross-gender behavior and therefore a possible indication of lesbianism.[11] Although contemporary psychiatric wisdom was slowly moving away from connections between "mannishness" in women and homosexuality, prevailing popular attitudes still linked the two, and the "mannish" woman became the public symbol of the social/sexual category "lesbian."[12]

The image of the "mannish woman" was not only imposed by the medical establishment, but was also in part embraced and re-created by lesbians as a means to assert an explicitly sexual identity. Historian Esther Newton has characterized some female homosexuals' adoption of male images in the early twentieth-century as a mode of breaking through nineteenth-century assumptions about the sexless nature of women and offering an alternative, sexual vision of women's relationships with one another.[13] Furthermore, in Madeline Davis and Liz Kennedy's study of working-class lesbian communities in the mid-twentieth century, the authors suggest that by manipulating the hierarchical distinction between male and female and masculinity and femininity, butch women and their femme partners found a way of challenging heterosexual hegemony and publicly expressing their love for one another.[14] Within this context, "mannish" or butch women and butch/femme dyadic relationships within the WAC were distinct targets of hostility, accusations, and discharge proceedings, and simultaneously formed the foundation of visible lesbian communities in the women's corps.

Not all lesbians, however, were considered equally threatening; class and cultural divisions made some same-sex female relationships more acceptable than others. While butch/femme couples were the most recognizable lesbians during the 1940s, historian Leila Rupp has argued that their culture defined only one tier of a class system of relationships between women that existed in the twentieth-century. Rupp suggests that while butch/femme was a largely working-class phenomenon, it was paralleled by the continuation of traditions of "romantic friendships" between white middle-class and upper-class women.[15]

Cultural perceptions of butch/femme women and their less visible middle-class and upper-class counterparts helped define both the spectrum of lesbian relationships during this period and the limits of public tolerance of same-sex female affiliations. The use of degeneration theory by Richard von Kraft-Ebbing and Havelock Ellis to describe different categories of homosexuals formed the basis for some of these judgments. Both Kraft-Ebbing and Ellis labeled "masculine" women as the most degenerate lesbians, while Ellis went on to develop a continuum marking female "romantic friendships" as the least degenerate.[16] Thus, although female "romantic friendships" came under stricter scrutiny throughout the twentieth-century, many white middle and upper-class women forming same-sex relationships were culturally perceived as sexually respectable.[17] They were able to do so largely because they structured their relationships in relation to contemporary standards of white, middle-class, sexual morality, including their deemphasis of explicitly sexual components in their ties to other women.

At the same time, butch working-class lesbians were the subject of hostility and criminal charges. The differential treatment of butch/femme women vis-à-vis those women involved in "romantic friendships" paralleled assumptions as to the class-based nature of heterosexual behaviors.   Contemporary Euro-American middle- and upper-class cultural attitudes toward working-class people ascribed to them a more vulgar and obvious sexuality and assumed their greater sexual immorality. Both the greater visibility and assumptions about sexual aggressiveness contributed to the general hostility toward butch women. In the same manner, assumptions as to the inherent sexual respectability of white middle- and upper-class women were part of the greater tolerance shown their relationships with one another.

The formal and informal procedures for dealing with "suspected" lesbians within the women's corps were consistent with this larger framework and supported WAC leaders' overall emphasis on the recruitment of white middle-class women into the WAC. "Romantic friendships" were often "tolerated," although not encouraged; so long as they remained invisible to the public they were not considered a threat to the larger aims of the WAC sexual regulatory system, which defined threats to the public legitimacy of the corps as the primary criterion for punishing sexual misbehavior. Rooting out lesbians who maintained their "femininity" and did not call attention to themselves would have made the "lesbian problem" more visible to the public than the WAC leadership desired.[18]

"FEMALE SOLDIERS" AS CROSS-DRESSERS

In response to public concerns about female homosexuality within the women's corps, WAC leaders created a framework in which "masculine" appearance and behavior, not only sexual acts between women, were the key criteria for defining the "lesbian threat" within the corps. Servicewomen's position within these debates can be viewed through the metaphor of the "cross-dresser," a "woman" assuming a "masculine" identity, by embracing the role of soldier and the male garb that went with it. But unlike the cross-dresser, who might "pass" without being discovered, GI Jane's secret was "out" and Wacs, whether heterosexual or homosexual, were forced to negotiate within cultural and medical frameworks that viewed their desires to enter the army and their role within the WAC as possible evidence of lesbianism.

Public fears that female soldiers would become "masculinized" or that a women's corps would attract "mannish" women were in part supported by the military's acceptance of contemporary psychiatric theories naming gender inversion as one of the major criterion for distinguishing lesbians. WAC psychiatrist Major Albert Preston, for instance, contended that women's desire to enter the military was in itself proof of their "masculine" identification.[19] Psychiatrists like Preston linked cross-gender behavior in women, including their aspirations to "male" occupations and/or adoption of male dress with sexual "confusion," a code word for rejection of femininity and heterosexuality. As a result, the "mannish woman" came to signify the "lesbian" because her behavior, job, and/or appearance manifested elements designated as exclusively masculine.[20] Within this framework, military women's masculine appearance, as defined by the uniforms they wore, and their movement into an institution that defined American manhood, seemed clear cause for alarm.[21]

WAC appearance played a crucial role in public accusations of lesbianism and informed the responses of the WAC Administration to allegations that the military "masculinized" women. In particular, the WAC uniform was the focus of constant public criticism during the war. Public opinion surveys addressing the WAC made it clear that many civilians felt that the WAC uniform was the most "unfeminine" and "unattractive" of all the services.[22] The masculine appearance of the WAC uniforms was due in large part to the fact that the Philadelphia Quartermaster's Depot for most of the war based its patterns and sizes for women's attire on male models.[23] Consequently, the WAC uniforms simply could not compete with the tailored WAVES uniforms which were available at women's clothing stores. Navy women could purchase their uniforms, and be individually fitted for them as opposed to their army counterparts, who were issued military garments based on regulation sizes.[24]

In a 1944 segment of the popular military camp comic strip "Male Call," the strip's creator, Milton Caniff, explored the interaction between his femme fatale protagonist, "Miss Lace," and a WAC private. The segment's title, "Know Which Army You're In" aptly described this cartoon's four-frame content as "Miss Lace" awakens from an evening's sexual encounter and is startled by the sound of a female voice in bed beside her. Somewhat shocked, she stares at the uniform hanging on the chair next to the bed as the WAC private in bed with her asks her what's wrong. "Lace" replies, "They should have more distinctive insignia on those WAC uniforms!"[25]

Although this particular segment was censored by the army and therefore not distributed to military camp newspapers, it suggests in a humorous fashion the correlations between masculine appearance and female homosexuality, in particular the explicit connections between women in uniform and lesbianism. The predicament of "Miss Lace" arises from a case of mistaken identity—her assumption that army uniforms are worn only by men. Caniff's cartoon suggests that WACs wearing army uniforms were "passing" in a very concrete sense, if they can be mistaken for men by "Miss Lace," a perennial male GI favorite. Moreover, Caniff's casual treatment of the lesbian Wac also implies that the presence of lesbians within the women's corps was well known.

Throughout the war the WAC administration made attempts to create a "feminine" look for female soldiers. Brightly colored accessories, including scarves and gloves, were added to the women's uniform and off-duty dresses were designed, all in an effort to make Wacs look less "masculine."[26] The WAC director and her staff also encouraged the creation of informal policies that cautioned against the adoption of "mannish hairstyles" while simultaneously advocating the development of a "feminine" WAC pompadour courtesy of Elizabeth Arden salons.[27]

The controversy surrounding the issuance of trousers to female soldiers exemplified the connections between male attire and male power, and between mannishness and lesbianism. "Wearing the pants," like "wearing the uniform," was a symbol of women's usurpation of the types of power and status conventionally associated with men, and servicewomen donning trousers generated anxieties among male military personnel as to their own positions and authority. In the European Theater of Operations trousers never became an official part of the field uniform. Pants were suggested as part of the WAC uniform in Europe because they were warmer and were superior to skirts in preserving servicewomen's health during European winters. They were rejected, however, because of the adverse reactions of male military personnel and commanders. Enlisted men and male officers complained that the experimental "trouser outfits" initially issued to Wacs were "bulky...unbecoming...and could not be tailored to the female figure," making it difficult to distinguish between male and female soldiers.[28] One civilian woman urged the WAC to adopt trousers as part of the official women's uniform, but also suggested that they be distinguished from those worn by men by a "slightly different shade of color." She believed this would "help ease the mental anguish and embarrassment of men," by assuring a distinction between female and male soldiers that she feared would otherwise be perceptible only by "looking at their hair." She concluded that "properly handled the WAC members could eliminate any feeling on the part of the male officers and men that they [women] were trying to wear the pants."[29]

The sight of female soldiers in trousers also highlighted the "problem" of female masculinity. Wacs in New Guinea adopted makeshift trousered uniforms and wore them throughout the war because they provided much better protection than skirts against heat rash and insect bites endemic to the area. In June 1945, however, Colonel Hobby issued orders requiring Wacs serving in New Guinea to wear skirts, though most enlisted women opposed the plan.[30] Throughout the war the WAC director went on record against the adoption of slacks, saying that she preferred women to wear skirts "to avoid rough or masculine appearance which would cause unfavorable public comment."[31] The efforts of Colonel Hobby and her staff to "femininize" the appearance of female soldiers, including the prohibition of "mannish" hairstyles and pants, were aimed at subverting the connections between the masculine aspects of some women within the WAC and the presence of lesbians and in effect created one set of parameters for identifying and eliminating lesbians from the women's corps.

CREATING AND IMPLEMENTING WAC POLICIES ON HOMOSEXUALITY

Most WAC policies that affected lesbians were not specifically addressed toward female homosexuals but fell within the larger WAC regulatory system addressing female sexuality in general. The predominant concern of this design, based in corps regulations regulating women's "conduct," was to portray women within the corps as sexually respectable and to eliminate those whose behavior or appearance undermined this goal. Within this paradigm, sexual agency in general was defined as a threat to the legitimacy of the women's corps, no matter *who* was the object choice of the female sexual actor. Wacs who acted on their sexual desires were violating both gender and sexual norms as the potentially "masculinizing" effect of the military on women was defined not only as women's taking on male characteristics, appearance, and power, but also as women's adopting an aggressive, independent, and "masculine" sexuality.[32] Throughout the war, Colonel Hobby's efforts to address the "problem" of female masculinity were aimed at women whose dress, demeanor, and/or behavior linked them with the popular cultural stereotype of the "mannish lesbian" who was by definition a sexual agent. Both of these frameworks had affected lesbians within the corps.[33]

The procedures developed by WAC officials for evaluating applicants to the corps did not specifically address lesbians until the war was near an end. Because the WAC was a volunteer organization whose requirements for enlistment were much higher than those used by the army to rate men, military leaders and psychiatrists affiliated with the women's corps believed that the process of self-selection would be sufficient for screening out "undesirables."[34] Yet, while no formal system for identifying lesbians existed, the WAC *did* develop and use screening procedures that were partially aimed at detecting and rejecting lesbian applicants to the corps. This informal setup focused on class background, education, personality, and behavior and worked to eliminate women who demonstrated characteristics culturally associated with female homosexuality. WAC policies for selecting women for the first Officer Candidate class and for subsequent officer training included criteria for the exclusion of women whose manner was "rough or coarse," whose build was "stocky or shapeless," and whose demeanor, including dress and "voice type," was "masculine."[35] While these policies did not name *lesbians* as persons to be refused admission to the corps, WAC leaders' efforts to eliminate "masculine" women from the corps most likely resulted in some female homosexuals being denied entrance.

Policies that explicitly identified lesbians as persons to be rejected developed slowly over the course of the war and were usually part of broader strategies aimed at rejecting any woman whose behavior suggested sexual deviance. In November 1942, the director's office issued a memo to the adjutant general that addressed the "enrollment of auxiliaries…of doubtful reputation" and called for increased emphasis on the "examination of enrollees" in order to "keep out those individuals who are known to have very bad traits and habits."[36] The "questionable moral standards" of the enrollees described within subsequent reports to the adjutant general were defined in large part by references to heterosexual promiscuity and homosexuality. In response to Colonel Hobby's request, the adjutant general issued confidential instructions to all service commands ordering them to revise their recruiting procedures to include inquiries into the applicants' "local reputation." These instructions also listed nine "undesirable habits and traits of character" that recruiting officers should look for when interviewing applicants, including "promiscuous association with men" and "homosexual tendencies."[37]

The adjutant general's "confidential instructions" to army commanders within the U.S. were the first to contain explicit references to homosexuals as individuals that should be excluded from the corps.   Numerous euphemistic references to lesbians, however, were used as benchmarks by WAC recruiters in screening applicants during the same period. WAC recruiters, for example,   were asked to intensify their inquiries into applicants' motivations for joining the women's corps, in order to "get under the patriotic motive." One question recruiters were encouraged to ask was if part of the applicant's motivation was to "be with other girls." This question was aimed at "catching" women of "questionable" character, in particular, lesbians.[38]   Simultaneously, representatives of the WAC's civilian advertising agency recommended changes in the WAC recruiting pamphlet that would serve to deemphasize the all-female aspects of the WAC environment.[39]

In developing subsequent screening procedures that addressed female homosexuals Colonel Hobby received needed support for her efforts when the U.S. Surgeon General appointed Major Margaret Craighill to oversee the health and welfare of the women's corps.   Major Craighill, a psychiatrist, believed strongly that a psychiatric examination of prospective Wacs was necessary to determine women's fitness for admission to the corps.   Their combined efforts resulted in a WAC Selection Conference held July 27—29, 1944, with the intent to improve screening procedures. The conference yielded a new WAC Selection Policy that required recruiting officers to reject applicants when there was evidence of "promiscuity or behavior difficulties" and included provisions for army or WAC psychiatrists' evaluations of recruiters' reports before a candidate was enlisted.[40]

The most explicit antilesbian policy of the war came on the heels of this conference when the War Department issued specific instructions to guide military psychiatrists in their evaluation of prospective recruits. This manual (TB MED 100), entitled "WAC Recruiting Station Neuropsychiatric Examination,"   gave   medical   examiners   general background on the difficulties servicewomen might encounter and provided a list of specific criteria for rejection. A section defining the "object of neuropsychiatric examination" warned psychiatrists to "be on guard against the homosexual who may see in the WAC an opportunity to indulge her sexual perversity...and cause no end of difficulty."   Although offering no specific criteria for identifying lesbians, the authors did suggest that an applicant's appearance was key to such a diagnosis, noting that "homosexuals are quickly detected in the WAC" and "they should be excluded at the time of examination."[41]

WAC policies addressing homosexuality within the corps, like the screening procedures, were fashioned as part of the general measures for handling sexual agency of any kind.   These informal procedures were described in the sex hygiene course created by Major Craighill. The lectures and pamphlet that defined this course were intended to instruct officers in the "proper" modes of handling cases of venereal disease, pregnancy, heterosexual sexual relationships, and homosexuality as they arose in their commands. The entire program was designed to discourage actions that might bring negative publicity to the WAC. Officers were told to deal with issues of homosexuality in much the same manner as heterosexual promiscuity, advocating guidance and informal measures to control servicewomen's behavior, with discharge used only as a last recourse.[42] The pamphlet explained that WAC officers should expect some degree of homosexuality within their commands but advised them to handle such occurrences with "fairness and tolerance." They were further informed that, "if there is any likelihood of doubt, it is better to be generous in your outlook, and to assume that everyone is innocent until definitely proved otherwise."[43]

While this model suggests an extremely tolerant attitude toward homosexuality within the WAC, the behavior, appearance, and class background of individual lesbian actors were often used as criteria for determining which lesbians would be deemed threatening to the corps. WAC policies encouraging tolerance for same-sex relationships were aimed at those associations that stayed within the nonsexual rubric of female "romantic friendships"— relationships between middle-class, "feminine" women that, even if erotic, were not visibly sexual.[44]

Although the information distributed to WAC officers on how to identify homosexuals within their units was full of contradictions, it is clear that "mannish" appearance and behavior were used as the major criteria for identifying female homosexuals in the corps. While the creators of the sex hygiene course cautioned against conflating "mannishness" and homosexuality, explaining that "many homosexuals are indeed the very opposite in appearance of masculinity," they also described female homosexuals in ways that explicitly linked the appearance of "latent masculine characteristics" in women with lesbianism and continued to refer to lesbians as women who "attempt to take on characteristics of the opposite sex."[45]

The basis for the WAC's supposedly "tolerant" framework for dealing with homosexuality lay in WAC leaders' concerns with the image of the corps. Colonel Hobby felt that the adverse publicity generated by investigations and court-martial of lesbians within the WAC could only hurt the corps. Thus, while army regulations provided for the undesirable discharge of homosexuals, discharge proceedings specifically on the grounds of homosexuality were rarely initiated against lesbians in the WAC. In fact, WAC officers were warned to consider this action only in the most extreme of situations.[46]   Colonel Hobby felt that such proceedings would only result in intensive public scrutiny and disapproval of the women's corps. Instead, WAC leaders suggested that officers use informal methods of control, including shifting personnel and room assignments and transferring individuals to different posts. On several posts informal WAC policies prohibited women from dancing in couples in public.[47]

WAC directives encouraging less public methods for dealing with lesbians were joined by explicit prohibitions against witchhunting. Prohibitions against witchhunting, however, should not be interpreted as reflective of sympathy or understanding of lesbians. Because lesbianism was so visible a threat to the legitimacy of the corps, "witchhunting" was in itself understood to undermine the WAC publicly to a greater degree than the persistence of lesbian practices among some individuals. Officers were warned of the adverse effect rumor and innuendo might have on the reputation of the corps and the morale of the women involved, and were thereby ordered to have "definite evidence" before proceeding against any "suspected homosexual."[48]   Yet female officers sometimes acted on suspicion only, caught between instructions to seek the "prompt removal" of "active homosexuals" who were "addicted to the practice" and the knowledge that "sufficient evidence" to accomplish this was often "very hard to obtain."[49]

Some heterosexual Wacs themselves, moreover, entered the army with sufficient fears of "masculine women" and lesbians to contribute significantly to the explosiveness of public accusations. The information given to officers concerning the appropriate means of addressing homosexuality was not passed on to enlisted women, who occasionally acted on their own suspicions concerning their peers. "Any girl with marked masculine tendencies, any two girls with close friendships," commented Major Craighill, "were under suspicion and were practically convicted by a whispering campaign, with little opportunity to defend themselves." Craighill felt that the tendency of some Wacs to spread "false rumors" that might lead to witchhunts was "frequently a worse problem" than the actual presence of lesbians.[50]

Given the difficulty of obtaining "definite evidence" of a servicewoman's lesbianism, suspicion based on gossip and rumor was sometimes enough to eliminate enlisted women and officers from the WAC. Because of the many strictures on servicewomen's behavior, lesbian soldiers, unlike their gay male counterparts, were vulnerable to charges more easily proved than homosexuality, such as "drinking to excess" or being drunk in public. Thus, in the women's corps, where female soldiers' conduct was the subject of constant scrutiny and comment, Wacs whose "homosexual tendencies" or "masculine" appearance might be insufficient to convict them in a court-martial proceeding could find themselves discharged for other socially "deviant" behaviors. In the case of Lieutenant Martha B. Hayes,[51] "suspicion of homosexuality" was a sufficient reason for her superiors to "encourage" her to resign her commission, although the investigating officer reported that there was "not sufficient evidence to support disciplinary action."[52] WAC officials' attempts to punish Lieutenant Hayes for her lesbian desire went beyond pressuring her to leave the service; WAC and Army officials tried to ensure that Hayes would receive a dishonorable discharge, although there was insufficient proof of her homosexuality to guarantee such an outcome in a formal hearing. To accomplish this, WAC investigators asked Lieutenant Hayes to resign her commission "for the good of the service." Officers who tendered their resignations with this condition were released from the WAC, but their discharge was "other than honorable." The dishonorable circumstances of their discharge would become a part of their permanent record, affecting future employment opportunities and making them ineligible for veterans benefits. Lieutenant Hayes resisted this attempt to penalize her behavior; although she agreed to resign her commission, she refused to qualify her request and accede to a dishonorable discharge. While some WAC and male army officials recommended refusing her resignation for this reason, the decision of WAC headquarters was that the need to remove her from the WAC "without delay" was the chief priority; she was separated from service under honorable conditions.[53]

Military service provided arenas that offered women both economic autonomy and a social space away from the constraining environments of their home communities, in which they felt freer to explore their sexuality and sexual desires.[54] Some women discovered their sexual attraction for women during their wartime military service. Others joined the women's corps to be with other women, already certain of the direction of their desires. Still others chose to act as heterosexuals. Women joining the WAC formed their own attitudes toward homosexuality and acted on their sexual choices. In doing so, they were all forced to negotiate within the regulatory framework created by Colonel Hobby and the WAC administration, a framework that, while condemning women's sexual agency generally, also continued to characterize homosexuality as the most sexually deviant behavior for women.

Although servicewomen, unlike their male counterparts, did not have to deal with explicit questions about homosexuality in the screening process, many found themselves nonetheless grappling with issues of homosexuality raised by the rumors surrounding the corps and the presence of lesbians in their units.[55] Ex-Wac Martha Ward recalled that, "when we knew of it [homosexuality], it was talked about but quietly. For many of us it was our first knowledge of it." "I didn't know what the word [homosexual] meant until I went in the service," commented another former enlisted woman.[56] For some women, this "new" awareness generated questions about their own sexuality or led to a tolerant attitude toward sexual diversity. For others, it gave them a language of heterosexual privilege with which to expand their own authority within the confines of the women's corp.

While some historians have argued that even servicewomen who weren't lesbians tended to treat homosexuality with a "who cares" attitude, in fact heterosexual Wacs' responses to lesbianism fell along a continuum ranging from condemnation to acceptance.[57] Certainly there were heterosexual servicewomen who were sympathetic or supportive of lesbian friends. Remembering with regret the undesirable discharge of a lesbian friend, Ex-Wac Bessie Weaver recalled "a secretarial friend who came and cried on my shoulder after having to serve as court reporter at a court-martial for a woman we had known and liked so much."[58] Some Wacs claimed that "no one really cared" whether a woman was homosexual. Other servicewomen, however, attested to a general atmosphere of distrust at some posts, in which even a rumor about alleged lesbianism was assumed to threaten the status of the WAC unit as a whole, thereby encouraging harsh control or condemnation of suspected lesbians. "Homosexuality was a problem whenever it was believed to exist," claimed former Lieutenant Colonel Anne Clark. "The members of a unit were shamed by even a rumor of it within their unit and very conscious of public rumors about servicewomen's characters."[59]

The greatest challenges to lesbians' relationships and positions within the corps were presented by army and WAC investigations of "suspected" homosexuals. These inquiries, both formal and informal, produced some of the most trying situations for lesbian soldiers. During these investigations, army and WAC officials used a variety of coercive methods to obtain proof of suspected homosexuality. One of the most effective means employed by WAC officials was to pressure enlisted women to inform authorities about other lesbians in their unit. In May 1943, white WAC Lieutenant Georgia Joyce began an informal investigation of suspected homosexuals at the WAC installation in Daytona Beach, Florida. According to two white WAC first sergeants who were undesirably discharged as a result of Joyce's inquiries, the lieutenant had approached them several times and asked if they would help her substantiate some rumors and gossip concerning the involvement of officers and noncoms in homosexual activities. The sergeants claimed that they were "embarrassed and surprised" by Joyce's questions but thought that she had singled them out because they were familiar with both past and present personnel at Daytona Beach. Sergeant Joan Pound also contended that when she asked Lieutenant Joyce why she wanted such "gossip" and if she was going to "use it against someone," Joyce became angry and defensive and said that she wanted to know for her own "personal information and to satisfy her own curiosity." Pound said that Joyce asked them to disregard her greater rank and frequently sought them out for ostensibly social reasons. During these encounters Joyce "continually and persistently approached the subject at every opportunity." Obviously, Lieutenant Joyce attempted to "befriend" the sergeants in order to gain their trust with the intent of encouraging them to incriminate other women at Daytona Beach.[60]

At this point in her informal investigation, Joyce took the evidence she had gathered to army regimental headquarters and was given official sanction for her activities. Once Lieutenant Joyce received this authority, she brought four women up on charges of homosexuality, including Sergeant Pound and Sergeant Norma Chambers. The sergeants claimed that their arrest was due to their involvement in a "framed trap" with two female officers. After their arrest, they were confined in separate hotels for 11 days and not allowed to speak to anyone except the investigating officer. They felt this situation deprived them of the opportunity to vindicate themselves while giving Lieutenant Joyce the chance to "strengthen her case." Both women believed that Lieutenant Joyce had violated their rights and argued that her sole motive in the investigation was "personal gain."[61]

While it is impossible to ascertain Lt. Joyce's motives for launching this investigation, the results are clear. Joyce was promoted and transferred to a prestigious posting in the inspector general's office; Sergeants Pound and Chambers were undesirably discharged for "habits and traits of character that serve to render their retention in the service undesirable." Yet Pound and Chambers clearly believed that they were entitled to better treatment by the WAC and deserved more than disgrace and dismissal. They wrote their congressman, outlined their situation, and asked him to pressure the army into reopening the investigation. In defending themselves, the sergeants incorporated the WAC discourse of toleration, arguing that the situation at Daytona Beach lent itself to "abnormal relationships" and "false allegations" "because of the inactivity and lack of normal social contact." They also claimed that they "could have implicated a lot of people in protecting their character and reputation but chose to uphold the Corps." Despite their efforts, their case was not reopened, and evidence suggests that officials from the WAC and the adjutant general's office did not even reexamine the information given during the court-martial, fearing to stir up unnecessary publicity concerning homosexuality in the women's corps. As a result, Pound and Chambers' desire for reconsideration was denied, while Lieutenant Joyce received a letter from the adjutant general's office complimenting her on "carrying out an undesirable and disagreeable assignment which aided in unearthing an unwholesome situation involving a group of members of the Women's Army Corps."[62]

In a similar situation, African-American servicewoman Frankie Casey wrote to Colonel Hobby, requesting that the director reopen the case that had resulted in her undesirable discharge. Casey, like Sergeants Pound and Chambers, felt that her treatment by the military, especially by WAC officers, was unfair and that she had a right to demand redress. She claimed that while stationed at Fort Bragg she and several other women in her company were ordered by their WAC commanding officer to see the post psychiatrist. His questions indicated to Casey that they had been sent to him "so that he could determine if we were or were not homosexual cases." Several days later Casey was presented with hearing orders and subsequently discharged for homosexuality. According to Casey, her commanding officer, Captain Harriet White, regularly called WAC enlisted women into her quarters and promised them compensation in return for giving her information about other women's homosexuality. Casey also claimed that White forced servicewomen to sign incriminating statements and that during her court-martial one of her friends, Technical Sergeant John Eva Lawrence, "denied she knew anything about the statement she was supposed to have signed." Casey alleged that after her friend's denial, Captain White took Lawrence to the judge advocate's office and "frightened her to death, that if she did not stick to her statement in the case she would be given a dishonorable discharge."[63]

Given the embattled position of the women's corps in general, Captain White's actions reinforced the overall position of WAC administrators that women whose conduct "reflected badly" on the corps should be removed. Her actions may also have signaled her understanding of the precarious situation of African-American women within a largely white organization and reflected her desire to protect that position by eliminating those who posed a threat to it. Her rank as an officer gave her the power to do so. The relationships between African-American officers and enlisted women were often not only scenes of solidarity on the basis of race but also arenas in which conflicts rooted in differential status and rank were negotiated. In her letter to Colonel Hobby, Casey asked that Hobby not "refer" her case to Major Harriet West, the ranking African-American member of the director's headquarters staff, because West and Captain White were friends and "nothing will be done about it." In this light, Casey's appeal to Hobby, like Pound and Chambers' petition to their congressman, can be understood as a desire to gain sympathy and support from someone whose position placed them outside the power structures they believed responsible for their dismissal. For Pound and Chambers, who blamed the WAC and army for their plight, an appeal to civilian authority made sense. For Casey, who considered African-American WAC officers culpable, an entreaty to the white WAC director was equally understandable. Although Pound and Chambers did not succeed in getting their case reopened, their congressman's queries on their behalf warranted a response from the army. In Casey's case, her letter to Hobby resulted in the director forwarding her file and discharge records to the Secretary of War's Discharge Review Board for reevaluation. Unfortunately, there is no evidence as to whether or not her discharge status was changed as a result of this evaluation.[64]

"Undesirable" discharges stigmatized former servicewomen in the eyes of their families and larger communities, denied them all veteran's benefits, and made it difficult for them to get jobs.[65] Most employers required that job applicants who had served in the military bring in their discharge papers as a condition of employment. Undesirable discharges, printed on blue paper, labeled women like Pound, Chambers, and Casey as social misfits, and most employers were unwilling to hire individuals whom the military had deemed unacceptable. As Casey wrote, "I can't get work with this blue paper—to whom do you think I would present it?"[66] This situation most likely affected women who did not have a college education more severely. Even if they wanted to "hide" their military service and their blue discharges, they still needed references from previous employers. More importantly, they could not directly refer to job skills they learned in the military that might have made them more hireable.

While Captain White was depicted by Casey as typical of African-American WAC officers in her behavior toward enlisted women, evidence suggests that other African-American officers were more tolerant of incidences of homosexuality. Captain Charity Adams, commanding officer of the only African-American WAC unit in the European Theater, recalled her reaction to army directives that she and other unit commanders "be alert to homosexual activity." She understood that such relationships probably existed in her unit but also judged suggestions from army headquarters that she make "surprise inspections during the hours when troops were in bed" unnecessary. She believed that as long as her unit performed well, there was no need for her to unduly examine enlisted women's behavior. Her philosophy is captured in her statement: "I cannot swear to the kind of social activity that took place with all the members of the 6888th, but I will swear that the efficient performance of the unit was not impaired."[67]

The construction of the "lesbian threat" in the WAC that I detail above requires we look beyond formal regulations addressing female homosexuality and analyze the many ways in which lesbianism was informally addressed within the women's corps. These more informal and often contradictory procedures were shaped by public concerns about a female presence within a powerful male institution and characterized by an intense focus on female masculinity as *the* marker of "deviant" behavior. While some formal policies, such as those prohibiting "witchhunting," seem to suggest tolerance, characterizing WAC policies as generally tolerant of lesbians misses the extent to which corps leaders targeted "masculine" women and tried to eliminate "suspected" lesbians with the least publicity possible. Through screening procedures focused on excluding "masculine" women and the practice of discharging women whose "homosexuality" was suspected but could not be proven by invoking the more stringent regulations governing Wacs' social behavior, WAC leaders were able to address what they defined as the "lesbian threat" to the corps with a minimum of publicity to the issue. Consequently, understanding the position of lesbians within the World War II Women's Army Corps demands that we situate them, not only like their gay male counterparts as homosexuals in the military, but also, unlike their gay male counterparts, within their precarious site as women within a male military.

NOTES

This article is adapted from Leisa D. Meyer, *Creating G.I. Jane: Sexuality and Power in the World War II Women's Army Corps* (New York: Columbia University Press, 1996), chapter 7.

1.   May 28, 1944, Captain Ethel F. Hoffman, Headquarters USAFISPA, to Lt. Colonel Jessie Pearl Rice, Deputy Director, WAC, Washington, D.C., File: 314.81, Box 57, Series 54, RG 165, NA.
2.   The Women's Army Auxiliary Corps (WAAC) existed from May 1942 to September 1943, when it was replaced by the Women's Army Corps (WAC). Throughout this article I use the acronym WAC to refer to the organization and Wac (lower case) to refer to individuals within the

corps.   In addition, to avoid repetition I use the terms "corps" and "women's corps" interchangeably with WAC.   To avoid confusing terminology, I use the acronym WAC in all discussions of the women's corps during World War II.

3.   In a recent essay, historian Donna Penn argues that much of the historical work on lesbians has been of two types, either a "gendered history that is desexualized or a sexual history that is degendered," the former generated by scholars within the field of women's history, the latter by historians of homosexuality. Donna Penn, "The Meanings of Lesbianism in Post-War America," *Gender & History* 3, no. 2 (Summer 1991): 190—203.

4.   See John D'Emilio and Estelle Freedman, *Intimate Matters: A History of Sexuality in America* (New York: Harper & Row, 1988), 260—261.

5.   Jack Kofoed, *Miami Florida News* (20 May 1942), in Center for Military History Manuscript Files, Mattie Treadwell's Background Files, Box 9, RG 319, NA.

6.   July 13, 1942, Mrs. Walter Ferguson on the appointment of Oveta Culp Hobby as director, WAAC. File: Newspaper Clippings, WAAC 21-40, Box 8, Oveta Culp Hobby Papers, Library of Congress (LC).

7.   Esther Newton, "The Mythic Mannish Lesbian: Radclyffe Hall and the New Woman," in *Signs: The Lesbian Issue*, ed. Estelle B. Freedman, Barbara C. Gelpi, Susan L. Johnson, and Kathleen M. Weston (Chicago: University of Chicago Press, 1982), 16.

8.   Interview of Colonel Oveta Culp Hobby by Joan Younger of the *Ladies Home Journal* . File: *Ladies Home Journal*, Article on WAC, 1952, Box 9, Hobby Papers, LC.

9.   Mattie Treadwell, *The U.S. Army in World War II, Special Studies, The Women's Army Corps* (Washington, D.C.: Office of the Chief of Military History, 1954), 625.

10.   As historian John D'Emilio has observed, the theories of Sigmund Freud, Havelock Ellis, and Richard von Kraft-Ebbing all linked "proper sexual development" to conventional definitions of "femininity" and "masculinity" and described women's deviations from prescribed "feminine" gender norms as one possible sign of female homosexuality. John D'Emilio, *Sexual Politics, Sexual Communities: The Making of a Homosexual Minority in the United States, 1940—1970* (Chicago: University of Chicago Press, 1983), 16—17. See also D'Emilio and Freedman, *Intimate Matters*, op. cit., 193—4.

11.   Medical theories that addressed the female sexual invert in the early twentieth century for the most part named gender inversion as a primary characteristic of female homosexuality.   Although historian

George Chauncey argued in early articles that the issue of sexual object choice came to dominate over gender inversion as a primary criterion for diagnosing a woman as homosexual, it is clear that the "mannish" woman continued as the popular lesbian archetype for most people. Indeed, Chauncey has indicated in later discussions of this issue that the shift from gender inversion to object choice in the discourse on "female deviance" was always confused and never complete. George Chauncey, "From Sexual Inversion to Homosexuality: The Changing Medical Conceptualization of Female Deviance," in *Passion and Power* , ed. Kathy Peiss and Christina Simmons (Philadelphia: Temple University Press, 1988), 87—117.

12. Newton, "The Mythic Mannish Lesbian," op., cit. See also Penn, "The Meanings of Lesbianism," op. cit., for a discussion of this point.

13. Newton, ibid., 7—27.

14.   Elizabeth Lapovsky Kennedy and Madeline Davis, *Boots of Leather, Slippers of Gold: The History of a Lesbian Community* (New York: Routledge, 1993).

15. Leila Rupp, "Imagine My Surprise: Women's Relationships in the 20th Century," in *Hidden from History: Reclaiming the Gay and Lesbian Past*, ed. Martin Duberman, Martha Vicinus, and George Chauncey, Jr. (New York: Penguin Books, 1989), 398. Much of the discussion of lesbians generated within the field of women's history has focused on these "romantic friendships" and women's homosocial networks. See Lillian Faderman, *Surpassing the Love of Men: Romantic Friendship and Love Between Women from the Renaissance to the Present* (New York: Morrow, 1981), Blanche Wiesen Cook, "Historical Denial of Lesbianism," *Radical History Review* 20 (1979): 60—65; Blanche Wiesen Cook, "Women Alone Stir My Imagination," *Signs* 4 (1979): 718—739; and Adrienne Rich, "Compulsory Heterosexuality and Lesbian Existence," in *Powers of Desire*, ed. A. Snitow et al. (New York: Monthly Review, 1983), 177—205.

16. Newton, "The Mythic, Mannish Lesbian," op. cit.,16.

17. Rupp, "Imagine My Surprise," op. cit., 407. Moreover, George Chauncey contends that degeneration theory embodied white, middle-class assumptions concerning the class nature of sexual morality.

18. Laws addressing gender disguise and women's adoption of male dress are far more relevant in analyzing the cultural construction of lesbianism historically than are sodomy laws. The latter have been connected by historians of homosexuality to the emergence of a gay male identity and are especially pertinent to discussions of male homosexuality within the military. Because such laws were rarely used to prosecute lesbians or lesbian sexual acts, historians of homosexuality generally have concluded that criminal law overlooked lesbians. Yet, while lesbian civilians were rarely prosecuted for sexual acts, those who adopted male

dress were subject to criminal charges under urban morals codes for cross-dressing. For examples of works that discuss sodomy laws as the precursor to constructions of homosexuals as a species of people, see Michel Foucault, *The History of Sexuality Vol. 1* (New York: Pantheon, 1978), and Allan Berube, *Coming Out Under Fire: Gay GIs During WWII* (New York: Free Press, 1990). For works dealing with the laws against cross-dressing, see " 'She Even Chewed Tobacco': A Pictorial Narrative of Passing Women in America," in *Hidden from History* , ed. San Francisco Lesbian and Gay History Project,185—87,192, and Marjorie Garber, *Vested Interests: Crossdressing and Cultural Anxiety* (New York: Harper Perennial, 1993).

19. Major Albert Preston, Jr., *History of Psychiatry in the Women's Army Corps* (Spring 1946) 4, File: 700, Box 143, Series 54, RG 165, NA.

20. Newton, "The Mythic Mannish Lesbian," op. cit.; Julie Wheelwright, *Amazons and Military Maids: Women Who Dressed As Men in Pursuit of Life, Liberty and Happiness* (London: Pandora Press, 1989), 153—4.

21. In 1934 German psychologist Magnus Hirschfeld, President of the World League for Sexual Reform, drew a direct connection between women's desire to enter the military and their potential homosexuality. Hirschfeld believed that female soldiers, because they engaged in the "most extreme" cross-gender behavior, were the most confused sexually. Ibid., 153.

22. 8 February 1944, Letter Commanding General Fourth Air Forces to Commanding General Western Flying Training Command, RE: Results of January 1944, Gallup Poll, 249-50, Section V, 4th Air Force Historical Study, #V-4, Box 450.01-13, 1941-45, Vol. 1, Air Force Center for Historical Research, Maxwell Air Force Base, Montgomery, AL. See also, 24 April 1944, Maxson F. Judell to Colonel Hobby, RE: Uniforms, and 21 February 1944, James E. Dunlap to Colonel Hobby, RE: Uniforms, Box 21, Series 54; 8 November 1948, Memo for the Record, From: H.M. Boutell, Major, GSC, Chairman, Subject: Plans and Policy Committee Meeting, 27 October 1948, Item #3 "Discussion: Uniform Consideration," File: WAC Committee Chairman's Book, Box 222, Series 55; All in RG 165, NA; "Reform for a Uniform," *Colliers* 113, no. 2 (June 1944): 82; Treadwell, *U.S. Army in World War II*, op. cit., 158—66.

23. Treadwell, ibid., 156—58.

24. Ibid., 160—61.

25. Milton Caniff, "Know Which Army You're In," in *Male Call Rejects Featuring Miss Lace* , ed. Peter Poplaski (Princeton, WI: Kitchen Sink Press, 1987). "Male Call" was distributed by the Camp Newspaper Service and appeared in over 3,000 military newspapers in the United

States and overseas. I am indebted to Allan Berube for bringing this material to my attention.

26. Historian, WAC Section, Headquarters, Fourth Air Force, 1 January 1944—40 September 1945, 46, Historical Section Files, 249—50, Section V, 4th Air Force Historical Study, #V-4, Box 450.01-13, 1941—45, Vol. 1; 73, Part Two: "Plans and Policies," chapter 2, "Supply," File: Study of the WAC in the ETO, V.I, Box 502.101—3—11 (43-45) ETO, Air Force Center for Historical Research, Maxwell Air Force Base, Montgomery, AL.

27. Berube, *Coming Out Under Fire* , op. cit., 59—61. Correspondence: 19 May—15 October 1943, Elizabeth Arden Corporation on WAAC Hairstyles, File: 062.001, 1942—43, Box 9, Series 54, RG 165, NA.

28. 73, Field Uniform, Part Two: "Plans and Policies", chapter 2, "Supply," File: Study of the WAC in the ETO, V.1, Box 502.101—3—11 (43—45) ETO, Air Force Center for Historical Research, Maxwell Air Force Base, Montgomery, AL.

29. 11 March 1942, Miss Louisa Givogre, Los Angeles, to the Adjutant General, RE: WAAC Uniforms, Box 19, Series 54, RG 165, NA.

30. Historical Record of WAC Detachment, Headquarters, USASOS, June 1945, Historical Record C-2417, D-1, AFWESPAC, Box 7, RG 319, NA.

31. Treadwell, op. cit., 38. Although historian Lillian Faderman has argued that pants and the public acceptance of women wearing them became a symbol of a lesbian "style" in the 1940s, wearing slacks in the WAC was always contested. Lillian Faderman, *Odd Girls and Twilight Lovers: A History of Lesbian Life in Twentieth-Century America* (New York: Columbia University Press, 1991), 126.

32. D'Emilio and Freedman, *Intimate Matters*, op. cit., 260, 288—289; Elaine Tyler May, *Homeward Bound: American Families in the Cold War* (New York: Basic Books, 1988), 69.

33. Army policies addressing male homosexuals and WAC procedures for dealing with lesbianism differed during World War II. Historian Allan Berube has meticulously documented the influence of modern psychiatry on the development of the U.S. Army's antihomosexual apparatus. The most significant change in army policies toward male homosexuality was a movement away from long-standing regulations criminalizing sodomy, and thus punishing identifiable homosexual acts, and toward policies that defined the homosexual soldier as mentally ill and therefore in need of psychiatric treatment and rehabilitation, not imprisonment. Berube contends that this change allowed the military to cast a substantially wider net in screening for homosexuals and thus affected a much larger number

of gay men than had the original sodomy restrictions. Berube, *Coming Out Under Fire*, op. cit., 8—33. It should also be noted that Berube makes clear in his study that this change was not smooth nor complete during the war and that some gay men continued to be imprisoned under the older sodomy regulations.

34. Preston, *History of Psychiatry* , op. cit., 8—10.

35. "Waac News," *WAAC Newsletter* 1, no. 33 (5—12 June 1943), 3, Fort Des Moines, IA, Box 212, Series 55, Rg 165, NA.

36. 19 November 1942, Memo for the Adjutant General, Appointment and Induction Branch, Attention: Recruiting and Induction Section, Colonel Sailor, Subject WAAC Recruiting, From: Lt. Colonel G.T. Gifford, Director, Personnel, WAAC, File: Enrollment of Auxiliaries with Physical Defects or of Doubtful Reputation, Box 111, Series 54, RG 165, NA. I am indebted to Allan Berube for bringing this document to my attention.

37. 5 December 1942, Tab A, Memo to the Adjutant General, Appointment and Induction Branch, Attention: Colonel Sumner, Subject: Enrollment of Auxiliaries with Physical Defects and Doubtful Reputation, From: 3rd Officer, Virginia Beeler Bock, Executive Officer, Personnel Division, WAAC, For the Director; 15 December 1942, Lieutenant General Somervell, Adjutant General to Commanding General, All Service Commands, Subject: Enrollment of WAAC Auxiliaries with Doubtful Moral Standards, File: Enrollment of Auxiliaries with Physical Defects or of Doubtful Reputation, Box 111, Series 54, RG 165, NA. I am indebted to Allan Berube for bringing these documents to my attention.

See also 15 December 1942, Report from Colonel J.A. Hoag, Commandant, Fort Des Moines, IA, First WAAC Training Center, To: Director WAAC, Subject: Summary of Pending Disciplinary Cases, 1st WAAC Training Center, Fort Des Moines, IA, File: 250.1, Box 48, Series 54, RG 165, NA.

38. Berube, *Coming Out Under Fire*, op. cit., 30.

39. "Life in the WAAC," File: 062.001, 1942-43, Box 9, Series 54, RG 165, NA. That some women's desire to join the women's corps in order to "be with other girls" was an indication of possible lesbianism was also addressed by a U.S. Air Force personnel officer after the war. In his report on the future utilization of the WAC in the Air Force, he argued that "group living" was a problem for most "normal, healthy women" who joined the armed services. He went on to note that although there were many women who "enjoyed" such situations, "they are not the type of women we are looking for or desire in our establishment." Major John L. Harris, *The Utilization of the WAC Within the Regular Air Force* (1948), Air

University Air Command and Staff School Thesis, Air University Library, Maxwell Air Force Base, Montgomery, AL.

40. Preston, *History of Psychiatry,* op. cit., 9—10. See also Treadwell, op. cit., 602—606.

41. TB MED 100, War Department Technical Bulletin, 1944, "WAC Recruiting Station Neuropsychiatric Examination," File: 320.2, Box 64, Series 54, RG 165, NA. See also Berube, *Coming Out Under Fire,* op. cit., 32.

42. Lecture Series on Sex Hygiene for Officers and Officer Candidates, WAAC. See in particular "Sexual Relationships" and "Homosexuality," 45—55, Box 145, Series 54, RG 165, NA.

43. WD Pamphlet 35-1, 25, Box 145, Series 54, RG 165, NA.

44. See Berube's discussion of this point, although he does not address class as an issue in defining which same-sex relationships were perceived as "queer" and which were seen as acceptable. Berube, *Coming Out Under Fire,* op. cit., 44—45.

45. Lecture Series on Sex Hygiene for Officers and Officer Candidates, WAAC, "Homosexuality," 53—5, WD Pamphlet, 35—1, 24—5, Box 145, Series 54, RG 165, NA.

46. WD Pamphlet 35—1, 26. Lecture Series on Sex Hygiene for Officers and Officer Candidates, WAAC, "Homosexuality," 53—55, Box 145, Series 54, RG 165, NA.

47. Berube, *Coming Out Under Fire,* op. cit., 59—61. See also WD Pamphlet 35—1, 26.

48. WD Pamphlet 35—1, 26. Lecture Series on Sex Hygiene for Officers and Officer Candidates, WAAC, "Homosexuality," 53—5, Box 145, Series 54, RG 165, NA.

49. War Department Pamphlet 35-1, 27, Box 145, RG 165, NA.

50. Margaret D. Craighill, "Psychiatric Aspects of Women Serving in the Army," *American Journal of Psychiatry* 104 (October 1947): 228.

51. All names, other than those of male and female military administrators, used in the case studies in this article are ethnically matching pseudonyms.

52. 8 May 1944, Lt. Martha B. Hayes, Case #5; WDWAC 201, 11th IND, War Department Office of Director, WAC to Commanding General, Army Service Forces, Attention: Director of Military Personnel, File: Data WAAC Officers, Box 201, Series 55, RG 165, NA.

53. Ibid.

54. D'Emilio and Freedman, *Intimate Matters,* op. cit., 260, 288—289. See also John Costello, *Love, Sex and War: Changing Values, 1939—45* (London: William Collins, 1985) and Berube, *Coming Out Under Fire,* op. cit., 6. See also May, 69.

55. Berube, ibid., 22; Faderman, *Surpassing the Love*, op. cit., 125.

56. Meyer Oral History Questionnaire, #4 and #11, Martha Ward and Anne Brown, Question #29.

57. Faderman, *Surpassing the Love*, op. cit., 125.

58. Meyer Oral History Questionnaire, #18 Bessie Weaver, Question #29.

59. Meyer Oral History Questionnaire, #12, Florence Fox, #18, Bessie Weaver; #7, Anne Clark, Question #29.

60. 7 December 1943, Letter from Former 1st Sergeants Joan G. Pound and Norma L. Chambers to Congressman John M. Coffee; 19 December 1943, Honorable John M. Coffee to Colonel Oveta Culp Hobby, Director, Women's Army Corps, File: 330.14, Box 91, Series 54, RG 165, NA.

61. 7 December 1943, Letter from Former 1st Sergeants Joan G. Pound and Norma L. Chambers to Congressman John M. Coffee; 19 December 1943, Honorable John M. Coffee to Colonel Oveta Culp Hobby, Director, Women's Army Corps, Letter Major General F.E. Uhl to Honorable John M. Coffee, File: 330.14, Box 91, Series 54, RG 165, NA.

62. 7 December 1943, Letter from Former 1st Sergeants Joan G. Pound and Norma L. Chambers to Congressman John M. Coffee; 19 December 1943, Honorable John M. Coffee to Colonel Oveta Culp Hobby, Director, Women's Army Corps, Letter Major General F.E. Uhl to Honorable John M. Coffee; Memo, Lieutenant Colonel R. Hippelheuser, Assistant Adjutant General to 1st Lieutenant Gloria Joyce Gomila, WAC, Subject: Result of Investigation Conducted at 2nd WAC Training Center, Daytona Beach, FL;   Report, Lieutenant Colonel, Assistant Adjutant General to Commanding General, Army Service Forces, Attention: Director Women's Army Corps, File: 330.14, Box 91, Series 54, RG 165, NA.

63. 30 April 1945, Letter from ex-Wac Frankie Casey to Colonel Oveta Culp Hobby, WAC Director, File: C, Box 26, Series 54, RG 165, NA.

64. Letter from ex-Wac Frankie Casey to Colonel Oveta Culp Hobby, WAC Director, File: C, Box 26, Series 54, RG 165, NA.

65. For an extensive discussion of the development of "undesirable" discharge policies by the military during World War II, see Berube, *Coming Out Under Fire*, op. cit., 139, 141, 149—176.

66. 30 April 1945, Frankie Casey to Colonel Oveta Culp Hobby, File: C, Box 26, Series 54, RG 165, NA.

67. Charity Adams Early, *One Woman's Army: A Black Officer Remembers the WAC* (College Station: Texas A & M University Press, 1989), 180—81.

Figure 10. Japanese-American children in internment camp. Sally Sakai-Tsutsumoto holding David Arai at Camp Harmony 1942.

TEN

The Silent Significant Minority
Japanese-American Women, Evacuation, and Internment During World War II

Ivy D. ARAI

Overwhelmed by desperation, you watch your husband and three sons board a train for an unknown destination. Only the pregnant and ill women have been left behind. The agony from separation proves practically unbearable. With your husband and sons hundreds of miles away, you give birth to your only daughter, Joanne Arai, a Sansei [third-generation Japanese-American], in a converted horse stall. Born in a barn on August 22, 1942, Joanne is later known as a "camp baby." Expectant mothers and people needing medical attention crowd together in this barn. The home of hay, horses, and hogs has been turned into a makeshift hospital for Japanese-Americans. The farmyard stench permeates the atmosphere. Crude facilities combined with the lack of doctors and nurses escalate concerns over the health of your future child as well as your own. With only one or two Japanese-American doctors, you fear that when your time comes, no one will be available to help you. Bringing a child into the world could not have occurred at a worse time. Home is nonexistent, and your only possessions are what you can carry. A numbered identification tag dangles from your clothing. Animals that roamed this Seattle Puyallup fairground only a few months ago had worn similar tags. The U.S. government orders you to assemble at this location, now called "Camp Harmony." This place is far from harmonious. Wailing children and sobbing, confused adults create a solemn environment. Their world has been turned upside down. In this time of crisis, families band together. Your pregnancy has isolated and severed you from your family. Alone in this hostile world with only your newborn daughter, you hope for the reunification of your family.

This was the experience of my obaasan (grandmother) Nobu Arai, a Nisei (second-generation Japanese-American), during World War II. The internment of 110,000 Japanese, of whom 70,000 were U.S. citizens, on the West Coast from 1941 to 1946 represents a tragedy in American history.[1] However, history, like the government that decided to evacuate

Japanese-Americans on the basis of race, tends to generalize aspects of the internment. Not only did the internment camps differ by location, but the evacuees varied by age, generation, previous area of residence, and sex. Although every individual's account of life behind the barbed wire was unique, similar circumstances existed. Many published accounts have overlooked the experience of Japanese women, however. Frequently, historians have used Japanese-American women's perspectives as anecdotal evidence to illustrate a broader, masculine—oriented issue. In this essay, the emphasis on women offers unique insight into the wartime internment experience. By capturing the personal histories and memories of Japanese-American women, we can draw a more complicated historical picture of the divisions within American society that persisted, and were even exacerbated during World War II, despite the need to unify and to mobilize the home front. By focusing on the history of everyday life and the war's disruption of community and family bonds, we can understand the full extent of the impact that the violent uprooting of the Japanese-American population had on social and cultural formations, especially gender relationships within the segregated community, and upon relations between the Japanese-Americans and American society as a whole. Japanese-American women's experience of internment during World War II, further demonstrates the extent to which militarization of the society not only restructured family relations, but also racial relations within the United States. This essay also underscores the way that wartime disruption of traditional family and community structures could at once render women victims of racial prejudice and state violence, but also loosen the bonds of patriarchal authority that restricted their power and possibilities within their traditional families and communities.

Drawing on oral interviews, memoirs, newspaper articles, and general historical references, I argue that a transformation in Japanese gender roles occurred as a result of the internment experience. Women, depending on age and generation, experienced different degrees of liberation and oppression. A woman's repressed role in the Japanese culture was somewhat relaxed during camplife. Many Japanese women freed themselves from their passive role and pursued untraditional self-interests. As we will see, internment and evacuation brought rewards as well as hardships for Japanese women.

"WALK TWO STEPS BEHIND A MAN": JAPANESE WOMEN'S TRADITIONAL ROLE

Traditional Japanese culture expected the woman to "walk two steps behind a man."[2] This popular saying depicts the woman's status in Japanese society. Japan's patriarchal traditions transferred to Japanese gender relations in the United States. Over time a fusion of Japanese and American cultures gradually relaxed the confines of Japanese gender roles. Women no longer walked two paces behind a man, but their inferiority remained evident. In the beginning, Issei (first-generation Japanese) women came to the United States to meet their husbands or future mates through a picture-bride practice.[3] Some women welcomed this "Japanese wife's life" in America because the migration offered freedom from demanding relatives at home.[4]

Similar to the expectations of women in Japan, Japanese women in the United States were primarily responsible for maintaining the upkeep of the home and the rearing the the children. Japanese mothers played a crucial role in the development and character of their children. Mothers stressed the difference between right and wrong. They taught children the proper way to do things—for example, how to eat, act, and dress.[5] Japanese mothers shaped children's morals in a traditional home, however, at the expense of their own self-worth. At the same time, each woman held the role of dutiful wife.

Japanese gender relations at the time provided a host of ambiguities, with women constantly being torn between the roles of mother and wife.[6] Japanese women were not only expected to repeatedly exhibit self-sacrifice for their children but to cater to their husbands' every request. Basically, wives were subordinate to both their husband and their children. Inside the home a woman exercised a greater degree of authority, because maintaining the household and children relied on her efforts. However, outside the home a woman's influence appeared nonexistent.[7] This public behavior along with strong kinship ties spurred popular cultural stereotypes labeling Japanese women as unassimilable, passive, silent, and submissive.

Until the end of the nineteenth-century when Japan began to industrialize and poor, single, women temporarily entered into the silk-spinning mills until they married, Japanese women's domestic role strictly limited their contact with the outside environment. Women hardly interacted with other women and men outside of their extended family since their sole concerns revolved around this close-knit arena. Few women in Japanese communities worked beyond marriage, and rarely did activities center on women's interests. Women's controlled, isolated environment reflected Japanese men's dominance in gender relations.

A woman's inferior status within the Japanese community was not entirely unlike the situation of Anglo-American women. During the 1940s, a defined patriarchal society still dominated American culture. Generally, men served as the providers while women acted as the homemakers. In the rare case women decided to work, the greater majority of employment opportunities for women were limited to menial jobs. In the prewar years Japanese-American women experienced a double exclusion. Racism also restricted Japanese-American women's freedom and position. By the beginning of the war, dominant American culture began the slow revision of women's role in society. Thus the expectations for a woman in America did indeed differ from those of traditional Japanese culture. As Japanese women came into greater contact in the United States with western values, Japanese-American women confronted a dilemma. Some Japanese-American women endured an inner conflict concerning their role in society as a result of the greater opportunity available in the United States.[8] Some women were attracted to the new possibilities open to American women, but their ambitions or dreams for themselves remained contained by their traditional culture. The evacuation and internment of Japanese-Americans both compounded this confusion, and served as a catalyst for change.

PATRIOTIC PARTICIPANTS: JAPANESE-AMERICANS VOLUNTEER FOR THE WAR EFFORT

Japanese-American women found their loyalties further divided following Japan's bombing of Pearl Harbor on December 7, 1941. Wartime hysteria and anti-Japanese attitudes enflamed American society. Posters advertising "How to tell your friends from Japs" speckled numerous West Coast cities.[9] The negative backlash caused Japanese women to demonstrate their loyalty to the United States. Immediately following Japan's attack, pressure within the Japanese community forced women to momentarily divert attention away from the home to participate in a unified coalition in support of America's war efforts. Women contributed to wartime activities by volunteering at local Red Cross chapters to roll bandages.[10] The Japanese-American Citizen's League (JACL) involved women in their patriotic campaigns to prove Japanese-American allegiance to the United States. Women helped gather and sign petitions and pledges.[11] Mass demonstrations and bomb fund-raising efforts in San Francisco, Los Angeles, and Seattle included women participants.[12]

These forms of protest by the Japanese community called upon the support and efforts of women. Some may consider the involvement by women in patriotism campaigns an act of desperation by male leaders of the Japanese-American community. Indeed, Japanese-American men did seek the participation of women in building a visible coalition against racist sentiment. Yet just the inclusion of women in public activities represented a gradual balancing of gender roles. The bombing of Pearl Harbor temporarily liberated Japanese-American women from their domestic sphere.

The larger public, however, ignored Japanese efforts to demonstrate their loyalty to America. Before internment, signs of suspicion and exclusion manifested themselves. In Seattle, white mothers protested the employment of two Japanese-American women in school offices within the district. School officials responded to the complaints, saying that "the girls, being American born, have the same right to employment as white citizens."[13] At the time, working Japanese women were rare. The Seattle school district had hired these two women because discrimination had forced the women to work for a lower salary. Yuri Ike, one of the office "girls" at Franklin High School, professed their loyalty:

> As American working girls we are loyal to our country and to our jobs. But if our fellow citizens feel that our employment in schools menaces our country's welfare, we will step down. We hope, however, we will be able to stay and earn our living, but whatever the decision is, we'll accept it without complaint.[14]

Yuri Ike's avowal of her allegiance to America and her accepted possible resignation exemplified the attitude of many Japanese-American women during this racially divisive period.

Many Japanese-American women harbored feelings of "racial guilt," the guilt of being a race loathed by their fellow citizens.[15] This insecurity exploded following the bombing of Pearl Harbor. In her memoir, Monica Sone, a Nisei woman from Seattle, explained her debilitating reaction to the surprise attack:

> I felt as if a fist had smashed my pleasant little existence, breaking it into a jigsaw puzzle of pieces. An old wound opened up again, and I found myself shrinking inwardly from my Japanese blood, the blood of the enemy. I knew instinctively that the fact that I was an American by birthright was not going to help me escape the consequences of this unhappy war.[16]

If women carried "racial guilt" unconsciously, the Pearl Harbor attack unburied these uncomfortable feelings.

As society grew increasingly suspicious of Japanese-Americans' loyalty, the Nisei took drastic measures to distance themselves from Japan. Women witnessed a massive destruction of family belongings associated with the Japanese culture. Nobu Arai watched her husband, Allen, bury his samurai swords and flags in their backyard, erasing any symbols that might tie the family to Japan.[17]

EXECUTIVE ORDER 9066: EXCLUSION AND INTERNMENT

Anti-Japanese sentiment eventually obscured any Japanese-American efforts to display loyalty to the United States. Swiftly, only 3 months after the bombing, President Franklin D. Roosevelt codified the hatred toward

Japanese-Americans by invoking Executive Order 9066 (EO9066) on February 19, 1942. EO9066 instructed military commanders to evacuate and intern all Americans living on the West Coast with at least one-sixteenth Japanese blood.[18] Roosevelt justified EO9066 by expiating racial unrest, claiming the order would protect Japanese-Americans. Although Japanese-Americans cooperated with this decision, their thoughts did not necessarily reflect their actions. Shocked or in a state of denial, many felt a "wholesale rejection by other Americans."[19] Monica Sone recalled her disbelief and anger:

> Once more I felt like a despised, pathetic two-headed freak, a Japanese and an American, neither of which seemed to be doing me any good. The Nisei leaders in the community rose above their personal feelings and stated that they would co-operate and comply with the decision of the government as their sacrifice in keeping with the country's war effort, thus proving themselves loyal American citizens. I was too jealous of my recently acquired voting privilege to be gracious about giving in, and I felt most unco-operative.[20]

The silent resignation by women like Monica Sone resulted from their following the initiatives of Japanese men. The leaders of Japanese-American organizations like the JACL decided how the community would respond to EO9066. Women's inferior status within the Japanese community left many voiceless. Even though Monica Sone felt "uncooperative," she succumbed to the passive actions desired by male Japanese leaders.

Not every American harbored anti-Japanese sentiments. Sally Sakai-Tsutsumoto, a Sansei from Seattle and 10 years old at the time, remembered how her Scandinavian neighbors felt saddened by the evacuation order and offered to house the Sakai family.[21] The federal government, however, prohibited families from harboring the Japanese. Etsuko Sunimoto-Mizokuchi, a 21-year-old Nisei from Seattle, recalled how the president of the local home loan bank aided the Sunimotos during this crisis. He rented out their house and put the money in savings for their later use.[22] Etsuko considers her family lucky compared to relatives like Tamayo (Tama) Arai-Sakai, who had their possessions and property robbed from them.[23] Many Issei lost their farms at a profitable time when the crop was ready to harvest.

Many Japanese-Americans felt uncertain about their future, so families moved in together. Several families living in one home created a base so everyone could evacuate together.[24] While Japanese-Americans isolated themselves within their homes, military troops established stations to monitor Japanese activity.   In Seattle, the military converted the Garfield High School track field into a temporary army camp.[25]

All Japanese persons living on the West Coast had approximately 3 weeks to store, sell, or pack belongings for their incarceration in one of the ten government internment camps that had been established inland.[26] The Sunimotos could not sell their flower shop because "no one would buy from a Japanese."[27]   Those Americans who purchased Japanese possessions and property paid a shamefully low price.   In Los Angeles, greedy Americans waited in lines outside Japanese homes to profit from their inevitable losses.   Etsuko remembered her younger brother Toshio's anger at the degrading situation:

> Someone offered him ten dollars for his brand new car. Toshio exclaimed [that] "he would rather throw it away before he gives it up for five dollars." He then asked the bus driver [who] was taking the Japanese to the assembly centers if he could follow and leave his car at the front gate.   Toshio did, and the government gave him two hundred dollars, which was a good deal since he originally paid three hundred and fifty dollars.[28]

Toshio's frustration and bitterness reflected common Japanese-American attitudes at the time.   The insensitive, malicious, and opportunistic behavior of many Americans shocked the Japanese.

DESTINATION UNKNOWN: GOVERNMENT OFFICIALS ROUND-UP JAPANESE-AMERICANS

Japanese-Americans abandoned their homes, farms, professions, and possessions for the "manure stall" living conditions of the assembly centers.[29]   Taking only what they could carry, a maximum of 100 pounds per person, the Arai family, along with thousands of other Japanese-Americans headed to an unknown destination.[30]   In a few weeks, the world for Japanese women in the United States was in turmoil.   Violent discrimination segregated the Japanese population, and they became prisoners within a nation based on the ideals of freedom and individual civil rights.   Women's control over their children's and their own future seemed unattainable.   The sudden emotional burden and stress took its toll on many Japanese-American women.

The chaos at the assembly centers compounded women's primary feelings of confusion.   Japanese-Americans experienced a quick transition from the security of their homes to an unknown, overpopulated environment.   Government officials at Camp Harmony, for example, divided the camp into three sections: two parking lots and the main fairground.   Japanese needed passes to see relatives and friends in other sections.[31]   Families who resided in the parking lot sections considered themselves lucky, being free from horse stall living conditions. The Arais, who arrived later than the Sunimotos, lived in this main fairground section. Tama Arai-Sakai dunked the heads of her younger daughters, Sally and Katie, in buckets of water to wash out the lice they contracted from playing in the horse stalls.[32] The change from the private, familial atmosphere of the home to a communal setting with thousands of strangers terrified many Japanese women. Consolidating thousands of dislocated individuals into a minuscule area fueled already present fears. The lack of space prevented any opportunities for privacy. At Camp Harmony the atrocious circumstances forced over 100 families to share one washroom.[33] Sally Sakai-Tsutsumoto recalled:

> There was a crawl space above the toilets. I remember seeing a little boy peering down and watching people go to the bathroom. I thought, "That punk little kid." I will never forget the total lack of privacy.[34]

Black tar-papered barracks provided extremely cramped conditions. Government officials gave newly married couples the privilege of using a curtain to separate themselves from neighboring families. Each barrack housed approximately thirty-two to forty-eight people in a total of four to six rooms.[35] Artist Miné Okubo described the horrendous conditions at the Santa Anita racetrack in southern California:

> The rear room had housed the horse and the front room the fodder. Both rooms showed signs of hurried whitewashing. Spider webs, horse hair, and hay had been whitewashed with the walls. Huge spikes and nails stuck out all over the walls. A two-inch layer of dust covered the floor, but on removing it we discovered that linoleum the color of redwood had been placed over the rough manure-covered boards.[36]

Initially, the women's reactions to internment involved feelings of confusion, anger, resignation, and especially culture shock. Many had never come into contact with so many Japanese people. The confined boundaries and the dense population overwhelmed many, like Mary Okumura, a Nisei from California:

> Just about every night, there is something going on, but I'd rather stay home because I am just new here and don't know very much around. As for the people I met so many already, I don't remember any. I am not even going to try to remember names because it's just impossible here.[37]

At first, some felt awkward about the forced interaction, as they were accustomed to private, familial settings. However, the common internment experience laid the foundations for bonds between Japanese-Americans who would have otherwise been strangers. For many young Nisei women, the experience generated friendships. Japanese-Americans gradually extended relations to individuals outside the family. Kinship ties steadily encompassed the entire Japanese community. This enforced isolation proved crucial in the development of lasting communal ties and the transformation of gender relations.

The feeling of community was shortlived, however, as the residents of the assembly centers were again uprooted. Thousands of Japanese-Americans from these centers were next transferred to internment camps. Evacuees traveled to one of ten relocation centers: Tule Lake and Manzanar in California; Poston and Gila River in Arizona; Topaz in Utah; Minidoka in Idaho; Heart Mountain in Wyoming; Granada in Colorado; and Rohwer and Jerome in Arkansas. The confusion and hysteria multiplied as thousands boarded trains headed for unknown destinations. At this time, pregnant mothers like Nobu Arai found themselves separated from their families.

The departure reinforced the federal government's refusal to recognize Japanese-American loyalty. Steadily, Japanese-Americans realized the seriousness of the government's proposed actions. The evacuation and internment orders were no longer considered a cruel joke or a mistake. American citizenship, for the Japanese, became irrelevant. Their terrifying fate was sealed. To withstand the hardships, many adhered to the traditional Japanese philosophy of *shikataganai* —"you can't help it."[38] This belief influenced Japanese-American women's passive response to the evacuation and internment. Instead of challenging and obsessing about the day's events, they accepted things as they happened, living one day at a time.

"WE LIVE SO CLOSE TO FREEDOM, YET SO FAR FROM IT": ISOLATION AND HUMILIATION

To further the humiliation and shock of many Japanese-Americans, the government kept the trip to the internment camps a secret. Blinds covered the windows, so no one would see the removal of the Japanese-Americans from the West Coast.[39] The government as well as the Japanese feared that people might shoot at the trains.[40] For women who believed EO9066 to be a hoax due to government wartime hysteria, this joke became cruel reality.

As if the desert surroundings failed to ensure Japanese-American isolation, barbed wire fences complete with armed guards encompassed each of the ten internment camps. The camp's militarized appearance shocked the internees. Miné Okubo wrote, "We live so close to freedom, yet so far from it."[41] The fence and the guard towers established a prison atmosphere. Lili Sasaki, an Amache, Colorado, internee, remembered her disbelief at the sight of armed military patrols:

> I always thought to myself, "Would those GIs actually shoot my daughter if she happened to go near the fence?" I was almost tempted to say, "Go on there, Mimi. Go out there and pick that flower over there." See if the GIs...[42]

Internees felt threatened by the guarded surroundings. Looking after themselves and their children was especially worrisome for mothers. Because the welfare of the children remained their first priority, the guns presented a danger in this supposed "protected" environment. Despite several protests, however, the fences remained. The prison construction of the camp blended with the hostile natural surroundings. In addition to the armed guards and barbed wire, residents at Camp Minidoka learned that the fence had been electrified.[43] Treated like criminals, Japanese-Americans began to better understand the scope of the government's racist intentions.

In addition to the watchful soldiers with bared bayonets, Japanese-Americans were numbered and lettered. The procedures of incarceration humiliated and appalled women evacuees. Fumi Ihsida at the Tanforan center felt disgusted at being tagged "like criminals."[44] When her family received a number upon their arrival, the impact of the internment "really hit" her.[45] The revelation of their dehumanizing experience occurred step by step for many Japanese women, due to the swiftness of the evacuation process.

The transition from home to camp life introduced unthinkable hardships. To begin with, the desert environment contrasted with the moist, heavily vegetated surroundings of the Pacific Northwest. Sally Sakai-Tsutsumoto remembered how the wind was like nothing anyone had ever encountered in Seattle, throwing sand everywhere so that they could even taste sand in their mouths.[46] The extreme seasons made the adjustment to camp difficult. As a child, Sally recalled how the rain transformed the desert environment into a puddle of mud and the mud swallowed people's shoes. A person's boot would get stuck in the mud and the foot would slip out.[47]

The overcrowded environment made mothers' supervision of children difficult. The extraordinary amount of free time, along with the loss of societal rules and expectations, gave way to children running wild. Because the children remained the mothers' foremost responsibility, the loss of control was especially trying. Mary Tsukamoto, a 27-year-old Nisei at the time of the evacuation, described the stressful situation at the Jerome, Arkansas, camp:

> The young ones reacted in predictable ways. They cried a lot and demanded attention. Older ones were noisy and quarrelsome; teenagers acted wild and tried to be independent. A few angry, rebellious youths caused problems for all of us. They stayed out past curfew, ran around shouting loudly and refused to obey regulations, and generally embarrassed us.[48]

The adjustment to camp life resulted in the loss of family structure. As children and adolescents broke away from rigid parental guidance, mothers also experienced a relaxation in their self-sacrificial duties. The large mess halls reflected the disintegration of family unity. Family members began to eat separately: mothers with young children, fathers with other men, and older children with peers.[49] The loosening of familial expectations resulted in child and teenage cliques. Sally Sakai-Tsutsumoto described the peer pressure for young children and teenagers to eat together:

> If you saw your friends, you ate with them. Peer pressure existed against eating with your parents. Young kids stayed clumped together. This aided in deterioration of the family.[50]

Discipline and guidance proved an arduous task for mothers where privacy remained nonexistent. Internment eradicated the usual incentives to behave according to traditional customs. Juvenile delinquency increased, and gang activity developed.[51] The physical dislocation of Japanese-Americans disrupted parent/child relations.

The sudden loss of familial control perpetuated Japanese-American women's confusion. Miné Okubo explained her disbelief and resentment of America's decision to intern Japanese-Americans. She blamed the internment on race.[52] After all, the United States was at war with Italy and Germany, yet the government neglected to intern Italian and German-Americans. Other women accepted their circumstances as the unfortunate result of war. These women felt thankful for anything that lessened the degree of tragedy.

The dislocation generated a sense of instability. Despite government assurances, many internees were apprehensive. In the face of the government's distrust of Japanese-Americans, the internees became wary of the government's intentions. The ways in which the government degraded Japanese-Americans prior to their arrival at the internment camps transformed many of the women's feelings of optimism to pessimism. Assumptions of the worst possible scenarios infected the minds of many

Japanese-American women like Lili Sasaki:

> We didn't know what to expect in the camps. We didn't know if
> we were going to stay there forever, or if we were going to be sent
> back to Japan. Or if something real bad, and Japan was winning,
> they might kill us all. If Japan did start to win, I think the camps
> could have been invaded. Some of the hot-headed ones would
> have said, "Blow them up." That was a frightful thing. It could
> have happened because there was prejudice.[53]

There were good reasons for Japanese-Americans' fears. U.S. government
officials did indeed discuss whether to send "disloyal" Japanese back to
Japan. Usually by choice, some Japanese did return to Japan.

Viewing the barricaded camp structure, many Japanese women realized
that only racism could have spawned such an undesirable fate. Many
believed that the government had made a rash decision to intern all West
Coast Japanese. At the time, women wondered what could prevent other,
more extreme measures from occurring, for example the extermination of
all Japanese-Americans. Despite these worries, the women toiled,
attempting to make the most of their meager, hostile surroundings.

The adjustment to camp life introduced a variety of hardships. Food,
shelter, privacy, and other things individuals generally took for granted
became main sources of discontent. Lili Sasaki complained of the horrid
food situation:

> We got so tired of camp food. And it got so we couldn't stand
> looking at the women's magazines with all of the jellos and cakes.
> We wanted to go home and bake a cake or something. They just
> handed you a tin plate all mixed up in one. And we missed
> Japanese tea. We got the orange pekoe type. When we got out,
> Japanese tea tasted bitter.[54]

The repetitious, bland meals reminded Japanese-American women of their
oppressive conditions. Although camplife relaxed their domestic
responsibilities in areas such as food preparation, the women felt
restricted. They not only longed for the comforts of home but desired the
appreciation and attention from their families for cooking incredible
meals. At home, Nobu Arai, for instance, had prepared elaborate meals
for her family. She would make soup stock from boiled kelp and would
scoop the meat out of fresh crabs for salads.[55] Women like Nobu Arai
spent a great deal of time preparing food. Although time seemed
unlimited at the camps, cooking was a communal effort with limited
resources. The abundance of mutton and the lack of better meat
transformed the traditional diet of Japanese-Americans. Some women

worked and cooked in the large mess halls. Instead of preparing food for a small family, the portions served 250 to 300 individuals. Cooking for women became an organized group effort, with restricted creativity and resources. These restrictions placed on food preparation—such a fundamental symbol of ethnic identity, and women's traditional role— underscored the degree to which internment eroded Japanese-American women's dual identity as women and preservationists of ethnic integrity.

How women made the awkward, cramped living quarters livable represented a remarkable feat in itself. All ten camps shared similar physical characteristics. At Camp Minidoka in Idaho, twelve tar-papered barracks formed rows for forty-two blocks, housing approximately 9,000 evacuees.[56] Each barrack measured 20 feet by 100 feet, with eight people in each of the four to six rooms.[57] The partitions between the rooms failed to reach the ceiling. Noise was inescapable and privacy an impossibility. Sand constantly seeped through the thin tar-papered walls, making cleanliness a chore. Bored children easily poked holes through the room dividers.[58] These homes failed to meet the minimum standards for military housing. A U.S. judge, later asked to review the camp living conditions, found prisoners in federal penitentiaries better housed than the Japanese-Americans.[59] In the end, the limited area encouraged outside activity and the barrack became merely a place to "hang your hat and sleep."[60] This dispersion of individuals perpetuated family disunity.

Women found no improvement in privacy at the internment camps. Writer Michi Weglyn summarized the crowded conditions by stating, "Evacuees ate communally, showered communally, defecated communally."[61] Large showering rooms erased any efforts to behave modestly. People had to wait in long lines for one of the eight showers in an open room. The doorless stalls and shadeless windows made routine cleanliness a humiliating, public, chore. Some women carried a shower curtain with them, while others bathed in their underclothes. Older women preferred bathtubs to showers.[62] One woman from Tanforan went as far as to take her baths in the washtubs.[63] The communal showering rooms robbed women of their femininity.

The public restrooms at the internment camps offered little improvement over the conditions at the assembly centers. People had to travel over a block just to reach the cold, dark, smelly, buggy restrooms.[64] The distance, lack of privacy, and filth made going to the bathroom an inconvenience. Some internees avoided the humiliation and the journey by reverting to the old technology of the chamber pot.[65] They would use a bucket instead of the restroom, emptying the improvised chamber pot in the morning. The process of exposing camp residents' most private moments to public scrutiny, and observation, further accelerated the deterioration of their individual identity, as well as their position within the traditional family structure.

DECLINING HEALTH AND WEAKENING GENDER DIVISIONS

Women discovered new hardships as a result of the inadequate communal resources. Laundry represented an extremely arduous task. Not only were the barracks usually a considerable distance from the washing rooms, but the laundry tubs were often too low. One Nisei woman believed that "the people who built [the washing tubs] must have thought Japanese women were awfully short for [the tubs were] only eighteen inches from the ground."[66] The heavy lifting in domestic chores and field work instigated health problems. Rheumatoid arthritis plagued some interned women.

Many women suffered preventable health problems due to the inferior medical facilities at the assembly centers and camps. Tama Arai-Sakai was 40 years old and 4 months pregnant when she miscarried at the Puyallup, Washington, assembly center.[67] Tama's health declined in subsequent months due to inadequate medical expertise and resources. As a child, Sally Sakai-Tsutsumoto explained her confusion over her mother's illness:

> I arrived [at] camp on Mother's Day. I had saved my pennies and purchased a picture for my mother. She was in the hospital and I thought she was going to die. My aunties kept asking my mother, "Are you going to die?" In that era, mothers did not talk to their kids much. No one would tell me anything.[68]

The medical facilities had few doctors and nurses. Often people's health problems were overlooked or mistreated.

The transition to camp life could be considered more disruptive for Japanese-American women than men. A woman's subordinate position to her husband or father steadily deteriorated in the camps. The change was especially drastic for first-generation Issei women who held on to traditional Japanese values. Born and raised in America, the Nisei possessed different perspectives, which helped them somewhat in their new roles. The Nisei generation had sparked this transformation in gender roles even before the internment. Issei mothers had encouraged their sons and daughters to become more Americanized. Deeply embedded stereotypes and discrimination toward the Japanese influenced this assimilationist trend. Some parents had purposely decided not to pass on the Japanese language to their children, in hopes of Americanizing younger generations.[69] Nisei women, unlike their Issei mothers, had the benefit of an American education. Besides academics, an education fostered a social transformation through the intersection of cultures. Young Japanese-American women enjoyed a life outside the realms of the family and home.   Internment restricted interaction with non-Japanese peoples, but the isolation accelerated the change in gender roles.

The War Relocation Authority (WRA) attempted to treat women and men as equals.[70]   Camp facilities, including the showering rooms, made no distinction between male and female use.   The clothes issued to internees, from navy pea jackets to army coats, also made no distinction between the sexes.[71]   The WRA offered similar employment and wages to males and females.   Crude medical facilities provided no advantages or special treatment for either sex.   At times, this lack of gender differences increased the hardships for women (e.g., the demanding physical labor). However, the camps' enforced levelling of identity influenced the collapse of rigid gender roles.

The reaction to this degree of equality varied among Japanese women. Older Issei and Nisei women with strong Japanese traditions felt especially alarmed and confused by the gender transformation.[72]   Younger generations readily accepted the change and took advantage of the window of opportunity, transplanting, in some cases, old values into a new context. Education, for instance, had been considered very important for young men in the Japanese-American community before the evacuation. During internment, this avenue of personal independence often actually became open to Japanese-American women for the first time.

During internment, a college education became nearly as accessible for women as men.   The pursuit of a college degree meant an escape from internment.   In 1943 the WRA granted men and women students the choice to leave for a college education.   Many young women took advantage of this opportunity and left interned family members to seek a higher education.   A study in Valerie Matsumoto's *Japanese American Women During World War II* found that a third of the first 400 students to leave the camp for college were women.[73]   Women who left for college heightened their sense of independence and promoted a bold level of personal liberation.

When women decided to relocate, other factors besides their own educational advancement had to be considered.   Some felt obligations toward the upkeep of their family, including caring for elderly parents and relatives.   Silent resignation to women's expanding liberties signaled a cultural revolution for Japanese-Americans.

Time encouraged Japanese-American women to express their creativity through arts and crafts.   Leisure activities included sewing, embroidery, painting, and carving.   Older women, like Nobu Arai, taught younger women, like Etsuko Sunimoto-Mizokuchi, to sew dresses and knit.[74] Women artists, like Miné Okubo, recorded a sense of camp life from a woman's perspective.   Lili Sasaki recalled this creative transformation within the Japanese community:

> For the first time, they became creative, because they had the time.
> Which proved time is [of] the essence for everybody.   If you don't
> have time, you have no time to be yourself.[75]

In the past, Japanese-American women had little time to themselves, bearing the burden of caring for the children, maintaining the household, and satisfying their husbands' every whim.   Internment was contradictory. On the one hand, camplife introduced new hardships.   On the other, internment offered personal liberation for many women.   Older Issei women, like Etsuko's mother, Toyo Arai-Sunimoto, compared the internment to a vacation: "She [Toyo] worked hard in the flower shop and at camp she never cooked; instead, all she did was knit and sew."[76]

Various women's clubs and classes developed.   They sponsored activities specific to women's interests, such as lessons in flower arranging, cooking, and, most significantly, instruction in reading and writing English.[77]   The Japanese-American community continued to place a heavy emphasis on their children's education.   Young Nisei women had already acquired an American education.   Time and isolation in the camps now allowed for older women's educational instruction.   Issei women especially appreciated these opportunities that were otherwise unavailable and unattainable.   Learning the English language would help to eradicate some cultural barriers that previously had separated Japanese and Anglo communities.

The communal environment especially relaxed older Japanese-American women's domestic responsibilities.   This decline in expectations and the increase in freetime facilitated female sociability.   Women's clubs exemplified the developing networks between women.   At Tanforan, Charles Kikuchi described the positive effect camp life had on his mother:

> Mom is gradually taking things into her own hands....For 28 years
> she had been restricted at home, raising children and doing the
> housework. Now she finds herself here with a lot of Japanese, and
> it has given her a great deal of pleasure to make all of these new
> social contacts.[78]

At last, older Japanese women relinquished their self-sacrificial expectations and devoted time to themselves.

The breakdown in rigid gender roles allowed women to pursue job opportunities not formerly available.   Each camp functioned like a model city administered by various departments.   Within every camp specific departments managed aspects of community life (e.g., accounting, agriculture and medical care, mess hall service, and the weekly newspapers).[79]   Whites headed these departments, which employed interned Japanese men and women for minimal monthly wages. General Dwight Eisenhower referred to these departments as "work corps."[80] Internees produced the necessities for the camp as well as war materials for sale in the open market, again underscoring their position as victims and participants in the war effort.

Time allowed women to experiment with a variety of work experiences. Some women assumed the respected position of teacher. In the relocation camps, teachers, as well as doctors and other professionals, were at the top of the pay scale, earning as much as $19 a month.[81] Women who worked as waitresses and latrine cleaners earned $12 a month.[82]   Etsuko earned $3.50 a month as an assistant to a Portland, Oregon, kindergarten teacher.[83]   Superior teacher salaries placed some women on the same financial level as men.   Women who had no experience teaching volunteered.   Many were shocked by their own assertiveness in seeking employment.   After volunteering for a teaching job, Mary Tsukamoto described her surprise to her unusually aggressive, spontaneous behavior:

> Immediately after these brave words, I realized what I had done as I...wondered if I had gone mad under the Fresno sun.   How did I dare think I could teach!   I walked back to Section H with my head spinning.   I could not even tell Al [her husband] what I had done.[84]

Women like Mary Tsukamoto realized an undiscovered sense of confidence when competing with men for jobs.   This idea of self-worth and importance flourished behind the barbed wire.

Many women understood how teaching served as a means of uplifting the Japanese community.   Japanese-Americans considered education crucial for assimilating in and adapting to American culture.   Internment provided time for Japanese women to explore various occupational fields. For women who already assumed tremendous domestic and parental responsibilities, the transition to teaching was an attractive, rewarding challenge.

The internment experience enabled women to establish a recognizable presence within the Japanese community.   For the first time women aggressively extended their activity beyond the home.   Some women exhibited their new sense of independence by participating in the WRA work leave program beginning in May 1942.   Most Japanese-Americans toiled as field laborers.   In 1943 Etsuko left camp and worked for an Idaho farmer picking onions and potatoes.[85]   Farmers employed Japanese-Americans whenever they needed extra help and paid by the hour.

Sporadic outside work opportunities allowed young Nisei women to earn extra money. Although domestic work comprised the majority of nonagricultural jobs for Issei and Nisei women, a trend toward clerical, secretarial, and factory work evolved. The program allowed Sumi Arai-Kawaguchi to temporarily leave her Camp Minidoka residence to work as a stenographer in the nearby town.[86] Many young Nisei women easily adapted to leaving their family. Some believed that internment would end soon, because of the government's concerns regarding the camps' growing expenses.[87]

GENDER TENSIONS GROW AT CAMP HARMONY

The confidence women obtained from the collapse of rigid gender roles bred tensions between the sexes. While many men felt emasculated by internment, some women developed a sense of empowerment. To an extent, a reversal of gender roles occurred. Internment restricted a man's control over his own actions as well as those of his family's. Some men responded to their sudden inadequacy by regressing to a passive personality. The experience broke the spirit of Allen Arai, who possessed a master's degree in architecture from Harvard University. His daughter, Joanne Arai-Mar, explained how, after the evacuation and internment, "he never got the respect he deserved."[88] This relaxation of power forced women to assume a more dominant presence within the family and community. Women provided stability in a time of constant change and rising male insecurities.

When the War Department decided in January 1943 to draft Japanese-Americans, the women's elevation in status was put to the test.[89] Approximately 33,000 Japanese-American men served in the army during the war, leaving thousands of women to fend for themselves and their family.[90] A mother had to assume both roles of parenting. The community's emphasis on the men fighting in the war often overshadowed the enormous responsibilities of the women at home.

Women experienced a sense of confusion as a result of their husbands and sons joining the U.S. military. Many realized the need for the men to participate in America's war efforts. However, fighting for a nation that resented one's actions seemed to increase the level of danger. Unlike other American women with loved ones fighting the war, Japanese-American women harbored concern over the military's treatment of their men. The intense discrimination against Japanese-Americans on the home front could easily transfer to their men overseas. Many women, like the men who enlisted, had divided feelings concerning Japanese-Americans' involvement in the military. They realized the "bitter injustice of being plucked out of a concentration camp" to fight in a battle in which their own country viewed them as enemies.[91] Etsuko explained her brother

Toshio's reaction to being drafted, as well as her own confusion and bitterness:

> Lots of men volunteered for the draft. Girlfriends felt sad. My brother was softhearted, kind and could never kill anybody....He told me, "I don't want to die." One week after his eighteenth birthday, he was inducted into the U.S. army. It was when I was saying good-bye to him [that] the impact of his actions really hit me. This is not fair. This is wrong. Hundreds are dying over there and here my brother wears a U.S. uniform and [a] guard sits...watching us with a gun. I really grew up then.[92]

Other women shared the men's perspective of wanting to prove their patriotism. The success of the all-Nisei 100th Infantry Battalion and the 442nd Regimental Combat Team in the European war provoked the U.S. government to give "loyal women the opportunity to serve their country."[93] In 1943 Japanese-American women volunteered for the Women's Army Corps (WAC). Nisei WACs worked at bases all over the country, in medical detachments, in Military Intelligence School, in the Public Information Office, and as typists, clerks, and researchers in occupied Germany and Japan.[94] Women joined the WACs for the same reason men served in the military: to prove their Americanism. A Nisei from the Heart Mountain internment camped explained her motivations for volunteering and the controversy surrounding her decision:

> I felt that the Nisei had to do more than give lip service to the United States and by joining the WACs I could prove my sincerity....After all, this is everybody's war and we all have to put an equal share into it. I don't know why the Nisei objected so much to my joining the WACs....Most of the Nisei girls said that they would not join because they would never be able to get married then.[95]

Dispelling the myth, most Nisei eventually married. Women at the time expected to marry in their early twenties. Nisei women and their parents assumed they would marry other Japanese-Americans. Unlike their elders, though, Nisei women hoped to choose their husband and marry "for love."[96]

The Nisei women's assertiveness and sense of independence surprised the Japanese community. The emotional strength necessary for Japanese-American women to endure the rigors of internment contrasted with their feeble stereotypical image. An uprooted community requires flexibility on the part of both men and women. Determined acts of protest negated overgeneralizations of Japanese-American women as silent. Mary

Tsukamoto's aggressive letter writing campaign to the WRA Director, Dillion Meyer, President Roosevelt, and his wife, Eleanor, served as her lifeline to the outside world.[97] Women, like Mary Tsukamoto directed their new sense of liberation to inform government officials about camp life and question the motives for internment.

Mitsuye Endo exemplified aggressive protest against the government. A Nisei from Sacramento, California, she utilized the legal system to challenge the evacuation and detention of Japanese-Americans. On April 2, 1942, Mitsuye was dismissed from her California State government job without due process of law. In July 1942, she filed a petition for a writ of habeas corpus in the U.S. District Court, requesting to be released from the internment camp, thereby reclaiming her liberty.[98] Three years and 11 days after the bombing of Pearl Harbor, on December 18, 1944, the U.S. Supreme Court ruled that the evacuation of Japanese-Americans was constitutional based on "military necessity."[99] The Court further decided that any American citizen, like Mitsuye Endo, with undeniable loyalty should not be detained.[100] Mitsuye Endo's actions proved crucial in influencing the War Department to revoke exclusion orders. A few hours following the Endo ruling, the army declared the West Coast exclusion orders revoked.[101] Her independent efforts set a legal precedent. Mitsuye Endo's perseverance and determination influenced the fate of all Japanese-Americans.

LOOSENED TIES TO FAMILY AND COUNTRY: THE NEW JAPANESE-AMERICAN WOMAN ENTERS POSTWAR AMERICA

Women held the fabric of the Japanese-American community together during a period of crisis. The evacuation and internment of Japanese-Americans brought hardships as well as rewards to the women involved. Life behind the barbed wire transformed gender roles. In some cases, the internment accelerated women's liberation. The experience differed for younger and older women. Female children enjoyed a relaxation of parental guidance and developed strong relations with peers. In some ways, internment for older women offered a refreshing break from the demanding domestic and familial duties of the past. Young Nisei women felt the most liberated by taking advantage of college and work-leave opportunities. Women of all ages discovered varying degrees of independence.

World War II called into question Japanese-Americans' loyalty to the United States. Suspicions of espionage fueled the government's decision to intern the Japanese. Before the evacuation and during the internment, women demonstrated their developing sense of confidence through patriotic activities. Whether women volunteered for the JACL, wrote petitions, or joined the WAC, the traditional role of homemaker steadily disintegrated. To a degree, women's patriotic efforts undermined Japanese families. A focus outside of the home created instability within family relations. Children matured with decreased maternal supervision. Husbands lost a measure of spousal attention, generating marital tensions. The irony of Japanese-Americans' seemingly unyielding loyalty to America shocked other citizens. The 100th Infantry Battalion and the 442nd Regimental Combat Team typified this irony. Although women could not fight in the war, young Nisei women actively participated in patriotic campaigns. Betrayed and incarcerated by their own nation, Nisei women relentlessly exhibited their support to the United States. Their faith in America could involve a passive acceptance of government orders or an attempt to assimilate by seeking a college degree. As many young women struggled to Americanize or establish a level of financial independence, the rigid gender roles of the past dissolved. One of the women featured in this essay, Etsuko, spent only a few months at Camp Minidoka and left her family behind to work on a farm and later a flower shop in Salt Lake City until 1946.[102] Work-leave programs and college offered an escape from internment for Etsuko and others.

Today when Sansei, like my auntie Joanne and father, David Arai, discuss "camp," the experience seems unfathomable. How older generations endured the difficulties, discrimination, and psychological stresses amazes younger Japanese-Americans. Through passed down oral accounts, interviews, and readings, Yonsei (fourth-generation Japanese-American), like I, can learn about an overlooked tragedy in American history.

One would believe that bitterness afflicts the Japanese-American community, since 90 percent of the Issei had died before the 1988 repatriations and redress, when President Ronald Reagan issued an official apology to the Japanese-American community. Surprisingly, the *shikataganai* philosophy flourishes. The now 76-year-old Etsuko, for example, sees the internment as a wartime disaster and maintains that President Roosevelt had to sign EO9066.[103]

By taking life one day at a time, Japanese-American women endure. Collecting oral histories from the aging generation, the younger generation of Japanese-Americans transmits knowledge of past hurtful events to present and future generations. In so doing, we help to inscribe the history of racism in the main of American history, and reclaim the loyalty and contribution of our ancestors to the American past and present. By recapturing the particular experiences of Japanese-American women during internment in World War II, we learn how racism and military concerns conspired to marginalize and threaten the rights of citizenship of Japanese-Americans. We also learn of some of the larger historical processes that have conspired to redefine our traditions as Japanese, women, and Americans. I am no longer blind to the hardships of my female ancestors. No generation of Japanese-Americans should feel ignorant of their historical and familial roots. The two are intertwined. The internment of Japanese-Americans during World War II unleashes a plethora of painful, sometimes perplexing, thoughts. We must remember and grow from their sufferings and sacrifices. I write to keep their memories alive.

NOTES

1. Allan R. Bosworth, *America's Concentration Camps* (New York: Norton,1967), 18.

2. David Y. Arai, interview by author, Seattle, April 20,1996.

3. Yuji Ichioka, *The Issei: The World of the First Generation Japanese Immigrants, 1885—1924* (New York: The Free Press, 1988), 164.

4. Christie W. Kiefer, *Changing Cultures, Changing Lives* (San Francisco: Jossey-Bass, 1974), 14.

5. David Y. Arai, interview by author, Seattle, 28 April1996.

6. Monica Sone, *Nisei Daughter* (Seattle: University of Washington Press, 1979), 148.

7. Kiefer, *Changing Cultures*, op. cit.,179.

8. Ibid., 223.

9. Elizabeth Becker, "Seattle-Postcard: Private Idaho," *The New Republic* 4 May 1992, 9.

10. Mary Tsukamoto and Elizabeth Pinkerton, *We the People: A Story of Internment in America* (Elk Grove, CA: Laguna Publishers, 1988), 23.

11. Carey McWilliams, *Prejudice Japanese-Americans: Symbol of Racial Intolerance* (Boston: Little, Brown, 1944), 113.

12. Jerry Stanley, *I Am an American: A True Story of Japanese Internment* (New York: Crown Publishers, 1994), 13.

13. *The Seattle Post-Intelligencer*, 24 February 1942.

14. Ibid.

15. Mei T. Nakano, *Japanese-American Women: Three Generations 1890—1990* (Berkeley, CA: Mina Press, 1990), 127.

16. Sone, *Nisei Daughter*, op. cit., 145—146.

17. Kenji Kawaguchi, interview by author, Seattle, 20 May 1992.

18. Estelle Ishigo, "Nowhere to Go: Views from Inside an American Concentration Camp by Internee No. 14744," *California* 9 (October 1969): 375.

19. McWilliams, *Prejudice Japanese-Americans,* op. cit., 171.

20. Sone, *Nisei Daughter,* op. cit., 158—159.

21. Sally Sakai-Tsutsumoto, interview by author, Seattle, 22 April 1996.

22. Etsuko Sunimoto-Mizokuchi, interview by the author, San Leandro, CA, 3 May 1996.

23. Ibid.

24. Sakai-Tsutsumoto, interview, op. cit.

25. Ibid.

26. Phil Sudo, "They Took Away Our Rights," *Scholastic Update,* 8 December 1989, 16—17.

27. Sunimoto-Mizokuchi, interview, op. cit.

28. Ibid.

29. Katherine Bishop, "Treating the Pain of 1942 Internment," *New York Times,* 19 February 1992.

30. Kawaguchi, interview, op. cit.

31. Sunimoto-Mizokuchi, interview, op. cit.

32. Ibid.

33. McWilliams, *Prejudice Japanese-Americans,* op. cit., 137.

34. Sakai-Tsutsumoto, interview, op. cit.

35. Valerie Matsumoto, "Japanese-American Women During World War II," *Frontiers* 81 (1984): 8.

36. Nakano, *Japanese-American Women,* op. cit.,138.

37. Matsumoto, "Japanese American Women," op. cit., 8.

38. Deborah Gesensway and Mindy Roseman, *Beyond Words: Images from America's Concentration Camps* (Ithaca, NY: Cornell University Press, 1987), 15.

39. Tsukamoto and Pinkerton, *We the People,* op. cit., 41.

40. Sunimoto-Mizokuchi, interview, op. cit.

41. Bill Hosokawa, *Nisei: The Quiet Americans* (New York: William Morrow, 1969), 332.

42. Gesensway and Roseman, *Beyond Words,* op. cit., 58.

43. Michi Weglyn, *Years of Infamy* (New York: William Morrow, 1976), 90.

44. Audrie Girdner and Anne Loftis, *The Great Betrayal* (London: Macmillan, 1969), 147.

45. Ibid.

46. Sakai-Tsutsumoto, interview, op. cit.

47. Ibid.

48. Tsukamoto and Pinkerton, *We the People,* op. cit., 89.

49. Matsumoto, "Japanese-American Women," op. cit., 8.

50. Sakai-Tsutsumoto, interview, op. cit.

51. McWilliams, *Prejudice Japanese-Americans,* op. cit., 173.

52. Gesensway and Roseman, *Beyond Words,* op. cit., 66.

53. Ibid., 88.

54. Ibid., 115.

55. Arai, interview, op. cit.

56. Girdner and Loftis, *The Great Betrayal,* op. cit., 217—218.

57. Matsumoto, "Japanese-American Women," op. cit., 8.

58. Gesensway and Roseman, *Beyond Words,* op. cit., 112.

59. Smithsonian Museum exhibit, "A More Perfect Union: Japanese-Americans and the U.S. Constitution," 28 April 1996.

60. Nakano, *Japanese-American Women,* op. cit., 138.

61. Girdner and Loftis, *The Great Betrayal,* op. cit., 166.

62. Hosokawa, *Nisei,* op. cit., 332.

63. Girdner and Loftis, *The Great Betrayal,* op. cit.,166.

64. Sakai-Tsutsumoto, interview, op. cit.

65. Ibid.

66. Girdner and Loftis, *The Great Betrayal,* op. cit., 167.

67. Sakai-Tsutsumoto, interview, op. cit.

68. Ibid.

69. Arai, interview op. cit.

70. Page Smith, *Democracy on Trial: The Japanese American Evacuation and Relocation in World War II* (New York: Simon & Schuster, 1995), 196.

71. Hosokawa, *Nisei,* op. cit., 351—352.

72. Smith, *Democracy on Trial,* op. cit., 196.

73. Matsumoto, "Japanese-American Women," op. cit., 10.

74. Sunimoto-Mizokuchi, interview, op. cit.

75. Gesensway and Roseman, *Beyond Words,* op. cit., 104.

76. Sunimoto-Mizokuchi, interview, op. cit.

77. Smith, *Democracy on Trial,* op. cit.,196.

78. Ibid., 195.

79. Matsumoto, "Japanese-American Women," op. cit., 9.

80. Hosokawa, *Nisei,* op. cit., 339.

81. Matsumoto, "Japanese-American Women," ibid.

82. Tsukamoto and Pinkerton, *We the People,* op. cit., 99.

83. Sunimoto-Mizokuchi, interview, op. cit.

84. Tsukamoto and Pinkerton, *We the People,* op. cit., 93.

85. Sunimoto-Mizokuchi, interview, op. cit.

86. Arai, interview, op. cit.

87. Sunimoto-Mizokuchi, interview, op. cit.

88. Joanne Arai-Mar, interview by author, San Leandro, CA, 4 May 1996.

89. Jacobus tenBroek, Edward N. Barnhart, and Floyd W. Matson, *Prejudice, War and the Constitution* (Berkeley, CA: University of California Press, 1968), 149.

90. Stanley, *I Am an American*, op. cit., 69.

91. Nakano, *Japanese-American Women*, op. cit., 168.

92. Sunimoto-Mizokuchi, interview, op. cit.

93. Nakano, *Japanese-American Women*, op. cit., 169.

94. Ibid., 170.

95. Dorothy Swaine Thomas, *The Salvage* (Berkeley, CA: University of California Press, 1952), 319.

96. Matsumoto, "Japanese-American Women," ibid.

97. Tsukamoto and Pinkerton, *We the People*, op. cit., 139.

98. Dillion S. Myer, *Uprooted Americans* (Tucson: The University of Arizona Press, 1971), 268.

99. Hosokawa, *Nisei*, op. cit., 427.

100. Myer, *Uprooted Americans*, op. cit., 270.

101. Ibid., 267.

102. Sunimoto-Mizokuchi, interview, op. cit.

103. Ibid.

(Tsuguji Fujita, Courtesy of The Pacific War Art Collection)

Figure 11. "Japanese prefer dishonor on Saipan."

ELEVEN

Turning Women into Weapons
Japan's Women, the Battle of Saipan, and the "Nature of the Pacific War"

Haruko TAYA COOK

Bold headlines in the morning papers of July 19,1944, told the Japanese public of another major battle fought and lost:

ALL MEMBERS OF OUR FORCES ON SAIPAN MEET HEROIC DEATH REMAINING JAPANESE CIVILIANS APPEAR TO SHARE FATE

The *Asahi Shimbun*, the nation's leading newspaper, ran the official announcement from Imperial General Headquarters, issued at 5:00 P.M., the previous afternoon:

1. It is acknowledged that our forces on Saipan Island carried out the last attack with their total forces from early morning on July 7th and trampled the existing enemy. Some members advanced to the vicinity of Tapochau Mountain, bravely engaged in combat, caused extreme damage, and attained heroic death by the 16th.

2. It appears that the remaining civilian Japanese on Saipan Island always cooperated with the military, and those who were able to fight participated bravely in combat and shared the fate of officers and soldiers.[1]

Few Japanese reading the story, or hearing the news whispered between neighbors, could have fully appreciated what terrible consequences awaited. But the disclosure that Japan had lost a key outpost in its Mandate territories, which had been colonized by Japanese following World War I, trumpeted as a cornerstone of the defensive perimeter girding the empire, and was only 1,500 miles southeast of Tokyo itself, was for most confirmation that the war had entered a new stage. Despite all the assurances of their government, the vaunted defense perimeter that was to have kept at bay American ships and planes had now been deeply pierced, exposing the home islands themselves to attack.

Interested Japanese citizens, tracking the course of the war on maps in their homes and suffering under increased economic privation due to the accelerated effects of the submarine blockade, could draw for themselves grave conclusions about the war's course. The fall of Saipan did not come suddenly, but only after a long series of reverses that had followed the successes of the early stage of the war. With the exception of a brief period filled with victory and clear triumphs at the beginning of war in China and then again in the Pacific, the Japanese people had heard little good news from the front.

War had become a part of the daily routine for the people of Japan. Some, like Nogami Yaoko, a well-established novelist, had confided their building unease and growing concerns to their diaries. In the spring of 1944, she had written of her odd feelings of acceptance: "The severe enemy air attacks have been repeated and two, new [enemy] landing areas were established along the western coast of New Guinea.[2] However, we were calm even when we read this kind of report or articles. Nobody seems to care." This was to her "an astounding change" from the public attitude she had observed even a year earlier, when Attu fell in April 1943, and the whole country had seemed galvanized by the news that the entire garrison had died in battle.[3]

In her entry for June 7, Nogami noted the invasion of northern France by the U.S. and British forces on June 6, and followed the news with interest. From mid-June she recorded reports of attacks on the Marianas, and her attitude toward the conflict seemed to shift. No longer could she view it as a distant war; now it was one in which she was directly involved. By June 15, according to her diary, she had braced herself for the sound of the air raid warnings that would fill many of her nights to come.[4]

From other sources, too, it is clear that, despite Prime Minister Tōjō's bellicose claim that Saipan was an impregnable fortress, many Japanese were prepared for the announcement that the Americans had moved one step closer to Japan itself. The news of the ouster of Tōjō's government and the naming of General Koiso Kuniaki as his successor, with Admiral Yonai Mitsumasa as navy minister and virtual deputy prime minister, soon followed, but these developments were greeted by few with any enthusiasm. The war would continue.

A WINDOW ON THE LAST MOMENTS ON SAIPAN

One month after running the official news of the fall of Saipan, the *Asahi Shimbun* ran large block-character headlines that riveted the reader's eye:

THE HEROIC LAST MOMENTS OF OUR FELLOW
COUNTRYMEN ON SAIPAN SUBLIMELY WOMEN TOO
COMMIT SUICIDE ON ROCKS IN FRONT OF THE
GREAT SUN FLAG PATRIOTIC ESSENCE ASTOUNDS
THE WORLD[5]

The next day, August 20, 1944, headlines in the *Mainichi Shimbun*
proclaimed that Japanese women:

CHANGED INTO THEIR BEST APPAREL, PRAYED TO
THE IMPERIAL PALACE, SUBLIMELY COMMIT SUICIDE
IN FRONT OF THE AMERICAN DEVILS SACRIFICE
THEMSELVES   FOR   THE   NATIONAL   EXIGENCY
TOGETHER WITH THE BRAVE MEN[6]

The *Yomiuri Hōchi*, another major daily, was also emblazoned with the
story:

WOMEN COMBED THEIR HAIR AND PUT ON MAKE-UP
IN DEPARTURE FOR DEATH PURIFIED THEIR BODIES,
PRAYED TO THE SUN FLAG, AND COMMITTED GROUP
SELF-EXPLOSION BY HAND GRENADE[7]

From where did such stories come? Why were they appearing across
the Japanese press more than a month after the battle on Saipan had died
down, long after General Tōjō had been replaced, and at time when the
next grim battles in the Pacific were in the offing? As difficult as it may
be to credit, the origin of these stories was an article by the American
reporter Robert Sherrod in the August 7, 1944, issue of *Time* magazine.[8]
Entitled "The Nature of the Enemy," Sherrod's single-page account of
events on Saipan, part of the issue's wider treatment of the Marianas
invasion and campaign, was one of the most stunning pieces of war
reportage from the Pacific, filled as it was with graphic, unforgettable
images, and powerful questions.[9] While at times maudlin and always
partisan, Sherrod's account purported to be an investigation of the
extraordinary stories the author said he had heard of suicides among some
of the 20,000 civilians on the island, of whom the United States had
interned some 10,000.

"The Nature of the Enemy"—a work by an American journalist—was
to inspire Japanese correspondents overseas to file stories on the battle

Sherrod depicted in his description. Passing through the news rooms and censors in Japan, massaged and replayed, those pieces became the foundation for an unprecedented orgy of glorification of death splashed across the front pages of all the major daily newspapers. Those reports, reactions to them, and the national spiritual mobilization campaigns they fostered established new standards of behavior and commitment for Japan's civilians in the grim wartime conditions their country confronted in the late summer of 1944.

The first story to appear was credited to special correspondent Watanabe in neutral Stockholm, Sweden, and appeared on page one of *Asahi Shimbun* on August 17. It began:

> The facts that all of our loyal and courageous officers and soldiers defending Saipan Island died in action and that even the Japanese civilians who were able to fight participated in combat and shared the fate of the officers and soldiers, were reported worldwide through the announcement of the Imperial General Headquarters July 18, and their loyal, courageous and noble acts have impressed the world. [Now] it has been reported that noncombatants, women, and children have chosen death rather than to be captured alive and be shamed by the demon-like American forces. The world has been astounded by the strength of the fighting spirit and patriotism of the entire people of Japan.[10]

Correspondent Watanabe continued, "An American correspondent, Sherrod," reported the "suicides of our fellow countrymen on Saipan in detail," although, Watanabe added, the "heroic" ends of Japanese were "incomprehensible" and "mystic" to the Westerners. Watanabe stated that Sherrod feared that the suicides of the civilians meant that "the whole Japanese race would choose death to surrender."[11]

While criticizing Sherrod's article as "meant for the lowbrows" and "dramatized in parts because it was written for American readers," the veteran Japanese journalist chose to borrow a report from an American magazine, because of the lack of information available to him regarding the "heroic end" of the noncombatant civilians and "the last moments of [our] fellow countrymen in Saipan."[12] His article included long sections in quotation marks and comments on the American report, which were interspersed with Watanabe's own interpretations for his readers.

The article out of Sweden under a Japanese journalist's byline did not accurately reflect the *Time* article, however. Instead, it was an elaborate construct. All quotations, events, images, and statements in Sherrod's work that might have conflicted with the primary Japanese theme that civilians would willingly die rather than surrender or submit to their enemies were carefully edited out. Missing were Sherrod's poignant mention of a Japanese school boy desperately fighting to stay afloat after his resolve to drown was overcome by a futile desire to live. Gone, too, were mentions of a Japanese officer "hacking at the necks" of his men to kill them or a Japanese sniper mercilessly "drilling" a father and his wife who had led his children to the edge of the sea, only to falter and begin to turn back. Cut were the gory images of Japanese "blowing their insides out" or dashing themselves to death on the rocks of Marpi point. In place of such passages, editors and perhaps censors had inserted other images and pared away any doubts about Japanese civilian resolve and any mention of Japanese military cruelty or indifference to both combatants and noncombatants.

The Americans, too, were stripped of humanity in the edited version. They were made to simply gape in ignorant stupefaction at the "glories" of the Yamato race *in extremis*.[13] The official author of the *Asahi* article asserted that the "American reporter does not grasp the fact that the large number of valuable lives sacrificed [has already begun] to bear fruit by creating an incomparable stimulus to their fellow countrymen toward total armament."[14] Sherrod took them merely as "death," said Watanabe, when, instead, they had to be viewed as "lives that would remain in the spirits of our fellow countrymen and inflame as many as one hundred million," a reference to the notional population of Greater Japan.[15]

Sherrod built his article around a central question, which was raised in the final section. But first he asked:

Death for 80,000,000? What did all this self-destruction mean? Did it mean that the Japanese on Saipan believed their own propaganda which told them that Americans are beasts and would murder them all? Many a Jap civilian did beg our people to put him to death immediately rather than to suffer the torture which he expected. But many who chose suicide could see other civilians who had surrendered walking unmolested in the internment camps. They could hear some of the surrendered plead with them by loudspeaker not to throw their lives away.[16]

After mentioning that the "marines have come to expect almost anything in the way of self-destruction from Japanese soldiers," and noting that the troops had read how Japanese newspapers praised the "dauntless courage" of Japan's Attu garrison commander, which merely "consisted in destroying himself,"[17] the *Time* correspondent declared that "none were prepared for this epic self-slaughter among civilians. More than one U.S. fighting man was killed trying to rescue a Jap from his wanton suicide."

Sherrod's article concluded with a short paragraph incorporating his vital question:

Saipan is the first invaded Jap territory populated with more than a handful of civilians. *Do the suicides of Saipan mean that the whole Japanese race will choose death before surrender?* [emphasis added] Perhaps that is what the Japanese and their strange propagandists would like us to believe.[18]

Although phrased as an interrogatory, clearly the readers of *Time* and those of *Life* magazine which published a versions later that month (accompanied by photographs by that magazine's photographers "documenting" "eyewitness" statements)—were being prepared, and perhaps deliberately, for the actions American forces would "have to take" that could lead to the destruction of the Japanese people as a whole. After all, if the Japanese do not distinguish between combatants and noncombatants, why should we? Sherrod seemed to ask.

Naturally, the last section of Sherrod's piece was not quoted in Japan exactly as written. The *Asahi* inserted a large headline in the article that covered over half of the front page of the August 19 edition: "Prefer Death to Surrender" replaced *Time*'s "Death for 80,000,000?" "Self-destruction" was translated as *gyokusai*, and "their own propaganda" was dropped.[19] The third sentence was rendered "Many Japanese civilians preferred death, rather than capture and torture, and resolutely killed themselves." The last two sentences of the above-quoted paragraph were completely excised. Watanabe's "translation" ended,

Saipan is the first invaded Japanese territory populated with many civilians. Thus, the success of Japanese noncombatants on the islands shows that [the] Japanese, the whole race, choose death before surrender.

The *Yomiuri Hōchi* and the *Mainichi Shimbun* reported the same news, one day later, adding only the a detailed map, also datelined Stockholm. Their use of the *Time* article was similar, although each paper showed recognizable variations in wording and style, reflecting different reporters or editors, and at least giving the appearance of independent confirmations that the story from the battle front was real. The *Yomiuri* version emphasized the death of all on Saipan; it called for revenge:

Oh, what heroism and loyalty! Are there anyone who would not pray for the last moment of their noble fellow countrymen without tears and indignation? Look, American demons, we, one hundred million, will become the demons of revenge! The loyal spirits of our brothers on the isolated island in the southern ocean call to us, covered in blood....The children of the Emperor will resolutely crush the American demons. We must answer their loyal spirits calling to us.[20]

The complete omission in the Japanese accounts of any indication that any Japanese civilians had surrendered stands out as well. Sherrod wrote that at least 10,000 civilians were being held on Saipan and said that "many who chose suicide could see other civilians who had surrendered walking unmolested in the internment camps," or "could hear some of the surrendered plead with them by loudspeaker not to throw their lives away."[21]

In addition to the sensational and twisted treatment of the *Time* article, Japan's leading newspapers drew on noted intellectuals to comment on the deaths of civilian women on Saipan, turning their deaths into weapons directed at the Japanese civilian population. In the August 20, issue of *Yomiuri*, for example, the poet Saitō Ryū wrote how pleased and proud he was of how Japanese women and children had behaved on Saipan. Saitō turned to Japanese history for parallels, identifying, Ōbako, a woman whose husband and son were killed by an enemy of Yamato (Yamato is the ancient name for Japan in the 4th—7th centuries. During the war years it was used as a synonym for Nippon or Japan.) in Korea in A.D. 562. According to the *Nihongi*, an ancient history of Japan, Ōbako became a captive, but took her own life.[22] To Saitō, the women of Saipan stood on the cliffs above the Pacific and waved their sleeves praying toward the mother country just as Ōbako did nearly fourteen centuries before. Moreover, these "Ōbako of Shōwa" "held their children firmly in their arms, dying together."[23] In a concluding paragraph, the poet urged all Japanese women to be prepared for "beautiful death" when the enemy nears the main islands of Japan.[24]

Such articles also appeared in the *Yomiuri*. Dr. Hiraizumi Kiyoshi of Tokyo Imperial University echoed the sentiment:

The women and children of Saipan taught us how splendid the power of blood and tradition was, and they gave us courage which will grow one hundred, no, one thousand times, and will live in the minds of the one hundred million.

In the *Mainichi*, Saitō Fumi, Saitō Ryū's daughter and a noted poet in her own right, pledged:

I swear to the sisters of Saipan that we will fight to the end with the pride of the women who fought to the last in a sea of blood, and with the encouragement of death, and together with the spirits of the women who have fallen beside the soldiers.[25]

Streaming tears, expressions of pride, and protestations that such acts were the vindication of "the Japanese race," "the true nature of Japan," and "unprecedented in history" filled the public pages.   Commentators emphasized repeatedly that the women of Saipan were not of samurai families. Takayanagi Mitsuhisa of Kokugakuin University expressed his emotions when he declared, "I am deeply moved to learn that the blood of the great race will shine with a brilliant light when the time comes."[26]

Not all Japanese accepted these notions approvingly, of course. Critic and foreign policy expert Kiyosawa Kiyoshi's diary—itself one of the most remarkably complete personal accounts of the war—recorded his denunciation of such sentiments on August 20, 1944: "Japanese can neither objectively write articles nor read them." Moreover, he summed up for his diary the intellectuals' accounts of the deaths of women on Saipan, contemptuously as "Feudalism—the influence of ancient warriors—In the time of the airplane, a great admiration for *hara-kiri*!"[27]   Yet neither Kiyosawa nor any other leading figure publicly questioned the message implicit in the articles about the "*gyokusai* on Saipan," that in the face of such praise for the acts of their fellow citizens, all Japanese civilians were now expected to be ready for this kind of death.

What might otherwise appear to be a matter of journalistic rivalry— just jumping on a good story—was likely something much more. There is strong evidence that substantial parts of Japan's leadership—not only commanders of the armed forces, but members of the so-called peace group— were seeking to prepare the Japanese public to carry out such a destiny rather than to give up their own war or their hold on political leadership and control of the Japanese people.

ANOTHER FRONT: POLITICAL STRUGGLES BETWEEN THE GENERAL AND THE SENIOR STATESMEN

While the military battles between U.S. and Japanese forces were grinding on and the toll in human lives was mounting on Saipan, political struggles triggered by the defeat of the Japanese forces intensified. A battle for political leadership in Japan was fought behind the doors of the Imperial Palace and in the chambers of the Tōjō cabinet members and the senior statesmen who were behind Emperor Hirohito.[28]   A pessimistic assessment of the war's future course at last had activated statesmen close to the Court. Their secret debates were about who should take responsibility for the loss and how blame for defeat in the war could be kept from being affixed to the emperor, in whose name the war was fought.

The senior statesmen's primary candidate for full responsibility was General Tōjō Hideki, the prime minister. The diaries of Prince Konoe Fumimaro (himself prime minister through much of the Sino-Japanese War of 1937—1941) and Hosokawa Morisada (Konoe's son-in-law and father of future anti-Liberal Democratic party prime minister Hosokawa Morihiro) show a willingness to "blame Tōjō for everything."[29] They also reveal a shocking callousness to the suffering of the Japanese people as a whole. Lord Keeper of the Privy Seal Kido, the emperor's closest adviser—and a diarist himself—believed Tōjō should be left in his position until the last moment. Hosokawa quoted Kido as having said to Konoe:

> Judging from today's circumstances, the people don't know the [true war] situation at all. After the retirement of the Tōjō cabinet, people might not follow a cabinet that would change a direction even if it were created. Although regrettable, after [the people] have experienced bombings once or twice and suffered a landing on the Homeland, the people would move in that direction. Then, we can change to a peace cabinet.[30]

This extraordinary view—that the people were not ready for peace and had to be softened up by further suffering and even invasion—was coming from one of those makers of Imperial cabinets usually identified as a peace advocate!

On July 2, even before the official "final charge" on Saipan, Prince Konoe sized up the situation as follows:

> The army and navy have both concluded that defeat is unavoidable. But today they are at the stage where they don't have [the] courage to say so publicly.

Konoe then argued that "the enemy was making Tōjō the ringleader of the war, parallel to Hitler, and were focusing their attacks on him. Thus, he should be kept in his position in order to avoid responsibility for the war being placed on the Imperial House."[31] Konoe had showed a willingness to consider creating a new intermediary cabinet as early as June 25, around the time the Japanese government and high command decided Saipan was indefensible. "The end is almost in sight," he wrote, "but it is still necessary for the people to resign themselves to the point where they will accept that as unavoidable. An interim cabinet which could conduct a fleet battle still might be necessary."[32]

The story of how Tōjō Hideki was indeed pushed from office only after he met a steely curtain of silence from everyone from Hirohito to

Kido has often been told. His last efforts to effect a thorough reshuffling of his cabinet and his willingness to give up many of the posts he had accumulated since October 16, 1941, were not enough to save him.[33] The prime minister was forced to resign on July 16, 1944. The appointment of Admiral Yonai Mitsumasa, a former prime minister, as naval minister in the cabinet under General Koiso Kuniaki created to succeed Tōjō reflects the thinking recorded by Konoe.

In these private words of some of the key leaders closest to the Japanese Imperial Household may be seen the true concern of Japan's leaders in early July 1944. It is difficult to say whether the death of civilians on the islands of the Marianas ever entered the minds of the military and political leaders of Japan. They seem to view enemy bombings of the cities and people of Japan, and even enemy landings in the home islands, as a necessary prerequisite for the Japanese people to accept the forthcoming defeat of the nation. After that, these leaders imply, they intended to come out as the "peacemakers," saving Japan, and more importantly, the Imperial House itself, from the consequences of their own earlier decisions.

The Battle of Saipan and the Saipan experience were to be instrumental in the peace process. But it would take the Japanese political and military leadership—including formal and informal government leaders—more than a year to implement their "plan." Saipan was seized upon as the ideal tool to mobilize the Japanese public to this newly defined purpose. By turning the people's minds toward death, they might be prepared for several months of struggle, while the statesmen sought to convince the Allies that the Japanese public was indeed prepared to fight to the last citizen. This would provide a formidable bargaining counter to use against the American demand for unconditional surrender that threatened the position of the Imperial House and the very lives of Japan's wartime leadership.

It is vital when considering the consequences of such thinking to recall that the vast majority of the one million Japanese civilian casualties in the war, and perhaps more than half of the military deaths—over one million—occurred in the last 12 months of the conflict. Between July 1944 and August 1945, as Japan's leaders sought to protect themselves and the institutions they claimed to serve, the people of Japan were in fact sacrificed under a national slogan that was eventually refined as "One Hundred Million Die Together," a natural extension of the illusory image of Saipan's civilians embracing death together with their soldiers, in service to their emperor.

THE REALITIES OF THE SAIPAN *GYOKUSAI*

The notion of *gyokusai* was first introduced into the Pacific War in

May 1943, when American forces retook the outpost of Attu in the Aleutians, seized by the Japanese in the complex operation that had culminated in the Imperial Japanese Navy's disaster at Midway in June 1942. The term—made up from two ideographs with literal meanings of "jewel" and "smashed"—was derived from a sixth-century Chinese classic telling of the morally superior man who would rather destroy his most precious possession than compromise his principles.[34] Rather than the meaningless deaths of a garrison overwhelmed by superior numbers and firepower, the final charge of the Japanese garrison under Colonel Yamazaki on Attu island was transmogrified into an act of heroic self-sacrifice and given the name *Attu gyokusai*. The phrase had poetic resonance and soon caught on as a euphemism with wide application.[35]

The most important point to be made about the Saipan *gyokusai* is that it did not happen. At least it did not occur to the extent, or in the way, it was reported. Nor did what took place on Saipan—especially at Marpi Point and places now called in the tourist trade "Banzai Cliff"— support the conclusion that all Japanese civilians were prepared to die rather than surrender. Despite horrible scenes of suicide and murder, fear and misery, desperation and despair, the facts do not support the stories of the mass death on Saipan. In order to grasp the magnitude of what happened, and what application of this particular term to the events on Saipan has meant, we need to ask who killed themselves on Saipan, why the term *gyokusai* was applied to that battle, and inquire as to what that tells us about the importance of Saipan to the understanding of the final year of death in the Pacific.

From where did the idea originate that the garrison on Saipan, and ultimately the entire population of the island, should "destroy themselves"? The Imperial General Headquarters Army Section Confidential War Diary [*Rikugun Daihon'ei Kimitsu Sensō Nisshi*] for June 24, 1944, contains the following entry, accompanied by a detailed criticism of why operations on Saipan had not gone as hoped:

> The Saipan Defense force should carry out *gyokusai*. It is not possible to conduct the hoped-for direction of the battle. The only thing left is to wait for the enemy to abandon their will to fight because of the "*Gyokusai* of the One Hundred Million."[36]

Saipan was the jewel in the crown of Japanese South Seas Mandates at the beginning of the Pacific War. These islands, former German colonies awarded to Japan after World War I, had been developed gradually since the first settlers from the Japanese empire began arriving.[37] Saipan was not fortified before the war. Indeed, the first large-scale military force was not assigned to the island and its neighbors until an army billeting party arrived in February 1944. Far from being an "impregnable fortress" as Tōjō is reported to have called it, construction of defensive installations had barely begun when the Americans landed and what efforts had been made had been drastically limited by shortages in construction materials, especially concrete and lumber.

The largest town on the island was Garapan, often called "the Tokyo of Saipan," located at the foot of Mt. Tapochau. Home of the South Seas Agency branch for the Marianas before the war, it held some 160 shops, two movie theaters, a post office, schools, an agricultural laboratory, a Catholic church, a Buddhist temple, a Shintō shrine, and the judiciary building of Garapan. Ten miles of roads, 18 feet wide and built from crushed coral reef, ran through the town. Among the shops were 47 houses of prostitution, employing as many as 277 women, broken into two classes—31 *geisha*, with presumed artistic abilities, and 246 "saké servers"—divided by ownership and patronage among the different groups, each serving different economic, social, and ethnic clientele.[38] The major industries were moderate-scale sugarcane growing and sugar processing, tuna catching and drying, and the mining of mineral phosphates for fertilizer that was needed increasingly in Japan.

The civilian population at that time was approximately 29,000, comprised of 22,000 Japanese, 1,300 Koreans, and 5,000 islanders.[39] The vast majority of the Japanese were from Okinawa prefecture and were themselves seen by main island Japanese as second-tier citizens. One visitor from Japan, the novelist Ishikawa Tatsuzō, described them as "Japanese gypsies."[40]   Below the Japanese on the social scale were the Korean subjects of Japan and the Kanaka and Chamorros peoples, whose islands, the Marianas, were before the coming of European and Asian colonists.

Most of the island's civilians were still on Saipan when the American forces landed. Although evacuation efforts had begun in March 1944, the sinking on March 6 of *Amerika Maru*—one of the first two evacuation ships—with the loss of all but two of 500 women and children aboard, deterred others from attempting the 5-day passage back home until May 31, when both the *Chiyo Maru* and the *Hakusan Maru* sailed, only to be sunk a few hundred miles north of the islands. Able-bodied men under 60 and above elementary school age could not leave and became increasingly important in the late efforts to scrape together organized defensive positions despite shortages of cement and any building materials for reinforced shelters.[41]

The precise number of civilians, including settlers, natives, and military employees—extremely difficult to determine accurately—was probably between 16,000 and 20,000 when the American V Amphibious

Corps stormed ashore on Saipan. While the military forces of Japan were given priority in food and water allocation and were nearly annihilated in fighting with the advancing Americans, the civilians, who had been frightened out of Garapan by the early bombings, soon found themselves exposed to the full wrath of American and Japanese firepower. Some surrendered on encountering American forces and soon began their lives as captives in camps for survivors established by the Americans at Susupe.[42]   So intense was the fighting, and so difficult was the American advance that, at least at first, these camps were little better than enclosed wastelands, with little food and medicine.[43]   Much of the food needed to sustain life in the camps had to be grown within them, even months later.

Other civilians were driven along with surviving Japanese troops to the northern part of the island, where nearly 4,000 were eventually cornered. It was in this part of Saipan, near Marpi Point that most of the civilian suicides and killing of civilians by Japanese forces and American close-in assaults took place. Such scenes as those described by Robert Sherrod were given pictorial life by the great Japanese war artist Fujita Tsuguharu in his massive painting *The Day of Gyokusai on Saipan Island.* The painting seemed a complete confirmation and actualization of the very essence of the ecstasy in death of the Yamato race. It portrayed dark-skinned natives and Yamato women nursing infants gathered at the edge of the island heights. Young women, mere girls, really, are shown grasping each another in grim embrace as they plunge daggers into one another's sides, while a defiant rifleman stands in full view of the enemy and aims one last shot at them and a woman hurls herself from the stark cliffs to their rear as the next in line kneels toward Japan in prayer.[44]

Examining the history of the Battle of Saipan closely, it is clear that a third group of noncombatants wandered around the mountains of Saipan seeking any available shelter, hiding, and searching for food. Some still hid in the hills until well beyond the end of the battle, a few civilians remaining at large until the end of the war, in danger not only from American search parties hunting down still-resisting Japanese soldiers but also from those same Japanese troops. In all, at least 15,000 civilians survived the battle.[45] Despite the focus on their acts, those who killed themselves or were killed or murdered in the desperate final moments of the battle, especially women and children, in reality numbered about 1,000. To these tragic final deaths must be added several thousand others killed in the course of the more than monthlong battle.

As terrible as those last figures are to contemplate, and as awful a human tragedy as each death was, this was not total self-annihilation, this was not *gyokusai* !   Many thousands survived, most of them openly choosing surrender to death. Battered civilians in excess of 10,000 and more than 1,000 military men were captured and returned to Japan after the war. Use of the term *gyokusai* allowed the conductors of this war to finalize the destruction of many lives in a glorified tone that combined a sense of tragedy and a resulting feeling of both lamentation and righteous indignation.

While news of *gyokusai* on Saipan spread through the main islands of Japan, wounded and starving soldiers still were wandering in the mountains of Saipan chased by U.S. strafing parties until they were made into "war dead" or fell into enemy hands. Thousands of noncombatants were also still roaming until they were captured by or surrendered to the U.S. forces. Back in Japan, all on the island were viewed as "heroic dead." Following the war the first repatriation ship carried about 1,000 to the main islands of Japan. In the second stage of repatriation, 10,000 survivors were taken to Okinawa. Noda Mitsuharu, a sailor who was captured after the "final charge" on July 7, found his own grave had been erected back at home when he returned and his name erased from the family registration.[46] The fate of the Koreans among the internees is still undetermined.[47] All those survivors of the Battle of Saipan were made into living ghosts by erasing them from the memory of the living world and remain "missing" in most accounts and public memory to this day.

SAIPAN: THE DEFINING BATTLE

Saipan was the battle that defined the character of the Pacific War. Americans—soldiers, policymakers, and the folks on the home front—learned what many took to be "the nature of the enemy" along the sharp coral promontories and the towering cliffs at Marpi Point. After the island's capture by American forces, Japan's leaders and propagandists presented their version of events there to the public as a vision of the nature of the war they were fighting and as a glorification of the national spirit.

"I have always considered Saipan the decisive battle of the Pacific offensive," wrote Holland M. ("Howling Mad") Smith, the U.S. Marine Corps general who commanded the assault that began on June 15, 1944. As he contemplated the 16,525 U.S. casualties, including 3,426 killed and missing, which accounted for nearly 25 percent of his command's total strength of 67,451 men, Smith declared after the war that its seizure made Allied victory absolute.[48] Although final figures for Japanese casualties on Saipan vary considerably, with American sources identifying 23,811 "enemy buried" and 1,780 captured (838 Koreans), with some 14,560 civilians taken into custody,[49] according to one Japanese source, of the 43,682 military defenders from all units, 41,244 died in the Battle of Saipan (June 15 to July 10, 1944).[50]

Such horrendous military losses are cause enough to remember Saipan, but for the future course of the Pacific War—and for those who made decisions based on estimates of how Japan, the Japanese, and their leaders would perform—the deaths of 1,000 or more civilians (multiplied by propaganda, indifference to individual suffering, and desperation) would ultimately prove the most significant statistic of all.

In the year after Saipan's fall in July 1944, and in the subsequent half century, portrayals and interpretations of the Battle of Saipan have helped define how American strategy and victory, Japanese resistance and defeat, and the subsequent horrors of war in the Pacific were justified to history. Saipan—the battle and the mythology of the battle—helped forge an unholy alliance of national stereotypes and self-justifications. America's conviction that a demand for unconditional surrender and ruthless willingness to exact the highest possible toll in enemy lives, military or civilian, was the only guarantee of a certain victory in the end was to guide U.S. policy through the firebombings of Japan's cities, the invasion of Okinawa, and the atomic devastation wrought on Japan in lieu of the contemplated invasion. The strategy in Japan that exploited the image of Saipan and the Marianas amounted to a threat of national self-destruction and suicide embraced by Japan's leadership to stave off abject surrender and acceptance of American demands at any cost.

NOTES

1. *Asahi Shimbun*, 19 July 1944. The announcement was followed by a rather lengthy description of the situation on Saipan by the reporting directors of the Imperial Army and Navy at the Imperial Headquarters.

2. These were marking the advance of General MacArthur's slowly developing offensive in the southwestern Pacific.

3. Nogami Yaoko, *Nogami Yaoko Zenshu: Dainiki, Daihachikan Niki 8* [The Collections of Nogami Yaoko: The Second Period vol. 8, Diary 8] (Tokyo: Iwanami Shoten, 1988), 272.

4. Ibid., 316.

5. *Asahi Shimbun*, 19 August 1944.

6. *Mainichi Shimbun*, 20 August 1944.

7. *Yomiuri Hōchi*, 20 August 1944.

8. See *Time*, 7 August 1944. The Marianas campaign was covered extensively. Sherrod's piece, "The Nature of the Enemy," appeared on 27.

9. *Life* magazine dealt with Saipan and the Marianas in the August 28, 1944, issue and married Sherrod's earlier *Time* article—stated to be an eyewitness account from Saipan—with the strong photographs by *Life*'s own photographers Peter Stackpole and W. Eugene Smith, 75—83. The result was doubly shocking confirmation of Sherrod's main themes. The four photos of an attempted backing away from "group suicide" by a father, mother, and their four children foiled by a Japanese sniper seemed to confirm stunningly Sherrod's version of the events, 80—81.

Almost as horrifying was the photo captioned "As a Jeep Bears Wounded Yank to Rear, Bulldozer Scoops Grave for Some Saipan Japs" on the page following a photo of a grave marker for an "Unknown" U.S. Marine of the 4th Division, 82—83.

10. *Asahi Shimbun*, 19 August 1944.

11. In the brief introduction to Sherrod's piece, it is perhaps possible to locate the source of this line in Watanabe's article: "In this dispatch, *Time* Correspondent Robert Sherrod describes the gruesome deeds, incomprehensible to the occidental mind, which followed the U.S. victory," 27.

12. See *Time*, 7 August 1944, 27.

13. The first story cited referes to a detachment of marines on amphibious tractors who tried to capture seven Japanese on a coral reef:

As the amphtracks approached, six of the Japs knelt down on the reef. Then the seventh, apparently an officer, drew a sword and began methodically to hack at the necks of his men. Four heads had rolled into the sea before the marines closed in. Then the officer, sword in hand, charged the amphtracks. He and the remaining two Japs were mowed down. *Time*, 7 August 1944, 27.

The *Asahi* "translation" reads a little differently. Six out of seven men committed suicide on the reef, and one, apparently an officer, even from a distance, charged toward the amphtracks brandishing his sword with a subordinate, and he and his subordinate attained their heroic ending being strafed by the American forces. *Asahi Shimbun*, 19 August 1944, 1. A drastic rewriting took place here, making the text more palatable to the readers back home in Japan. Moreover, the numbers do not add up.

14. *Asahi Shimbun*, 19 August 1944, 1.

15. That there was an ongoing "dialogue" between the American and Japanese press was shown even in Sherrod's article. Indeed, both American and Japanese journalists used enemy reports to heighten the drama and verité of their reports. When Sherrod needed to substantiate his claim that Japanese actions were deliberate, he referred to Japanese newspapers and their tale of the "dauntless courage of Captain Yamazaki"—the commander on Attu who led the final charge. He disparagingly noted that it was "only in the seventh paragraph it is revealed that Captain Yamazaki's courage consisted in destroying himself." Having said that "the marines had come to expect almost anything in the way of self-destruction from Japanese soldiers," Sherrod continued, "But none were prepared for this epic self-slaughter among civilians. More than one U.S. fighting man was killed trying to rescue a Jap from his wanton suicide."

16. *Time*, 7 August 1944, 27.

17. Ibid.

18. Ibid.

19. The euphemism *gyokusai* is most often rendered in English in a heroic image, such as "sacrificial battles," "death-before-surrender," or "self-sacrificial battle." The term became a device for propagandists in Japan to turn horrific suffering and near useless death into a heroic, and acceptable, sacrifice for the sake of the country. See Haruko Taya Cook and Theodore F. Cook, *Japan at War: An Oral History* (New York: The New Press, 1992), 14—15, 263—65, for discussions of how the term was applied. It will be discussed further below.

20. See the front pages of *Yomiuri Hōchi* and *Mainichi Shimbun* for 20 August 1944.

21. *Time*, 7 August 1944, 27.

22. See W.G. Aston, translator, *Nihongi: Chronicle of Japan from Earliest Times to A.D. 697* (Tokyo: Charles E. Tuttle, 1972), 85. Her husband was Tsukinokishi Ikina. She composed:

> Of the Land of Kara,
> Ōbako
> Waves her head-scarf,
> Turning toward Yamato.

23. See Hyōgoken Kindai Bijutsukan and Kanagawaken Kindai Bijutsukan eds., *Egakareta Rekishi* [The Images of the History in Japanese Modern Art] ("*Egakareta Rekishi*"-ten jikko iinkai, 1993), 100, for a wooden statue of Ōbako.

24. See the August 20, 1944, issue of *Yomiuri Hōchi*. The author noted, "Despite the fact that they were neither brought up in the family of warriors, nor the wives of warriors," like Ōbako and the wife of Hosokawa Tadaoki, who stabbed her two children and committed suicide when they were surrounded by the enemy, Saitō declared, the women of Saipan "achieved a sublime and grand last moment, by coloring red the rocks of the South Ocean," with "sublime Japanese blood." Saitō does not bother to provide an explanation of a life of Hosokawa's wife. Her life history is quite complex. She is also known as Hosokawa Gracia (1564 –1600). She was a convert to Christianity and is also known as the very model of the virtuous warrior wife. She was a third daughter of Akechi Mitsuhide and was married to Hosokawa Tadaoki, the eldest son of a daimyo [a wealthy Japanese landowner]. Her husband refused to support her father when Akechi killed Oda Nobunaga (1534—1582). She was obliged to retire to the countryside and eventually allowed to live in Osaka by Hideyoshi (1536—1598) who ruled as the second of Japan's three great unifiers of the late sixteenth century and who brought about the end of feudal civil wars. There she was baptized and became a Christian. Hosokawa Tadaoki later sided with Ieyasu (1542—1616). When Ishida Mitsunari (1560—1600), who had disputed with Tokugawa Ieyasu for leadership of Japan on the death of Hideyoshi, attempted to capture her as a hostage, a retainer of the family executed her on orders of Hosokawa Tadaoki. See *Japan: An Illustrated Encyclopedia*, vol. 1. (Tokyo: Kodansha, 1993), 567.

25. See the front page of the August 20, 1944, issue of *Mainichi Shimbun*. See the third page of the August 20, 1944, issue of *Asahi Shimbun* for these comments of Takayanagi Mitsuhisa, a professor at Kokugakuin University.

26. See the third page of the August 20, 1944, issue of *Asahi Shimbun* for these comments of Takayanagi Koku, a professor at Kokugakuin University.

27. Kiyosawa Kiyoshi, *Ankoku Nikki, 1942—1945* [Diary of Dark Days, 1942—1945] (Tokyo: Iwanami, 1990), 221—222. We can also note that Kiyosawa left his diary in his residence in Karuizawa out of fear that its contents might be revealed were it in his Tokyo home (201). He wrote how the reporting director of the Imperial Navy invited the representatives of various circles, including "liberals," in order to discuss "how to heighten the fighting spirits of the people."

28. Such reports were numerous. For example, see also Nogami Yaoko, *Nogami Yaoko Zenshu,* op. cit., 377—379. At the time these articles appeared, Nogami Yaoko was in Kitakaruizawa as a part of her regular summer stay. She made no comment on the *Time* article, perhaps because she did not read newspapers regularly, filling her entries of August 19 and 20 instead with details of a barter of ten eggs for some of her children's clothing, her comments on her reading of a work by the Chinese radical writer Lu Xun, the notation that she had completed writing a short piece called "A Memory of Miss Haruko," and her effusive appreciation of her "luxurious" breakfast of bread with butter and a few cups of Indian tea with milk and sugar. But on August 21 she related a story she heard about a woman who had boarded an evacuation ship from Saipan with her 3-year-old child after having given birth to a second child just 2 hours before it sailed. The ship was torpedoed en route and despite an order to abandon the ship without children, she floated in the sea with her two children, hanging to a float until eventually all three were rescued. Rather than write of deaths, of which she may not have heard, she asserted the value of the will to live.

29. Bōeicho Bōei Senshishitsu, *Senshi sōho, Daihon'ei Rikugunbu (8): Shōwa 19-nen made* [War History Series, Imperial General Headquarters: Army Division, Part 8: Up to 1944] (Tokyo: Asagumo Shinbunsha, 1974), 445—518. Konoe quoting *Nikki,* 26 June 1944, 496.

30. Ibid., quoting Hosokawa Morisada *Nikki,* 26 June 1944, 497.

31. Ibid., quoting Konoe *Nikki,* 2 July 1944, 497—498.

32. Ibid., quoting Konoe *Nikki,* 8 July 1944, 499.

33. Robert J.C. Butow, *Tōjō and the Coming of the War* (Stanford, CA: Stanford University Press, 1961), 431—433, gives a bare-bones version.

34. John W. Dower, *War Without Mercy: Race and Power in the Pacific War* (New York: Pantheon Books, 1986), 231—33 and 352—353 notes 61—64, discusses one interpretation of the origin of *gyokusai* and its development. Dower dates the phrase *ichioku gyokusai* ("the shattering of the hundred million like a beautiful jewel") from April 1945. Actually, it appeared at least as early as June 24, 1944, when it was used in the *Daihon'ei Kimitsu Sensō Nisshi* that day. See Mikano Hirosuke, *Higeki no Saipan. Zettai Kokubōken no hōkai* [The Tragedy of Saipan: The Collapse of the Absolute Defense Zone] (Tokyo: Futowaaku Shuppansha, 1992), 118.

35. Kiyosawa Kiyoshi, *Ankoku Nikki,* op. cit., 39—40. Yet the phrase did not answer all questions about such actions as Attu to observers, even in Japan. On May 31, 1943, Kiyosawa Kiyoshi noted in his diary that following the previous day's broadcast of the news of the *gyokusai* of Japanese forces on Attu by Imperial General Headquarters, "Today's papers tell us that at the end only a hundred and a few score remained, that the wounded committed suicide, and the healthy charged [into the enemy]." Rather than accept the story, Kiyosawa set down in his diary this thought: "If they were not people related to the military, the following questions would come up and become social problems." Criticizing such events, he asks why headquarters did not dispatch more men, although it was reported that Colonel Yamazaki did not request even one more soldier. Isn't the lack of reflection of their strategy leading to all strategic failures? he asked. What is the meaning of "gyokusai-ism"—a phrase he coined—as seen on Attu? "Next, it will be Kiska," he wrote.

It appears we have one division there. *Gyokusai*-ism will deprive them of their lives. Is this good for the nation? This will be an issue in future. The general public may not make any inquiry into such things. Oh, stupid general public!

Perhaps Kiyosawa was able to foresee what lay ahead for the people of Japan. While the High Command did eventually evacuate the Kiska garrison prior to an American descent on the island, Kiyosawa remained angry at the Japanese public for their seeming indifference to news he felt should have shocked them into demands for clarification.

36. Mikano Hirosuke, *Higeki no Saipan,* op. cit., 116—118.

37. See Mark R. Peattie, *Nan'yō : The Rise and Fall of the Japanese in Micronesia, 1885—1945* (Honolulu: University of Hawaii Press, 1988).

38. Yamada Akiko, *Ianfutachi no Taiheiyō sensō* [The Pacific War of the Comfort Women], cited in *Saipan muzan: "Gyokusai" ni tsuieta "umi no Mantetsu"* [The Remains of Saipan Dreams: The "Manchurian Railway of the Sea" which Died in "*Gyokusai*"], ed. Suzuki Hitoshi (Tokyo: Nihon Hyoron sha, 1993), 180.

39. Suzuki Hitoshi, *Saipan muzan,* ibid., 179. See also Hirakushi Takashi, *Nikudan!! Saipan-Tinian Sen: Gyokusai sen kara seikanshita sambō no shōgen* [Human Bullets!! The Saipan Tinian Battle: The Testimony of a Staff Officer Who Returned from a *Gyokusai* Battle] (Tokyo: Kyōei Shobō, 1979), 266.

40. Ishikawa Tatsuzō, "Kokai Nisshi" [Ocean Diary] in *Ishikawa Tatsuzō sakuhin-shu* dai nijusankan [Ishikawa Tatsuzō Collection, vol. 23 (Tokyo: Shinchosha, 1973), 405—7.

41. Hirakushi, *Takashi Nikudan!!*, op. cit., 266. Horie Yoshitaka, *Higeki no Saipan tō* [The Tragedy of Saipan Island] (Tokyo: Hara Shobō, 1967), 80—81. Those in the northern part of the towns were run by Japanese from the main islands, with one run by a Korean. In southern Garapan they were segregated—one for Okinawans, five for Tokyo people, two from Fukuoka, and one owned by Koreans. See also Bōeichō Bōei Kenshūjō Senshishitsu [Self-Defense Agency, Self-Defense Research Institute, War History Office], *Senshi Soshō* [War History Series], vol. 6, *Chūbu Taiheiyō rikugun sakusen, 1: Mariana gyokusai made* [Army operations in the Central Pacific, Part 1: Up to the Mariana *gyokusai* (Tokyo: Asagumo Shimbunsha, 1967), hereafter cited as BBKS. *Chūbu Taiheiyō rikugun sakusen, 1: Mariana gyokusai made*, 618, says total evacuees numbered 2,300.

42. See Suzuki Hitoshi, *Saipan muzan*, op. cit., 198—201.

43. Many American accounts refer to the plight of the Saipan captives in piteous terms and speak of the lessons learned for the coming battle of Okinawa. Few speak fully of the truly terrible conditions in the American camps as the battle raged on the island. Many, many internees died of disease and malnutrition, and deaths were very common. More than 1,000 are documented to have died in captivity.

44. Naruhashi Hitoshi et al., eds., *Taiheiyō sensō meigashū* [The Pacific War Art Collection] (Tokyo: Nobel Shobō, 1967),128—29.

45. BBKS, op. cit., 618, gives the total number of civilians on the island at the end of July as about 15,700, including Koreans. The camp was divided into four: islanders, Japanese, Koreans, and military men and civilian employees of the Army (*gunzoku*).

46. Noda Mitsuharu, interview with the author.

47. Suzuki Hitoshi, *Saipan muzan*, op. cit., 206.

48. General Holland M. Smith and Percy Finch, *Coral and Brass* (New York: Scribner, 1949), 181—182, quoted in Samuel Eliot Morison, *History of United States Naval Operations in World War II*, vol. 5: *New Guinea and the Marianas, March 1944—August 1944* (Boston: Houghton Mifflin, 1953), 339—340. Such general views of the importance attached by Tokyo to Saipan may be seen in many official and semi-official sources, for example, Carl W. Hoffman, USMC, *Saipan: The Beginning of the End* (Historical Division HQ, U.S. Marine Corps, 1950), Jeter A. Isely and Philip A. Crowl, *The U.S. Marines and Amphibious War* (Princeton, NJ: Princeton University Press, 1951), and Philip A. Crowl, *United States Army in World War II:* Vol. 2. *The War in the Pacific;* Part 9. *Campaigns in the Marianas* (United States Army, Office of Military History, 1960).

49. Morison, *History of United States Naval Operations*, op. cit., 339.

50. Kuroha Kiyotaka, *Taiheiyō sensō no rekishi* [History of the Pacific War], vol. 2 (Tokyo: Kōdansha, 1989), 143—46. See Cook and Cook, *Japan at War*, op. cit., 291—292.

Part III
1946–Present

(*al-Dabbur* magazine cover, December 6, 1943)

Figure 12. Lebanese liberation celebrated, 1943.

TWELVE

Gender, War, and the Birth of States
Syrian and Lebanese Women's Mobilization During World War II

Elizabeth THOMPSON

In December 1946 a prominent Lebanese feminist named Imilie Faris Ibrahim published an article entitled "New Horizons for Lebanese Women." With the end of World War II, and with the end of more than a quarter century of French colonial occupation earlier in the year, Ibrahim heralded a new era for women. She foresaw women's liberation in "the pervasive spirit of progress in the world and the new opportunities afforded women in the new international order," particularly in the international law of the new United Nations, which called for legal equality among men and women, and in the advent of new household appliances, which would free women from housework so that they might engage more fully in economic and political life. Ibrahim urged women not to abandon the new roles they had adopted in the struggle for liberation from France, but rather to expand their political and economic roles in the service of national progress: "Women's concern is to share with men in the building of a new society."[1]

World War II had opened new possibilities for national liberation and profound social change. During the war, Syria and Lebanon shared with the other home fronts the experience of deep state penetration and reorganization of economy and society. Paradoxically, even as the French state claimed new powers over society, it became more vulnerable to challenge, as French rule was weakened when the Germans occupied France. The dual processes of liberation struggle and wartime economic transformation produced a highly charged moment of national reinvention that opened debate on every aspect of social and political life. Perhaps nowhere else in the world were the terms of independence so closely tied to the war's conditions.

The legacy of World War II and the liberation from France would not, however, bring parity—or even clarity—to gender relations in independent Lebanon and Syria. The new states were born in 1946 in profound uncertainty about their future political and social order, an uncertainty that was preeminently expressed in the ambivalent place of women in both the legal structures of the new countries and in the political ideologies that posed competing visions of the family in national life. Debates about the relationships among women's rights, family, and nation both defined and divided the major parties that emerged during the war. Should women carve out their place in the citizenry primarily as mothers, devoted to rearing new generations of citizens and represented in public affairs through male household heads? Or should women participate, as Ibrahim urged, in public affairs alongside men, in a workforce and citizenry organized around individual rights rather than the family unit? Were the roles of mother, worker, and citizen complementary or contradictory? Gender lay at the very core of conflicts over the basic structure of the new polities. Women's status would become not only a litmus test of their rival visions of the nation-state but also the price of compromise between them at the dawn of independence.

The conditions of the "birth" of these independent states would define gender relations in Syrian and Lebanese public life for several decades to come. This is because wartime policies and rights won from the French institutionalized a gender regime within the newborn states. Groups mobilized not only to capture the state but to redefine it by establishing a new agenda of mutual rights and responsibilities between the state and the citizenry. They believed that the state was the principal arena in which their newly independent society would be realized and organized. Because both Syria and Lebanon were ruled by a unified government headquartered in Beirut, and because mobilization centered on this state, the goals and patterns of mobilization and reform resembled one another.

Because of the paucity of historical documents from the wartime years, we can at this point sketch only the general outlines of the terms upon which men and women entered independence.[2] We cannot, for example, fully detail organizational structures of the groups that mobilized. But we can, from government reports, memoirs, interviews, and journalistic accounts, identify the major goals and major players in the conflict, as well as the laws and reforms that were implemented by the time the last French troops departed. The story that emerges suggests that women's efforts to mobilize on many fronts were undermined by the fact that their very presence in political affairs was questioned.

THE WAR AS OPPORTUNITY FOR MOBILIZATION

Syria and Lebanon were created out of former provinces of the Ottoman Empire, which had been defeated in World War I. France ruled Syria and Lebanon from 1920 under the authority of the League of Nations, which granted the French a mandate over the territory. Mandates were intended as a temporary period of tutelage by advanced countries to prepare new nations for self-government. In most respects, however, the French ruled Syria and Lebanon as they had ruled their other colonies and resisted all pressures to end their "temporary" tutelage. However, two major changes occurred during World War II: French rule was drastically weakened, and economic crisies bred mass discontent. The war thus provided both the opportunity for oppositional groups to mobilize against the state and the conditions within which these groups would formulate and seek to realize their goals.

At first, the war brought little change to daily life in the Levant. In contrast to recruitment in France's North African colonies, Syrian and Lebanese men were not mobilized to fight the war in Europe. The French did, however, suspend the Syrian and Lebanese constitutions in July and September 1939 and arrest opposition leaders, particularly those sympathetic to the Soviet Union and Germany. Military repression stifled protest.

Dramatic change came in June 1940, with the German invasion of France and the imposition of Vichy rule in Syria and Lebanon. By late 1940 the region sank into economic crisis. Critical markets and sources of income and supplies were lost when the border with British Palestine was partially closed and the Syrian branch of the Iraqi petroleum company's pipeline was shut off. Inflation and food shortages touched off violent confrontations with the state. Bread riots and hunger marches were met by Vichy tanks in the streets of Aleppo and Damascus. Protests spread to Lebanon in March 1941 forcing the resignation of President Emile Eddé, who had cooperated with the Vichy government. The Vichy high commissioner, General Henri Dentz, made initial efforts toward economic planning, a rudimentary rationing program, and pay raises.

Vichy rule lasted one year. In June 1941, British and Free French forces occupied Syria and Lebanon to block rising German influence in the Middle East. The Free French at first justified their ousting of Vichy with the promise of imminent independence. They then contradicted that promise by making it clear they intended to rule with a firm hand, demonstrated in a much-publicized visit by Charles de Gaulle that summer. But Free French rule was severely weakened by the fact that they could make only tenuous legal claims to the right to rule under the League of Nations mandate and because they depended heavily on British troops.

Opposition movements mushroomed with vigorous campaigns against the postponement of independence and continued shortages and inflation. Under British pressure, the Free French were forced to permit elections in the summer of 1943. But when the newly elected Lebanese president and prime minister sought to make good on Free French promises of autonomy by introducing changes to the constitution, the Free French arrested them. This provoked huge street demonstrations and an international scandal. Again, under British pressure, the Free French were forced to release the politicians and, in January 1944, to begin handing over control of government ministries to the Lebanese and the Syrians. By January 1945 Syrian and Lebanese nationalists controlled their entire governments, except for the military. The last French troops left in 1946.

While the British played a decisive role in loosening the French grip on their governments, Syrians and Lebanese themselves shaped the terms of independent rule. The major political movements had emerged, and been suppressed by the French, in the 1930s. The nationalists who took power in 1943—1944 were paradoxically the strongest and most weakly organized group. They were elite landowners and businessmen from families that had been prominent in politics since the last decades of Ottoman rule. They used their wealth and prestige to build personal power bases, as patrons of clienteles usually based in a single city and in districts where they owned land. They did not command national political parties in the modern sense.

The nationalists' main opponents, in contrast, built more sophisticated organizations to mobilize followers through ideology. The Communist party in both Syria and Lebanon grew rapidly in the late 1930s and 1940s, mainly among students and urban workers and in alliance with labor unions. A grassroots, populist Islamist movement had spread since the 1920s and by 1939 had built a powerful and increasingly centralized leadership structure. Based primarily in cities, the Islamist groups recruited middle- and lower-middle-class civil servants, professionals, and merchants through social welfare programs, mosques, and schools. In Lebanon, Christian groups were also powerful, particularly the Maronite church, the paramilitary Maronite organization called the Phalanges, and the French Jesuits.

Political mobilization during the war, then, generally ranged from leftist networks of the Communist party, university students, and labor unions to socially conservative organizations often affiliated with religious groups. The nationalists espoused a motley assortment of political views, which ranged from socially conservative to secularist, progressive, and even socialist, loosely united by their central demand for independence from France. They were also united, in the eyes of the communist left and populist Islamist right, by their wealth. Both communists and Islamists explicitly opposed the economic and political dominance of nationalist elites. The nationalists generally defended the social order produced in the previous 75 years by colonialism and integration with the world economy, which had benefitted landowners and harmed peasants, artisans, and small merchants.

Women's mobilization was also rooted in the prewar period, most deeply in literary salons and educational and charitable groups established before and during World War I. Membership in these groups was mainly from the middle and elite classes. Many of the women were daughters, wives, sisters, and mothers of prominent nationalists. In the late 1920s they formed two umbrella political organizations, the Lebanese Women's Union and the Syrian Women's Union, each of which united dozens of smaller cultural and charitable groups and sponsored conferences on women's issues. Both were headquartered in Beirut and Damascus and maintained close contacts with one another. Both were loose federations of a highly decentralized structure led by a committed core of several dozen elite women, with hundreds of others called in intermittently when demonstrations and conferences were staged. The women's movement in Syria and Lebanon did not produce an outstanding charismatic leader, in contrast to the centralized movement headed in these years by Huda Sha'rawi in Egypt. This in part reflected the Levantine movement's breadth and democratic nature, as leadership rotated regularly among elected presidents. However, the expansion of the women's movement was inhibited by the very small size of the middle and upper classes in the region, by the low rate of literacy, and by the fact, to be detailed below, that women's very presence in public affairs was hotly debated. Given these limitations, the level of women's mobilization is all the more remarkable.

Their small size forced the women's unions to adopt a different strategy from men's groups. Men could recruit much larger numbers through a broader network of male spaces in mosques, in the market, and at workplaces and schools. Women did recruit in girls' schools and among cultural and charitable groups, but they could not call out the numbers men could in demonstrations. They also did not have access to parliament or government office as a vehicle of protest. Women's strategy, then, focused on symbolic acts, journalism, and formal petitions to governments to advance their goals. They buttressed these efforts with alliances with male-led groups, mainly nationalists. A minority of elite women, like Imilie Faris Ibrahim, affiliated with the Communist party. The Communist party was unique in that it had organized a formal women's wing. "The Communist party is the only party where woman has a place," declared Rugina Khayta at a 1943 rally.[3] It was the main vehicle through which lower class, working women were organized, mainly among those working in factories organized by labor unions. Yet other women mobilized mainly in alliance with religious groups, in Christian and Muslim charities. There were women who undoubtedly sympathized with Islamist populism, but we have little record of their activities, as they appear to have worked in circles quite distant from the women's unions.

Because of its indistinct and fluctuating organizational structure, women's wartime mobilization is better studied by focusing on goals, and on the actual rights won from the state, rather than focusing on the institutions themselves.   Women mobilized in distinct roles as soldier-citizens, workers, and civic-minded mothers.   While women's goals in each of these guises overlapped, each one tended to prioritize the women's agenda differently.   In their guise as militant patriots, women's union leaders sought explicitly to parley their service into voting rights.   As workers, women sought equal rights in the workplace.   And as mothers, a broad spectrum of women sought varied claims to authority in social affairs.   While this essay intends to suggest the broader spectrum of women's mobilization, it will focus mainly on the arenas in touch with the women's unions, and mainly on the cities where they were most active, in Beirut and Damascus.

WOMEN AS SOLDIER-CITIZENS: THE CAMPAIGN FOR POLITICAL RIGHTS

Elite Lebanese and Syrian women had sought women's right to vote since the end of World War I.   Proposals for suffrage had been debated and defeated in the Syrian Congress three months before the French occupation in 1920, and in the Lebanese parliament in 1924.   At that time, Syrian and Lebanese women had perceived that the rights of citizenship around the world seemed to fall upon soldiers who defended their country militarily.   They used their own experience, as charity workers in World War I, and the example of Nazik Abid, a Syrian nurse who participated in the battle against French occupiers, to demonstrate their claims.   (Abid was dubbed by some the Joan of Arc of the Arabs.)   Opposition to women's suffrage had come mainly from conservative rural landowners and tribal leaders, and from religious leaders, groups that would continue to be prominent in politics with French support.   They argued that granting women the vote would upset the entire social and legal order. They reminded lawmakers that Islamic law required women to obey their husbands and valued women's testimony as half that of men.   While in the 1930s women repeatedly petitioned their governments to reopen the issue, no serious movement or parliamentary debate occurred.

Indeed, by the 1930s, the women's unions had all but set aside political goals, as they shifted their strategy toward an alliance with nationalists and focused on preparing younger women to participate in the hoped-for independent nation.   Adile Bayhum al-Jazairi, a leader of the Syrian Women's Union, had since the 1920s run a prominent girls' school that emphasized Arab culture in its curriculum.   She had married into one of the most prestigious families in Damascus, the Abd al-Qadirs, descended from an Algerian resistance hero who was deported to Syria in the mid-nineteenth century. Al-Jazairi cooperated in numerous nationalist protests, recruiting women to join and even lead demonstrations and write petitions. Her belief was that if girls were trained as good citizens, and if women demonstrated their patriotism, male nationalists would heed their call for the vote. "Her first priority was the fight for independence, and the second was for women's rights. My mother didn't believe in revolution—she believed in evolution," recalls her daughter, Amal al-Jazairi.[4]

The women's unions also organized a number of international conferences in the 1930s, which produced resolutions proclaiming women's right to vote and to act as political representatives in parliament, as well as proposals to broaden women's education and reform personal status laws to enhance women's rights in marriage, divorce, and inheritance. These resolutions received courteous support of progressive nationalists, although they were not implemented by the nationalists who had gained government positions in the mid-1930s.

By 1938 women like al-Jazairi began to question the wisdom of their alliances with male-led organizations. Al-Jazairi's patience had worn thin, as women's issues were continually ignored. She and other Syrian and Lebanese women attended a women's conference in Cairo that year, which sought to reaffirm women's political participation with referenda proclaiming their support for Palestinians, then engaged in a revolt against British rule. When al-Jazairi returned from the 1938 conference, she vowed to place women's goals on an equal and simultaneous footing with the fight for independence.

Women's union leaders had further cause for concern when some nationalists forged closer ties with increasingly powerful Islamist groups, which focused their battle against the French on opposition to women's presence in public and to a proposal to institute civil registration of marriage. Furthermore, nationalists' prestige had fallen in the late 1930s in both Syria and Lebanon, as they had failed to secure an independence treaty from France, and as impending war seemed to postpone renewed efforts. Syrian nationalists joined the Islamists' demonstrations in March 1939, with pamphlets that warned: "The French want to take from you your wives, your daughters, and your children!"[5] Thousands of Muslim women and men demonstrated in the streets of Syrian and Lebanese cities, and the French high commissioner was forced to issue a public retraction on the radio. The price of alliance and liberation increasingly appeared to be the reaffirmation of religious and male authority over women.

World War II brought a renewed campaign for women's political rights by the women's unions. Women again joined violent confrontations against the French. But now, they carried their own banners proclaiming the names of women's groups, and they publicized their participation in the anti-French conflict as qualifications for suffrage. Three incidents in the later war years highlighted the new suffrage strategy: women's protests in November 1943 against the arrest of the Lebanese president and prime minister, their highly publicized attendance at a 1944 feminist conference in Cairo resulting in a new Arab Feminist Union, and Damascene women's battlefield service against the French in May 1945.

In Lebanon the suffrage campaign climaxed in 1943. In June a group of prominent Lebanese women petitioned the Lebanese president to place the question of women's suffrage on the ballot in that summer's elections. The president refused, telling them the issue should be taken up by the elected government. But in September the newly elected president, Bishara al-Khuri, also decided to postpone the issue of women's vote. When al-Khuri and other officials were arrested in November for asserting their political autonomy by seeking to change the constitution, Lebanese women seized the opportunity to prove they deserved full citizens' rights.

According to a participant in the events, Eugenie Elie Abouchdid, women gathered daily during the crisis in Beirut, at the houses of arrested ministers, and marched to foreign embassies with petitions for international intervention. While young men organized armed militias in protest, women staged their own military battle on November 16. More than 200 women marched that day, escorted by the men's militias, through the town to the residences of the Greek Orthodox bishop and the mufti, the highest Muslim official, where they were blocked by French and Senegalese troops with bayonets and tanks on a narrow street. The women stood their ground in what they viewed as a climactic national battle. On November 23, after the French had backed down, victory marchers gathered to hear speeches by the released politicians and their wives. Representatives of the women's union conferred their congratulations on the government. Mrs. Bishara al-Khuri, wife of the Lebanese president, was proclaimed by other speakers at the rally as "The Mother of the Lebanese People."[6]

Lebanese women's leaders sought to translate their confrontation with armed soldiers into political gains. Eveline Bustros, a prominent writer and president of the Lebanese Women's Union between 1942 and 1946, had led some of the 1943 demonstrations. She called them the supreme expression of Lebanese women's patriotic vocation, which was equal to, and sometimes surpassing, that of men.[7] Rose Shahfeh, former head of the Lebanese Women's Union, urged women to seize the opportunity opened in 1943 to attain full political rights: "The Lebanese Women's

Union has taken an active part in the Lebanese political movement, with excellent results. This proves that if women interest themselves in political life, they can be productive."[8]   Another union leader, Ibtihaj Qadoura, proclaimed in a 1945 speech: "Woman is no longer solely for the home, because the whole world can no longer do without her services."[9]

The momentum begun in 1943 carried through the next year, as Lebanese and Syrian women's union leaders attended another Arab women's conference in Cairo in December 1944.   The conference sought explicitly to highlight women's claims to political participation, above and beyond their reiterated calls for social reforms.   The conference called on Arab governments to hire women for what were considered men's jobs and to name them to parliaments, to grant women the vote, and to suppress usage of feminine suffixes in the Arabic language in favor of neutral usage. It buttressed these demands by proclaiming the establishment of the Arab Feminist Union, comprising member unions from Egypt, Lebanon, Syria, Palestine, Transjordan, and Iraq.   The Arab Feminist Union was the symbolic vehicle of women's contribution to the Arabs' national struggle against colonial rule and was designed specifically to complement the formation, at about the same time, of the Arab League of States.

Damascene women would have their own opportunity to position themselves as soldier-citizens worthy of the vote in violent battle against the French in May 1945.   That month, 200 women demonstrated against the continued presence of French troops, calling for a Syrian national military.   They did so not just as nationalists, but by carrying banners representing women's groups. When fighting broke out, the women acted as auxiliaries to male rebel soldiers. "Everyday women would distribute food to rebels all around Damascus.   On the last day, the day the Parliament was bombed [by the French], they bombed the old fortress which was used as a prison at the time.   Adile Bayhum [al-Jazairi] and Widad Quwwatli were elderly by then, and it was their turn to distribute food," recalls one of the activists, Nadida Cheikh al-Ard.   The women could not make their way home because the fortress lay in their path. "They went into the orchards to hide, and met up with the prisoners who had just escaped from the fortress."   Cheikh al-Ard says the two women were congratulated widely for their bravery in enduring a night alone not just with strange men, but criminals at that.[10]

Although these symbolic acts of soldierly combat inspired enthusiasm in the press and in discrete rallies, they did not result in the building of a sustained mass movement that might have given the women's suffrage cause the weight it needed to match their opponents in the political arena. They also did not result in women's suffrage at independence.

Upon their return from Cairo in late 1944, for example, Syrian and

Lebanese delegates met ridicule in the press and deaf ears among their nationalist allies, who now controlled their governments. When meetings were held in 1945 to organize the Arab League, only men were designated as representatives. The Arab Feminist Union (AFU) nonetheless sponsored a reception for the new league, at which the AFU president, Egyptian feminist Huda Sha'rawi, objected to women's exclusion. The Syrian prime minister, Faris al-Khuri, responded by praising women for their role as the rear guard of the male vanguard of the Arab army and called women the "ornament of man."[11]

Auxiliary roles in what was cast as a male soldiers' victory over colonialism seemed to bring women only auxiliary status as citizens. In 1946 in Lebanon, a proposal to grant the right to vote to a small number of educated women never even reached the floor of parliament for a vote (partial suffrage would eventually be granted in 1953). Syrian women's far more explicit alliance with military causes would pay off only after a military coup in 1949 ousted conservative nationalists. The coup's leadership promised an era of progress and also introduced limited suffrage for educated women. These belated and limited victories only underscored how women entered independence on terms quite different from male citizens, who had enjoyed universal and unconditional suffrage since the 1920s.

Women's failed bid for the vote as soldier-citizens underscores the broader context of their effort to attain a place in the civic order. Their defeat rules out one commonly cited reason for the failure to attain the vote under the French: that the suppression of women's suffrage in the French metropole blocked it in French colonies as well. DeGaulle decreed French women's right to vote before World War II ended, but Syrians and Lebanese did not rush to do the same. This suggests that internal forces of resistance to women's suffrage had as much to do with suppressing women's political rights as colonial forces did. Indeed, as we turn to women's mobilization for economic and social rights, it becomes clear that women's vote would have undermined the construction of new traditions of women's dependency on men at work in these arenas. When Faris al-Khuri called woman the auxiliary and ornament of man, he placed women implicitly in a role both subordinate to and dependent on men, within marriage and family.

WOMEN AS WORKERS: THE STRUGGLE FOR ECONOMIC RIGHTS

A month after the French departed, on June 27, 1946, a Lebanese female tobacco worker, Wardah Butrus Ibrahim, was shot dead by police during a strike. At the tobacco factory, south of Beirut, the workers' union had demanded implementation of laws protecting salaries and family support allowances.   But their employers claimed that since the laws had been adopted under French rule, the laws did not apply in independent Lebanon.   On June 16 a group of women union members formed a picket line to block shipments of tobacco from leaving the plant.   On June 27 the company forced a truck guarded by gendarmes through picket lines. The women sought to block it by laying down in the road, and the gendarmes opened fire.   In addition to Ibrahim's death, twenty-seven workers, including thirteen women, were wounded in the bloody confrontation.[12]

During the war, increasing numbers of women mobilized as workers. Lower-class women had long worked outside the home, particularly in services such as domestic help and in bathhouses.   But the war also returned employment to thousands of other women who had lost jobs in the previous two decades as homeworkers and in family businesses hurt by competition from increased foreign imports.   Particularly devastated had been textile and clothing workers, as markets had been flooded with inexpensive European-made fabrics and clothing.   When fighting in World War II disrupted international markets, Syrian and Lebanese women stepped in to produce at home much-needed clothing, handicrafts, and food products.   In addition, a small proportion of women had since the late 1930s obtained jobs in the emergent industrial sector. Several thousand women worked in the tobacco, textile and food-processing plants that expanded in wartime, especially in Lebanon.   Their numbers in industry remained small relative to the mobilization of women in Europe and the United States, however, because men were not withdrawn from the labor force for military service and because the level of industrialization was still low.   Nonetheless, urban women's contribution to wartime production, and to the economic welfare of their families, had grown to be quite significant.

A second new trend in women's work was the employment of middle class and elite women.   Hundreds began working as schoolteachers after World War I, and expansion of state schools in the 1940s increased their numbers further.   A few pioneering women began working in the professions in the late 1930s and during the war, as journalists, lawyers, and doctors.

It was labor unions and the Communist party, rather than the elitist women's unions, that mounted the most sustained and powerful campaign for increased economic rights from the state for all workers, including women.   Their reasoning was that women's production was necessary for progress and that women's labor qualified them as full-fledged citizens. Imilie Faris Ibrahim, the prominent communist and feminist quoted above, argued in an article published in December 1943 that women deserved the vote because they work hard for the good of the country, at factory jobs and in the fields.[13] Women workers' attainment of economic rights, however, differed from men's, as they became the object of public policy not just as workers but as women as well.

The French mandatory state had reluctantly come to intervene in the issue of women's labor just 5 years before the war. In 1934—1935, under pressure from the International Labor Organization and the Permanent Mandates Commission, the French drafted and pushed through the Lebanese and Syrian parliaments protective labor legislation limiting women's hours, assuring maternity leave, and banning women from workplaces with heavy machinery and dangerous substances. Labor unions supported the measures, both because they included the 8-hour workdays they had been seeking for all workers and, it seems, because the laws appeared to secure high-paying industrial employment for men in a time of high unemployment. The precise impact of the laws in the Levant is unclear. Government records report that families objected to the loss of women's wages, and women concealed the number of hours they worked from inspectors.[14] The laws certainly helped to reduce women's entry into new industrial sectors at a time when their employment in home and family industries was declining due to increased imports.

The construction of women as a separate and inferior category of worker along with children, was a significant political and economic step. Women carried their diminished legal and economic status into the critical 1940s, and the ambiguity of the state's position on women's labor was only accentuated by the changes in government during the war. Vichy's family-and-tradition propaganda was replicated in the Levant's French newspapers and among conservative political circles, rekindling movements to remove women from their jobs and to restrict them to domestic roles. In November 1940 the newspaper *Bayrut* ran a story entitled "Why France Kicks Spouses Out of Jobs." The reason, according to a radio broadcast by the minister of labor in Lyons, was that married working women rob wealth from men and other families.

In early 1941 the Lebanese Bar Association sought to ban women's membership in the bar. Invoking the spirit of Vichy, the association's board rejected the membership application of a woman who had graduated from law school that year. General Dentz, the pro-Vichy high commissioner, not surprisingly, approved of the bar's decision. But critical press coverage forced the bar to revise its decision, allowing unmarried women to join the association and practice law. Two women were immediately admitted, Imma Qashu' and Alice Karam.[15]

The Free French at first vowed to reverse Vichy policy and advance a liberal position in defense of women's work. In May 1943 they publicized a showcase munitions complex called De Gaulle Park in the press, featuring 100 Lebanese women who had joined the war effort. In photos, the women wore white laboratory coats. They were quoted as saying they were happy to give up their sewing machines and typewriters to manufacture truck parts.[16]

Women in the civil service and industrial sector legally shared in the rights won by unions during the war. The Free French implemented a broad package of programs providing minimum wage guarantees and accident insurance to civil servants and workers in large industries, with explicit provision of the benefits to both female and male workers on the principle of equal pay. This was a partial fulfillment of demands made by unions for more than a decade. But as labor unrest continued, these benefits were expanded and guaranteed formally at independence in 1946 in comprehensive labor codes passed by both countries. Both codes guaranteed labor's right to form unions and to strike, affirmed women's right to work, and assured women various benefits including, in Lebanon, a woman's right to paid maternity leave and to a pension when she quit her job to marry.

In addition to labor protection laws, massive labor strikes pressured the Free French into adopting family welfare programs. These included cost of living allowances and supplementary family allowances for child support. Cost of living allowances were critical in offsetting inflation, adding anywhere from 45 percent of salary for the highest-paid workers to 250 percent for the lowest-paid. The family allowances were awarded to workers with dependents, providing a schedule of wage bonuses according to the number of children in the family. They amounted to a family wage that paid household heads more than single workers for the same job. Benefits were by law available to workers of both sexes.

However, the spirit of equality went little beyond the letter of the law. Few women seem to have benefited substantively or directly from either the labor protections or the welfare programs. Most women worked outside of the government and industrial sectors covered by the policies; indeed, the women had been excluded from industry precisely because of the 1934—1935 protection laws. Most women schoolteachers worked in the private sector; those who worked in state schools were routinely paid less than men. And because of pressures to quit working upon marriage, a large percentage of middle-class working women were unmarried teachers who lived with their families and contributed their earnings to support the household. Because there was almost always a male member of the family also working, these women did not, in general, qualify for family allowances. Reflecting the virtual exclusion of women, government documents routinely referred to the family allowance recipients as pères de famille (fathers of the family).

There is reason to believe that women's exclusion was not merely an oversight. Perhaps because the family allowance program seemed to favor the construction of families around male household heads, profamily groups tended to support it. Vichy prejudice against women's work did not disappear in 1941, particularly in Lebanon. In the same month that the labor package was announced, May 1943, the top French university in the Levant, St. Joseph University, held a much-publicized lecture series entitled "The Lebanese Family," in which speakers denounced individualism and called on women to quit their jobs and have more children. Lectures called for more state support to fathers.

In sum, while women moved into the labor force in large numbers, women workers received a disproportionately smaller share of labor benefits from the state. If the 1946 labor codes were manifestos of workers' rights as citizens, then the legal differentiation between male and female workers implied a legal differentiation between their rights as citizens. State labor and welfare policies represented an unstable compromise between policies focused mainly on aiding all workers, and so indirectly supporting their families, and policies that sought the state's direct support of family units headed by male breadwinners with women and children as dependents.

The issue of women's work also split the women's movement. The Women's Social Democratic League, founded in Beirut in 1943 and funded primarily by the state and by private French and Maronite donors, pledged to support higher wages for fathers than bachelors and to discourage women from working, because working women took jobs from fathers and neglected their maternal duties. And while they did not condemn women's work, neither did the elite leaders of the women's unions give high priority to women's right to work in their many manifestos. Their position may have in part reflected a class bias. There is no doubt that many elite women sought through charities to help poor women support their families. Nadida Cheikh al-Ard, mentioned earlier in connection with the May 1945 rebellion, ran a program that supplied sewing machines and materials to poor rural women outside Damascus. The Women's Social Democratic League, too, planned a crafts school to teach poor women skills. But these groups did not advance work as a right for women, but rather as a sorrowful necessity for the poor. They promoted, rather than battled, the underlying tendency of public policy, which was to construct women as auxiliaries to, and dependents on, male household heads. This partly reflected the fact that the cultural ideal that women should not work, unattainable for poor women, was a normative reality for the elites heading the women's unions. Women like Wardah

Butrus Ibrahim, shot during a labor strike to defend economic rights won during the war, existed in a world far from that of the women's movement's leaders.

Class was likely only part of the reason for the women's unions' maternalism and indifference toward women's right to work. Maternalism was also partly a political strategy, as elite women sought desperately to define a role in public affairs for women that would not excite opposition by challenging men's roles either at home or in the workplace. It was a defensive strategy adopted in the face of mounting opposition to women's presence, not just at work, or in a voting booth, but generally in public affairs by the increasingly powerful Islamist movements. We now turn to women's mobilization as civic-minded mothers, and why this became the dominant discourse surrounding women's place in the civic order.

WOMEN AS MOTHERS: THE DEMAND FOR SOCIAL RIGHTS

On June 2, 1942, a group of 300 Muslim women in Aleppo, Syria's most northern city, led 2,000 protesters against the high price of bread on a march to the governor's office. Police were mobilized to stop the march, and ten women were injured. In 1942 and 1943 women in Aleppo, Beirut, and Damascus were mentioned more than a dozen times in French police reports as the principal participants in demonstrations against wartime economic policy. In perhaps their crowning achievement, the leaders of the Lebanese Women's Union led a boycott that shut down Beirut's markets in February 1944, forcing merchants to reduce prices.

No other role was as widely adopted in women's wartime mobilization as that of mothers. As guardians of family welfare, they demanded state action to make basic necessities available and affordable. Common women who led lives far from the women's unions salons and conferences turned out in large numbers. Their activism contrasted sharply with images of their passivity during the First World War, when they and their children had been featured in the press as the tragic and helpless victims of the famine, that had killed up to a half million people. When World War II broke out, all Syrians and Lebanese over age 30 recalled the nightmare of that famine, and feared its return. This time, however, women appeared determined to take their fate into their own hands.

Motherhood as the basis for making claims upon the state was a far older role than that of worker, and far more common than that of soldier-citizen. Poor women had often led bread riots in Ottoman times. Wealthier women had begun, in the 1880s, to take their motherly duties outside their homes, by organizing charities and girls schools. New in the period of French rule was the elevation of motherhood to political significance. "[Woman] was created to raise distinguished men and loyal youths who will revive the nation and [Islamic] religion," proclaimed a

1931 Damascus student journal.[17] "In motherhood is the power to increase the capacity of the male population and the power and life to establish a new nation," wrote Rose Shahfeh, a leader of the Lebanese Women's Union, in 1939.[18] Even the communists joined in. Mythical models of the Soviet woman who works in the morning, does charity work in the afternoon, reads before dinner, and cares for her children in the evening were regularly printed in their official magazine.[19] While social conservatives, especially religious groups, vaunted maternalism as a separatist ideology, placing mothers' importance for the nation squarely within the home, others, including women's unions, sought to extend mothers' importance in public affairs, in an ideology of civic motherhood.

Indeed, the women's unions had not only justified their demand for suffrage on the basis of their battle scars, but also justified it by asserting the importance of mothers to the nation. At the 1944 Cairo conference, they sought explicitly to extend mothers' skill and duty to a wider public arena, in pledges that mother-citizens would work to guard public morals, particularly in combating drug abuse, gambling, and prostitution. But mothers' involvement in wider public affairs also required, in their view, reform of the legal terms of motherhood: freedom to choose marriage partners and to marry at a later age; greater access to education; more power to obtain divorce and child custody; guarantees of inheritance rights. The terms upon which motherhood was defined (here called social rights) were essential keys to economic and political rights and to the full participation of women in their nations' future.

The proposal to reform religious laws covering women's status drew stiff opposition from some, but not all, religious leaders. While some distinguished Christian clergy and Muslim scholars supported moderate change, populist religious leaders of both religions led campaigns against reform—as seen in the 1939 civil marriage conflict. These movements extended their criticism of increased women's rights in marriage and divorce to include criticism of women's increasing freedom of movement, which they claimed contradicted their proper duties as mothers. Indeed, in the years since World War I women had claimed a greater presence in public spaces, as increasing numbers of them took jobs outside the home, attended school, traveled across the city by tramway, attended new movie houses, and participated in demonstrations and public gatherings of all types. Women's mobility was, in the eyes of religious populists, the most glaring threat to family integrity and male authority.

The debate over the proper role of mothers flared into impassioned and sustained conflict as Syria and Lebanon approached independence. The reason lay in the very conditions of colonial rule and in the backlash against the progressive diminution of religious authority in the previous century. In the name of social and political progress, the Ottomans had dramatically reduced the Muslim clergy's long-standing control over the court system and education. By 1914 their sphere of influence in social affairs was virtually restricted to matters regarding personal status—marriage, divorce, inheritance. Muslim clergy saw their status plummet further after World War I, when French Christian rulers occupied the territory.

The terms of French rule, however, broadened the basis for the politicization of religion around gender issues. The mandate charter, as set by the League of Nations, prohibited the French from interfering with local law and custom. This in effect meant that while the Ottomans had acted freely to diminish the power of the clergy, the French could not. Religious groups based their protests of French rule and policy precisely on this provision, claiming to protect local custom. And the local custom over which they enjoyed power was precisely that area of the law that most concerned women's civil status.

In promoting their notion of civic motherhood, then, the women's unions confronted not just tradition but also the reinvention of a more powerful religious conservatism as a product of colonial rule. The women's unions did not see themselves as acting against religion. On the contrary, they framed their reform proposals within the discourse of noted religious scholars who had been promoting Islamic reform since the turn of the twentieth century. What they faced in the Islamist groups, however, was a populist response to elitist reforms coupled with the class-based tensions that fueled the rise of their movements. Among Christians in Lebanon, the reform of women's status did not encounter a specifically legalist opposition, but rather an array of conservative maternalisms espoused by the powerful Maronite church, and by politicians, clergy, and paramilitary groups influenced by Vichy and fascist ideals of domestic motherhood, as expressed in the 1943 St. Joseph University conference on the family.

In Syria the populist Islamist campaign climaxed in 1943—1944, when Islamist groups succeeded in banning women from movie theaters in one city (Hama) and staged a violent demonstration against a mixed-sex charity ball to be held at the French Officer's Club in Damascus. The demonstration ended when police shot two protesters dead. Syrian nationalists, now in control of the government, canceled the ball and later further appeased Islamists by not implementing personal status reforms demanded by the women's union after the 1944 Cairo conference. Although nationalists had gained control of the government, their personal clienteles were increasingly vulnerable to the challenges of the better organized Islamist movement.

Women fought back for their right to appear in public, a right critical not just to entertainment but to their ability to work and participate in charities and politics. Indeed, during the war, women for the first time organized collective campaigns to promote unveiling. A group of Muslim women in the city of Hama, where Islamists had successfully banned them from cinemas, petitioned the government in Damascus shortly afterward for permission to leave their homes unveiled, and met opposition from the same *shaykhs*. In 1944, in the southern Lebanese city of Sidon, a women's cultural group staged a collective unveiling at one of their meetings, provoking such an uproar that the city shut down for 2 days. The women were then barred from the school where they usually met by the Maqased, a relatively moderate Muslim educational foundation.

Despite opposition, a mass level of support appears to have emerged for the reforms in social rights proposed by the women's unions, reforms that would enable mothers to exercise their concerns in public. By 1945 observers noted that the familiar black, veiled silhouette of women in the street was quickly disappearing. The dramatic change was ascribed primarily to the removal of foreign power: As long as the French had ruled, veils had been symbols of resistance and protection of local custom. For these thousands of women, national liberation seemed to fuel hopes of personal freedoms as well.

This terribly complex political conflict around mothers' proper role helps explain a puzzle of the war years. Why weren't women's unions able to capitalize on the wartime mobilization of women—particularly as mothers—to achieve the social rights they demanded at the 1944 Cairo conference? Were not the hundreds of mothers who regularly took to the streets to demand state protections for their families the potential mass base for the elitist women's unions? If every woman could not be a soldier, or if the number of working women was too small to form such a base, should not motherhood have been the key to mass mobilization?

Contemporaries and later historians have blamed the women's unions themselves, for being elitist, lazy, and poorly organized. Leaders met in luxury in one another's homes or at fancy hotels. They divided their time among many different activities and did not concentrate energy where it might be most profitable. Charity benefits were often merely occasions to socialize. The demonstrations led by women were organized on an ad hoc basis, with little infrastructure to build continuity and sufficient numbers of loyal adherents.

While this focus on the internal failings of the women's movement may be partially justified, our view of the political context in which the movement acted suggests compelling external reasons for its inability to organize mothers. The structural limitations to women's ability to assemble and to participate politically were built into religious laws ossified by the terms of the French mandate and reinterpreted in conservative terms by religious groups empowered by the mandate with autonomous jurisdiction over those laws.

Thus, on what might have been the most fertile ground for recruitment, maternalism, the women's unions were stymied. Motherhood was indeed praised almost universally at independence as an important moral and social influence on the nations' progress. But motherhood as it remained defined made it extremely difficult for the women's unions to pursue their goals of extending mothers' influence into the wider public arena. The stalemate on the issue of social rights paralleled and aggravated women's ambiguous claims to economic and political rights as well. In all three areas, women's gains were offset by the construction and institutionalization of new forms of dependency on men.

CONCLUSION

Women mobilized on many different fronts, asserting themselves in a variety of roles in the fight against French rule and in their efforts to survive the hardships of a wartime economy. Through the efforts of women like Imilie Faris Ibrahim and Wardah Butros Ibrahim (no relation), women had secured a significant, if small and contested, place in the workforce with rights guaranteed at least in law. Through the efforts of Adile al-Jazairi and the many women teachers and school directors like her, Syrian and Lebanese women were gaining far more education than they would ever have. And through the symbolic acts of the women's unions, women's patriotism and importance in the new nations was at least rhetorically affirmed.

But the conditions of colonial rule and war confronted women with more contradictions and higher trade-offs than men faced. Women's claims to social and political rights had by the 1940s become the crucible in which rival visions of a new political order were tested, among the three major movements of the war years: Arab nationalists, religious groups, and Communist party/labor unions. Each of the groups advanced its own version of the time-honored adage that the basis of a healthy nation is a well-ordered family. Gender lay at the center of political contestation. Gender also informed the structure of political life. The terms of the mandate and French policy had structured the political playing field to ensure the dominance of male, and often patriarchal, interests, through the protection of local (religious) law, through the promotion of a new urban and male workforce in public works programs that became the basis of union organizing, and through the incorporation of patriarchal leaders—tribal, religious, and landowning—into government.

Women's attempts to organize as players in politics were hampered by their marginalized or subordinate status in the arenas that gave birth to the unprecedented mass mobilizations of the period: in schools, in workplaces, in street demonstrations, at mosques, in parliaments, and in courts. Their contested civic and social status, evidenced in the conflicts over their very presence in public spaces, aggravated their efforts to organize for political and economic goals. Likewise, women's relatively meager economic resources could not support the kinds of organizations built by union dues or donations from nationalist landowners. These circumstances weakened women's position in the debates over the future shape of nation and role of citizen.

While only a minority of women were labor activists or feminists, thousands more women moved into employment during the war, asserted a public presence, and supported bread riots with new political demands on the government to guard family welfare. Women in these years had quietly asserted a civic role that, while not fully recognized in law, knitted together communities and families in distress. Most of these women were pious, and they likely abhorred the secular nationalist-religious cleavage in politics. Their civic identity and rights as citizens were burdened by trade-offs that did not burden men's struggle for rights in the new nations. Men generally did not risk violation of religious morals in seeking national rights.

Imilie Faris Ibrahim's postwar predictions about the opportunities for women afforded by the United Nations and household appliances would bear little fruit, as world unity was split by the Cold War and liberation struggles, and as the promise of prosperity in independence seemed to fade. And as this essay has suggested, international influence likely would not have cut through the web of conflicts surrounding women's status. Far more determinative to women's rights were the domestic political structures bequeathed by colonial rule and the wartime liberation struggle. In both countries, the construction of rights and motherhood as either/or choices rather than as complementary civic roles emerged from the major parties' contest for power. The compromise between religious and secularist visions of the family in the political order would in effect compromise women's economic, social, and political rights for decades to come.

NOTES

1. Printed in the Lebanese communist magazine *al-Tariq* [The Path], 24 December 1946.

2. The lack of documentation is due mainly to the destruction of government documents during the war, to censorship of the press, and to the economic difficulty of publishing in wartime. In addition, many surviving government documents are unavailable to the public, as French archival regulations block their release for 60 years.

3. *al-Tariq* 20 (29 December 1943).

4. Personal interview with Amal al-Jazairi, Damascus, 28 October 1992.

5. As reported in a letter from High Commissioner Gabriel Puaux to the Ministry of Foreign Affairs in Paris, dated 22 March 1939.

6. Eugenie Elie Abouchdid, *Thirty Years of Lebanon and Syria (1917—1947)* (Beirut: Sader-Rihani, 1948), 132—67.

7. As quoted in the preface to a reprint of Takieddine el-Solh's 1926 novel *La Main d'Allah* (Beirut: Dar an-Nahar, 1988), xxiv.

8. *Les Echos*, 13 December 1944, 2.

9. Quoted by the French police, the *Sûrété générale*, in report no. 1994, dated 24 May 1945.

10. Personal interview with Nadida Cheikh al-Ard, Damascus, 9 October 1992.

11. As quoted in Margot Badran, *Feminists, Islam and Nation: Gender and the Making of Modern Egypt* (Princeton, NJ: Princeton University Press, 1995), 246.

12. Jacques Couland, *Le mouvement syndical au Liban, 1919—1946* (Paris: Editions Sociales, 1970), 351—55.

13. Imilie Faris Ibrahim, "Sawt al-Mar'a: Haquq Jadida" [Women's Voice: New Rights], *al-Tariq* 2 no. 20, (29 December 1943): 15—17.

14. Ministère des Affaires Etrangères, *Rapport à la Societé des Nations sur la situation de la Syrie et du Liban (Année 1936)* (Paris: Imprimerie Nationale, 1937), 30; Couland, *Le mouvement syndical*, op. cit., 239.

15. *Al-Nahar*, 13, 16, and 29 March 1941.

16. *Le Jour*, 22 May 1943.

17. "The Hijab: Woman and Her Duty," *Lisan al-Talaba* 3 (August 1931): 3.

18. "Motherhood Is My Role: What It Is and How I Use It to Serve My Nation," *al-Amali* 1 no. 22, (27 January 1939): 4—8.

19. See, for example, "The Duty of the Arab Woman in the Current War," *al-Tariq* 1 no.14, (15 August 1942): 17—19.

(Courtesy of Antonella Fabri)

Figure 13. Resettled Mayan refugees working in the tourist trade.

THIRTEEN

Silence, Invisibility, and Isolation
Mayan Women's Strategies for Defense and Survival in Guatemala

Antonella FABRI

Before the signing of the peace accords on December 29, 1996, Guatemala was engaged in a devastating civil war that lasted 36 years. The army and the guerrilla or revolutionary forces (URNG) were the protagonists of this ongoing struggle that caused social fragmentation in different sectors of the civil society. Indigenous people, women, and children experienced the most severe repercussions, as many of these survivors continue to live their lives in fear. Among the various consequences of this war, in this essay I concentrate on the conditions resulting from internal displacement and the strategies of survival adopted by indigenous people in Guatemala City. In particular, I focus on the testimony, as given in 1991, while I was conducting my fieldwork research in the capital city, by a Mayan Quichè woman, Rosa. In 1982, after the assassination of her father and brother by the army, Rosa moved from her village in Quiche`, in the western highlands of Guatemala, to Guatemala City. In the capital Rosa's life changed drastically. Away from her family, alone with her children, she had to face the hardships of poverty and discrimination. In the new environment Rosa came to reflect upon her experience and reconsider her own history. Rosa's life, although unique, has many features in common with the lives of other internally displaced indigenous people who, in order to escape the violence in the countryside, found refuge in the anonymity of the city.[1]

After she left her village, Rosa became an activist in two popular organizations, first GAM (Mutual Support Group for the Relatives of Disappeared People) and later CONDEG (National Committee of Guatemalan Displaced People). The traumatic shift of her displacement to the city was accompanied by the acquisition of a consciousness of her role as a Mayan displaced woman during the years of terror and transition to democracy in Guatemala.

The event that has greatly contributed to enhance the stress already present in the recent social conflicts in Guatemala is the violence of the 1980s witnessed by many of the indigenous communities, who were caught in the conflict between the Guatemalan army and the revolutionary forces.[2] Displacement is one of the consequences of the Guatemalan war, primarily waged in the highland regions that were mostly populated by indigenous people of Mayan descent who were forced to resort to displacement as a strategy of survival. Guatemala has been engulfed in civil war for thirty-six years, in a conflict that, like Peru's and the more recent uprising in Chiapas, Mexico, has had a strong ethnic component. The counterinsurgency war, which affected indigenous communities, was particularly destructive between 1978 and 1985, leaving over 100,000 civilians dead or "disappeared" and over a million displaced, according to official records.

Military repression that started in the 1960s targeted those Indian communities which had created local cooperatives and educational programs. Such organizations, perceived by the government as revolutionary, were actually a response to the impoverishment of Indian communities caused by the state's own policies of land division.

The military repression of the 1980s, which largely affected the Indian population, is probably one of the worst examples of ethnic cleansing in the history of Central America. Many of the survivors of the violence fled to Mexico, Canada and the United States. Others went to Guatemala City with the hope of not being pursued by the army.

My studies have centered on the relation between state violence and the construction of identity by Mayan people in Guatemala through the process of displacement from the 1980s to the present. In particular, my focus is on the construction of identity through the personal memories of displaced people as expressed in their testimonies. A central concern of my work has been the way different forms of identities are represented and perceived by Mayan people who have been affected by displacement. Rosa—although extremely vocal and aware—is only one voice among these people.

STRUGGLE FOR SURVIVAL

I first met Rosa in Guatemala City in 1989 when she was 36 years old. She was living in one of the dreariest parts of town, within 10 feet of the railroad tracks, in a cardboard house. She had lived in the city since 1982, when she left her community in Quichè, one of the departments or provinces in the western highlands. She told me that she had lost both her father and her brother, suspected of being guerrillas and part of the revolutionary movement and who had thus been killed by the army. Her husband abandoned her and the children before she left her village, and she had not seen him since.

While she was earning her living as a maid at the house of some wealthy family in the city, one of her daughters, 15 years old at the time, was employed in a *maquila* factory. This was one of the many Korean-owned sweatshops that have become a pretty constant characteristic in the lives of many young indigenous women of the capital who are willing to work for next to nothing just to have a job. Rosa enjoyed working at GAM; (Support Group for the Relatives of Disappeared People), she faithfully attended all the meetings, organized some of the events, and became very articulate in expressing her social and political perspectives. She felt proud of being in a position that one day would enable her to "change things," as she put it, and do something for people like herself. The memory of her lost relatives and home in Quichè was always very vivid. Rosa would often talk about the death of her brother and father, of the impact that these experiences had on her life, and of the pain that she was still suffering.

Her life in her community centered on the everyday chores generally assigned to women. In her story she resented not having had more freedom to play and to go to school. Most of her time, in fact, had been devoted to taking care of her brothers. She remembered how much she would enjoy, as a little girl, being with her peers and her older brother and the times when she used to sing in the chorus with them. Those happy times were interrupted by her growing up and getting married to a man who later revealed himself as one of the causes for her suffering. Rosa experienced loneliness for the first time when she left the house of her parents to go and live with her husband, a man who not only never loved her but also deprived her of the joy and freedom of being with her family.

> Little by little time went by and my parents forgot about me, that I was at home alone and very unhappy because my husband didn't give me a good life. He always fought with me. He used to drink a lot and hit me. His family was also there. They didn't love me either. I couldn't go out of the house, visit anybody, not even my mother. He was jealous of my brother and he forbade me from seeing him.

Rosa's brother was among the people who decided to create one of the cooperatives in his village. The work that he was trying to carry on was devoted to improving the "future of the community," according to Rosa. The goal was to build a road and create a committee in charge of the children's education and a medical center, because the closest one was in a town that was a considerable distance from the village. In the 1980s any organization was perceived by the army as threatening, and its members were assumed to be communists who wanted to subvert the status quo that the military government wanted to maintain.[3] Rosa, as a woman, was relegated to traditional domestic roles.   Soon after the murder of her brother, she decided to leave the village with her children, because her life, just for being related to somebody who had been labeled a rebel, was in danger.   Her husband had already left her.   Rosa, unlike many other displaced people who were able to survive the violence, had not been left numb by the experience of death.

The story of Rosa outlines the trajectory of the redefinition of identity or self-representation by a Mayan displaced woman. This testimony stands out from others that I have collected not only because it deals with the recounting of witnessed and suffered experiences of violence but also because it addresses the existential dilemma of the place of Mayan women in the present history. This quotation from another Mayan displaced woman exemplifies Rosa's situation:

> For some of us the condition of displacement began several decades ago, but for the majority it started at the beginning of the eighties. Most of us left the communities and hid in towns and cities, mostly in the capital, in order to safeguard our lives. Since then, we have been living in fear and endured a lot of suffering.

THE MAYAN PEOPLE OF GUATEMALA

The label "Mayan" is highly problematic, since there are twenty-two different Mayan groups and languages alive today. According to most accounts of the demographics of Guatemala, there are two main ethnic groups: Indians, or *Indigenas*; people of Mayan descent, and ladinos, referring to people of mixed blood and Western culture, the descendants of Spanish settlers who make up the elite aristocracy of the ruling coalition. The Indian population is estimated to be about 60 percent of the total population, but this is a figure that is difficult to pinpoint because of the debatable criteria used in the census data to define the categories that "constitute" an Indian.   Moreover, Indian people living outside their villages are denied their "Indianness" and thus mistakingly perceived as ladinos, or, more specifically, as Indians who lost their culture. This phenomenon, known as ladinization, marks especially those Indians who have integrated or are trying to integrate themselves into the urban, industrialized world.   The meaning of the concept and the implications of ladinization cannot be fully grasped without first understanding the sharp ethnic divisions of Guatemalan society that are a legacy of a long history of racism.

The Guatemalan state, although defined by government officials as multicultural and multiethnic, has instead tried to deny the presence of indigenous people.[4] A recognition of the plurality within the borders of

Guatemala has not dissuaded those in power from crafting and implementing pervasive and brutal policies designed to homogenize the population, even if this has meant ethnocide. In this respect, Mayan leader Demetrio Cojti suggests that Guatemala is "a multi-national society whose political unit, represented by the state, is administered by *ladinos*."[5]

The name "Maya," which can be read as a site of resistance against the project of assimilation of the Indians to the Guatemalan state, has only recently been included in contemporary accounts of the political-economic situation in Guatemala. In this sense, one can surmise that "Mayan culture," the way it is understood today, has been fashioned in the last 15 years or so and narrated differently by divergent factions (e.g., Mayan popular organizations and the Mayan cultural intellectual movement).

Guatemala City has the highest rate of Mayan internal refugees. Studies conducted on this topic estimate that 21.3 percent of indigenous people displaced themselves in Guatemala City between 1977 and 1990.[6] I started my fieldwork in the capital in 1990, when the most brutal period of violence was over, but the people had not yet abandoned the fear that they directly experienced during periods of daily terror. Given the sensitive political situation in which displaced people lived, I concentrated my collection of data on testimonies of Mayan women who wanted to narrate their experiences to a foreigner in the hope that their voices could overcome the silence imposed by the official history.[7]

> We don't talk to anybody [,] one of the people whom I interviewed said. We don't tell anybody who we are; otherwise we wouldn't last even a week. We tell these things to you in order to make you understand our situation, since you are an anthropologist. We want people outside of Guatemala to know about us. I believe that this conversation won't stay here, it will be of some use....I want to know what others who hear about us think of this.

Testimonies are narratives that express an ongoing critical positioning of oneself as an individual within social organization and vis-à-vis the dominant culture. This process of "reinvention" is mediated by the outsider, that is, the anthropologist. I decided to focus primarily on women's testimonies for two main reasons: (1) I wanted to explore why most of the people in grassroots organizations were women, although the main roles of the organizations were occupied by either men or ladino women; and (2) I was aware that often ethnographies had overshadowed women, especially Mayan women, and downplayed their roles in contemporary society.[8]

Considering the still existing risk of talking about displacement and asking individuals why they chose to move to the capital, I decided to work with people in grassroots organizations, some of the few Guatemalans who made a point about speaking out of their own condition. The Mayan women who narrated their lives to me identify the organizations as a "safe place," where they can articulate their experiences both to foreigners and to their *compañeras*.

Memory, the vehicle of these narrations, assumes a crucial turning point in the present conditions of those people who have lost their homes. It enables these survivors to contest the fixed notions of ethnicity and gender in the map of national categories, categories that are super-imposed by the dominant ideology. Through the telling of their testimonies, these women redefine their place in history as well as their concepts of identity and gender, thus crossing the border of those identities imposed by the ideology of the nation-state. I chose to focus on testimonies of Mayan women because most of the displaced population of Guatemala City is constituted by Mayan women and because Mayan women generally are perceived as the bearers of "traditional" Mayan culture yet are denied any specific place outside that "authentic" milieu. Both in the Guatemalan discourse of women's rights and in the Mayan movement, Mayan women have been superseded by what are perceived to be more "urgent" problems, such as Mayan identity as a whole and ladina feminist claims.

Of the nearly 100 testimonies that I collected, I here present one, in which the author, Rosa, analyzes the place of Mayan women in relation to the ethnic question. The testimony that she recounted, along with her experience of displacement, constitutes a fracture that causes a shift in her consciousness and therefore the prelude for the redefinition of her place or identity within a new context. What she expressed is the notion that identity, or one's place in history, is not fixed but fluid and always in a process of making. Anthropological studies of Guatemala have in part contributed to create stereotypes of the indigenous population that at times tend to be overtly paternalistic. By looking at personal life histories, specifically testimonies, and paying attention to the perception and practice of identities within Guatemala's recent history, one senses how old definitions and categories are no longer sustainable. Moreover, as Rosa's activist work suggests, the unexpected rise of new social movements based on heterogeneous cultural identities forces us to question notions of culturally homogeneous nation-states. The condition of displacement, within a context of a continuing war, is one manifestation of the disruption of master narratives, that is, the unity of the nation.[9]

CROSSING THE BORDERS: MAYAN IDENTITY OF AND IN DISPLACEMENT

> We are the ones who are in need. We are like a plant which has been snatched away and not yet planted, for it doesn't stick any longer into the soil. We are like a dog who's waiting for a bone that never comes.

These words by a displaced Mayan man clarify the uprootedness that characterizes the condition of displaced people.[10] The symbol of the plant is even more meaningful in the case of indigenous people, because a tree, the oak, is a Mayan symbol of life as suspended between the sacred realms of earth and sky. This relation between the people and the sacred elements is then broken and denaturalized so that "uprootedness" comes to denote displaced people as dislocated from a popular image of identity and marks them as the antithesis of good citizens. The lives of displaced people become suspended between the impossibility of return and the hardships they encounter in the new place. People who have lost their relatives during the years of the most brutal violence in their communities of origin are denied a fixed place and doomed to wander from one place to another. Furthermore, they are denied any identity other than that of a subversive.

The absence of a fixed place and conditions of liminality and fragmentation become the bases upon which the displaced person, as Other, even more so if Mayan, creates "multiple forms" of identity.[11] Identity, in its multiple representations, becomes a trope of displacement itself, since the individual remains invisible by assuming a disguise that, while it complies with the required and enforced image, defies localization and transparency.[12] The lack of localization that characterizes displacement marks these Maya as the "cannibals" of the nation-state, that is, people who are corroding the national image of unity.[13] The representation by the army and government officials in the period preceding the democratic opening, in 1986, of displaced Mayas as subversives and "deviants" fits a sort of imagery of degeneration from the romantic idea of the "noble savage," which I call the "proper" Indian. The latter is the repository of the old values and traditions that constitute the main asset for the national tourist business.[14] Here, Indian otherness is located in traditional communities, clothed in traditional *trajes* (the colorful *huipiles*), and thought to be deaf and dumb, being unable to speak and understand Spanish. One of my Mayan friends, referring to the tourist industry, said:

> The habit of wearing traditional clothes is often just a show; that's not what one wears for everyday activities. The practice of wearing and showing *tipicas* in certain circumstances has more of a business connotation.

In fact, many Indians are not hired when they show up at the work place in their traditional clothes. Thus Maya are erased from the present since they become identified with a past that does not exist; they are deprived of "coevalness," to use Johannes Fabian's term.[15]

While doing fieldwork in the capital, somebody asked me about the topic of my research. I vaguely responded by saying that I was looking at the changes and adaptations of indigenous people in the urban environment, and my interlocutor remarked that there are no indigenous people in the city. "Here," he said, "everybody is ladino." Contrary to this person's opinion, the Maya are indeed present in Guatemala City, but it is also true that many of them try to hide their "indigenous characteristics" to defy discrimination and thus be able to get jobs and to prevent them from being recognized by *ortejas*, spies of the army. The latter case especially applies to those who are in the city in order to avoid the compulsory military service of the civil patrol system in their villages.[16] Hence, silence, invisibility, and isolation are assumed by these Maya people as strategies of defense and survival.

Displacement, or migration, is a form of travel. All travels, whether in the form of migration, tourism, or pilgrimage, entail a departure and a movement to another place. This other, foreign place is liminal and marked by antistructural qualities and activities.[17] Travel, such as in pilgrimage—but unlike migration—is not complete until the return home, or the original place of belonging. The "travel" of displaced people has no return: The disruption of the departure implies further expropriation and threat of the unknown.[18] Thus, while the pilgrim or tourist returns to his or her normal life, the displaced is forced to dwell in a liminal state. From the point of view of the *desplazados*, the return to the communities is both feared and desired. However, once they leave their communities they become "stigmatized." Leaving is, in fact, perceived both by the military and by the civilians as a declaration of culpability, like the open confession of a rebel.[19]

Especially in the capital, displaced people are like foreigners. Nonetheless, everyday life for the displaced becomes what Mircea Eliade identifies as an act of foundation: The displaced person reconstitutes a new identity in the effect of estrangement.[20] Identity is a social place: It expresses one's relation with nature and introduces an order.[21] The passage from the place of origin to the city implies disorientation, as expressed by a Quichè Mayan living in the capital:

> We had to abandon our homes, leave behind our belongings and move to the capital....We go there under very unfortunate conditions: I don't know the work here, I don't know the city, I get lost here.

The experience of displacement is expressed as a form of mutilation that imposes an experience of exclusion and absence. The city lacks reference points and restricts the individual to an ambiguous relation with the environment. The link with the condition of origin is missing, as is expressed by a Caqchikel Mayan man:

> It is very important to have a place and it seems that those people, the indigenous, do not have the right to have one.

It seems that displacement is experienced as misplacement. It represents a condition that compels the individual to blockout the past and to live like a foreigner in a hostile place.

> Here, we don't know where we are; it is difficult to relate to places outside our communities.

In the condition of displacement, the surrounding space becomes "disorganized"; the more one distances oneself from the village, the more one is at loss and out of control.[22] There is no return to the place of one's own past, or to the normal life and identity that are there situated. Thus the city comes to represent the end of the journey, that is, the final and yet liminal stage in the quest for safety and economic improvement. For many other displaced people, though, this "travel" represents a catalyst for a process of change. In contrast with the communities of origin, where people are characterized by cultural homogeneity, the the ethnic diversity of the city challenges the assertion of one's identity. In other words, in a foreign place where individuals have to face cultural differences and discrimination; one's identity is continuously challenged and contested.

To the witnesses of violence, testimonies offer a chance to reappropriate the denied space of memory and reterritorialize their misplaced identities under new forms. Testimonial narratives constitute memories of a traumatic history and representations of national politics. This is visible in the testimonial narratives, through which indigenous displaced people establish the authority of their interpretations. These individual stories help to confer authorial identity on the "personas" who are both protagonists and narrators of the testimonies.[23] In a situation of crisis, such as the one of displacement, the narrators reelaborate their historical role. The deprivation of a place triggers a new perspective, which focuses on a newly acquired consciousness of one's role in society. The telling of one's own story is experienced by narrators as a form of liberation, as a tactic of resistance and survival, because it becomes a way to give meaning to the historic present. This is how Rosa introduced a part of her story:

Every song has its words. I sing my personal song. It has words too.
It is good to have the awareness of saying what I am going to tell
you. My mind is very clear....What I am going to tell you is just a
small story.

Rosa then talked about her present situation, relating it to a wider history,
the history of many other displaced women. Memory, by rephrasing the
past in terms of experience, seems to have the ability to disrupt dominant,
official versions of history which render displaced people responsible for
their own sufferings.[24]

ROSA

Rosa's narrative raises the issue of the location of Mayan women in the
Guatemalan nation-state. Why does Rosa feel that she has to distance
herself from her community—a "traditional" Mayan community—in
order to acquire a new identity? More importantly, why is Rosa's
transgression against the traditional coupling of women's identity to their
ethnic identity perceived as destabilizing certain seemingly fixed identities?

Rosa, like other displaced women, decided to break the silence even
under the risk of being abducted or killed. The narration of her
experiences to me, a *gringa*, made her the subject of a transgression, since
she broke the tacit rule of not talking about what she has witnessed. At the
same time, she acquired space, a public forum that empowered her, in her
words, to "help [author her] own history."

The consciousness Rosa acquired in the grassroots organizations
paralleled her finding a place, that is, her return "home." This enabled her
to think and act from a relatively stable place, that of a displaced Mayan
woman. Her conditions as a displaced person provided her with a political
identity from which to make certain claims. Rosa crossed the boundaries
imposed on gender and ethnic identities and revealed the "unnaturalness"
of these categories. She showed how the placement of markers of identity
shifts through interactions, practices, confrontations, and accidents of
history and how that difference does not annul identity. For Rosa, history
started when she began wondering about her own story as a Mayan, as
displaced, and as a woman.

Our houses here are little; the ones we had have been taken away from us. When we had all those problems we had to displace ourselves and run away. In the beginning, I found a job making tortillas. I used to carry twenty quetzales [about three U.S. dollars] of tortillas over my head and the baby on my shoulders. At that time, they had to show me the directions, since I couldn't read the names of the streets. The lady I worked for always used to reproach me. Truth is, it's a shame when one doesn't know how to read....Sometime I would say: My God, why the father of these children had the heart [to leave] us? Why did he abandon them and never come back? It was when thinking about all this that I would come home tired. Men never take women into consideration, never do they worry about the needs of their children. This is the sickness of being a woman. [We don't] have an education that allows us to fight for our rights in front of the law. Thus men go with other women and make them miserable too. What we have to do, then, all of us women, is to make a history of all women of all Central America in order to claim our rights with the authorities. We have to teach men to respect us, because never has the dignity of women been respected....Never have the voices, the histories of women, been listened to by the authorities, the men, the husbands. Women's histories are left in oblivion.

This quote points out the different stages of the acquisition of consciousness. Rosa traced three main blocks on which she organizes her experiences: her past personal experiences, the consideration of her situation at present, and a reflection on problems related to women's condition. At the end of this quotation she offered a statement of action that confirmed her choice to become a political activist. In fact, Rosa's participation in the struggle of first GAM, then CONDEG (National Committee of Guatemalan Displaced People), changed her life since these organizations offered her a new understanding of the conditions of Mayan people, specifically the role of women in her country. In Rosa's own words:

Now I am seeing a reality. I am seeing the situation in which I live. I am seeing a situation which becomes everyday harder and harder. I am worse than the situation itself and I ask you to help me make my history as an indigenous [person] and as a woman, because nobody has ever paid attention to us. Only the men have talked and had the courage to get organized, but I now realize because I have suffered in my own flesh pain, hardship, and sadness.

Rosa's life seems to rest on a structure lent by divergent, yet complementary, experiences. These experiences are organized around categories of "learned" and "known." While the former refers to Rosa's life in the capital and her experiences in GAM and CONDEG, the latter involves the traditional knowledge that shaped her way of being within her community. In the category of the "known" are Rosa's childhood experiences, such as the hard work when she was 6, the house chores, the food preparation. All these memories, although pervaded by a sense of hardship and fatigue, could summon a sense of happiness. Hence, the "known" represented what is "natural," that is, what is immersed in the everyday reality and practice of the past. However, when Rosa stepped out from her memories and faced her present life, the good things of the past assumed a different perspective: The "known" came to embody a life that did not deserve to be lived. Rosa's sadness and sense of doom were expressed in terms of a baggage that was useless in her new condition of displacement. At that point, Rosa blamed her community and the people close to her for not having provided her with the "right" knowledge:

> History is like this, when I started thinking that women's lives have never been taken into account. Women don't have the chance of getting an education. I never did have the opportunity of taking advantage of my youth. Our father told me to go work and then to take care of our brothers....But later I started thinking that I can't read, write, do nothing.

Thus, by discarding the knowledge that was valuable in her community, Rosa affirmed that everything that she had learned was thanks to her *compañeros* in the organization. However, her assertion that she did not know anything needs to be interpreted within the basic structure of the whole narrative. Rosa was in fact emphasizing her recent political and social awareness. This is reinforced by the chronological division of part of the testimony between a "before" and an "after" that refers to the violence of the 1980s, when she was in her mid-twenties. Furthermore, she related these experiences to the genocide that occurred in the early history of Guatemala, starting with the Spanish invasion, or "conquest."[25]

For Rosa, as for other displaced people, violence constituted the point of departure from her community and the prelude to her consciousness. The sphere of the ethnic was revisited under Rosa's new understanding of her place in tradition. Her criticism was against her community as well as Guatemalan society. In particular, her critical considerations focused first on an ethnic perspective, then on women's conditions, and finally, on Mayan women. Women, especially Mayan, are assigned the role of producers and guardians of the culture at all levels of society: by giving birth to children, providing for the needs of daily subsistence, taking care of the young, elderly, and sick, and maintaining tradition through clothing, religion, customs, etc. When the community is threatened or suddenly absent, these role assignments do not change. In the case of Rosa, she came to realize that women's roles are not just imposed upon by the men in particular communities, but that these roles are deeply imbedded in the construction of society as a whole.

Rosa traced gender subordination to the influences of Spanish invasion, which deeply influenced the structure of gender roles in Mayan communities. This focus appears to be crucial in Rosa's understanding of her subordinate position within the family, the community, and Guatemalan society in general:

> 1992 will be the anniversary of 500 years of women's exploitation, since, according to our elders, before there was no such discrimination; there was happiness and joy before the arrival of Cristobal Colón.

It is with Spanish colonization that Rosa's "history" begins, or rather, the history of her dislocation from history. The past is the time of both her lost joy and the beginning of her sorrows. By stressing the practice of discrimination against women—and particularly against Mayan women—since the time of the invasion, Rosa detected a fracture in history that occurred 500 years ago. Her life was therefore marked before she was even born. At this point, in her narrative, Rosa started coming to terms with her identity as fixed in the past history of Guatemala, a past that she had not directly experienced but that she felt a part of. Now, away from her community, she realized the meaning of history in terms of what history had taken away from her, first as a woman and then as a displaced Maya. The fracture in her established, or "proper," identity thus occurs when she perceives herself as Other, as an outsider even within her community.

In her narrative, Rosa broke away from the "paralyzing" concept of identity that had made her the object of two cultures: the ladino and the Mayan. By contesting and redefining her Mayan identity Rosa thus does not discard it, but rather recovers the sphere that has been denied to her, that is, the sphere of the "learned." Her "traditional" community has failed, according to her perspective, to provide her with the place that she deserves. Thus Rosa presented her knowledge within her community as worthless and the "learned," which comes with pain and suffering, as a condition of reality that has provided her with the consciousness that identity is acquired by struggle and not by ascription or consent. In conclusion, Rosa's testimony represents the process of change in the perception of identity, which is crucial in the understanding not only of personal narratives but also of the national politics of ethnic and gender identities.

Rosa's life history shows that the act of recounting one's own traumas might be interpreted as a reappropriation of space and time, through a translation in terms of transposition and superimposition of another story. The story narrated in the testimony represents a supplement both of the state's or official version of history, which does not include these stories, and of the individual's history, because the traumatic experiences have psychologically and symbolically fragmented the continuum of life. Thus memory stands as a fragment, a ruin, a moment of fracture in relation to the way in which wholeness and the real are otherwise represented. Testimonies show that presence can be reconstituted on that fracture; they disrupt and undermine the concept of totality by offering pieces, ruins, fragments as viable historical representations. The circulation of truths through testimonial writing is, in turn, an effect of power. Testimony, in this context, represents a disturbance of the official history, a trope of substitution, which provides the victim with an Other frame of knowledge that is different from the one enforced by the nation-state.

Narratives of violence, or testimonies, provide a reinsertion of Mayan identity in a reconstructed temporal and spatial frame.[26] This is, again, apparent in Rosa's testimony and in her way of responding to acts of violence by organizing and protesting against the state.

NOTES

1. It has been estimated that by 1990, 100,000 to 250,000 of the total population of Guatemala (8,663,859) had been internally displaced. AVANCSO, Politica institucional hacía el desplazado interno en Guatemala: Cuaderno de Investigación (Guatemala City, Guatemala: AVANCSO, 1990).

CONDEG (National Committee of Guatemalan Displaced People) estimates that between 100,000 and 150,000 people were displaced in the capital city. The highest rate of migration, 60 percent, occurred between 1977 and 1990, years with the most intense military repression. See Santiago Bastos and Manuela Camus, *Quebrando el silencio* (Guatemala City, Guatemala: FLACSO, 1993), and *Sombras de una batalla: Los desplazados por la violencia en la ciudad de Guatemala.* (Guatemala City,

Guatemala: FLACSO, 1994). The majority of the displaced population in the capital originates from the indigenous rural areas of the central and western highlands.

2. See David Stoll, *Between Two Armies in the IXIL Town of Guatemala* (New York: Columbia University Press, 1993).

3. According to various Human Rights Commissions, since 1980 political violence resulted in 100,000 civilian deaths, 40,000 disappearances, the destruction of 450 villages, 250,000 orphans, 45,000 widows, over 100,000 refugees, and one million internally displaced people. Tom Barry, *Inside Guatemala* (Albuquerque, NM: Interhemispheric Education Resource Center, 1992). The army campaign against guerrilla activities in the highlands was started and promoted by General Lucas Garcia, who became president through electoral fraud in 1978; Rios Montt, who seized power by a military coup in 1982; and General Oscar Mejia Victores, who was in power between 1983 and 1985. When the Christian Democrat Vinicio Cerezo won the election in 1985, he established hopes for a democratic government. However, after he took office in 1986, human rights violations continued. To date, despite of the presence of the United Nations Human Rights Commission (MINUGUA) and the peace transaction between the army and the revolutionary forces, Guatemala is still a country where military repression perpetuates a state of terror.

4. The signing of the Accord on Identity and Rights of Indigenous Peoples in 1995 has constituted one of the major gains in the implementation of democracy.

5. Demetrio Cojti Cuxil, *La configuración del pensamiento politico del pueblo Maya* (Quezaltenango, Guatemala: Asociación de Escritores Mayanses de Guatemala, 1991), 4.

6. See AVANCSO, *Politica institucional hacia el desplazado interno en Guatemala*, op. cit., Bastos and Camus *Quebrando el silencio.*, op. cit., and *Sombras de una batalla:*, op. cit.

7. By "official history," I refer to the media's and government's records of episodes related to political violence that are usually reported either as lawful repression of subversive and criminal attacks or as occurrences of ordinary violence.

8. See Brenda Rosenbaum, *With Our Heads Bowed*, vol. 5 (Austin: University of Texas Press, 1995); Christine Eber, *Women and Alcohol in a Highland Maya Town* (Austin: Texas University Press, 1995); Tracy Ehlers Bacharach, *Silent Looms: Women and Production in a Guatemalan Town* (Boulder, CO: Westview Press, 1990); Emily Smith-Ayala, ed., *The Granddaughters of Ixmucane': Guatemalan Women Speak* (Toronto: Women's Press, 1991); and Margaret Hooks, *Guatemalan Women Speak* (London: Russel Press, 1991).

9.   Some analyses interpret the ethnocide counterinsurgency campaigns of the early 1980s as an attempt to impose a homogeneous image of national identity onto the Mayan population. Although it is questionable that the Mayans have been spared inclusion in the nation, voices from all parts of the political spectrum, including the popular movement, call for national unity to solve the ethnic problem.

10.   AVANCSO, Politica institucional hacía el desplazado interno en Guatemala, op. cit. Displaced person, or *desplazado*, is the category by which those who stayed in Guatemala define themselves. The others are defined as "refugees" by international organizations in support of their conditions.

11.   It is interesting to notice that, for the Guatemalan Center of General Statistics, these are the determining factors that account for national identity:

(a) local sense of belonging

(b) social role of the ethnic group to which the individual belongs

(c) objective criteria of identification in use

(d) individual's autoidentification

The erroneous concept that identity is an unchangeable category has been utilized in Guatemala and imposed upon Indian people. Such a concept has greatly contributed to promote stereotypes and discrimination against the Mayan population. Change, as well as difference in time and space, is still often denied to indigenous people. As a result, this "claustrophobic" operation offers a type of identity that can only perpetuate the Same, (i.e., a frozen identity because it can only reiterate itself). Thus the Maya become a dialectical counterpart that is either negated or utilized and fetishized in order to reinforce an ethnocentric concept of self by the ladino ethnic group.

12.   This clarifies the phenomenon of what has been referred to as ladinization, or the supposed assimilation of Indians by the dominant *ladino* culture. See Richard Adams, "La Ladinización en Guatemala," Integración Social en Guatemala: *Seminario de Integración Social Guatemalteca* 3 (1959): 213—44. The concept has been used to define those members of the Mayan community who adopt ladino cultural markers such as, the Spanish language, Western clothes, and ladino names. If, on the one hand, ladinization is acceptable for the Guatemala nation-state because it would eliminate Indians who are supposedly hindering the

process of modernization, then on the other hand, Indians are still supposed to maintain their visibility as "authentic" museum pieces or memories of a long gone past. Many Indian people today, especially those living in cities, have chosen to adopt Western or ladino cultural markers in order to avoid discrimination and be identified by government spies. This latter form of control applies to those internal refugees who escaped from their villages in order to survive.

13.   My use of the word "cannibal" echoes recent debates on the "cannibalistic" image of Indians. See Michel De Certeau, "Montaigne's 'Of Cannibals': The Savage 'I' in *Heterologies: Discourse on the Other*, ed. Michel De Certeau (Minneapolis: University of Minnesota Press, 1986); Stephen Greenblatt *Marvellous Possessions*. (Chicago: University of Chicago Press, 1991); Peter Hulme, *Colonial Encounters* (New York: Routledge, 1992); and Anthony Pagden, *The Fall of Natural Man: The American Indian and the Origin of Comparative Ethnology* (Cambridge: Cambridge University Press, 1982).

During the colonial period, the Spaniards referred to the Indians as cannibals and used this description to justify their crusade in the name of civilization and Christianity. This image persists today because the indigenous people are partially perceived as the "cannibals" of the nation-state, as obstacles to development, and as an embarrassment to the country. See Antonella Fabri, "(Re)Composing the Nation: Politics of Memory and Displacement in Mayan Testimonies from Guatemala," (Ph. D. dissertation, State University of New York at Albany, 1994).

14.   This quote from one of the most popular Mayan intellectuals exemplifies the image of Indians that the Guatemala nation-state wants to perpetuate:

The Indians are hated and loved at the same time. They are admired for their glorious historic past but despised and neglected in the present. May live the Indians who built the pyramids of Tikal! May live the Indians who made the stelas of Quirigua'! But...what about the four millions of Indians who live in the highlands? Well, "let them die." One admires the art of contemporary Indians, their music, culture, etc., but nobody acknowledges the person who is owner and creator of such expressions. Further, while the Indians are considered as the repositories of "national authenticity" they are forced to remain subdued or to assimilate.

Demetrio Cojti Cuxil, *La configuración del pensamiento político del pueblo Maya* (Quezaltenango, Guatemala: Asociación de Escritores

Mayanses de Guatemala, 1991), 9 (my translation).

The following anecdote clarifies the role of the Mayan people in contemporary Guatemalan society: In a restaurant in downtown Guatemala City I noticed that all the waiters and waitresses were wearing traditional Mayan clothing, even though they were not indigenous. When I asked one of the waiters why they were wearing those clothes, he answered: "Este es un ambiente tipico" ["This is a touristic place"]. Such a scene is not atypical in Guatemala: Mayan art, autochthonous rituals, and *trajes* (typical clothes) constitute the image that any tourist in Guatemala expects to capture.

15. Johannes Fabian, *Time and the Other: How Anthropology Makes Its Object* (New York: Columbia University Press, 1983).

16. The system of paramilitary civilian self-defense patrols, in which men from indigenous communities were required to serve, was instituted as a counterinsurgency strategy by General Efrain Ríos Montt in 1982. The Demilitarization Accord, signed in September 1996, eliminated this system.

17. Victor Turner, "The Center out there: Pilgrim's Goal," *History of Religions* 12 (1972):191—230. See also Victor Turner and Edith Turner, *Image and Pilgrimage in Christian Culture: Anthropological Perspectives* (New York: Columbia University Press, 1978).

18. Georges Van den Abbeele, *Travel as Metaphor* (Minneapolis: University of Minnesota Press, 1992), xv.

19. People who escaped their villages either had some relative murdered by the army (as in Rosa's case) or had refused to become part of the civil patrol system. In either case, they were considered subversives by the government.

20. Mircea Eliade, *The Sacred and Profane* (Orlando, FL: Harcourt Brace Jovanovich, 1959).

21. Franco La Cecla, *Perdersi: L'uomo senza ambiente* (Florence, Italy: Laterza, 1988).

22. I found the sensation of being lost to be one of the main characteristics of displaced people, who relate their migration to the city to the overbearing terror in their communities. In contrast, the migrants who left their communities to improve their education and/or economic conditions have a clear and "clean" (i.e., acceptable) social status. However, the distinction between economic migrants and displaced people is sometimes hard to assess, because some give the economic explanation as a reason to live in the city in order to avoid any suspicion.

23. Antonella Fabri, "Memories of Violence, Monuments of History," in *The Labyrinth of Memory: Ethnographic Journeys,* ed. J. Climo and M. Teski (Westport, CT: Greenwood Publishing Group, 1995).

24. According to Michel Foucault, testimonial narrative becomes "neither a composite work nor an exemplary text, but rather a.... confrontation, a power relation, a battle among discourses and through discourses." Michel Foucault, *The Archeology of Knowledge* (New York: Tavistock, 1975), x. Defamation, misleading information, and total silence on events dominate official versions of massacres, torture, and disappearances. The Guatemalan press is a monopoly of the government's and army's institutions. Until recently, before the signing of the peace accords, journalists were abducted and tortured. On February 28, 1996, for example, a reporter of a local radio station in Guatemala City had been kidnapped, then released, after having been tortured and warned that "freedom of the press has its price." Other attacks have often been explained by the press and by other official sources as examples of street violence. More famous examples of manipulation of events are the Guatemalan government's and army's officials attempts to cover the truth about the torture and murder of guerrilla leader and American lawyer Jennifer Harbury's husband, Efrain Bamaca, which occurred in 1992. In the case of Sister Dianna Ortiz, a U.S. citizen kidnapped in Guatemala and brutally tortured and raped on November 2, 1990, the Guatemalan defense minister stated that the victim fabricated her detention because she was secretly a lesbian who had been injured in some sort of lovers' quarrel. The murder in 1991 of Myrna Mack, a Guatemalan anthropologist who was investigating the issue of Guatemalan refugees, was given the institutional explanation that she had been the victim of street violence. At present, the truth about these events in which the army is directly implicated is being disclosed thanks to the work of local human rights organizations and the United Nation's mission for the verification of human rights violations, in whose reports these episodes of violence are denounced. Personal testimonies have played a central role in the assessment of the real version of historical facts, and the ongoing exhumation of clandestine cemeteries testify to the army's brutal repression in the 1980s.

25. Mayan people who have acquired a consciousness of their colonial past refer to the Spanish invasion as "the conquest."

26. Issues of the interplay between memory and history, and the role of testimonial narratives, are broadly discussed in my doctoral dissertation, "(Re)Composing the Nation," op. cit.

Figure 14. "Unleash the fury of women."

FOURTEEN

"It's Right to Fight"
Women Insurgents in Peru

Carol ANDREAS

During a decade of civil war in Peru, counterinsurgency specialists made radical reversals in their estimates of the strength of the Communist party (Partido Comunista del Perú or PCP), often called Sendero Luminoso or "Shining Path." In 1983, 3 years after the PCP's initiation of guerrilla warfare, a leading "senderologist" wrote: "As for Sendero, the combination of the [government's] military offensive, declining popular support [for Sendero], and continued political isolation is likely to spell defeat."[1] Nearly a decade later observers assessed the situation quite differently: "If the military's counterterror campaign were pushed to its logical conclusion and Sendero proves to be as resilient and adaptive as suggested here, it could...end in a guerrilla victory."[2]

President Alberto Fujimori of Peru, faced with the prospect of an imminent takeover of the capital city by the rural-based Maoist insurgency, disbanded the country's parliament in April 1992. He dismantled the court system, arbitrarily arrested opposition leaders and intellectuals, and conducted sweeping raids in schools, workplaces, and neighborhoods inhabited by the poor. During the first week of May, government troops assaulted a women's prison on the outskirts of Lima, killing and wounding hundreds of prisoners who had gained public attention by performing an elaborate stage production inside the prison celebrating International Women's Day and the advance of the PCP-led Popular Women's Movement (Movimiento Femenino Popular).

Although these desperate actions received worldwide condemnation immediately after these events, Fujimori was praised for providing attractive incentives to foreign investors, measures deemed necessary to assure Peru's reacquisition of loans from international creditors. A Shining Path victory would have brought an end to such neoliberal economic "reforms."

The U.S. government was restrained from increasing overt aid to Peru's military because of public concerns regarding extreme human rights violations by the armed forces and the national police in Peru. However, covert aid to Peruvian security offices was stepped up. An elaborate program of espionage led to the capture of the PCP's top leader, Abimael Guzman (known as "Chairman Gonzalo"), who was found living above the dance academy of prima ballerina Maritza Garrido Lecca. Among those arrested with him were Garrido Lecca and her husband, along with three women identified by the government as members of the PCP's Central Committee: Elena Iparraguirre, Laura Zambrano, and Maria Pantoja Sanchez.[3]

The images of PCP leaders—admired by many of Peru's disenfranchised poor and by other revolutionaries around the world— were shown on television for the first time after years of scornful representation by the press as savage "terrorists." Efforts to dehumanize them before the public included issuing prisoners striped suits never before seen in Peru. Guzman was "demasculinized" by calling attention to his paunch and his various illnesses. PCP women were declared "more macho than macho." A *New York Times* article quoted a female psychoanalyst who portrayed senderista women as "almost like robots" in their political role, "but when you switch to other subjects, they return to becoming mostly normal people."[4]

Opinions about the "normality" or "abnormality" of a radical movement challenging the authority of a corrupt and incompetent government depend mostly on the class position of those making such judgments. More than half the population of Peru lives in acute poverty, exacerbated by government programs to stem inflation and bring about greater integration into the global capitalist economy. Epidemics of cholera, typhoid fever, tuberculosis, and other diseases associated with poverty and malnutrition affect all those living without secure employment—more than two-thirds of the population of Peru. Polluted water and land poisoned by mining operations or made sterile by deforestation and overgrazing are only a few of the consequences of "modernization" and "development." Increasing orientation toward production for export, which began in the 1950s and was further stimulated by agrarian reform (including the U.S.-inspired "Alliance for Progress"), caused disintegration of subsistence agriculture and rapid urbanization. Social unrest brought about replacement of elected governments by military governments—and vice versa—a process that has been going on throughout the twentieth century. Regardless of who has been in power, the majority of the people have been excluded from effective participation in the decisions that affect their lives.

Most intellectuals in Peru acknowledge that women especially have reason for dissatisfaction in both their private and their public roles. Women who live in the Andean highlands in particular have been victimized by foreign intervention and conquest, which has undermined their own historical positions of authority and threatened the survival of their communities. Peru's present civil war began in the high puna of central Peru—an arid plateau region of the Andes, regarded as "women's territory"—where the last battle against the Spanish occurred almost two centuries ago.

The Communist party of Peru (PCP) originated within a student movement led primarily by women. Augusta La Torre, the daughter of a landowning family who had migrated to the central sierra city of Ayacucho during a time of peasant unrest, was a founder of the Movimiento Femenino Popular, of which she was elected head in 1965. By all accounts she was the group's most successful organizer—intelligent, dedicated, and much admired. While studying at the Universidad San Cristobal de Huamanga, La Torre married Guzman, a charismatic philosophy professor. According to numerous sources, Augusta La Torre and other student leaders persuaded Guzman—whom they regarded as a brilliant theoretician—to help them put his ideas into practice.

Both Guzman and La Torre left Peru's traditional Communist party after traveling to China and Albania, as did other prominent residents of Ayacucho, including a professor of literature, Catalina Adrianzén, and her husband Antonio Diáz Martinez, author of *Ayacucho, Hambre y Esperanza* [*Ayacucho, Hunger and Hope*].[5] In 1970, after several internal splits, their group emerged as the vanguard of the Revolutionary Student Federation (FER), following in the "Shining Path" of José Carlos Mariátegui.

Mariátegui had been mentor of the Peruvian Left since the 1920s. Before his death, at the age of 35, he had written numerous essays, edited a literary journal, and founded peasant and worker organizations that were forerunners of the Communist party of Peru. Among his writings are several essays on women's emancipation in which he identifies three tendencies within feminist movements:

It should not be surprising that all women don't unite in a single feminist movement. Feminism, of necessity, comes in different colors. Three general tendencies can be identified: bourgeois feminism, petit-bourgeois feminism, and proletarian feminism. Each of these formulates feminist demands in its own way. The bourgeois feminist tries to find common ground with the interests of the conservative class. The proletarian woman bases her feminism on faith in the revolutionary masses who struggle for a new society. Class struggle—which is an historic fact and not a theoretical assertion—is reflected in feminism. Women, like men, are reactionaries, centrists, or revolutionaries. They can't, therefore, fight together in the same movement....This feminist plurality isn't just a theoretical formulation. It can be seen in practical deformations. Feminism per se is essentially revolutionary. The thought and action of those who consider themselves feminists and conservatives at the same time lack real coherence.[6]

An early publication of the PCP's Movimiento Femenino Popular— said to be written largely by Catalina Adrianzén—is titled *El Marxismo Mariátegui y el Movimiento Femenino* [*The Marxism of Mariátegui and the Women's Movement: For a Class Line in the Popular Women's Movement*].[7] Other publications from the early 1970s are a translation of *Love in a Communist Society*, by Russian revolutionary Alexandra Kolantai, and *Rima Riyña Warmi [Women Speak Out]*, a magazine published in both Quechua and Spanish.

The second volume of *Rima Riyña Warmi* included a statement of Principles that came out of the Popular Women's Movement of Ayacucho in the early 1970s (see the appendix at the end of this chapter). In passionate language, the document expresses the conviction that women's struggles must be based on self-reliance and cannot be separated from those of the oppressed masses. The document emphatically asserts that women are central actors in history. The figure that most represented the ideals of the movement was Micaela Bastidas, the commander of the forces that fought against the Spanish in 1780—1781. She was the wife of the last puppet Inca emperor, Tupac Amaru II.[8]

The principles outlined in *Rima Riyña Warmi* represent a point of view that continued to be espoused by PCP women throughout the following decades. Specific resolutions addressing the problems of women were published following conferences of peasant women, working women, and women students organized by the Movimiento Femenino Popular before the PCP was forced "underground" in 1976. It was at this time that serious preparation for a peoples' war began, requiring members to reassess their dedication to a long-term struggle against the state, regardless of the consequences for them personally.

Theoretical articles about women's oppression and women's liberation, as well as news features about women, appeared regularly in *El Diario Marka* after this Lima newspaper became partisan to the PCP in the mid-1980s. The authors of these articles were engaging in a polemic with other feminists who failed to acknowledge the limitations of legal reform and who did not take seriously the actual priorities of poor women.

Janet Talavera became coeditor of *El Diario* in 1986 after graduating from college with a degree in journalism. She was arrested in 1989, charged with "apology for terrorism," and killed by government troops that stormed Canto Grande prison after Fujimori's 1992 *autogolpe*, whereby he dissolved parliament and instituted military rule under his personal authority. During Talavera's tenure as editor of *El Diario*, the newspaper was continually suppressed by the government, its presses destroyed, and its director and other writers and staff arrested. Nevertheless, it was said to be more widely distributed than any other newspaper in the country before it was banned by the government and forced into clandestinity.

Perhaps more important than the party's official and semi-official publications have been the poetry, songs, and theatrical productions employed by the PCP to provide education and inspiration and to communicate with sympathizers. A week after several hundred senderistas were summarily killed by government troops following a prison uprising in 1986, members of Peru's Committee of Family Members of Political Prisoners and the Disappeared held a benefit cultural event in Lima's Campo Marti. A military band of the Peruvian government tried to drown out the program honoring victims and survivors of government repression. The band played to an audience of zero on adjacent bleachers, aiming loudspeakers across the wall into the Campo Marti arena. The military band finally left after 6 hours, at which time a popular theater group began performing a play about domestic violence and the affectations of "macho" and "femme" in an urban shantytown. In the play, young people conspired to resolve family and neighborhood problems, finally banishing the worst offender (i.e., the abusive and recalcitrant husband and father) and recruiting others (mostly women and children) to join the revolution.

While the PCP's political line emphasizes unity among the oppressed masses, in effect its organs of popular power do not hesitate to take up the cause of women who are victimized by men of their own class. Cadre whose families are in crisis are given support from comrades and time off from other duties in order to attend to their families' needs.

In the 1970s members of the PCP debated tenaciously with other self-proclaimed Maoists who maintained that women's problems with men would be dealt with "after the revolution."[9] The PCP was also critical of the bureaucratic women's organizations of the traditional Communist party.[10] Trotskyist parties were less hostile toward the PCP's feminism but disagreed with the senderistas' focus on organizing for a prolonged people's war. Some called for a Cuban-style *foco* warfare (instead of establishing people's committees throughout the countryside), or for general insurrection aimed at overthrowing the government; in practice, men resisted women's full integration into party organizations.[11] Eventually, many women left these political parties to join feminist movements or to support the women of the PCP.

The PCP left its base at the University of Huamanga to organize clandestinely in the countryside at the same time that General Francisco Bermudez replaced Juan Alvarado Velasco as head of the military government that had assumed power in 1968. Many members lived in their own villages of origin between 1976 and 1980, married, and took up farming and other occupations. Most often they were schoolteachers and, members of SUTEP (Sindicato Unico de Trabajadores en la Educación Peruana), the country's most militant union. Those who did not know Quechua, the predominant language in the Peruvian Andes, dedicated themselves to learning it.

Economic conditions worsened in Peru during this period, and repression against popular organizations grew. Finally, the military agreed to rewrite the Peruvian Constitution and hold general elections. The PCP declared the Constituent Assembly that rewrote the Constitution a fraud and objected to provisions for military authority that remained as part of the Constitution itself. They declared war on the government by burning ballot boxes in the Ayacucho village of Chuschi in 1980 and began challenging directly the authority of the state and of semi-feudal institutions in the central sierra.

Gamonales, big landowners, who had usurped communal land and municipal authorities linked with outside commercial interests were overthrown. Wherever possible, the national police were driven out of villages; provincial authorities were forced to resign their posts. All this was accomplished essentially without bloodshed and with widespread support among residents of the region. "People's Committees" were established in a number of villages as the nuclei of a "New Democratic Republic." These committees administered redistribution of land, helped organize agricultural production (promoting collective farming where feasible, a practice already common in indigenous communities), and reoriented market relations to better satisfy the needs of local populations.

Because of women's predominant role in subsistence agricultural production and the outmigration of men seeking work in industry, women far outnumbered men in Peru's countryside. This was especially true in the highest altitudes, where women herded animals and lived separately from men during much of the year. People's Committees established in the villages of Ayacucho and surrounding *departamentos* were predominantly female, as were the Popular Schools established to educate potential PCP cadre. Women and men were taught to become aware of exploitation and subjugation based on gender in economic, social, political, and ideological terms and to reject practices that were denigrating to women in their families and communities.[12] Women held rights and responsibilities equal to those of men in the party and were as likely as men to lead military assaults on police outposts in order to secure weapons for the use of guerrillas—a practice that continued to characterize the movement as it expanded into other parts of the country. In fact, all those who become full-fledged members of the PCP had to secure their own weapons by participating in such assaults.

The Peruvian government was slow to react to events going on in the central sierra. Members of the PCP were arrested but were often able to escape from jail with the help of comrades. President Fernando Belaúnde Terry eventually succumbed to pressure from the military, backed by both the United States and the Soviet Union, sending nearly 5,000 police and army troops into the area.[13] Borrowing counterinsurgency tactics developed by the United States in Vietnam and elsewhere, he also began secretly organizing paramilitary groups in order to divide the peasantry and reduce government casualties in the fight against guerrillas. Many peasants were forced to flee their villages, spreading insurrection to adjacent regions and escalating tension within the ranks of the military.

In January 1983 eight journalists were massacred in an Ayacucho village while investigating reports that the government was organizing "self-defense" units (*rondas*) in the area. Witnesses to the killing were "disappeared." The sister of a young man who had been killed while serving as a guide to the journalists was arrested. Years later, when a new government was in power, the case of the journalists' death was brought to trial.[14] The guide's sister, Juana Lidia Argumedo García, was then released from jail to testify at a hearing. Like most women who became political prisoners in Peru, she suffered rape and torture as a form of intimidation before her court appearance. Nevertheless, she accused the military of the 1983 massacre. She was subsequently offered asylum outside the country; instead of leaving Peru, she organized a music group, La Libertad, which performed for striking miners and grassroots organizations of the poor.

Many others risked their lives—and many lost their lives—providing support to guerrillas in the form of legal services, medical attention, transportation, and housing. Socorro popular (popular assistance) became an essential activity organized mostly by women who felt impelled to provide services for fighters in the guerrilla army and for those accused of "terrorism" or "apology for terrorism."

Best known among the heroines of the Peruvian revolution is Edith Lagos, a young woman who left high school to become the first military commander of the PCP. She became famous for her impassioned speeches in the plazas of the towns and villages where people gathered together to hear about the revolution. She is credited with playing a major role in a spectacular assault on an Ayacucho prison in March 1982, freeing nearly 300 prisoners.[15] Lagos, herself, escaped prison five times before being killed in captivity that same year, at the age of 19. At her funeral in Ayacucho, which was attended by some 30,000 people despite of a state of siege declared by the government, her sister read a poem Lagos had written before her imprisonment. The poem, which speaks of wildflowers growing over her tomb, became a *huayno* (folk song of the Peruvian highlands). When Martina Portocarrero, an Ayacucho artist who left the country under threat because of her sympathy for guerrillas, returned in 1987 to tour her homeland, she sang this folk song—"Hierba Silvestre"— drawing immense crowds wherever she went. Edith Lagos's tomb was later vandalized, but the site of her burial is a revered symbol of the idealism of youth and the fight against injustice.

Predictions that the PCP would never expand successfully in urban areas, nor in jungle and coastal regions of Peru, were put to rest by the mid-1980s; more than two-thirds of the country came under military occupation or a state of emergency (including the city of Lima, where at least one-third of Peru's population resides). Even more surprising to many, the preponderance of women at all levels of the organization continued to be evident wherever the party's influence was established. According to both PCP and counterinsurgency sources, women have comprised approximately 90 percent of the party's leadership and a majority of its cadre ever since the organization's inception. While in other political parties the "woman question" was discussed as a way of attracting female support, within the PCP the more practical matter was how to engage the talents and loyalties of men without endangering the party's commitment to fight against the subjugation of women. Men who showed sympathy for the PCP were sometimes derided by others as *sacos largos* (men who don't fit into their suitcoats). Those who were conscious of their roots in indigenous culture, where masculinity is not equated with machismo, were less likely to be threatened by such epithets. Women challenged men to give up "alienated" lives for commitment to the party. The rejoining of women and men who had been separated by economic dislocation was a major preoccupation of the PCP. This was not simply a vision for a future society; lives were transformed through participation in People's Committees.[16]

The PCP began organizing bases in Lima in the mid-1970s among factory workers, office workers, teachers, health workers, household workers, sanitation workers, construction workers, street vendors, and students. The party's Popular Schools functioned openly at that time.[17] Comites de Lucha (Struggle Committees, forerunners of People's Committees) were organized in some of the city's oldest shantytowns. Each family was invited to send one or two people to attend neighborhood meetings at which survival issues—water supply, sanitation, transportation, health, and education—were discussed and appropriate action taken. Uneducated housewives were taught to read and write.

Organization occurred rapidly in newer shantytowns established on the outskirts of Lima in the 1980s. Members of indigenous communities fleeing government repression in the countryside were arriving in large numbers, already educated in the ideology of the party. One shantytown in Ate Vitarte—Raucana—located near the central highway leading into the mountains, was completely off-limits to the government for several years. A nearby factory was bombed by guerrillas when troops attempted to penetrate the walls residents had built surrounding the area. Men and women fought with rocks and burning tires; they dug trenches across roads to keep the military out. Residents produced their own food, dug their own wells, and built houses out of mud and brick. Raucana schoolchildren being interviewed by a reporter were shown on TV; when asked who was the president of Peru, they said, "Presidente Gonzalo!" Employing his *nom de guerre*, the children thus revealed their aspirations and affection for the PCP party leader, Abimael Guzman.

Senderistas had a harder time consolidating support for the revolution in shantytowns where women's groups outside the party had been politically active. Already in the late 1970s, soup kitchens (*comedores populares*) had been set up in many poor neighborhoods by families that pooled resources to prepare inexpensive meals. During the 1980s electoral parties, churches, municipal governments, and foreign governments became involved in providing commodity aid for these programs and in some cases took over their administration. A "Glass of Milk" program was also set up, which became highly politicized. Corruption grew so much that the Catholic church withdrew from this program. Relief supplies sometimes disappeared before they reached *pobladores*. Among those who came under attack for corruption was Elena Moyano, one of the founders of the Women's Federation in Villa El Salvador, a shantytown where commodity aid was concentrated more than anywhere else in the country. Moyano gained office as vice mayor of Villa El Salvador and was able to manage millions of dollars of NGO (Non-Governmental Organization) monies. She accused her attackers of being members of the PCP; when they won elections in all the major community organizations of Villa El Salvador (including the Women's Federation itself), she refused to recognize the results. She was asked to resign her post. Instead, she called on the government to arrest her detractors and supported President Fujimori's plans to establish urban *rondas* (paramilitary groups) to keep the PCP from taking over neighborhoods and municipalities.

Elena Moyano was killed by a young female PCP guerrilla, an act that brought opprobrium from feminists who were not sympathetic to the agenda of the party and accelerated polarization that led up to Fujimori's assumption of dictatorial powers less than 2 months later.[18]

While militarization and polarization was growing in the cities, the PCP was expanding rapidly in the jungle. Some of those fleeing from war zones in the highlands sought refuge among colonists in parts of the jungle that had been opened up by previous governments for extraction of oil, minerals, fruits and grains, coffee, cocoa, and coca. The "march to the jungle" was already under way in the 1960s and was accelerated—with the help of U.S. AID—under the Belaúnde regime in the 1980s. Coca production overtook all other activity as demand for cocaine in the United States dwarfed the market for other products.[19]

The U.S. government, under the guise of its "War on Drugs," increased involvement with the Peruvian military—which was itself heavily involved in drug trafficking—and declared the PCP to be "narco-guerrillas." In fact, armed guerrillas fought abusive druglords as well as U.S. mercenaries and Peruvian government troops for control of the jungle territory. A PCP spokesperson declared:

> The Communist Party of Peru, since the beginning of armed struggle, has taken a radical position regarding the drug traffic. We are not drug traffickers, even less are we linked with them....It's true that the masses pay economically to sustain the struggle, according to their possibilities. We demand nothing of anyone, but they give even their lives and their blood, and contribute as they can, with conviction....We don't need money in great quantities. Not at all. The masses give us much more than this. Arms we take from the enemy....It's totally false that we have some kind of connection with the drug traffickers.[20]

Aside from ideological and military conflicts in the jungle, and the fact that the relation between growers and traffickers is always highly exploitative of peasants, the market for coca did bring in revenue originating outside the country. Unlike other political organizations in Peru, the PCP scorned assistance from foreign governments or other foreign agencies. Nor did they rob banks or kidnap people for ransom. But the principle of self-reliance has not meant that peasants were punished by the PCP for growing coca for export. Instead, at the urging of the party, farmers in "liberated territory" increased production of alternative crops in an effort to create a self-sufficient and self-sustaining economy in the jungle. Commitment to long-term economic survival of their communities contrasted sharply with the opportunism of those who were interested only in extracting the resources of the jungle for personal profit.

As the PCP appeared to be gaining over the combined forces of the U.S. Drug Enforcement Agency, drug traffickers, and Peruvian army and police, the Peruvian military—together with U.S.-based missionaries—attempted to organize natives of the jungle (*ashaninkas*) in paramilitary groups to fight guerrillas. A large majority of the ashaninkas joined PCP forces rather than fight under Peruvian military command; most who were armed by the government eventually escaped government authority.

In 1994 the Fujimori government began aerial bombardment of villages in the jungle and sent in thousands of troops to destroy People's Committees, causing massive dislocation of populations. However, the PCP became skilled in ambushing government vehicles and digging tunnels to escape encirclement by military troops. In 1998 (at the time of this writing), guerrillas, peasants, and native communities organized by the PCP continued to hold the upper hand in the region, as well as in mountainous regions contiguous with the jungle.

Elsewhere, repression took an enormous toll. At universities where senderistas once demonstrated daily and boycotted classes of professors they regarded as reactionary, the government intervened militarily. On one occasion, literally all students residing in a a dormitory called Micaela Bastidas were arrested in a predawn raid at Lima's San Marcos University. Lourdes Carpio, head of the university's faculty association, was arrested along with dozens of other university staff. In Huancayo and in Lima, scores of students and professors disappeared after being picked up by police. Their mutilated bodies were later found, but responsible authorities escaped prosecution.

While the government's terror campaign has affected the capacity of the PCP to engage in mass organizing and has robbed the movement of its most tested leaders, it has also exposed the regime and deepened the revolutionary commitment of those most affected. Even as the government claims to have dealt the movement a death blow, the number of people in Peru who boycott elections constantly increases. Public protest against the privatization of industries and the country's sellout to foreigners is on the rise. An imminent takeover by the PCP is no longer expected, but the movement's ideological premises are more widely accepted than ever before. The promise of the country's "salvation" through austerity and foreign investment is betrayed by super exploitation, which has meant increasing domestic violence, prostitution, sickness, and distrust of "politics as usual." The Maoist agenda of building a self-sustaining agrarian economy, one in which foreign capital plays, at best, a minor role, can no longer be regarded as a utopian vision. And the need for sustained class struggle, including a military overthrow of the regime, is widely understood. Women of the PCP define themselves—and their male comrades—as a vanguard of worldwide movements against global capitalist expansion. At the same time, they regard themselves as a vanguard of women's emancipation, which they believe can only be won through sacrifice and discipline.

At the time of this writing, the Fujimori regime holds prisoners regarded as top leaders of the PCP in complete isolation, in an underground cement bunker on the grounds of a military installation. Others are being kept in a new prison located high in Peru's *altiplano* (high plains), where they are subject to freezing temperatures and deprived of sunlight, medical attention, and sanitary facilities. They have no access to radio or newspapers.

Some prisoners (including Guzman) have allegedly called for peace talks with the government. But the war goes on, and bounties are out for anyone giving information leading to the arrest of a number of women and men thought to be members of the PCP's Central Committee. In widely distributed documents, the Central Committee categorically rejects the call for peace talks as an invention of the government, intended to demoralize and divide integrants and sympathizers of the PCP. A letter from the women's prison in Chorrillos, and another from the Committee of Family Members of Political Prisoners and the Disappeared, says the government is threatening the lives of those who do not support the "call for peace."

Of great concern to all who are protagonists in the people's war that has developed in Peru over a period of nearly three decades is the impact this war has had in other countries characterized by semi-feudal, semi-colonial relations, where Maoist insurgents follow events in Peru with great interest. In these countries, and in other places where resistance to global imperialism is not so highly developed, women are redefining the project of revolution to reflect more profoundly their own (gendered) interests as members of families and as peasants, workers, community leaders, artists, and intellectuals.

APPENDIX

DECLARATION OF PRINCIPLES, POPULAR WOMEN'S MOVEMENT OF AYACUCHO, 1973

The first appearance of classes, that marks the beginning of exploitation, also marks the beginning of women's subjugation: from slave to serf, from serf to worker. Today, wherever there is exploitation, women are subjugated, and this will only end when the roots of class subjugation are destroyed.

From the female slavery of yesterday to the formal equality of today we have seen centuries of quiet and tenacious struggle as well as mass violence that has brought great victories through battle without quarter. Societies develop in the midst of class struggle and the combativeness of the people brings progress.

The progress of women has been and is the progress of the people. Women have not been passive beneficiaries. They have been firmly decided, sisters in the cause of the oppressed, militants on the front lines; the trenches of combat everywhere are marked indelibly with their blood. Women are not apolitical and indifferent. Women of the people, especially, have been combatant revolutionaries.

The daughters of the oppressed classes—workers, peasants, and all those who toil—have made their names known among the greatest emancipators of history: Rosa Luxemburg and Liu Ju-lan are examples of international renown among revolutionaries; in our country, Micaela Bastidas.

Women are not passive, nor domestic adornments, nor apolitical instruments to be manipulated by others. Women who are embued with class consciousness are indefatigable fighters and decided militants.

Peruvian women, as part of the Peruvian masses, have been and are combative in popular struggles. They have been so throughout the history of our people. The history of our struggle as women is synthesized in one name, that of Micaela Bastidas.

Women today suffer oppression and exploitation, and these are rooted in the semi-colonial and semi-feudal situation of our country, a situation that presses like a mountain over our people and doubly so over women.

In our society where the masses are rising up against imperialism and feudalism, women are taking up their places in combat and crying out together with the cries of all our people at war. The fight of Peruvian women is that of all the oppressed and exploited; our enemies are the same. Our common battle cannot be contained, and our triumph will be the triumph of a free people.

Peruvian women have never refrained from combat; today our situation requires an even more profound commitment and even more widespread participation.

The dominant classes are deepening capitalist dependence and imperialism in our country; these same anti-democratic classes are applying conceptions that bring vertical control over us, organizing the masses in a corporativist state with the hope of undermining class struggle. They are promoting the organization of women outside the popular struggles of the masses and in favor of those who dominate us. In these conditions, the Movimiento Femenino Popular of Ayacucho is re-initiating our march to mobilize Peruvian women clearly, consciously, and militantly in a classist women's movement at the service of the National-Democratic Revolution.

Our tasks are guided by these basic principles:

• We can only succeed as revolutionaries by following the invincible light of Mariátegui Thought.

• The masses can only free themselves by their own efforts, and this can only be done if we are conscious of our creative role in history.

• In order to mobilize and organize it is necessary to study and to educate others; we must understand the concrete problems of the people and go among them agitating and propagandizing for revolution.

• We must use all the methods the proletariat has created and developed to further our organization, and we must become part of all the organizations of the proletariat.

• Women can only organize correctly if we do so following a class line, approaching women on the basis of their class interests.

• Without a clear political consciousness we will not be inspired to continue faithfully within the context of class struggle in our country.

• We must begin with the basic needs of the people and raise our political consciousness step by step, in the midst of struggle, recognizing what are the most pressing and concrete problems of the majority in order to reach a higher level of understanding.

• We will triumph in revolution only if we can unite all the oppressed classes and peoples, but the most important principle is self-reliance, to base ourselves in our own efforts.

Relying on these principles, the Movimiento Femenino Popular of Ayacucho, with the goal of organizing Peruvian women from a position of class, dedicate ourselves in a tenacious fight to unite with others who share our goals in creating a Movimiento Femenino Popular in the entire country, as part of the overall struggle among the masses of women, generated by the proletariat. Our struggle is guided by three characteristics: (1) adherence to Mariátegui's thought as (2) a mass organization with a class base, and (3) subject to democratic centralism.

NOTES

1.   Cynthia McClintock, "Sendero Luminoso: Peru's Maoist Guerrillas," *Problems of Communism* (September/October 1983): 34.

2.   Gordon McCormick, *The Shining Path and the Future of Peru* (Rand Report R-3781-DOS/OSD) (Santa Monica, CA: Rand Corp., 1990), 55.

3.   Iparraguirre, a longtime political leader in the PCP, became Guzman's companion after the death of his wife, Augusta La Torre.

4.   Nathaniel Nash, "Shining Path Women: So Many and So Ferocious," *New York Times*, 22 September 1992. In response to the U.S. media's negative portrayal of Peruvian guerrillas, a feminist sympathetic to the Shining Path movement wrote:

> The ado over Guzman's imperfect physique demonstrates refusal to allow revolutionists human frailty and mortality. It is as though Guzman's enemies expected him to be godlike, and were disappointed at the reality of a middle-aged, sedentary philosopher with psoriasis and kidney disease....These stories' hysteria about Sendero women stem from the realities that the women are communist revolutionists fighting against the established, U.S.-backed system, and that they are soldiers who kill. The truth is that women are not only capable of combat, and killing, but of leading in combat, and to say anything else is nonsense.

Brooke Williams, "Shining Path's Unmanly Men and Unwomanly Women: Revolution as an Unnatural Phenomenon"*New Directions for Women* (May/June 1993): 15.

5.   Antonio Díaz Martinez, *Ayacucho, Hambre y Esperanza* (Ayacucho, Peru: Ediciones Waman Puma,1969). Díaz Martinez was among those executed in a massacre of political prisoners at Lurigancho (Lima) in 1986. At the time of this writing, Adrianzén is reportedly ill and living in exile. Augusta La Torre—whose nom de guerre was "Norah"—died in 1988 of unknown causes. She is said to have had political differences with her husband before her death but was declared "most honored martyr of the revolution" at a party congress held that same year. A videotape of her funeral, showing Guzman together with other surviving founders and leaders of the party, was captured by the government in 1989; most of

those shown in the video are women, many of whom were taken prisoner in the following years.

6. José Carlos Mariátegui, *Temas de educación* (Lima, Peru: Biblioteca Amauta, 1973), 130. Mariátegui's views on feminism may have influenced the party's view of homosexuality as well. In response to queries regarding the PCP's alleged persecution of homosexuals, a Peruvian evidently authorized to speak for the party wrote:

> The problem is not one of a person's sexual orientation but rather the class position that they take....We can see that homosexuals have existed in all societies, some from birth, others converted by the social environment in which they live or have lived; the latter seems extremely influential to us. Our view is that homosexual orientation is not an ideological matter.

See (Lake Worth, FL) *Prison Legal News* (March 1994): 11—14.

7. The first edition of this booklet was published in 1974 by Editorial Pedagógica "Asencios," Lima.

8. Their movement was brutally suppressed. Micaela Bastidas had sent a note to her husband warning him that his delay in entering Qosqo would spell their death.

9. The largest organization claiming to represent Maoism in Peru at that time was called Patria Roja, whose members allied themselves with the Teng Hsiao-ping regime in China after Mao's death.

10. The pro-Soviet party in Peru was called PC-Unidad, which served as the propaganda arm of the Velasco military government.

11. All of these parties and organizations, which the PCP regarded as "reformist" or "revisionist," eventually became part of the Left Unity electoral coalition. By the mid-1980s several feminists affiliated with Left Unity ran unsuccessfully for Parliament. Others were operating relief programs and "self-help" business projects under the auspices of U.S. AID (Agency for International Development). A mostly male wing of Left Unity—which also included youth who defected from APRA, the governing party between 1985 and 1990—organized the Movimiento Revolucionario Tupac Amaru (MRTA), an armed organization that vied for power with the PCP in several regions of the country. The MRTA never attempted to penetrate the areas surrounding Ayacucho.

12. Juan Lazaro, "Women and Political Violence in Contemporary Peru," *Dialectical Anthropology* 15 (1990): 233—247.

13. Belaúnde was a U.S. ally since the 1960s, when the Green Berets helped put down insurrection in Peru during his previous tenure as president.

14.   Alán García was elected in a landslide vote in 1985, with Belaúnde's incumbent government receiving only 6 percent of the vote. Outrage over numerous village massacres in the countryside contributed to Belaúnde's unpopularity, but the García government continued with the brutal counterinsurgency campaign. His government was distinguished by the execution of more than 300 political prisoners in 1985 and 1986. Disappearances were more frequent than in any country in the world.

15.   Numerous conflicting accounts of this assault exist. An article in *El Mundo* (12 April 1995) says the woman who is thought to be the top intellectual leader of the party today, Yeny Maria Rodriguez Neyra, was among those who freed Edith Lagos from jail on that historic occasion.

16.   The larger question of historical resistance to global imperialism by women in Peru and the experiences that give rise to female political consciousness are the subject of my *When Women Rebel: The Rise of Popular Feminism in Peru* (New York: Lawrence Hill Books, 1985). For a summary of the structural factors, both economic and cultural, underlying women's predominance in Peru's insurgency, see my "Women at War," *NACLA Report on the Americas* 24, no. 4 (December/January 1990/1991).

17.   The PCP rarely put up candidates for union office; emphasis was placed on providing rank-and-file leadership.

18.   Another event that horrified many residents of Lima was a bomb blast in an upper-class district of the city that demolished the front of an apartment building, killing more that twenty people. The car bomb, intended by guerrillas to blow up a bank, had gone off prematurely because of a traffic altercation. The PCP paid a heavy price for this apparent disregard for civilian lives.

19.   One result of the booming overseas market for cocaine was the corruption of the local market for coca leaves in Peru. Coca is regarded as a sacred plant, along with the potato, both of which are associated with *mamapacha* (Mother Earth), the main deity of indigenous Andean peoples.

20.   *El Diario*, 7 September 1987.

"I tried to defend myself but I couldn't. They took my clothes, they hit me, they were pulling my hair. A few days later six soldiers came in. All of them raped me. They cursed me, insulted me, said there were too many Muslim people and said a lot of Muslims were going to give birth to Serbian children."

—From an account by an 18-year-old Bosnian woman in a hospital in Tuzla on January 1, 1993, reported in the *New York Times* by Barbara Crossette on Sunday, June 14, 1998.

FIFTEEN

Surfacing Gender
Reengraving Crimes Against Women in Humanitarian Law

Rhonda COPELON

Historically, the rape of women in war has drawn occasional and short-lived international attention. Most of the time rape has been invisible or has come to light as part of the competing diplomacies of war, illustrating the viciousness of the conqueror or the innocence of the conquered. When war is done, it is comfortably cabined as a mere inevitable "by-product," a matter of indiscipline, of soldiers revved up by war, needy, and briefly "out of control."

Military histories rarely refer to rape, and military tribunals rarely either charge or sanction it. This is true even when open, mass, and systematic rape and forced prostitution have been thought to shock the conscience of the world. In the mid-1970s an estimated 200,000 Bengali women were raped during the war of independence from Pakistan, yet, in the end, amnesty was quietly traded for independence.[1] The maintenance of concentration camp brothels for the rape of Jewish and Aryan women as well as rape in the course of conquest did not figure in the proceedings against high-level Nazis before the international military tribunal at Nuremberg,[2] just as the mass rape of German women by Allied soldiers went largely unredressed.[3] The response, however, to the "rape of Nanking," which refers to the brutal taking of Nanjing by Japanese soldiers through mass killings, public beheadings, looting, and rape of approximately 20,000 women in the first month, was unusual.[4] Rape was explicitly charged against the Japanese commanders, and it was discussed in the judgment of the international military tribunal in Tokyo.[5] But the Japanese army's alternative to open mass rape—the massive industrialization of sexual slavery on the battlefield—was a closely guarded secret. Only recently, the survivors from among at least 200,000 Korean, Filipino, Chinese, and Dutch/Indonesian women kidnapped and detained to serve as "comfort women" to the Japanese army have begun to tell their stories and demand redress.[6]

The fact that the rape of women in the wars in the former Yugoslavia captured world attention provides no guarantee that it will not also disappear from history, or survive, at best, as an exceptional case. The apparent uniqueness of the rape directed overwhelmingly against Bosnian-Muslim women as part of a genocidal campaign of "ethnic cleansing"[7] is a product of the invisibility of the rape of women in history as well as in the present. Geopolitical factors—that this rape is being perpetrated by white men against white, albeit largely Muslim, women, is occurring in Europe, and contains the seeds of a new world war—cannot be ignored in explaining the attention given to these rapes.[8] By contrast, the rape of 50 percent of the women of the indigenous Yuracruz people in Ecuador by mercenaries of an international company seeking to "cleanse" the land went largely unreported. Similarly, the routine rape of women in the civil wars in Rwanda, Peru, Liberia, and Burma, for example, has drawn only occasional attention.[9] Few in the West remember that the rape of Bengali women also had the distinct genocidal purpose of destroying their racial distinctiveness.[10]

Perhaps the most telling example of invisibility came to light in the Rwanda case. Nine months after the news of horrific massacres in Rwanda was front-page news, the massive scope of rape in that conflict was first reported in the European press. As a result of a mission by a French child psychiatrist, it was revealed that between 2,000 and 5,000 Rwandan women were pregnant and giving birth as a result of rape. This figure, confirmed by the Rwandan National Population Office, suggests that the overwhelming percentage of women who survived the massacre had been raped. Most of the women in the massacre, were sexually mutilated and killed. Women's shame and unwillingness to speak about rape only partially explains the deafening silence.[11]

Moreover, just as historically the condemnation of rape in war has rarely been about the abuse of women as a crime of gender, so the mass rape in Bosnia has captured world attention largely because of its association with "ethnic cleansing" or genocide. In one week, a midday women's talk show opened with the script, "In Bosnia, they are raping the enemy's women...," and a leading Croatian-American scholar, among others, insisted on the distinction between "genocidal" rape and "normal" rape. By contrast, our ad hoc Women's Coalition Against Crimes Against Women in the Former Yugoslavia characterized rape as a weapon of war, whether used to dilute ethnic identity, destabilize the civilian population, or reward soldiers. But for many, rape remains an inevitable by-product of war except when it is a vehicle of genocide.

The elision of genocide and rape in the focus on "genocidal rape" as a means of emphasizing the heinousness of the rape of Muslim women in

Bosnia is dangerous. Rape and genocide are separate atrocities. Genocide involves the infliction of all forms of violence to destroy a people based on its identity as a people, while rape is sexualized violence that seeks to destroy a woman based on her identity as a woman.[12] Both are based on total contempt for and dehumanization of the victim, and both give rise to unspeakable brutalities. Their intersection in the Serbian, and to a lesser extent, the Croatian aggressions in Bosnia defines an ineffable living hell for Muslim women. They must contend with the loss of their world, with the loss of self, with the loss of community, and with marginalization in diaspora.

But to describe the horror of genocidal rape as unparalleled is factually dubious and risks rendering rape invisible once again. Labeling rape as genocidal does not necessarily increase the likelihood that, when ethnic war ceases or is forced back into the bottle, the crimes against women, the voices of women, and their struggles to survive will be vindicated. Moreover, it significantly increases the likelihood that condemnation will be limited to this seemingly exceptional case; that women who are brutally raped for domination, terror, booty, or revenge in Bosnia and elsewhere will not be heard.

The creation of the International Criminal Tribunal for the Former Yugoslavia[13] makes it more difficult, but not impossible, to barter impunity for peace. The pressure of survivors and their advocates, together with the global women's human rights movement, makes it harder for the tribunal to ignore or marginalize sexual violence against women. Whether rape, forced prostitution, and forced impregnation of women will be effectively prosecuted before the ad hoc tribunal, and whether the survivors will obtain redress, will depend on constant vigilance. The situation presents a historic opportunity as well as a historical imperative, to insist on justice for the women of Bosnia and to press for a feminist reconceptualization of the role and legal status of rape under humanitarian as well as human rights law.

To do this, it is necessary to "surface" gender in the midst of genocide and, at the same time, to avoid dualistic thinking. We must critically examine the claim that rape as a tool of ethnic cleansing is unique, worse than or not comparable to other forms of rape in war or in peace, at the same time that we recognize that rape, together with genocide, inflicts multiple, intersectional harms.[14] This combination of the particular and the general is critical if the horrors experienced by women in Bosnia are to be fully understood and if that experience is to have meaning for women brutalized in lesser-known theaters of war or in the byways of daily life.

This article examines the evolving legal status of rape (and other forms of sexual violence, such as forced prostitution and forced pregnancy) in war, with attention to both the particular and the general as well as to the tension between them.[15] It focuses on two central questions of conceptualization. The first section addresses whether these gender crimes are fully recognized as war crimes under the Geneva Conventions, the cornerstone of what is called "humanitarian" law—that is, the prohibitions that have made war itself permissible. This requires examination of whether rape is viewed as a grave breach and whether, within that framework, it is treated as a form of torture. The second section explores whether the customary international legal concept "crimes against humanity" does or should distinguish between genocidal rape and mass rape for other purposes. It argues that in order to capture the multilayered relationship between gender and ethnicity in the campaign of sexual violence against women in Bosnia, as well as the gender element in all campaigns of sexual violence, the concept of crimes against humanity must be interpreted to encompass mass rape apart from persecution and be broadened to encompass persecution based on gender. The conclusion suggests some connections between the recognition of rape in war and rape in the time called peace.

IS RAPE A WAR CRIME?

Although news of the mass rapes of women in Bosnia had an electrifying effect and became a significant factor in the demand for the creation of the international tribunal, the leading question for a time has been whether rape, forced prostitution, forced pregnancy, and other forms of sexual abuse are "war crimes" within the meaning of the Geneva Conventions and the internationally agreed-upon norms that bind all nations, whether or not they have signed the conventions.[16] The proceedings before the tribunal are likely to settle this question, but not necessarily all the issues it presents.

The question is not whether rape is technically a crime prohibited in war. Rape has long been viewed as a criminal offense under national and international rules of war.[17] The 1949 Geneva Conventions, as well as the 1977 protocols regarding the protection of civilians in war, explicitly prohibit rape, forced prostitution, and any form of indecent assault and call for special protection of women during war, including separate quarters with supervision and searches by women only.[18] Yet it is significant that where rape and other forms of sexual assault are explicitly mentioned, they are categorized as an attack against *honor*.[19] Crimes of violence, including murder, mutilation, cruel treatment, and torture, are treated separately.

The conceptualization of rape as an attack against honor, as opposed to a crime of violence, is a core problem. Formal sanctions against rape range from minimal to extreme. Where rape has been treated as a grave crime in domestic laws, it has often been because it violates the honor of the man and his exclusive right to sexual possession of his woman as property. Thus in the United States the death penalty for rape was prevalent in southern states and was used against African-American men convicted of raping white women or, more precisely, white man's property.[20] Similarly, the media often refer to the mass rape in Bosnia as the rape of "the enemy's women." The enemy in this formulation is the male combatant in the seemingly all-male national, religious, or ethnic group.

Under the Geneva Conventions, the concept of honor is somewhat more enlightened: Rape is a crime against the honor and dignity of women.[21] The commentary explains that "[h]onour is a moral and social quality," respect for which is owed to "man because he is endowed with a reason and conscience,"[22] and describes rape as an "outrage...of the worst kind."[23] But this too is problematic. Where rape is treated as a crime against honor, the honor of women is called into question and virginity or chastity is often a precondition.[24] Honor implies the loss of station or respect; it reinforces the social view, internalized by women, that the raped woman is dishonorable. And while the concept of dignity potentially embraces more profound concerns, standing alone it obfuscates the fact that rape is fundamentally violence against women—violence against their bodies, autonomy, integrity, selfhood, security, and self-esteem, as well as their standing in the community. This failure to recognize rape as violence is critical to the traditionally lesser or ambiguous status of rape in humanitarian law.

The issue, then, is not whether rape is a war crime, but whether it is a crime of the gravest dimension. Under the Geneva Conventions, the most serious war crimes are designated as "grave breaches."[25] The significance of a war crime's categorization as a grave breach is threefold. On the level of discourse, it calls attention to the egregiousness of the assault. On a practical level, it is not necessary that rape be mass or systematic: One act of rape is punishable. Finally, only crimes that are grave breaches give rise to universal jurisdiction under the Geneva Conventions. Universal jurisdiction means that each nation has an obligation to bring the perpetrators to justice through investigating, arresting, and prosecuting offenders in its own courts or extraditing them to more appropriate forums.[26] The existence of universal jurisdiction also provides a legal rationale for trying such crimes before an international tribunal and for the obligation of states to cooperate. If rape is not a grave breach under the Geneva Conventions, some international jurists would argue that it can be redressed only by the state to which the wrongdoer belongs or in which the wrong occurs, and not by an international tribunal.[27]

The relevant portions of the Fourth Geneva Convention relating to the protection of civilians do not specifically mention rape in the list of crimes that are considered grave breaches, and the Tribunal Statute simply reiterates the convention's list. Included are "willful killing, torture, or inhumane treatment" and "willfully causing great suffering or serious injury to body or health."[28] Clearly these categories are generic and broad enough to encompass rape and sexual abuse.[29] ·But in addition to qualifying as simply "inhumane treatment," or even as "willfully causing great suffering or serious injury to body or health," it is important that rape be recognized as a form of torture in order to remove the ambiguity that is the legacy of sexism and to place the crimes against women on par with crimes against men.

When the Geneva Conventions were drafted, the view that torture was a method of extracting information was dominant.[30] The crime of "willfully causing great suffering or serious injury to body or health" was added to the list of grave breaches largely because the meaning of torture was so narrow.[31] Today, although it endures in popular thinking, the narrow definition of torture has been largely abandoned. The historian Edward Peters writes: "It is not primarily the victim's information, but the victim, that torture needs to win—or reduce to powerlessness."[32] Recent treaties, which reflect customary international human rights law, define torture as the willful infliction of severe physical or mental pain or suffering not only to elicit information but also to punish, intimidate, discriminate, obliterate the victim's personality, or diminish her personal capacities.[33] Thus torture is now commensurate with willfully causing great suffering or injury for a broader set of purposes.[34] It is not simply or necessarily the infliction of terrible physical pain; it is also the use of pain, sensory deprivation, isolation, and/or humiliation as a pathway to the mind. Indeed, in the contemporary understanding of torture, degradation is a vehicle and debilitation, a goal.[35]

It is thus entirely appropriate that the implementation of the Geneva Conventions today incorporate the contemporary understanding of torture rather than use the category of "willfully causing great suffering...," which, though perhaps equivalent, has no counterpart in human rights law. The commentary to common article 3 emphasizes that progressive interpretation of the meaning of torture is intended: "However great the care taken in drawing up a list of all the various forms of infliction, it would never be possible to catch up with the imagination of future torturers who wished to satisfy their bestial instincts; and the more specific and complete a list tries to be, the more restrictive it becomes."[36] This commentary also makes clear, in discussing the taking of hostages and the imposition of nonjudicial punishments, that condemnation can extend to practices that are both common and previously tolerated.[37] In addition, the commentary to the 1977 Protocol I specifically refers to the evolving concept of torture in international human rights law.[38] There is thus little doubt that the Geneva Conventions were intended to incorporate the evolving concept of torture in international human rights as well as humanitarian law. To remove the ambiguity surrounding the gravity of rape and similar forms of gender violence in both contexts, it is important that the category "torture" be used.

Although largely ignored until recently by human rights advocates, the testimonies and studies of women tortured by dictatorial regimes and military occupations make it clear that rape is one of the most common, terrible, and effective forms of torture used against women.[39] Rape attacks the integrity of the woman as a person as well as her identity as a woman. It renders her, in the words of Lepa Mladjenovic, a psychotherapist and Serbian feminist antiwar activist, "homeless in her own body."[40] It strikes at a woman's power; it seeks to degrade and destroy her; its goal is domination and dehumanization.

Likewise, the testimonies of women raped in the wars in former Yugoslavia, whether they were attacked once or forced into prostitution, make clear that rape is both a profound physical attack and a particularly egregious form of psychological torture. Their testimonies document the intersection of contempt for and conquest of women based on their identity as women and their national or religious/cultural identity. Croatian women are raped in revenge against their "Ustasha mothers," and Bosnian-Muslim women are taunted that they should bear "Serb babies." This frequent genocidal threat, carried out on the bodies and spirits of women, underscores the omnipresent threat, fear, and/or reality of pregnancy. Genocide entrains forced pregnancy—repeated rape and detention until abortion is no longer an option. The horror is only exacerbated by the fact that in Bosnia the rapists are, in many cases, former colleagues, neighbors, or even friends.[41]

Indeed, torturers know well the power of the intimate in the process of breaking down their victim.[42] Because rape is a transposition of the intimate into violence, rape by acquaintances, by those one has trusted, is particularly world shattering and thus a particularly effective tool of ethnic cleansing. It is no wonder that local Bosnian Serbs are being incited and, in some cases, recruited to rape. The stories of some of the perpetrators, notwithstanding their selfjustificatory quality, reflect the common methods of training torturers—exposure to and engagement in increasingly unthinkable violence and humiliation.[43]

The statute establishing the jurisdiction of the international tribunal largely tracks the Geneva Conventions' definition of grave breach and does not, therefore, list rape as such.[44] The creation of the tribunal was preceded by the condemnation of sexual violence against women in these wars in the Vienna Declaration of the World Conference on Human Rights as well as by the United Nations Commission on Human Rights.[45] The first papers filed by the prosecutor, however, raised serious doubt about whether rape would be treated as a grave breach.[46] In February 1995, due in no small part to the continuous monitoring of women's human rights advocates, the tribunal prosecutor filed two indictments that give prominence to the charges of rape and classify it as a grave breach, a crime against humanity, and a violation of the laws and customs of war.[47] Prosecuting rape as a grave breach should effectively expand the meaning of the Geneva Conventions and obviate the need for formal amendment.

The classification of rape as a grave breach in the indictments is thus extremely significant, but it is not without problems. Although the indictments recite as applicable the broad definition of torture contained in the U.N. Torture Convention,[48] the indictments charge rape as "willful infliction of great suffering," not "torture,"[49] despite the fact, as discussed above, that these two terms have become virtually synonymous. The failure to charge rape as torture perpetuates the ambiguity as to its status. Moreover, the use of terms particular to humanitarian law fails to make the connection with this most egregious violation of human rights.

Curiously, the prosecutor uses the category "torture" very sparingly in his indictments. Physical brutality, commonly understood as torture by other bodies charged with implementation of human rights prohibitions against torture, is charged as "willful infliction of severe suffering or physical or mental health damage."[50] For example, the most common forms of torture include beating, kicking, and the infliction of pain with ordinary objects such as canes, knives, and cigarettes. This is true of charges involving prisoners who were severely beaten, kicked, stomped on (often to the point of unconsciousness), left to die, forced to drink foul fluids, and/or otherwise abused.[51] Nor do the indictments appear to encompass the evolving understanding of psychological torture.[52] In other words, these early indictments fail to charge both rape and other common forms of torture as "torture."

These indictments characterize only one offense as torture: the sexual mutilation of a male prisoner. The case is gruesome—two prisoners were forced to bite off the testicle of another prisoner, who subsequently bled to death.[53] The general problem with the prosecutor's definition is illustrated by the fact that torture is charged only as to the mutilated prisoner; those who were compelled to enact the mutilation are viewed as having been subjected to inhumane treatment.[54] The sex-specific problem involves the differential treatment of sexual violence. What makes this sexual mutilation torture as compared to the repeated (or, indeed, one act of) rape of women over a period of months charged in the same indictment? It is hard not to attribute it to the sex of the decision-makers, to the difficulty that men have in empathizing with the female victim by comparison to the horror that surfaces so easily when male sexual abuse is the issue, and to the fact that the concept of rape as torture implicates men's sexuality and comfortable distinctions between voluntary sexual intercourse and rape. It cannot be disconnected from the fact that the damage of rape is unseen: The physical damage is largely internal, and the psychological is born in silence.[55] Finally, the distinction between male sexual mutilation and rape, which could also be viewed as a form of female sexual mutilation, must be linked to their differential prevalence. Because rape is so common in war as well as peace, it loses its shock value. It is the egregious in the everyday, obscured or naturalized by the banality of evil.[56]

This failure to charge rape as torture emphasizes the importance, from a practical as well as a moral perspective, of insisting that all rape, and not only mass or genocidal rape, be subject to the most severe condemnation and punishment. It is also important that the range of sexual violence, including forced prostitution and forced pregnancy, be explicitly charged as grave breaches, consisting of torture. The Vienna Declaration explicitly included forced pregnancy in its condemnation of the mass atrocities in the former Yugoslavia. Forced pregnancy must be seen as a separate offense against women as well as an act of genocide: The expressed intent to make women pregnant is an additional form of psychological torture; the goal of impregnation leads to imprisoning women and raping them until they are pregnant; the fact of pregnancy, whether or not aborted, continues the initial torture in a most intimate and invasive form; and the fact of bearing the child of rape, whether or not the child is placed for adoption, has a potentially lifelong impact on the woman and her place in the community.[57] Finally, it should be noted that under the Geneva Conventions as well as the tribunal statute, perpetrators are held responsible, whether or not they were officially ordered to commit the acts charged, and responsibility is imputed to commanders when they knew, or should have known, of the likelihood of rape and failed to take all feasible measures within their power to prevent or repress it.[58]

GENOCIDAL RAPE VERSUS "NORMAL" RAPE: WHEN IS WIDESPREAD RAPE A CRIME AGAINST HUMANITY?

"Crimes against humanity" were first formally recognized in the charter and judgment of the Nuremberg Tribunal; they do not depend on adherence to a treaty, and they, like grave breaches, give rise to universal jurisdiction. Since crimes against humanity can be committed in times of war or peace, it is irrelevant whether war in the former Yugoslavia is international or internal.

Rape has been separately listed, and forced prostitution acknowledged, as a "crime against humanity" in the statute of the International Tribunal.[59] This is not without precedent. After the Second World War, Local Council Law No. 10, which provided the foundation for the trials of lesser Nazis by the Allied forces, also listed rape as a crime against humanity. No one, however, was prosecuted.[60] Thus the Security Council's reaffirmation that rape is a "crime against humanity," and therefore among the most egregious breaches of civilization, is profoundly important. It is doubly important that the prosecutor has also charged rape as a crime against humanity.[61] But the meaning of this designation and its import for other contexts in which women are subjected to mass rape apart from genocide or "ethnic cleansing" are not clear. The danger, as always, is that extreme examples produce narrow principles.

The commentary to the statute on this aspect of the jurisdiction of the current tribunal signals this danger. It explains crimes against humanity as "inhumane acts of a very serious nature, such as willful killing, torture or rape, committed as part of a widespread or systematic attack against any civilian population on national, political, ethnic, racial, or religious grounds."[62] The prosecutor's indictments follow suit.[63] Several aspects of this definition deserve comment.

First, on the positive side, the statute correctly encompasses violations that are widespread but not necessarily "systematic." The law wisely does not require massive numbers but instead encompasses general frequency and patterns of abuse. Particularly with rape, numbers are unprovable: A small percentage of women will ultimately come forward, and the significance of rape threatens to become drowned in statistical claims. Moreover, the principle of responsibility under the statute, as well as in the customary law, does not require that rape be ordered or centrally organized. Commanders can be held responsible when widespread violence is known and tolerated.[64] In Bosnia, rape is clearly a conscious tool of war and genocide. Although it is politically and ethically important for the tribunal to investigate and prove the chain of command, it is likewise important that leaders be held legally responsible for acts of commission or omission, even without proof that rape was committed under orders.

Second, the commentary on the statute does rank rape with torture in terms of the gravity of the violence and its characterization as a crime against humanity. While this is important (and bears as well on the treatment of rape as torture under the grave breach category), it remains problematic that the statute lists rape and torture as distinct, instead of identifying rape as a form of torture.[65]

The third issue with the statute's definition of crimes against humanity, however, is its conflation of what were originally understood as two separate and independent criteria of crimes against humanity: gross acts of violence *and* persecution-based offenses.[66] Under the original concept, rape, if widespread or systematic, should independently qualify as a crime against humanity because it is a gross act of violence. By merging the criterion of gross violence with persecution-based offenses, the commentary could limit prosecution to rape that is undertaken as a method of persecution on national, political, ethnic, racial, or religious grounds. Since the tribunal statute lists rape and persecution separately, it is not clear, until put into practice, whether the original, broader understanding of crimes against humanity will prevail. But since widespread rape is a critical aspect of genocide against the non-Serbian populations in Bosnia, these prosecutions do not present a clear occasion for testing the sufficiency of widespread rape, apart from the recognized grounds of persecution, as a crime against humanity.

Acceptance of the conflation of rape and persecution, together with the absence of gender as a basis of persecution, would narrow the concept of crimes against humanity as well as jeopardize its application to women. This narrow view of crimes against humanity, which treats gender crimes as significant only when they are the vehicle of some "larger" persecution, is quite prevalent and requires critical examination.

The international and popular condemnation of the rapes in Bosnia tends to be either explicitly or implicitly based on the fact that rape is being used as a tactic of ethnic cleansing. Genocidal rape is widely seen, not as a modality of rape, but as unique. The distinction commonly drawn between genocidal rape and "normal" rape in war or in peacetime is proffered not as a typology, but rather as a hierarchy. But to exaggerate the distinctiveness of genocidal rape obscures the atrocity of common rape.

Genocidal rape often involves gang rapes, is outrageously brutal, and is done in public or in front of children or partners. It involves imprisoning women in rape "camps" and/or raping them repeatedly. These are also characteristics of the most common rape in war—rape for booty or to boost the morale of soldiers—and they are common characteristics of the use of rape as a form of torture and terror by dictatorial regimes.[67]

The notion that genocidal rape is uniquely a weapon of war is also problematic. The rape of women is a weapon of war when it is used to spread political terror, as in the civil war in Peru.[68] It is a weapon of war when, as in Bosnia and elsewhere, it is used against women to destabilize society and force families to flee. In time of war, women are the mainstay of the civilian population, even more than in peacetime.

The widespread rape of Haitian women as a weapon not of war, but of terror, in the recent virulent political repression in Haiti shares many of these characteristics. Haitian women were routinely raped in their homes, often repeatedly and in front of their children. They were raped because of their active or presumed resistance to the illegal regime or that of their partners or family members; they were raped simply because they lived in poor sections that had voted overwhelmingly for Jean-Bertrand Aristide and because, as women, they kept civil society functioning before and after men went into hiding. They were raped to render them powerless as well as to drive home the powerlessness of their male "protectors." As a result of this ultimate invasion of the security of person and home, many Haitian women fled their homes and went into hiding or exile. The brutalities visited upon them as women were not in the service of war or genocide, but the pattern is familiar. Now, unlike the Bosnian-Muslim women, many Haitian women can (and some are being forced by the lack of refuge elsewhere to) return to their communities. But the suffering, estrangement, memory, and mark of this trauma does not end with physical return.[69]

The rape of women, where permitted or systematized as "booty" of war, is likewise an engine of war. It maintains the morale of soldiers, feeds their hatred and sense of superiority, and keeps them fighting. For this reason, and to prevent the public outcry that attended open mass rape, the Japanese military industrialized the sexual slavery of women in the Second World War. Deceived by false offers of employment or taken forcibly, women were disappeared into "comfort stations" and, once there, were raped repeatedly and moved from battlefield to battlefield to motivate and reward the Japanese soldiers. Genocide was not a goal, but it is believed that 70 percent to 90 percent of these women died in captivity, and among the known survivors, none were subsequently able to bear children.[70] For similar reasons, the U.S. military in Vietnam raped Vietnamese women and established brothels, relying on dire economic necessity rather than kidnapping to fill them.[71] The testimonies of Bosnian Serbian rapists reveal a mixture of all these goals.[72]

At the same time, some aspects of the genocidal rape practiced in Bosnia are particularly tailored to the goals of driving women from their homes or destroying their possibility of reproducing within and "for" their community. When women are raped by men familiar to them, their trauma is exacerbated, as is their impulse and need to flee the community because trust and safety are no longer possible.[73] This is particularly true in Bosnia, where war and propaganda have made enemies out of neighbors.

The second and more distinctive feature of genocidal rape is the focus on women as reproductive vessels. The explicit and common threat to make Muslim women bear "Serbian babies" justifies repetitive rape and aggravates a woman's terror and potential unacceptability to her community. Bengali women were raped to lighten their race and produce a class of outcast mothers and children. Enslaved African-American women in the southern United States were raped to produce babies, bartered, sold, and used as property.[74] While intentional impregnation is properly treated as a separate offense, it should also be noted that pregnancy and the fear of pregnancy are an often unrecognized, yet common consequence and added harm of rape. In situations in which women are raped repeatedly, most fertile women will become pregnant at some point. When the U.S. Navy took overSaipan, at the end of World War II, for example, one observer reports that virtually all the women, who had been enslaved as comfort women for the Japanese army, were pregnant.[75] This appears to be true today for Rwandan women, together with the threat and reality of infection with HIV.

These distinctive characteristics do not therefore place genocidal rape in a class by itself; nor do they reflect the full range of atrocities, losses, and suffering that the combination of rape and ethnic cleansing inflicts. The women victims and survivors in Bosnia are being subjected to crimes against humanity based on *both* ethnicity and religion, and gender. It is critical to recognize both and to acknowledge that the intersection of ethnic and gender violence has its own particular characteristics.

This brings me to the fourth concern: the complete failure of the United Nations and the international community in general to recognize that persecution based on gender must be recognized as its own category of crimes against humanity. The crystallization of the concept of crimes against humanity in the wake of the Holocaust has meant that it is popularly associated with religious and ethnic genocide. But the concept is a broader one, and the categories of persecution are explicitly open ended, capable of expanding to embrace new understandings of persecution.

Historically, gender has not been viewed as a relevant category of victimization. The frequency of mass rape and the absence of sanctions are sufficient evidence. In the Holocaust, gender persecutions—the rape and forced prostitution of women, Aryan as well as Jewish, as well as the extermination of gay people—were obscured.[76] Gender combined with nationalistic superiority and hatred in the Japanese army's purposeful sexual enslavement of girls and young women as "comfort women." The growing involuntary trafficking of women presents a clearer case today. Without recognition of gender as a basis for persecution, sexual slavery would escape condemnation as a crime against humanity when it was shown that nationality or ethnicity was incidental.

The absence of gender as a basis for persecution is not, however, peculiar to the concept of crimes against humanity. A parallel problem exists in the international standards for political asylum, which require a well-founded fear of persecution, but do not explicitly recognize gender as a source of persecution.[77] The expansion of the concept of crimes against humanity explicitly to include gender is thus part of the broader movement to end the historical invisibility of gender violence as a humanitarian and human rights violation. The recognition of "social" and "cultural" persecution by the 1954 Draft Code of Offenses exemplifies this principle and should encompass gender.[78]

Moreover, the particular goals and defining aspects of genocidal rape do not detract from, but rather elucidate, the nature of rape as a crime of gender as well as ethnicity. Women are targets not simply because they "belong to" the enemy, but precisely because they keep the civilian population functioning and are essential to its continuity. They are targets because they, too, *are* the enemy—because of their power and vulnerability as women, including their sexual and reproductive power. They are targets because of hatred of their power as women, and because of endemic objectification of women, and because rape embodies male domination and female subordination.

The crime of forced impregnation, central to genocidal rape, also elucidates the gender component. Because under patriarchy women are viewed as little more than vessels for childbearing, involuntary pregnancy is commonly viewed as natural, divinely ordained perhaps, or simply an unquestioned fact of life. As a result, the risk of pregnancy in all rape is treated not as an offense but as a sequela. Forced pregnancy has drawn condemnation only when it reflects an intent to harm the victimized race. In Bosnia, the taunt that Muslim women will bear Serbian babies is not simply an ethnic harm, particularly in light of the prevalence of ethnically mixed families. When examined through a feminist lens, forced pregnancy appears as an assault on the reproductive self-determination of women; it expresses the desire to mark the rape and rapist upon the woman's body and upon the woman's life.

Finally, the fact that the rape of women is also designed to humiliate the men or destroy "the enemy" itself reflects the fundamental objectification of women. When a woman is attacked because she "belongs" to the enemy or because of her relationship to male targets, raping her is a means to humiliate, indeed, to feminize the men who are powerless to protect her. As such, she is also being attacked on the basis of gender, as man's property, lacking in separate identity, dehumanized, and subservient. In this common scenario, women are the target of abuse at the same time as their subjectivity is completely denied. The persistent failure to acknowledge the gender dimension of rape and sexual persecution is thus a most effective means of perpetuating it.

In sum, the international attention focused on Bosnia challenges the world squarely to recognize sexual violence against women in war as torture. Moreover, it is not enough for rape to be viewed as a crime against humanity when it is the vehicle of some other form of persecution even though gender is, in fact, usually intertwined. Sexual violence against women on a mass scale must also be recognized as a crime against humanity because it is invariably a persecution based on gender, sometimes exclusively or primarily so. The recent recognition in international human rights law of gender violence as a form of discrimination against women as well as a violation of women's fundamental human rights supports this expansion of the persecution bases of crimes against humanity.[79] This is essential if the women of Bosnia are to be understood as full subjects and not simply as objects in this terrible victimization and if the international attention focused on Bosnia is to have meaning for women subjected to widespread rape in other parts of the world.

CONCLUSION

Given the formidable pressure being brought to bear by women survivors and the women's movement globally, it may well be that some men will be indicted, subject to international warrants, or even tried before the international tribunal or national courts, at least if impunity is not again the price of peace. This would be precedent setting in international law and it would offer symbolic vindication to the untold numbers of women the war in the former Yugoslavia has rendered homeless in so many senses. Unless the gender dimension of rape in war is recognized, however, it may mean little for women where rape is not also a tool of genocide.[80]

Emphasis on the gender dimension of rape in war is critical not only to surfacing women as full subjects of sexual violence in war but also to recognizing the atrocity of rape in the time called peace. When women charge rape in war they are more likely to be believed, because their status as enemy, or at least as "the enemy's," is recognized and because rape in war is seen as a product of exceptional circumstances. When women charge rape in everyday life, however, they are disbelieved largely because the ubiquitous war against women is denied.

From a feminist human rights perspective, gender violence has escaped sanction because it has not been viewed as violence and because the public-private dichotomy has shielded such violence in its most common and private forms.[81] The recognition of rape as a war crime is thus a critical step toward understanding rape as violence. The next step is to recognize that rape in the presence of war or the imprimatur of the state is not necessarily more brutal, relentless, or dehumanizing than the private rapes in the so-called time of peace.

This is not to say that rape is identical in the two contexts. There are differences here, just as there are differences between rape for the purpose of genocide and rape for the purpose of booty. War tends to intensify the brutality, repetitiveness, public spectacle, and likelihood of rape. War diminishes sensitivity to human suffering and intensifies men's sense of entitlement, superiority, avidity, and social license to rape. War and armed repression carried out against civil society attacks whatever security, social supports, and routine existed for women in daily life. They rain terror from many directions and force many into hiding and flight.

But the line between war and "peace" is not so sharp. Gang rape in civilian life shares the repetitive, gleeful, and public character of rape in war. Marital rape, the most private of all, shares some of the particular characteristics of genocidal rape in Bosnia: It is repetitive, brutal, and exacerbated by betrayal; it assaults a woman's reproductive autonomy, may force her into hiding, to flee her home and community, and is widely treated as legitimate by law and custom. The lasting terror and shame of rape may change the psychological as well as physical landscape of a woman's life. Violation by a state official or enemy soldier is not necessarily more devastating than violation by an intimate.[82]

Every rape is a grave violation of physical and mental integrity. Every rape has the potential to profoundly debilitate, to render the woman homeless in her own body and destroy her sense of security in the world. Every rape is an expression of male domination and misogyny, a vehicle of terrorizing and subordinating women. Like torture, rape takes many forms, occurs in many contexts, and has different repercussions for different victims. Every rape is multidimensional, but not incomparable.

The rape of women in the former Yugoslavia challenges the world to refuse impunity to atrocity and to resist the powerful forces that would make the mass rape of Muslim women in Bosnia exceptional and thereby restrict its meaning for women raped in different contexts of war, official repression, and "peace." It thus demands recognition of situational differences without losing sight of the commonalities. To fail to make distinctions flattens reality, and to rank the egregious demeans it.[83]

NOTES

Permission to reprint this article is granted by the University of California, Hastings College of the Law, and *Hastings Women's Law Journal* where it appeared in vol. 5, no. 2 (Summer 1994): 243—266. Originally this article appeared as "Surfacing Gender: Reconceptualizing Crimes Against Women in Time of War" in *Mass Rape: The War Against Women in Bosnia-Herzegovina*, ed. Alexandra Stiglmayer (Lincoln, NK: University of Nebraska Press, 1994). Credit for extensive research into the historical and current understanding of war crimes and crimes against humanity is due to Krishna Stark and Ethan Taubes, 1992-1993 IWHR interns. Had there been more time to develop this earlier piece, we should have been coauthors. I also appreciate Marilyn Young's comments on the draft, as well as the ongoing collaboration with Jennifer Green and conversations with Felice Gaer, Vesna Kesic, Guadelupe Leon, Celina Romany, Indai Lourdes Sajor, Sara Sharett, Ann Snitow, and Dorothy Thomas, among others.

1. See Susan Brownmiller, *Against Our Will: Men, Women and Rape* (New York: Simon & Schuster, 1975), 78—86.

2. The London Charter, which created the Nuremberg Tribunal, did not list rape as an offense. Local Council Law No. 10, which was the basis for the prosecution of lower-level Nazis, did list rape as a crime against humanity. See Agreement on Punishment of Persons Guilty of War Crimes, January 31, 1946, Control Council for Germany, No. 3, 50—55 (adopted by the Allied powers on December 20, 1945, establishing the jurisdiction of military tribunals operating in the occupation zones). But no cases were brought on this ground, perhaps because the Allied forces were not innocent of this particular atrocity. See, generally, Adalbert Ruckerl, *The Investigation of Nazi War Crimes 1945—1978: A Documentation* (Heidelberg: C.F. Muller, 1979). See also Brownmiller, ibid., 31—113.

3. Brownmiller, *Against Our Will*, op. cit., 65—78 (reporting on rape by Russian, Moroccan, and U.S. armies and citing limited statistics on U.S. courts-martial for rape); Atina Grossman, "A Question of Silence: The Rape of German Women by Occupation Soldiers," *October* (April

1994): 43—63; Michael Walzer, ed., *Just and Unjust Wars* (New York: Basic Books, 1992).

4. See Leon Freidman, *The Law of War: A History*, vol. 2 (1972), 1061.

5. See R.J. Pritchard and S. Magbunua Zaide, eds., *The Tokyo War Crimes Trial*, vol. 1 (1981). The indictment charged "violation of recognized customs and conventions of war," including "mass murder, rape, pillage, brigandage, torture and other barbaric cruelties upon the helpless civilian population of the over-run countries." Commander Matsui, in charge of the capture of Nanjing, was found guilty of violations of the laws of war because he was aware of the atrocities, including the mass rape of women, and did nothing to stop them. Ibid. at 49, 814—816. Defendants Hirota and Admiral Toyoda were likewise charged with responsibility for massive atrocities, including rape. Ibid., at 49, 791—792. See also W.H. Parks, "Command Responsibility for War Crimes," *Military Law Review* 1 (Fall 1973): 69—70.

6. See, Ustinia Dolgopol and Snehal Paranjape, *Comfort Women: An Unfinished Ordeal: Report of a Mission* (Geneva, Switzerland: International Commission of Jurists, 1994), and Dan P. Calica & Nelia Sancho, eds., *War Crimes on Asian Women: Military Sexual Slavery by Japan During World War II—The Case of the Filipino Comfort Women* (Manila: Task Force on Filipina Victims of Military Sexual Slavery by Japan; Asian Women Human Rights Council—Philippine Section, 1993).

7. There is evidence that all sides have used rape of women in this conflict, but the most intensive use has been by the Bosnian-Serbs against Bosnian-Muslim women. Jeri Laber, "Questions of Rape," *New York Review of Books*, 25 March 1993, 4.

8. At the printing of this volume in June 1998, it is clear that the present tense still applies. Since the major initiatives of "ethnic cleansing" in ex-Yugoslavia between 1993 and 1995, rape has also been employed by Hutu troops against Tutsi women in what the international community now recognizes as a genocidal campaign in Rwanda. Other instances of civil war rape have been reported by women in Algeria. On June 16, 1998 the United Nations sponsored the first conference in Rome to begin defining rules for a permanent international court to prosecute crimes against humanity. The permanent international court is expected to model itself on the ad hoc tribunals, discussed here, that have been hearing allegations of war crimes, first in the Balkans and also in Rwanda. It remains to be seen how the precedents of the prosecutors in these tribunals, which elevated sex crimes to the level of genocidal and crimes against humanity, will be observed and how the international court will

treat rape independently of genocide. Clearly, rape continues as a weapon of "conventional" war. Thus I continue to use the present tense because the invisibility of rape is still pervasive.

9. Presentation of Guadelupe Leon, Panel on Military Violence and Sexual Slavery, 1993 U.N. Conference on Human Rights, NGO Parallel Activities, June 1993 (discussing the rape of the Yuracruz women); Americas Watch and Human Rights Watch, *Untold Terror: Violence Against Women in Peru's Armed Conflict* (1992); Asia Watch and Women's Rights Project, *Burma: Rape, Forced Labour and Religious Persecution in Northern Arakan* (1992); Shana Swiss, *Liberia: Women and Children Gravely Mistreated* (1991). See also Shana Swiss and Joan E. Giller, "Rape as a Crime of War: A Medical Perspective," *Journal of American Medical Association 270*, no. 5 (1993): 612.

10. See Brownmiller, *Against Our Will,* op. cit., 78—86.

11. See David Crary, "Generation of Rape Is Born in Rwanda: Doctor Describes Nightmarish Abortion Plight of Victims," *The Guardian*, 11 February 1995, 13; Lindsey Hilsum, "Rwanda's Time of Rape Returns to Haunt Thousands," *The Observer*, 26 February1995, 17.

12. The same is true in the less frequent case of rape against men, except that when a man is raped, the humiliation is accomplished by reducing him to the status of a woman. For this reason, rape, whether carried out against women or men, is a crime of gender.

13. The full title of the Statute of the International Tribunal is the International Tribunal for the Prosecution of Persons Responsible for Serious Violations of International Humanitarian Law Committed in the Territory of the Former Yugoslavia Since 1991. The statute is the annex to the Report of the Secretary-General Pursuant to Paragraph 2 of the Security Council Resolution 808, U.N. SCOR, 48th Sess., 7 para. 25, U.N. Doc. S/25704 (1993). The tribunal received authority to prosecute war crimes in Rwanda in 1994. Final Report of the Commission of Experts Established Pursuant to Security Council, Resolution 935, U.N. SCOR, 49th Sess., 40—52, U.N. Doc. No. S/1994/1405 (1994).

14. On the significance of the intersection of categories of oppression, see Kimberley Crenshaw, "Demarginalizing the Intersection of Race and Sex: A Black Feminist Critique of Antidiscrimination Doctrine, Feminist Theory and Antiracist Politics," *University of Chicago Legal Forum* (1989), 139.

15. See Theodor Meron, "Rape as a Crime Under International Humanitarian Law," 87 *American Journal of International Law* 87, no. 424 (1993) (exploring the treatment of rape in humanitarian law); Dorothy Q. Thomas and Regan E. Ralph, "Rape in War: Challenging the

Tradition of Impunity," 14 *SAIS Review* 81 (1994) (examining analytic questions presented by rape in different contexts of war); Deborah Blatt, "Recognizing Rape as a Method of Torture," *New York University Review of Law and Social Change* 19, no. 821 (1992) (arguing rape in detention should be viewed as torture); Kathleen M. Pratt and Laurel E. Fletcher, "Time for Justice: The Case for International Prosecutions of Rape and Gender-based Violence in the Former Yugoslavia," *Berkeley Women's Law Journal* 9, no. 77 (1994) (summarizing the factual background of war and rape in the former Yugoslavia and examining the applicability of humanitarian law); Adrien Katherine Wing and Sylke Merchan, "Rape, Ethnicity, and Culture: Spirit Inquiry from Bosnia to Black America," *Columbia Human Rights Law Review* 25, no. 1 (1993) (examining factual and legal implications of ethno-gender violence in both contexts); and Catharine MacKinnon, "Rape, Genocide, and Women's Human Rights," *Harvard Women's Law Journal* 17, no. 5 (1994) (emphasizing genocidal aspects of rape in Bosnia).

16. Report of the Secretary-General, op. cit., 9 para. 35, 10 para. 37.

17. See Yougingra Khushalani, *Dignity and Honour of Women as Basic and Fundamental Human Rights* (The Hague; Boston: Martinus Nijhoff Publishers,1982).

18. Geneva Conventions Relative to the Protection of Civilian Persons in Time of War, adopted 12 August 1949, arts. 3(1)(a), 3(1)(c), 27, 76, 97 [hereinafter Geneva Convention IV]; Protocol Additional in the Geneva Conventions of 12 August 1949, and Relating to the Protection of Victims of International Armed Conflicts, adopted 8 June 1977, art. 76 [hereinafter Protocol I]; and Protocol Additional to the Geneva Conventions of 12 August 1949, and Relating to the Protection of Victims of Non-International Armed Conflicts, adopted 8 June 1977, art. 4 [hereinafter Protocol II], reprinted in   Center for Human Rights, *Human Rights: A Compilation of International Instruments,* vol.1, 799939 (1993).

19. See, e.g., Geneva Convention IV, op. cit., art. 27, para. 2; Protocol II, op. cit., art. 4.

20. See, e.g., *Coker* v. *Georgia,* 433 U.S. 584 (1977).

21. Khushalani, *Dignity and Honour,* op. cit., 39—76.

22. Commentary IV: Geneva Convention Relative to the Protection of Civilian Persons in Time of War of 1958, International Committee of the Red Cross, art. 27 at 202 (commentary of Jean Pictet) [hereinafter 1958 ICRC Commentary].

23. Ibid., 205.

24. See, e.g., *Americas Watch and Women's Rights Project, Untold Terror,* op. cit., 10—16.

25. Geneva Convention IV, op. cit., art. 147.

26. Ibid., art. 145. It should be noted here that the concept of "grave breach" applies only to international conflict and not to civil war. Although there is some debate about whether the conflict in the territory of the former Yugoslavia is international or internal, the U.N. Security Council has indicated that it is an international conflict. Report of the Secretary-General, op. cit., 8, para. 25.

27. The concept of "purpose" should not be understood as requiring a showing of specific intent on the part of the perpetrator. Rather, it calls for an evaluation of the functions and effects of the violence. See Rhonda Copelon, "Recognizing the Egregious in the Everyday: Domestic Violence as Torture," *Columbia Human Rights Law Review* 25, no. 290 (1994): 325—331.

28. Geneva Convention IV, op. cit., art. 147; Protocol I, op. cit., arts. 11, 85(3).

29. Khushalani, *Dignity and Honour*, op. cit., 39—76. See also Alexandra Stiglmayer, "The Rapes in Bosnia-Herzegovina," in *Mass Rape*, ed. Alexandra Stiglmayer, op. cit.

30. The 1958 ICRC Commentary to the Fourth Geneva Convention explains:

> The word torture has different acceptations. It is used sometimes even in the sense of purely moral suffering, but in view of the other expressions which follow (i.e., inhuman treatment...and suffering, etc.) it seems that it must be given here its, so to speak, legal meaning—i.e., the infliction of suffering on a person to obtain from that person, or from another person, confessions or information....

1958 ICRC Commentary, op. cit., 598.

31. The 1958 ICRC Commentary defines this crime as referring to "suffering inflicted without the ends for which torture is inflicted....It would therefore be inflicted as punishment, in revenge or for some other motive, perhaps out of pure sadism...." Ibid., 599. Since the Conventions do not specify that only physical suffering is meant, it can quite legitimately be held to cover moral suffering as well.

32. Edward Peters, *Torture* (New York: B. Blackwell, 1985), 164 .

33. Convention Against Torture and Other Cruel, Inhuman or Degrading Treatment or Punishment, G.A. Res. 39/46, U.N. GAOR, 39th Sess., at 3, U.N. Doc. AIRES/39/46 (1984); Inter-American Convention to Prevent and Punish Torture, 9 December 1985, art. 2, 258, reprinted in J. Herman Burgers and Hans Danelius, *The United*

Nations Convention Against Torture: A Handbook on the Convention Against Torture and Other Cruel, Inhuman or Degrading Treatment or Punishment (Dordrecht; Boston: Martinus Nijhoff Publisher, 1988).

34. Copelon, *Recognizing the Egregious,* op. cit., 325—331.

35. Amnesty International, *Report on Torture* (1974).

36. 1958 ICRC Commentary, op. cit., 39.

37. Ibid. (stating that the Geneva Conventions intend to "prohibit practices which are fairly general in wartime . . . [and,] although...common...until quite recently,...are nevertheless shocking to the civilized mind").

38. Commentary on the Additional Protocols of 8 June 1977 to the Geneva Conventions of 12 August 1949, International Committee of the Red Cross, art. 75(a)(ii), at 873 (citing the General Assembly's 1975 Declaration on Torture, which expanded impermissible purposes by adding punishment and intimidation and noting the General Assembly's 1984 vote adopting the Convention Against Torture, which it described at that time as "without binding force of law, [but] nevertheless hav[ing] a real moral value").

39. See, e.g., Ximena Bunster-Burotto in *Surviving Beyond Fear: Women and Torture in Latin America* , ed. Marjorie Agosin (Fredonia, NY: White Pine Press, 1993), and *Women and Change in Latin America,* ed. June Nash and Helen Safa (South Hadley, MA: Bergin and Garvey, 1986), 297; F. Allodi and S. Stiasny, "Women as Torture Victims," *Canadian Journal of Psychiatry* , no. 2 (1990): 35—144; and Inge Lunde & Jorge Ortmann, "Prevalence and Sequelae of Sexual Torture," 336 *Lancet* (1990): 289. While not the subject here, the rape of men is also a devastating crime of gender, designed as it is to humiliate through feminization.

40. Testimony Before the Global Tribunal on Violations of Women's Human Rights, NGO Parallel Activities, 1993 World Conference on Human Rights, Vienna, 15 June 1993.

41. See Stiglmayer, *Mass Rape,* op. cit. (testimonies of women raped in Bosnia).

42. See Amnesty International, *Report on Tortures* (1973); Elaine Scarry, *The Body in Pain: The Making and Unmaking of the World* (New York: Oxford University Press,1985), 41; Judith Lewis Herman, *Trauma and Recovery* (New York: Basic Books,1992).

43. See Stanley Milgram, "Some Conditions of Obedience and Disobedience to Authority," *Human Relations* 18, vol. 57, no.1 (1965). On the training of torturers, see Amnesty International, *Torture in Greece: The First Torturers' Trial* 1975 (1977), and Mike Haritos-Fatouros, "The Official Torturer: A Learning Model for Obedience to the Authority of

Violence," *Journal of Applied Social Psychology* 18, no. 13 (1988): 1107. For examples of stories by the perpetrators of rape in Bosnia, see Stiglmayer, *Mass Rape*, op. cit.

44. Article 2 identifies as grave breaches "(a) wilful killing; (b) torture or inhuman treatment, including biological experiments; (c) wilfully causing great suffering or serious bodily injury to body or health." Report of the Secretary-General, op. cit., 10, para. 40.

45. "Violations of the human rights of women in situations of armed conflict are violations of the fundamental principles of international human rights and humanitarian law. All violations of this kind, including in particular murder, systematic rape, sexual slavery, and forced pregnancy, require a particularly effective response." Vienna Declaration and Programme of Action, United Nations World Conference on Human Rights, U.N. GAOR, 47th Sess., at 37, U.N. Doc. A/Conf.157/24 (Part 1) (1993) [hereafter Vienna Declaration]; United Nations Commission on Human Rights, Rape and Abuse of Women in the Territory of the Former Yugoslavia, E.S.C. Res. 1993/8, U.N. ESCOR, 45th Sess., Supp. No. 3, at 6061, U.N. Doc. E/CN.4/1993/122 (1993).

46. The first public mention of rape by the prosecutor was in an affidavit seeking deferral to the tribunal of the *Tadic* case, which had been previously within Germany's jurisdiction. *An Application for Deferral by the Federal Republic of Germany in the Matter of Dusko Tadic Also Known By the Names Dusan "Dule" Tadic*, Case no. 1 of 1994 (Trial Chamber, October 11, 1994). The affidavit gave decidedly secondary consideration to the conditions affecting women and to the severity of rape, for example, treating it as less serious than beatings or omitting discussion of it. At the hearing on the deferral application, Judge Odio-Benito questioned the prosecutor on these defamations, and an amicus brief, filed by the International Women's Human Rights Law Clinic, the Harvard Human Rights Program, and the Jacob Blaustein Institute, underscored the trivialization of violence against women. See *Re: Application for Deferral By the Republic of Germany in the Matter of Dusko Tadic Also Known By the Names Dusan "Dale" Tadic* (on file with author). The chief prosecutor acknowledged the value of this critique:

> We essentially concur with your comments as to the characterization of rape. The Declaration's discussion of rape does not sufficiently reflect our policy of equating rape to other serious transgressions of international law. Apart from the relevance to charges of genocide and crimes against humanity, rape and other sexual assaults will be prosecuted under the Statute's provisions for torture, inhumane treatment, willfully causing great suffering or

serious injury to body, and inhumane acts, and other provisions that adequately encompass the nature of the acts committed and intent formulated.

Letter from Justice Richard Goldstone, Prosecutor, to Rhonda Copelon, Felice Gaer, and Jennifer Green (November 22, 1994) (on file with author). While the indictment against Tadic is very responsive to the critique, it does not identify rape as torture, as discussed hereinafter.

47. *Prosecutor of the Tribunal* v. *Zeljko Meakic* [hereinafter *Meakic*]; *Prosecutor of the Tribunal* v. *Dusan Tadic* [hereinafter *Tadic*].

48. *Meakic*, at para. 14; *Tadic*, at para. 3.6.

49. In *Prosecutor of the Tribunal* v. *Zeljko Meakic,* the indictment charges the defendant Radic with five incidents of forcible sexual intercourse against "A" between late June and late July. Ibid., at paras. 22.2, 22.5, 22.8, 22.11, and 22.14. It charges the defendants Gruban and Kostic with willfully causing great suffering for repeatedly raping "F" during a 2 month period. Ibid., at paras. 25.1—25.2 and 26.126.2, respectively.

50. For comparative treatment of a charge of torture, see Burgers and Danelius, *The United Nations Convention*, op. cit. (discussing the legislative history of the U.N. Torture Convention and describing the most common forms of torture). See also Nigel Rodley, *The Treatment of Prisoners Under International Law* (Paris: UNECO; Oxford [Oxfordshire]: Clarendon Press; New York: Oxford University Press, 1987), and cases cited therein.

51. For example, paragraph 2.6 of the *Tadic* indictment describes the factual basis of the charges:

> Severe beatings were commonplace. The camp guards, and others who came to the camp and physically abused the prisoners, used all manner of weapons during these beatings, including wooden batons, metal rods and tools, lengths of thick industrial cable that had metal balls affixed to the end, rifle butts, and knives. Both female and male prisoners were beaten, tortured, raped, sexually assaulted, and humiliated. Many, whose identities are known and unknown, did not survive the camp....

Tadic, at para. 2.6.

52. Amnesty International has laid great emphasis on the psychological component of torture. Amnesty International, *Report on Torture* 3955 (1975). See also Rodley, *Treatment of Prisoners*, op. cit., 83—86; Burgers and Danelius, *The United Nations Convention*, op. cit., 177—78. Of

particular relevance here is the finding of the Human Rights Committee that a concert pianist was subjected to "severe psychological torture" because he had been threatened for hours with amputation of his hands by an electric saw, as a result of which he lost sensitivity in his hands and arms for almost a year and suffered continuing discomfort thereafter. See Report of the Human Rights Committee, U.N. GAOR, 38th Sess., Supp. no. 40, Annex 12, paras. 1.6 and 8.3, U.N. Doc A/38140 (1983) *(Estrella v. Uruguay)*. Applying *Estrella*, the threat of rape endured constantly by women in detention should be considered as a form of torture. The threat of rape, like the threat to amputate in that case, challenges bodily integrity in a way that is deeply connected to the most import aspects of personal identity.

53. *Tadic*, at para. 5.1.

54. By contrast, the mainstream understanding of torture recognizes that being forced to perform humiliating acts or to confess—that is, to cross the boundaries of civilized conduct—is a key method of breaking the will of the torture victim. See Amnesty International, *Report on Torture*, op. cit., 41—42. See also Haritos-Fatouros, "Official Torturer," op. cit.

55. This might be inferred from the fact that the indictments charge beating as willfully causing great suffering or serious injury to body or health, whereas repeated rape is viewed only as willfully causing great suffering. *Meakic*, at paras. 20.2, 22.2, 24.2, 25.2, and 26.2. On the other hand, a case involving kicking in the testicles, repeated beating, and kicking in the ribs, causing the prisoner to lapse in and out of consciousness, was charged as willfully causing great suffering. Ibid., at para. 29.2.

56. Hannah Arendt, *Eichmann in Jerusalem: A Report on the Banality of Evil* 2nd ed. (New York: Penguin Books, 1964), 93. This point is developed with regard to domestic violence in Copelon, *Recognizing the Egregious*, op. cit.

57. See, generally, Stiglmayer, *Mass Rape*, op. cit. See also Anne Tierny Goldstein, *Recognizing Forced Impregnation as a War Crime Under International Law* (Center for Reproductive Law and Policy, 1993) (examining forced impregnation under the Geneva Conventions and as a means of genocide and enslavement).

58. Protocol I, op. cit., art. 86; Report of the Secretary General, op. cit., art. 7, paras. 53—59 at 14—15.

59. Report of the Secretary-General, op. cit., art. 4, paras. 47—49, at 1171.

60. Khushalani, *Dignity and Honour*, op. cit., at 13—38.

61. *Meakic*, at paras. 22.4, 22.7, 22.10, 22.13, 25.4, 26.4, and 30.4; *Tadic*, at para. 4.4.

62. Report of the Secretary-General, op. cit., art. 4, para. 48, 13.

63. The indictments explain that the offense of "crimes against humanity" applies when the "alleged acts or omissions were part of a widespread or large-scale or systematic attack directed against a civilian population, specifically the Muslim and Croat population of the Prijedor district." *Meakic*, at para. 15; *Tadic*, at para. 3.7.

64. Report of the Secretary-General, op. cit., art. 7; Report of the International Law Commission, Draft Code of Offenses Against the Peace and Security of Mankind, U.N. GAOR, 6th Sess., op. cit., art. 2, at 11, U.N. Doc. A/1858 (1951) [hereinafter Draft Code].

65. The statute reads "torture or rape"; it could have read, for example, "torture, including rape."

66. See Khushalani, *Dignity and Honour*, op. cit., at 14—16. Article 6(c) of the London Charter, which established the Nuremberg Tribunal, defined "crimes against humanity" as follows: murder, extermination, enslavement, deportation, and other inhumane acts committed against any civilian population, before or during the war, or persecutions on political, racial or religious grounds...."

Agreement by the United States, France, Britain and the U.S.S.R., 82 U.N.T.S. 279, cited in Khushalani, ibid., at 14, no. 33. This clear bipartite definition was obscured somewhat at the same time as "social" and "cultural" were added as bases of persecution by the postwar proposal of the International Law Commission in article 2 of the Draft Code of Offenses Against Peace and Security of Mankind, which defines crimes against humanity as "[i]nhumane acts such as murder, extermination, enslavement, deportation or persecutions, committed against any civilian population on social, political, racial, religious or cultural grounds...."

U.N. GAOR, 6th Sess., op. cit., art. 2, at 13, U.N. Doc. A/1858 (1951), cited in Khushalani, ibid., at 31.

67. See Brownmiller, *Against Our Will*, op. cit.; Bunster-Burotto, *Surviving Beyond Fear*, op. cit.; Amnesty International, *Women in the Frontline* (1991).

68. See, generally, Americas Watch and Women's Rights Project, *Untold Terror*, op. cit.; Swill and Giller, op. cit., at 612.

69. See Haitian Women's Advocacy Network, et al., *Communication Respecting the Violations of Human Rights of Haitian Women*, submitted to the Inter-American Commission of Human Rights (October 1994) (on file with author); Human Rights Watch, National Coalition for Haitian Refugees, *Rape in Haiti: A Weapon of Terror* (July 1994) (on file with author); and The Situation of Democracy and Human Rights in Haiti, U.N. GAOR, 48th Sess., Agenda Item 31, U.N. Doc. A14815321, Add. 3 (1994).

70. Testimony of Bok Dong Kim before the Global Tribunal on Violations of Women's Human Rights, NGO Parallel Activities, 1993 World Conference on Human Rights, Vienna, 15 June 1993. See also Hearings Before the United Nations Secretary-General (25 February 1993) (testimony of Hyo-chai Lee, MA, Soon-Kum Park, and Chungok, MFA, Korean Council for the Women Drafted for Military Sexual Service in Japan); Lourdes Sajor, *Women in Armed Conflict Situations*, MAV/1993/ WP.1 (21 September 1993) (article prepared for Expert Group Meeting on Measures to Eradicate Violence Against Women, U.N. Division for the Advancement of Women) (on file with author).

71. Brownmiller, *Against Our Will*, op. cit., 92—93.

72. See, generally, Stiglmayer, *Mass Rape*, op. cit.

73. Ibid.

74. Angela Davis, *Women, Race and Class* (New York: Vintage Books, 1983), 172.

75. Author's personal conversation with D.B., April 1993.

76. See Brownmiller, *Against Our Will*, op. cit., 48—78, for a discussion of the unrecognized sexual violence against women on the part of Allied as well as Axis forces. See also Erwin J. Haeberle, "Swastika, Pink Triangle, and Yellow Star: The Destruction of Sexology and the Persecution of Homosexuals in Nazi Germany," in *Hidden from History: Reclaiming the Gay and Lesbian Past,* ed. Martin Duberman et al. (New York: NAL Books, 1989), 365—79 (noting the gender aspect of Nazi attacks on homosexuals reflected in the use of the pink triangle and charges of emasculation).

77. The U.N. Convention relating to the Status of Refugees recognizes persecution based on race, religion, nationality, membership in a particular social group, or political opinion. See Office of the U.N. High Commissioner for Refugees, *Handbook on Procedures and Criteria for Determining Refugee Status Under the 1951 Convention and 1967 Protocol Relating to the Status of Refugees*, U.N. Doc. HCR/PRO/4 (1979). The "social group" category is currently being expanded to encompass gender claims, but this is not enough. See Pamela Goldberg and Nancy Kelly, "International Human Rights and Violence Against Women," *Harvard Human Rights Journal* 6, no. 195 (1993): 206—08.

78. See *Draft Code*, op. cit.

79. See, e.g., Committee to End Discrimination Against Women, Recommendation No. 19, U.N. Convention on the Elimination of All Forms of Discrimination Against Women, 11th Sess., U.N. Doc. CEDAW/C/1992/L.1/Add. 15 (1992): "Gender-based violence...is discrimination within the meaning of article I of the convention." The section defines violence against women as "violence that is directed against

a woman because she is a woman or which affects women disproportionately. It includes acts that inflict physical, mental or sexual harm or suffering, threats of such acts, coercion and other deprivations of liberty." Ibid., Vienna Declaration, supra note 45, at paras. 36—44. See also Declaration to Eliminate Violence Against Women, G.A. Res. 104, U.N. GAOR, 48th Sess., op. cit., U.N. Doc. A/RES/48/104 (1994).

80. Moreover, as we discussed in "Affecting the Rules for the Prosecution of Rape and Other Gender-based Violence Before the International Criminal Tribunal for the Former Yugoslavia: A Feminist Proposal and Critique,"*Hastings Women's Law Journal* 5 (1994): 171, the effective prosecution of rape depends on "engendering" the Tribunal process in a number of ways: equal employment of women, including a substantial cadre of women and men with experience working with women traumatized by sexual violence; gender training of all personnel; and effective enforcement of procedural and evidentiary rules to prohibit prejudicial and unfair harassment and retraumatization of witnesses while preserving the defendants' legitimate rights to a fair trial. Beyond that, women (as well as men) survivors and victims of these atrocities deserve more than symbolic recognition; they deserve a commitment from the United Nations, through the tribunal process and otherwise, to provide compensation, albeit for the incompensable.

81. See, e.g., Charlotte Bunch, "Women's Rights as Human Rights: Toward a Revision of Human Rights," *Human Rights Quarterly* 12 (1990): 486; Rhonda Copelon, "Intimate Terror: Understanding Domestic Violence as Torture," and Celina Romany, "State Responsibility Goes 'Private': A Feminist Critique of the Public/Private Distinction in International Human Rights Law," both in *The Human Rights Of Women: International and National Perspectives* , ed. Rebecca J. Cook (Philadelphia: University of Pennsylvania Press, 1994).

82. See Herman, *op. cit.*; Copelon, ibid.

83. As the tribunal proceeds, you can write to United Nations Secretary-General Kofi Annan, to your country's ambassador to the United Nations, and to the judges and chief prosecutor of the tribunal, which is situated at the Peace Palace in The Hague. Three women justices now sit on the International War Crimes Tribunal for former Yugoslavia: Tribunal President, Gabrielle Kirk-MacDonald (United States), Registrar Dorothee De Sampayo (Netherlands) and Justice Elizabeth Odio-Benito (Costa Rica); the Chief Prosecutor is Justice Louise Arbour.

Contributors

Carol Andreas lives in Fort Collins, Colorado and is professor emeritus of sociology, University of Northern Colorado. She has authored a number of books in the areas of women's studies and Latin American Studies, including *When Women Rebel: The Rise of Popular Feminism in Peru* (Westport, CT: L. Hill, 1985). Her most recent publication is *Meatpackers and Beef Barons: Company Town in a Global Economy* (Niwot, CO: University Press of Colorado, 1994).

Ivy D. Arai earned her B.A. with honors at Princeton University. She is currently studying at the Georgetown University School of Law. Ivy grew up in Seattle and listened for years to her parents and grandparents' stories of life during the evacuation of Japanese-Americans from that city during World War II. Most recently she has worked on the Densho Project, a Seattle Japanese-American Legacy Project intended to recover the experiences of Seattle Japanese-Americans.

Annette Becker is author of *La Guerre et La Foi: De la Mort à la Mémoire 1914—1930* (Paris: Armand Colin, 1994). In English the translation is, *War and Faith: The Religious Imagination at War, France 1914—1930* (New York: Berg, 1998). She also published *Les Monuments aux Morts, Miroir de la Grande Guerre* (Paris: Errance, 1988). She is professor of history at the University of Charles de Gaulle/Lille III, and is codirector of the Historial de la Grande Guerre, the Center for Research on World War I. Her new book is, *Oubliés de la Grande Guerre. Humanitaire et Culture de Guerre: Populations Occupées, Déportés Civils, Prisoniers de Guerre* (Paris: Noësis, 1998). She edits a new journal, *1916—1918 Today.*

Haruko Taya Cook teaches Japanese history and war and society at Marymount College in Tarrytown, New York. She is the author of *Japan at War: An Oral History* (New York: The New Press, 1992). Her current project is a book provisionally titled *Japanese Women in the "Greater East Asian War": A Social and Cultural History.*

Rhonda Copelon is professor of law and director of the International Women's Human Rights Law Clinic at the City University of New York School of Law. Since the initial call for the creation of an International

War Crimes Tribunal, she has contributed, formally and informally, to the integration of a gender perspective in its work. Her recent writings in the field of international human rights include "Recognizing the Egregious in the Everyday: Domestic Violence as Torture," *Columbia Human Rights Law Review*, 25 (1994) and, with Rosalind Petchesky, "Toward an Interdependent Approach to Reproductive and Sexual Rights as Human Rights: Reflections on the ICPD and Beyond," in *From Basic Needs to Basic Rights: Women's Claim to Human Rights*, ed. Margaret A. Schuler (Washington, D.C.: Institute for Women, Law and Development, 1995).

Nicole Ann Dombrowski received her Ph.D. in modern European history from New York University in 1995. She is currently finishing a book *Families Under Fire: French Civilians and the German Invasion of France, 1940—1942* which analyzes the French state's provisions for civilian security during World War II. It documents how French civilians, especially women, children, and the elderly, survived the experience of becoming refugees in their own country at the time of the German invasion of 1940. She has been a lecturer in history at Princeton University, where she taught European intellectual and social history. She is currently assistant professor of European and family history at Towson University in Maryland.

Barbara Alpern Engel is professor of history at the University of Colorado, Boulder, where she has taught Russian history and modern European history since 1976. She received her Ph.D. from Columbia University in 1974. Her major publications include *Mothers and Daughters: Women of the Intelligentsia in Nineteenth-Century Russia* (Cambridge; New York: Cambridge University Press, 1983) and *Between the Fields and the City: Women, Work and Family in Russia, 1861—1914* (Cambridge; New York: Cambridge University Press, 1994). She is coeditor, translator and annotator with Clifford Rosenthal of *Five Sisters: Women Against the Tsar* (New York: Knopf, 1975, 1992); coeditor with Barbara Clements and Christine Worobec of *Russia's Women: Accommodation, Resistance, Transformation* (Berkeley, CA: University of California Press, 1991); and coeditor and annotator with Anastasia Posadskaia-Vanderbeck of *A Revolution of Their Own: Voices of Women in Soviet History* (Boulder, CO: Westview Press, 1998).

Antonella Fabri received her doctoral degree (Laurea) in foreign languages and literature from the University of Rome in 1983 and her Ph.D. in anthropology from the State University of New York at Albany in 1994. The title of her dissertation is "(Re)Composing the Nation: Politics of Memory and Displacement in Mayan Testimonies from Guatemala." She has taught anthropology at Bryn Mawr College and Princeton University and is currently assistant professor of anthropology at Drew University. In addition to her scholarly pursuits she has worked as a human rights observer for the United Nations' Mission for the Verification of Human Rights in Guatemala.

Susan R. Grayzel received her Ph.D. in Late Modern European history at the University of California at Berkeley. She is finishing a book, *Women, Culture and Modern War: Gender and Identity in Britain and France, 1914—1918*, that analyzes how transnational wartime concern with women's sexuality, reproductive capacities, and political rights led to new efforts to conceptualize gender and national identity. She is currently assistant professor of European social and women's history at the University of Mississippi.

Atina Grossmann is most recently author of *Reforming Sex: The German Movement for Birth Control and Abortion Reform, 1920—1950* (New York: Oxford University Press, 1995). She also coedited the volume *When Biology Became Destiny: Women in Weimar and Nazi Germany* (New York: Monthly Review Press, 1984). She is associate professor of history at The Cooper Union and teaches at the Institute for Research on Women and Gender at Columbia University.

Leisa D. Meyer is author of *Creating G.I. Jane: Sexuality and Power in the Women's Army Corps During World War II* (New York: Columbia University Press, 1996). She is currently assistant professor of U.S. history at the College of William and Mary, where she teaches courses in U.S. women's history, the history of sexuality, and U.S. military history.

Mindy Jane Roseman is coauthor of *Beyond Words: Images from America's Concentration Camps* (Ithaca, NY: Cornell University Press, 1987). She received her master's from Columbia University and her J.D. from Northwestern University School of Law in 1986. She is working on her dissertation, "Birthing the Republic: Midwives, Medicine and Morality in France, 1890—1920" and is a visiting researcher at Harvard Law School. She has served as the associate director of the Program on Gender and Culture at the Central European University in Budapest.

Elizabeth Thompson received her Ph.D. in history from Columbia University in 1995. She is the author of *Colonial Citizens: Gender, Class and Religion in French Syria and Lebanon*, forthcoming from Columbia University Press. Ms. Thompson has taught Middle East history at the University of California at Berkeley and is currently an assistant professor at the University of Virginia.

Helen Praeger Young returned to the academic world in 1972 at age 40 after raising her four children. She received a B.A. from Antioch College in 1973 and two masters from Stanford University in 1975 in East Asian studies and education. In 1979 she began work in China at the Beijing Broadcasting Institute training undergraduates as English teachers. Since 1986 she has been a member of the faculty of the Beijing Foreign Studies University, where she teaches U.S. social history, women's history and literature and history in the American Studies Program. She is presently an associate scholar at the Center for East Asian Studies at Stanford, where she is preparing an oral history of women on the Long March.

Index